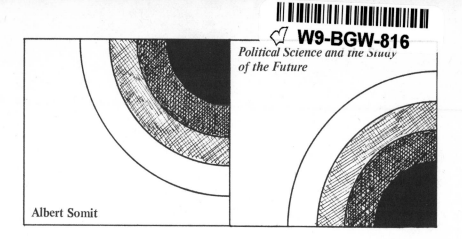

W9-BGW-816

Political Science and the Study
of the Future

Albert Somit

Political Science and the Study of the Future

Albert Somit

State University of New York at Buffalo

The Dryden Press
901 North Elm Street
Hinsdale, Illinois

Copyright © 1974 by The Dryden Press,
A Division of Holt, Rinehart and Winston, Inc.
Library of Congress Catalog Card Number: 73-2345
ISBN: 0-03-083633-6
Printed in the United States of America
45678 090 987654321

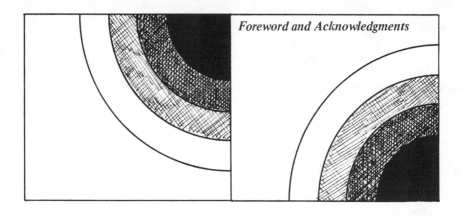

Foreword and Acknowledgments

Daniel Bell was most helpful in the development of this volume and has been characteristically generous with his counsel and his time. I am indebted to all the contributors for joining in this undertaking, for their good-natured tolerance of an occasional editorial suggestion, and for their patience as the book underwent a rather lengthy gestation period. I owe much to my research assistant, Mr. Steven Peterson, who contributed substantially to the final product, and with only an occasional murmur about "academic serfdom." Barb Chelikowsky gave generously of her thought, time, and secretarial skills, and I would be both ungrateful and rash not to make full acknowledgment thereof. Lastly, I am obligated to Dryden Press for providing ample confirmation of my earlier views about the efficiency with which the publishing industry is conducted.

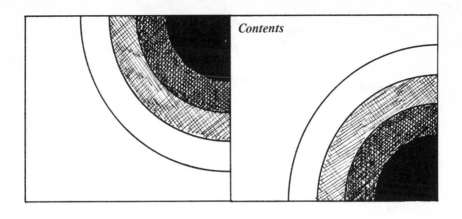

Contents

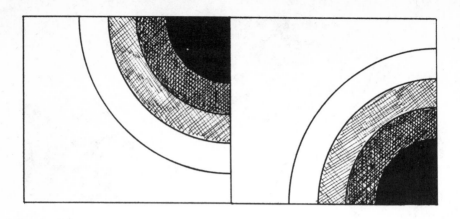

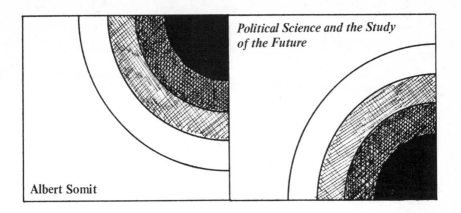

Political Science and the Study
of the Future

Albert Somit

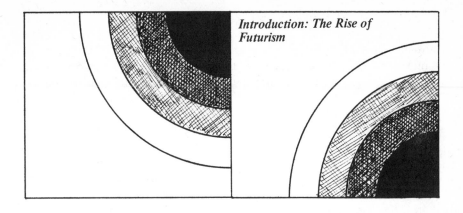

At least in part, the organization of this introductory chapter betrays my (previous?) shortcomings as a futurist. When I began to think seriously about this volume a half decade ago, I planned to open it with an explanation of "futurism"—a topic with which many of my readers, I assumed, would be relatively unfamiliar. That assumption could hardly have been more mistaken.

As we all know, futurism has "caught on" to a degree almost unprecedented even in the fad-prone social sciences. The items which make up its literature now number literally in the thousands. There are futurist bibliographies and, by 1970, there was a bibliography of futurist bibliographies.[1] Futurist courses in our colleges and universities numbered some 90 at the close of academic 1969-1970;[2] 150-175 by the end of the following year;[3] and they continue to proliferate. The language of futurism has become familiar coin of the realm. There are few practicing intellectuals today who would not recognize—if not actually employ—such once arcane terms as future shock, surprise—free futures, alternative futures, Delphi technique, inventing the future, scenario, etc.

In fact, futurism has taken on many of the characteristics not only of an intellectual movement but, as Nicholas Rescher has observed,[4] of an industry as well. There are at least a dozen futurist journals,[5] easily the same number of futurist associations,[6] and barely a month goes by without a national or international conference[7] devoted to one futures topic or another. There are notices of positions available for futurists, of futurists available for positions,[8] and of consulting organizations available to deal with futurist problems.[9]

As might be expected, there has quickly emerged a futurist Establishment: one can safely predict that on the program of any really important futurist conference will be such names as Robert Jungk, Daniel Bell, Bertrand de Jouvenel, Alvin Toffler, Hasan Ozbekhan, Johan Galtung, Dennis Gabor, Buckminster Fuller, Yehezkel Dror, John McHale, Theodore Gordon, Herman Kahn, and Nigel Calder.[10] And, as even a futurist could have foreseen, there have already emerged the Young Turks who argue, with equal fervor and implausibility, that since the future belongs to them, so should futurism.

Consequently, I need not linger over an explanation of futurism, but can proceed directly to the next two points which need brief discussion in this introduction. First, what factors might help explain the swift popularity of futurism? Second, and more germane to this volume, what factors contributed to the emergence of *political* futurism—*i.e.,* futurism as practiced by political scientists?

The Rise of Futurism

Any attempt to account for the rise of futurism raises the complex question of what is cause and what is effect. Here, as is so often the case, we can only say that there has been an interaction among several factors. Each of these, to some degree, serves as cause; each, to some degree, as effect. The logical dilemma so resolved, we can now note the diverse influences which appear to have been operative.

1. Chiliasm

Western civilization is approaching not only the end of the 20th century but, more important symbolically, the close of the second millennium A.D. What will the next *century* be like? What will happen in the next *thousand* years? The unexpected popularity of *Toward the Year 2000*[11] was probably both a symptom of, and a contributing factor to, this intense curiosity.[12]

2. Science Fiction and Utopianism

Hardly coincidental has been the boom in future fiction and science fiction.[13] Not long ago viewed as pap for mental adolescents, futures fiction and science fiction have now achieved intellectual respectability.[14] Successful science fiction authors have achieved the status of social pundits, and their views are eagerly solicited on present as well as on prospective issues. The ultimate imprimatur has come from professors of English, who have discovered a new significant literary genre. Courses in science fiction are a "must" in any department which prides itself on keeping abreast of contemporary currents; symposia, articles, and books on the subject appear apace. Science fiction has endured many vicissitudes; whether it can survive the embrace of our English departments remains to be seen.

Closely related is the recent vogue in *utopian novels.*[15] This is hardly surprising, for the two forms (science fiction and utopian novels) are closely related, and the distinction between them often turns largely upon the technological credulity demanded of the reader. In any event, the growing popularity of both fictional forms coincided with, and undoubtedly contributed to, the popularity of futurism.

3. Technological Forecasting

Turning to another area, there is a close interplay between the rise of technological forecasting and that of futurism. The staggering—as Alvin Toffler would have it, the "shocking"—technological advances of the past quarter century quite naturally gave rise to the question "what next?" But this query entailed more than mere curiosity. From the viewpoint of private industry, to *predict* techno-logical development implied the capacity to direct, plan, and even accelerate it as well. Nor was the matter of concern only to businessmen. As Sputnik demon-strated, there was, or there was thought to be, a close relationship between technological progress and national security. From both the public and the private sectors came mounting pressure to develop and refine the techniques whereby technological advances could be foreseen.[16] Since the techniques em-ployed in the one often overlap those utilized in the other, this thrust con-tributed almost as much to futurism as it did to technological forecasting.

4. Pollution and Attendant Problems

Post-1945 technological achievements, plus the concomitant surge in population, enhanced still further man's capacity to pollute his environment. Perhaps for the first time, Western public opinion became aware of the impending—or already existing—"ecological crisis." From all quarters came doleful predictions of what would happen if mankind did not resolve the twin problems of pollution and population. This sensitivity to one aspect of futurism naturally contributed to a greater interest in, and sensitivity to, other aspects. A somewhat more cynical viewpoint, I should add, recognizes a relationship between pollution and futur-ism but interprets it differently. The environmental crisis, it is argued, drove many people into futurism not so much to find a solution to the problem but rather to escape from it.

5. Rise of Policy Science

For the past quarter century, it has been unclear whether the human race would exterminate itself via nuclear warfare before, or only after, we had managed to despoil our environment beyond redemption. Under these circumstances, it is not surprising that there was an attempt to develop a specialized expertise for dealing with social problems. The resulting "policy science(s)" sought to develop techniques (a) for the analysis of social problems, (b) for finding solutions to these problems, and (c) for translating solutions into actual policy.[17] Impetus for this development came from the prestigious "think tanks" which advised the federal government (and later state and local agencies as well) on matters of public policy. Courses, curricula, and degree programs in policy science(s) soon appeared at the universities,[18] and, inevitably, a journal was published.[19] To the degree that policy science deals with long-range aspects of present problems, or with problems not yet upon us, it becomes almost indistinguishable from futur-ism.

6. Social Indicators

Pollution and population were not the only domestic problems faced by the United States during the past quarter century. Almost as serious were the decline of the city, racial discrimination, inadequate housing, the rising tide of crime, the inadequacy of our health delivery system, inflation, and, of course, poverty. Social scientists had long been aware that they lacked "yardsticks" which could satisfactorily measure either existing conditions, or the relative success or failure of public policy, in many of these areas.[20] Finally, in 1966, the federal government took official cognizance of this lack, and President Johnson ordered the Department of Health, Education and Welfare to develop a series of "social indicators." For obvious reasons, preceding and subsequent debates about the desirability of such indices were, to a significant degree, debates about futurism.

These, then, were some, but by no means all,[21] of the factors which in one fashion or another contributed to the rise of futurism over the past decade. The sequence in which they have been presented, I hasten to add, is not intended to rank them in order of importance.

There are some skeptics, candor requires me to observe, who would regard the above explanation as plausible but not persuasive. They believe futurism is a fad which is no more subject to rational explanation than any other fad. No doubt there is some element of truth in this view: social scientists, and perhaps other academics, are prone to faddism, and it would be naive to argue that this tendency has been totally inoperative.

But the objection really misses the point. Even if futurism is largely a fad, the question remains "why *this* fad rather than another?" Furthermore, even fads may yield constructive results. It would be unfortunate if those who hold to the faddist explanation permit it to prejudice their assessment of futurism's potential for enlarging our capacity to understand, and perhaps even to direct, the course of human events.

Political Futurism

Several of the foregoing factors contributed not only to the general popularity of futurism but, more specifically, to the interest it evoked among political scientists. Perhaps foremost among these was the movement, long advocated by Harold Lasswell[22] and his followers, toward a policy-oriented political science.[23] Although the discipline was rent by the post-1950 controversy over behavioralism, policy science was not one of the major issues dividing the disputants. Support for a policy-science orientation came, in fact, from both sides, although via different processes of reasoning.

Behavioralists were generally committed to the quest for a more scientific political science; and, for many sharing this commitment, it was fairly easy to move from the belief that political science should seek to become more scientific to the conviction that the resulting body of knowledge could—and should—be applied to the solution of society's problems. For others, policy applications offered a promising opportunity to develop a "harder" and more scientific discipline.[24] Needless to say, not all behavioralists concurred in this view.[25]

The anti-behavioralists arrived at a pro-policy science posture by a different route. Far better, they argued, that political science should concern itself with pressing social issues, should seek solutions to these issues, and should be committed politically and philosophically to the solution of these issues, than that it pursue the scientism, the sterile empiricism, and the even more sterile "normative neutrality" which they associated with behavioralism. But, in the anti-behavioral camp, too, there were doubts about the merits of an "applied" political science.[26]

If politics makes strange bedfellows, the politics of political science yielded equally improbable sleeping arrangements. The mid- and late 1960s saw the emergence of a highly vocal "New Left," whose rallying cry, in political science as in other disciplines, was a demand for "relevance"—i.e., for a political science attentive to the issues of the day.[27] The net result was a threefold pressure toward a greater policy orientation—from some of the anti-behavioralists, from the politically radical New Left, and, as previously noted, from within the behavioral camp itself.

However important the influence of a policy science orientation, other tendencies within the discipline also contributed to the growth of political futurism. The post-1945 period witnessed the emergence, within the field previously called "comparative politics," of a special concern with what came to be called "political modernization." Quite naturally, those working in this area sought to construct evolutionary models which could help explain political and social development in the emerging nations. From efforts to explain, it is a short step to efforts to predict future developments. And, in international relations, a somewhat analogous phenomenon occurred. The career of Herman Kahn evidenced how readily someone originally concerned with deterrence and conflict theory could move from that specialized concern to a more generalized interest in political futurism.

Still one more factor should be mentioned. The research enterprises of political scientists are largely dependent upon federal and foundation funding. Political scientists, to put it charitably, are not insensitive to the desires and objectives of those in a position to channel the flow of funds in one direction or another. In the past few years, there has been a growing disinclination to underwrite "pure" research; governmental agencies and the foundations have indicated by deed as well as by word that research should be increasingly addressed to "national needs." I would not suggest that the availability of support for applied research has of itself converted any significant number of political scientists into policy scientists and political futurists; at the same time, I think it would be erroneous to regard it as a deterrent.

Organization of Volume

As originally projected, this volume was to contain an introductory chapter and four major sections. If the developments of the past five years forced a modification of the introduction, the original fourfold schema remains. Since few of one's early notions about a book either do, or should, survive its completion, I have found this rather disconcerting. Nonetheless, no alternative model—and I have experimented with several—seemed to offer any notable advantages.

The first major portion of the volume, I felt, should present the argument for a futures-oriented political science. This has become *Part I — The Case for Politi-*

cal Futuristics. I will reserve specific comment on the items comprising this—and the other sections of the volume—for the opening pages of each "Part."

A second key section, I concluded, should describe for the reader the methods and methodologies available to the political futurist in his effort to anticipate the course of events yet to come. This material comprises *Part II – Tools and Techniques.*

The methodology available in theory to the futurist is one thing; the manner in which these devices have actually been brought to bear is another. Put somewhat differently, how have political futurists come to grips with specific problems? This matter is explored in *Part III – Case Studies,* which offers eight examples of applied futurism.

Political futurism (and indeed futurism itself) is still so young that its utility and validity remain a matter of controversy. A book on political futurism should, accordingly, provide for the expression of a less favorable viewpoint. This is the purpose of *Part IV – The Critique of Political Futuristics.*

The volume concludes with what I believe to be one of the better bibliographies of English-language literature compiled to date (July, 1972) in political futurism. Materials are presented under four headings: I – General Futuristics; II – Political Futuristics; III – Public Policy and Future Studies; and, IV – Methods of Future Studies. Lest the foregoing sound unnecessarily self-laudatory, let me hastily add that the bibliography is a collective effort, representing the combined labors of James Dator, University of Hawaii; Steve Peterson, State University of New York at Buffalo; Franklin Tugwell, Pomona College; and myself.

Notes

1. *The Futurist,* IV, 5 (October, 1970), p. 181.
2. *See* Eldredge, *infra,* pp. 292-312.
3. These include an experimental College of the Future at Fairleigh Dickinson University, *World Future Society Bulletin* III, 12 (December, 1970), p. 1; an Associate of Arts degree in "futuristics" at Alice Lloyd College in Kentucky, *World Future Society Bulletin* VI, 4 (May, 1972), p. 4; and a Ph.d. program at the Université des Sciences Sociales de Grenoble, *World Future Society Bulletin,* IV, 11 (November, 1971), p. 3.
4. "The Future as an Object of Research," *Rand Paper 3593,* 1967. Martin Shubik has described the futurists as "... a strange mixture of sociologists, technologists, physicists, and others, some charlatans, some poets, some meticulous workers, and others even geniuses. Most of them have considerable imagination. Many of their customers or semi-allies, however, belong to the penumbral areas of corporate or military management; and imagination there is often lacking." *Science,* 166 (5 December 1969), pp. 1257-58.
5. A basic list would include the following:
Analysen und Prognosen. Berlin Center for Future Research. 1968-.
Futurum. Germany. 1968-.
Technology Assessment. Marvin Cetron (ed.). The Hague, Netherlands: International Society for Technology Assessment. To begin Summer, 1972.
Perspectives. L. P. Singh (ed.). New Delhi: Indian Institute of Public Administration. 1965-.
The Futurist. Washington, D.C.: World Future Society. 1967-.

Futuribles. Paris: SEDEIS. 1961-65.

Futures. London: Unwin. 1968-.

Analyse et Prévision. Paris: SEDEIS. 1966-.

2000. Documentation Bulletin on Future Research. Netherlands. (Abstracts of future research).

Prometheus Project Newsletter. 1971-.

Trend. Cooperative School of Education at University of Massachusetts. (Annual publication on education).

Technological Forecasting. Elsevier Publishing Company.

In addition, there are:

Newsletter – Social and Human Forecasting. IRADES. Rome.

Newsletter of Alternative Futures Prospect. University of Illinois.

6. As of this writing (July, 1972), there were the following:

Swedish Association of Future Studies.

Israel Association for Futurology and Philosophy of Technics and Sciences.

Venezuelan Center for Studies of the Future.

Max Planck Institute for Future Research, Germany.

Ledoux Foundation for Studies for the Future, Paris, France.

Hague International Future Institute.

Futurological Society of Prague.

Institut fur Zukunftsfragen, Vienna, Austria.

Gesselschaft fur Zukunftsfragen.

Zentrum Berlin fur Zukunftsfragen.

Workgroup 2000, Amersfoot, Netherlands.

World Future Society, Washington, D.C.

International Futuribles Association.

Institute for the Future, Menlo Park, California.

Futurology Research Committee, Japan.

Academy for Research on Futures and the Society for Research on Futures, Denmark.

7. Including three international Futures Research Conferences: Oslo, 1967; Kyoto (1970); and Bucharest (1972).

8. *See*, for instance, *World Future Society Bulletin*, V, 1 (February, 1972), p. 1; and *The Futurist*, 5 (December, 1971), p. 250.

9. With such appropriate names as *Inter Future* and *Futuremics, Inc.* I am not quite sure how to classify the *Immortality Newsletter*.

10. This list, let me hastily add, is illustrative, rather than exhaustive, and is *not* intended to imply any necessary equality of status within the Establishment. Appropriately enough, Professor Billy Rojas of Alice Lloyd College, Pippa Passes, Kentucky, has published a compendium entitled "Who is Who in Educational Futuristics."

11. Daniel Bell reported that 100,000 copies of the *Daedalus* issue (Summer, 1967) which was entitled "Toward the Year 2000: Work in Progress" were sold. The report was also published in hardcover and softcover editions. Harvey S. Perloff, *The Future of the U.S. Government* (New York; George Braziller, 1967), pp. ix-x.

12. *See* Eldredge, *infra*, pp. 292-312.

13. I. F. Clarke, *The Tale of the Future* (London: Library Association, 1961). Also, of course, *see* the essay on science fiction by Dennis Livinston, *infra* pp. 230-245.

14. *The Futurist*, VI, 2 (April, 1972), p. 78.

15. *See* Frank Manuel, *Utopias and Utopian Thought* (Boston: Beacon Press, 1966), pp. xiii-iv. *The Futurist*, IV, 1 (February, 1970), p. 2, reports the establishment of a journal—*The Modern Utopian*—devoted to the subject.

16. A basic bibliography on technological forecasting would include the following items:

R. V. Arnfield (ed.). *Technological Forecasting.* Edinburgh: Edinburgh University Press, 1969.

Robert U. Ayres, *Technological Forecasting and Long-Range Planning*. New York: McGraw–Hill, 1969.

James R. Bright (ed.). *Technological Forecasting for Industry and Government*. Englewood Cliffs: Prentice-Hall, 1968.

Marvin J. Cetron. *Technological Forecasting: A Practical Approach*. New York: Gordon and Breach, 1969.

Erich Jantsch, *Technological Forecasting in Perspective*. Paris: Organization for Economic Cooperation and Development, 1967.

H. W. Lanford. *Technological Forecasting Methodologies: A Synthesis*. New York: American Management Association, 1971.

Joseph Martino (ed.). *An Introduction to Technological Forecasting*. New York: Gordon and Breach, 1972.

17. For a general overview of the field, *see*:

Yehezkel Dror. *Public Policy Making Reexamined*. San Francisco: Chandler, 1968.

Harold Lasswell. *A Pre-View of Policy Sciences*. New York: Elsevier, 1971.

Edward Shils. *Criteria for Scientific Development: Public Policy and National Goals*. Cambridge: M. I. T. Press, 1968.

18. Yehezkel Dror has been a leader in this movement. *See* "Teaching of Policy Sciences: Design for a Post-Graduate University Program," *Rand Paper P-4128*, 1969.

19. *Policy Sciences*. Amsterdam: Elsevier, 1970.

20. Major items in this literature would include:

Raymond Bauer (ed.), *Social Indicators*. Cambridge: M. I. T. Press, 1966.

Bertram Gross. *The State of the Nation: Social Systems Accounting*. London: Tavistock, 1966.

Bertram Gross and Michael Springer (eds.). *Social Intelligence for America's Future*. Boston: Allyn and Bacon, 1969.

Eleanor Sheldon and Wilbert Moore. *Indicators of Social Change*. New York: Russell Sage Foundation, 1968.

U.S. Department of H.E.W. *Toward a Social Report*. Washington, D.C.: U. S. Government Printing Office, 1969.

For additional bibliographic references, *see* the essay by Isabel Sawhill, *infra* pp. 114-127.

21. Other influences, according to Daniel Bell, were "a renewed optimism, stimulated by remarkable technological developments and the prestige of science, about possibilities of meeting basic human needs and of defining new, worthwhile, and realizable goals; greater interdependence in society created by new developments in transportation and communication; a national commitment to economic growth; and the development of a new intellectual technology—cybernetics, information theory, and so on—making long-range social and technological forecasting a more reasonable undertaking than before."

I would also add the interest evoked by advances in genetics and the realization that it might be possible, in the near future, to "breed to order," à la *Brave New World.*

22. In 1956, Lasswell had observed to his fellow political scientists that "part of our role, as the venerable metaphor has it, is scanning the horizon of the future with a view to defining in advance the probable impact of what is foreseeable for the navigators of the Ship of State." *American Political Science Review*, L, 4 (December, 1956), p. 966. *See also* his *The Future of Political Science* (New York: Atherton Press, 1963), and, of course, his essay on "The Future of Professional Political Scientists" in this volume, *infra* pp. 246-254.

23. "It can hardly be doubted that political science . . . is rapidly becoming enamored of the study of policy." Randall B. Ripley, book review, *American Political Science Review* LXIII, 4 (September, 1969), p. 918.

24. Austin Ranney, *Political Science and Public Policy* (Chicago: Markham, 1968), pp. 13-15, and Charles Hyneman, *The Study of Politics*. Urbana: University of Illinois Press, 1959), p. 5.

25. Some opposed it on the grounds that this would divert effort from the more

important task of building a more rigorous political science; others because they felt it would lead to a loss of scientific "objectivity."

26. This is essentially the position taken by James Charlesworth, *A Design for Political Science*, Philadelphia: American Academy of Political and Social Science, 1966), pp. 250-51.

27. *See* for instance, the report of the 1967 meeting of the American Political Science Association carried in *Science*, 157 (September, 1967), p. 1414.

28. In a later discussion, Bell identified *three* general methods of social forecasting: (1) analytical identification of future problems, (2) extrapolation of existing social trends "for which we have time series," and (3) construction of a model "in which the relevant independent variables and their dependent functions are identified." Perloff, *op. cit.*, pp. xi-xii.

29. For a somewhat different line of attack, *see* the paper by Fred C. Iklé, "Can Social Predictions Be Evaluated?," *Daedalus op. cit.*, pp. 733-58.

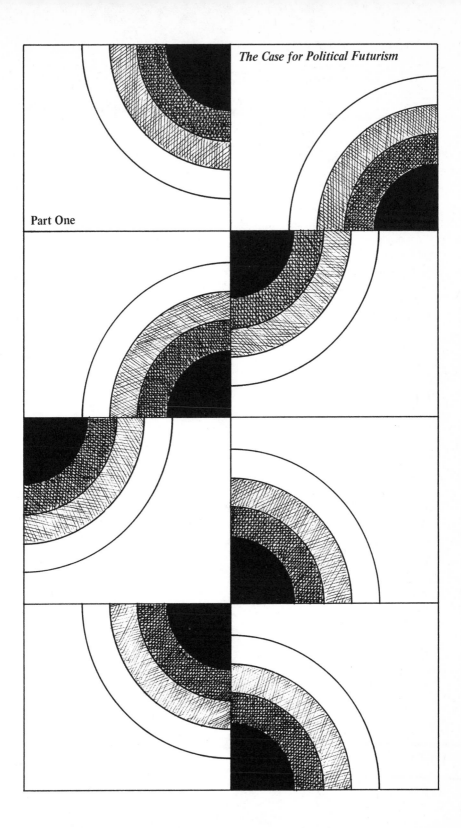

The Case for Political Futurism

Part One

The arguments in behalf of a futures-oriented political science are marshaled here in two quite different articles by two quite different authors. Bertrand de Jouvenel presents the case for political futurism as seen by one of our most distinguished political philosophers. This brief little essay, originally published in 1965, has since come to be regarded as one of the most seminal contributions to the literature.

Olaf Helmer, on the other hand, examines political futurism from the viewpoint of a non-political scientist. In an equally brief discussion, Helmer urges "a reorientation of political analysis toward the future." While de Jouvenel is concerned with the broad spectrum, Helmer focuses primarily on the benefits which could be derived by applying political futuristics to the formulation of foreign policy.

The de Jouvenel and Helmer essays, I feel, best fit into the structure of this volume. The case for political futuristics, however, has also been forcefully and ably argued by others. I call attention in particular to the items in the bibliography by Akzin, Flechtheim, de Jouvenel, and Polak.

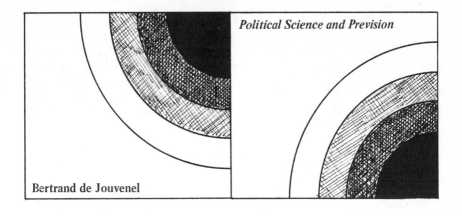

Political Science and Prevision

Bertrand de Jouvenel

The political scientist is a teacher of public men in the making, and an adviser of public men in activity; "public men," that is, men who are taught, invited or assumed to feel some responsibility for the exercise of political power; "political power," that is, concentrated means of affecting the future.

I

Obviously we can not affect the past, or that present moment which is now passing away, but only what is not yet: the future alone is sensitive to our actions, voluntary if aimed at a pictured outcome, rational if apt to cause it, prudently conceived if we take into account circumstances outside our control (known to decision theorists as "states of nature"), and the conflicting moves of others (known in game theory as opponents' play). A result placed in the future, conditions intervening in the future, need we say more to stress that decisions are taken "with an eye to the future," in other terms, with foresight?

Thucydides puts this utterance in the mouth of Archidamos, addressing the Assembly of Lacaedemonians on the eve of the Peloponnesian War: "For we that must be thought the causers of all events, good or bad, have reason also to take some leisure in part to foresee them."[1]

This can serve as our text: the greatest of historians warns us that we are the authors of our fate. It is levity in an individual to make a decision fraught with serious consequences to himself without forethought; but such levity turns to guilt in the case of the magistrate or citizen participating in a public decision the consequences of which will fall upon a great many. The political scientist then must recognize in foresight a moral obligation, to be felt and taught.

But saying that public decisions *ought* to be taken with foresight is a precept: how can we follow this precept unless we develop the corresponding *skill*? Knowing that foresight is required, the political scientist must therefore seek to develop that skill in himself, and in his pupils, and offer it to statesmen he has to advise. *Foresight is an expertise required in the political scientist*: that is my first point.[2]

Need I stress that expertise does not mean infallibility? A political scientist will often misread the course of events or miscalculate the consequences of a decision, but the frequency of his successful forecasts should be higher than that of the average politician or lay citizen; this is not a great deal to ask, and whoever denies that it can be achieved, thereby denies any practical value to political research. The moral philosopher who deems it his function to teach discrimination of what is best in an absolute sense, does not need to prove himself a good forecaster. But it is otherwise for one who presents himself as a student of behavior. Such a study must be called idle or unsuccessful unless it results in an increasing ability to state what is to be expected.

There is in every science a well known relationship between factual investigation and marshalling hypotheses, meant to account for the facts and assumed to have some predictive worth. It is true that there can be no certain knowledge but of the past: indeed the past is the realm of the "true or false," with which the future contrasts as the realm of "possibles," which are neither true nor false. Therefore only probable statements can be uttered regarding the future, but it is solely through such utterances that the sciences are of practical utility. As I shall stress, it pertains to the nature of the object that such statements should be least reliable in matters political. But if they are not to be attempted, the term "science" should be rejected: nor can we then think of the discipline as conferring positive bonus upon the body politic.

II

Since probable statements concerning the future are an outcome of factual investigations, they can, of course, concern only the realm of those phenomena which the student investigates. It is a verbal convention of our time that of two once synonymous terms, one of Latin, the other of Greek origin, both designating originally the whole of human relations, the word "social" has been retained to mean the whole, while the usage of the word "political" has been narrowed down to a part of these relations. In the meantime, however, the functions of government have grown more embracing: therefrom a non-congruence between the field of studies of the political scientist, and the field of concerns of the political magistrate. It follows that the kind of foresight which the political scientist may provide refers to but part of the phenomena the political magistrate has to deal with. This immediately suggests that it falls to other departments of the social sciences to provide complementary varieties of foresight, arising from their specific investigations, and relevant to some kinds of public decisions. It is indeed the practice of governments to consult experts other than political scientists, for the preparation of decisions concerning what Cournot very aptly called "the social economy." When it is future "traffic in towns" which forms the subject-matter of the decision, forecasts regarding the automobile population, the location of industry, the grouping of people, etc., are required of specialists quite other than political scientists.

This need not be labored and forms my second point. *Public decisions require a variety of foresights other than that of the political scientist.* We may well think of these diverse foresights being brought into play as each occasion demands. But there is a problem here, of no mean importance.

III

I shall introduce this problem by means of a concrete instance: the quotations here are from the *Survey of International Affairs* for the year 1930.[3]

Dr. Brüning became Chancellor of the German Reich in March 1930: "the Budget problem was by far the most untractable of all the problems with which Germany had to deal. . . . up to the time of writing [the Summer of 1931] it was only under the Chancellorship of Dr. Brüning that measures were taken of such a character as to promise real improvement. . . . The cumulative deficit was . . . the prospective deficit was. . . . Action was therefore urgent. Dr. Brüning met his immediate necessities by an emergency decree promulgated in July 1930, and, as the situation was not righted by this measure, it was succeeded by two further emergency decrees issued respectively in December 1930 and in June 1931." While drastically cutting down expenditure, these decrees also raised taxes. "Such were the draconian measures to which Dr. Brüning was obliged to resort. Their effectiveness in practice remained to be seen: their value as proof of the changed attitude of responsible German statesmen in the matter of public finance was beyond question or cavil."

Let me add that, on taking office, Dr. Brüning found three million unemployed: after two years of "draconian measures," he had six million; that he found 12 Nazis sitting in the Reichstag: after six months in office he saw their number raised to 107 (Sept. 30 elections), and soon after he left office (May 1932) the Nazis obtained 230 seats (July 31, 1932).

Now let us imagine a political scientist addressing Dr. Brüning in April 1930: "Ignorant as I am of public finance, I must assume that the measures which have been recommended to you by financial experts are the best for balancing the budget (which in fact they were not); ignorant as I am of economics, I cannot tell you what measures would effectively reduce unemployment: these are matters for different specialists. But it is my office to tell you that unemployment is a more serious evil than budgetary deficit, constitutes a more pressing problem, and that you should give it priority. Further it is my office to warn you that you will put the country in great political peril if you fail to address yourself to the major problem."

There is indeed a very heavy bill to be paid for the misinvestment of public attention, which is a very common fault of politicians. Consider the sad case of Dr. Brüning, an earnest and honorable man, who conscientiously and courageously addressed himself to what he deemed the major problem: but his ranking was quite mistaken, so that his virtuous efforts led to political disaster. This brings out the utility of properly ranking problems. Here I am not thinking of a lasting hierarchy in terms of values (however important that is) but of a here-and-now order of priorities, in terms of the costs of letting various problems fester and come to a crisis.

Politicians having proved remarkably poor judges of such priorities, a better judge is needed to redress their assessments: and this is a role for the political scientist, who to this end must operate as a "generalist," not only as a "specialist" among others. No matter that he is competent to deal only with certain problems, he must also be competent to appraise them all. And this role of "generalist" is logically linked with his role as specialist: because any social problem which is left inadequately attended will ultimately land in that court of passions and conflict which is his particular concern. He can be compared to a suzerain of the social field, who runs but a small part of the realm, but must oversee the whole, as any trouble arising in any other part must seep into his own. He is competent to request attention for a problem, and demand that experts competent therein be called. More than that, he is competent to state what questions they should answer, because he must be aware of interrelations between problems.

Another instance will serve to stress that aspect. Left alone after World War I to maintain the new map of Europe which Woodrow Wilson and Lloyd George had taken so large a part in drawing, France formed alliances with four Eastern Europe states, of which two, Poland and Czechoslovakia, were immediate neighbors of Germany. These alliances committed France to military intervention should Germany attack Poland or Czechoslovakia. Military intervention in what form? A mere glance at the map made it clear that effective intervention could occur in no other form than the invasion of Germany. Therefore these alliances required that the French army be shaped as an offensive instrument: exactly the reverse was explicitly decided, and a purely defensive apparatus was set up. So it was quite easy to foresee a good ten years in advance what happened in 1939: while practically the whole of the German forces was thrown against Poland, the French army sat uselessly on its defensive positions, having been designed for nothing else.[4] Not only was it easy to foresee but it was foretold behind closed doors by certain military leaders, and openly by some young civilians without authority. Now is this not again a clear case for the political scientist? Was it not proper for him to point out the discrepancy between the diplomatic policy and the military policy?[5]

I have chosen two instances of fatal mistakes, of which I can bear witness that they were perceptible at the time. Mistakes, one of which proceeded from a wrong priority of policies, the other from an incoherence of policies. Is it not the political scientist's role to take a view sufficiently panoramic to call attention to such blunders? That is my third point. *The political scientist is competent to appreciate priorities and consistency in policies the details of which he is incompetent to judge.*

IV

The foregoing statement means that the political scientist has to keep track of current and impending changes in non-political fields, and for this purpose to achieve a continual exchange of forward looking views with experts in these other fields. To take a simple instance, suppose that the balance-of-payments specialist foresees the necessity of slowing up the rate of wage increases. Some economists feel that this cannot be achieved otherwise than by a "squeeze," diminishing, as they put it, the pressure on the labor market—in more common parlance, maintaining a certain percentage of unemployment. Others, shocked by this prospect, reject that method and advocate an "incomes policy." Now the political scientist, informed of these views, foresees from the one procedure unpleasant political consequences; while the second poses a problem of political feasibility. Therefore such views are very germane to his concerns: indeed it may be the case that one policy seems to him inadvisable and the other impracticable, which may cause him to ask the economists for some other way: would a flexible exchange rate achieve the object?

As every change assumed to occur has repercussions in many fields, as every change devised has a variety of implications and calls for a variety of adjustments, it is clear that in a society characterized by rapid transformation, there is need for what I have called elsewhere a Surmising Forum where anticipations are confronted, and where incoherences discerned indicate measures to be taken, or alternatives to be considered. I do not propose to restate here the case for the Surmising Forum; all I need is to make the fourth point: *the political scientist must seek to coordinate anticipations.*

This attempt to overlook the whole field is useful for the long term, but it also meets a pressing need of the political scientist.

V

This overall watching allows him to detect sources of future political perturbances. *The political scientist should be a detector of trouble to come*: that is my fifth point.

Trouble is indeed his business. Who would deny that he is at his most useful if he warns of war or advises how to avoid it? That the foresight of the foreign policy expert revolves around the possibility of war, will be readily granted; but not so easily that the domestic equivalent of war must play the same central role in the speculations of the domestic expert. The contrast is understandable enough: the international system is thought of as a system of antagonism, the national system as one of cooperation. The very accent of words changes as we move from one system to the other. If we speak of a system of Powers (international), we use the capital to denote independent actors by their factual resources, their *means*; while if we speak of the system of powers (national), the powers we now refer to are *rights* to be exercised functionally in the service of the national whole.

"Home affairs," as the British tellingly put it, are supposed to be altogether quieter than foreign affairs. It is assumed that the institutions set up to take care of home affairs are and will remain adequate to cope with any problems arising: there is a political division whenever people strongly disagree as to what should be done, but this division is thought of as overcome when the matter has been settled by an established procedure of decision (such as a parliamentary "division").

The political scientist should be keenly aware that things are not so simple, but his function as teacher of institutions leads him to convey and therefore to adopt an optimistic vision. His first and foremost function is to address future citizens and potential magistrates, and fit them for participation in the management of public affairs, a management organized according to a certain system. This system must be described and explained to them, so that they shall feel "at home" in it, in the two senses of knowledge and acceptance; and it is surely of great importance to a republic that its citizens should have confidence in and respect for the form of its government. Political institutions, inherently precarious, are made solid and stable by belief, which must therefore be fostered; but, in the process of so doing, it is easy to become overconfident. It improves mores to think that what may not be done can not be done, but it deteriorates prudence. It is good that actions should run between the banks of established procedures, but it is dangerous that the imagination of the expert should be confined between these banks. To cite an admittedly extreme and caricatural instance of such confinement, it was apparently believed by those who called Hitler to the Chancellorship at the end of January 1933, that he would find himself quite paralyzed in this position by article 58 of the Weimar constitution, which stated that all government decisions should be taken by a majority of the members of the cabinet, wherein he was placed in a minority, having only two ministers of his own party! As I warned, this is an extreme and caricatural instance; it is not suggested that political scientists are prone to such mistakes. But it is true, surely, that, not only as teachers of good civic behavior, but also as law-abiding and reasonable men, they are not inclined to lend any great likelihood to strong departures from regular courses.

They are not prone to foresee dramatic events. Surely the United States is the country far the best endowed in political scientists—indeed possibly as many as nineteen out of twenty political scientists operating in the world today are Americans. It would be interesting to know what proportion of these political scientists foresaw—and how early—the sensational rise of McCarthy and his no less sensational collapse. Or again, what proportion foresaw the capture of the Republican Party by the Goldwater group.

This is not meant as a criticism: first, it is in any realm difficult to be a good forecaster; second, the difficulty is at its greatest in politics; last, and chiefly, political scientists have not, in general, deemed it their function to forecast, and when so doing they are apt to stress that they do so as citizens, not as scientists. The only purpose of my remark, therefore, is to note a psychological disposition, which I think would still be operative if political scientists were willing to adopt the view here advanced, that they should regard it as pertaining to their function to forecast, and should indeed regard such forecasting as a practical end-product of their science. Under such conditions, they would still, I think, be reluctant to foresee perturbation, disturbance, trouble. So, if this foresight of trouble is, as I think, the most important, a psychological effort will be required to overcome the tendency to project a relatively smooth course.[6]

That tendency is to be found also in other fields of social science: everywhere prevision resorts to projection of current trends and to reproduction of periodic changes. Economic prevision, to whatever degree of complexity it may be worked out, ultimately rests upon the assumption that certain structural relations are relatively invariant over time. It is natural enough that prevision should assume continuity and recurrence. Therefore it takes an effort to predict discontinuity, a break—in short, trouble.

VI

Political foresight requires study of political behavior: this sixth point is self-evident; every science studies the behavior of those objects about which it proposes to make statements of general and lasting validity, and therefore capable of being used for prediction, or anticipation. Nor is it necessary to advocate study of political behavior: this is presently the most esteemed compartment of political science.[7] Nonetheless something is to be said on this point.

"Behavioral studies," as they are called, are apt to deal with ordinary behavior: the word "ordinary" denotes at the same time, and very properly, what is not uncommon, and what fits into an order. Now times of trouble are characterized by extraordinary conducts: the behavior of the "force publique," when the independence of the Congo was proclaimed, came as a great surprise; no better, and no less surprising, was the behavior of the "gardesfrançaises" on the Fourteenth of July, 1789. Quite recently, some meticulous and respected German bureaucrats have been found out, to the shocked surprise of their colleagues, as the authors of most abominable actions in the days of the concentration camps: but for these historic events they might have lived irreproachable lives and no one would ever have imagined them capable of what they have done. Of course, saying that people would not have been criminal but for the occasion is not, as it is all too commonly taken to be, an excuse: the actions are their own and their features then made manifest were potentially there before. But it is a warning that the behavior we presently observe is not the only behavior of which the subjects observed are capable.

The instability of behavior is a great difficulty for political prevision. We know of course that a man's behavior is variable but in no realm is it as variable as in the political. And we get no inkling of behavior under "heated" conditions if we merely observe people under "cold" conditions, when they vote this way or that, attend meetings or not, move resolutions or raise their hands. Under heating, we observe that the same people are not then behaving in the same way; and further we must note that it is not the same people who then claim most of our attention. At all times, if people are ranked according to their degree of political activity, we find that such activity is high only in a limited number and falls off very rapidly as we consider greater numbers. "Heated" conditions are apt to increase the total surface included under such a curve, but they also substitute, for the most active minority under cold conditions, a minority made up of quite different persons.

Whatever the equality of political rights, so small is the share of total political activity performed by the great majority and so great that performed by a small minority, that the total hue and character of national political activity reflects that of the active minority. If that leading company then changes, the whole character of politics changes. And though the heat which changes behavior in the same people does pass away, the change in the people who impart their character to the total system may endure.

The great merit of an effective two-party system is that no man can rise to political importance otherwise than by a slow progress within one or the other party, a progress in the course of which he finds himself subject to screening by monitors at different stages of his rise. It is a major contribution to stability that the two parties conspire to persuade the public that between themselves they exhaust the possibilities. But the political scientist must be aware that, however salutary this belief, it does not correspond to reality: there are people floating in outer darkness who can, if the occasion arises, errupt upon the scene, casting out both of the small armies that have been engaged in a civilized duel. The heads carried away in the baskets attending the French guillotine represented the whole spectrum of opinions preceding the Revolution (also those which appeared in its course); the same has been true in the concentration camps of Soviet Russia and of Nazi Germany.

All this pertains to the process of "heating." To this, political scientists have given, if I may say so, quite inadequate attention; they have been very prone to regard this as inevitable when it has happened and unthinkable where it has not. That where it has happened it had sufficient cause, is of course true, but uninteresting; what is useful is to pin-point, if we can, what would have made a difference. It is now out of fashion for historians to stop their relation of events when they come to what seems to them a cross-roads, and to note that, from a different decision or action at this point, a different course of things might have followed. It may be that such exercises are unbecoming to historical science; they are surely in the highest degree suitable to political science.

Our science stands in great need of a systematic study bearing upon the occurrence of these "changes of state" here called "heating." Unless I am much mistaken, such a factual study would not confirm the breezy theory that they occur when necessary to allow the coming forth of a predetermined new order—that is, if and only if they serve a providential purpose; strange indeed is the unquestioned providentialism of agnostic philosophers of history.

I have noted that studies of behavior tend to disregard changes in behavior which attend "heating," and that too little attention is paid in them to what leads up to such "heating." Another remark is now called for, relative to normal conditions.

Political phenomena have by nature a tempo different from that of social phenomena. Let us take, for instance, people's attitudes toward the consumption of alcohol. Let us suppose that over time the proportion of teetotalers increases from a small minority to a majority. As a social phenomenon this can be continuous and carried to any degree without a break. But now consider teetotalism as politically militant. Then, as soon as the teetotalers have reached a majority, they will forbid drinking to the minority: a discontinuity, a break, and an occasion of "heating." Thus the diffusion of a political attitude gives rise to distinct events, as it does not in the case of a social attitude.

But the above illustration assumes a perfect democracy, where decisions are made by a popular majority; such is not the practice of any modern state. Indeed, the present trend is to entrust the major decisions to a single person: thus in the United States, while the Congress decides on the President's proposal how much financial aid should be given to South Vietnam, a military operation on North Vietnam can be decided upon by the President alone.

It follows therefrom that the political scientist, operating as "predictor," must pay to individual character an attention which is not called for in the case of the social scientist. A social phenomenon is the outcome of a very great number of individual decisions, an aggregate which reflects individual attitudes in proportion to their frequency. Social prediction can therefore safely neglect attitudes of a small minority—thus, for instance, Amish rejection of the motor-car is insignificant for estimates of future automobile sales—and the social predictor need not (as, indeed, he cannot) pay attention to idiosyncrasies. If interested in estimating the number of divorces next year, he will wave aside as irrelevant a tidbit of information regarding John's disposition to quarrel with Mary. It is not so in politics: an attitude relatively infrequent, such as rabid anti-semitism, acquires momentous importance if it pertains to a man who rises to the highest place. More generally, in the absence of any such extreme peculiarity, every little trait of the Prince's individuality acquires great importance, due to the "multiplier" of great power.

This has ever been recognized. We have centuries-old records of political forecasts in the form of diplomatic dispatches. While the ambassador owes his public character to his being the empowered spokesman of his sovereign, as soon as permanent missions abroad were established, they functioned mainly as listening posts, whence information was sent home, concerning political developments occurring or impending in the country of residence. These are the earliest "political surveys," of enormous value for the historian in that each describes a state of affairs, but also a source as yet untapped for the study of political surmising. The message of the political reporter is the more valuable the more it foretells; therefore, while conveying accomplished facts, the writer must also use them as raw material to convey a "transformed product," his surmise. The abundant diplomatic sources in existence are still to be used for the analysis of the surmising procedures they reveal. But it needs only the barest familiarity with them to remark the place occupied in such dispatches by the description of personal characteristics: the character of the Prince, those of his ministers and favorites, those also of possible successors.

What a change the simplest substitution of persons can make. Consider

Frederick the Great in January 1762: he writes to the marquis d'Argens: "If Fortune continues to pursue me, doubtless I shall sink," and suggests that unless a turn for the better occurs, he may next month take Cato's course: "Cato, and the little glass tube I have." But as he writes the turn has already occurred: Czarina Elisabeth has died, her nephew Peter has become Czar; a fanatical admirer of Frederick, he immediately relieves the pressure upon him by recalling the Russian troops. Peter's bare six months on the throne suffice to turn the tide.

Can we confidently say that personalities matter less in our own day? Why then did a shudder run through the West when the false news of Mr. Khrushchev's death was flashed? Even in the case of a liberal democracy, did we not find the very same men who interpret politics as a working-out of impersonal forces, expressing the utmost alarm at the prospect of a Goldwater presidency?

Personalities always matter in politics, and never have they counted for more than in our century, which has, at one and the same time, tended to collectivize the individual and to individualize collective power. From this has come, as it seems to me, an improved predictability in matters pertaining to the social economy, and a deteriorated predictability in matters specifically political. Far be it from me to exaggerate the freedom of action of the man who sits at the top of a nation. He is always "riding a tiger," but the way he rides it makes a very great difference indeed.

From these remarks it seems to follow that the methods which serve us well in the prevision of social change, which is continuous and insensitive to idiosyncrasies, cannot be suitable for political phenomena, which have different properties.

VII

It is a great ambition of modern social science to study phenomena without "insight"; an understandable ambition, this being the way which has led the human mind to phenomenal success in the physical sciences, which serve as the model and basis of all others. Standing in the way of such progress was the "pathetic fallacy," our apparently innate propensity to lend quasi-human personalities to objects. It is not helpful toward the control of floods to regard them as fits of anger in the river genius, who should therefore be appeased by gifts, perhaps human sacrifices. Our knowledge and mastery of nature have progressed as we have ceased to regard natural objects as whimsical persons, who behave according to their mood, and have come instead to regard them as "things" which behave as they are made to by circumstances. Containing as it does a most vigorous repudiation of animism, a depersonalization of objects, the Bible can be said to have helped to open the way for Western science.[8]

We find the eviction of "genii" historically associated with a procedure of inquiry which seeks to ascertain how the object behaves under varying conditions, and to derive from observed regularities assertions of predictive value. The procedure has its utmost practical value when it leads us to foretell with certainty how the object will behave under certain future conditions as they occur, and therefore also, what conditions we must create in order to make it behave as suits us. These great practical rewards of the method are fully attained when the object studied is a "thing" which must perforce "behave" in perfectly passive compliance to the conditions wherein it is placed. This being so, it is understandable that the method was extended to animals in consequence of Descartes's assertion concerning their "machine" character, and that Condillac and La Mettrie should have, by their views of man, encouraged its extension to him.

Whatever historical role the inclination to regard man as also a "mere thing" may have played in the extension to him of this method of inquiry, it is surely a mistake[9] to regard the validity of the method, applied to his case, as dependent upon this ontological assumption. In fact the very first finding from such an application is that men do not display that uniformity of behavior which we expect from "things." Thus an application, scandalous to some who regard it as debasing man to the status of "mere thing," in fact demonstrates that he is not such. But the method is not, in consequence, valueless: though we find in a number of men different conducts in the same circumstances, if we note the distribution of such conducts and its mode, and if we can find that over time this distribution and its mode change but little or shift but slowly, we have therefrom a predictive tool, as stressed by Quételet.[10]

Now a few words about "outwardness." The scientific method in respect to things has substituted for interpretations of their "genius" the examination of their performances. We attempt no sympathetic "understanding" of the thing's spirit but proceed by watchful "overstanding." In the metaphysical squabbles of social science, there is much argument for and against such "outwardness."

I can see no harm in observing a nation as one would an ant-heap; this just happens to be a hampering method. Were it the best, ethnologists who go out to investigate so-called "primitive peoples" should be strictly forbidden to learn the language of their hosts; for conversation conveys some insight into people's feelings, intentions, values. Thereby you lose the outwardness which some deem so essential.

Outwardness has indeed been used as a literary artifice by eighteenth-century wits, foremost among them Voltaire, to ridicule social behavior. If you look at conducts from an angle which annuls the values inspiring them and thus robs them of meaning, it is easy enough to make them appear nonsensical; thereby also they are made unpredictable. This is a clear warning not to press outwardness too far. The social scientist has to set the tangible behaviors he observes within the framework of prevailing beliefs and interests. An economist may dislike motor cars, he may, as a joke in the common room, describe weekends as an aimless buzzing of urbanites out of the hive, arising from a periodic perturbation of the regular courses therein: his forecasts must nonetheless rest upon men's known desires for cars. No forecasting is possible unless data about what people do are complemented with data about their feelings, wants, aspirations, judgments. These data may figure but implicitly in a model, which then assumes either their invariance over time, or that their changes will follow a certain ascertainable course.

But it is quite otherwise for the political forecaster: he has to focus upon feelings, attitudes, judgments, because these, in his field, undergo swift and vast changes, with major factual consequences. How soon, how very soon it was after Hitler's last stand in Berlin, that I heard an ADA group in New York acclaim Mayor Reuther's formula: "Berlin is the outpost and symbol of freedom!" What a reversal of significance! Did it occur because the national interest of the United States demanded it? I have no patience with those who explain the emotional attitudes of actual people by the rational interest of collective entities: it is rather the other way round. Is it credible that the anti-Soviet revulsion of the United States soon after the end of hostilities was inspired by the national interest? If so, surely, in the last weeks of the war, the American troops should have been urged to gain as much ground in Germany and in Czechoslovakia as was possible, and to keep it. But no, the policy of containment came as an aftermath of a change in the affective valuation of Stalinist Russia.

History would be different—indeed there would be very much less of History as commonly understood—if policies corresponded to a relatively stable conception of the national interest. For instance, consider Britain's "war or peace" relations with Hitler over a period of less than five years. March 1936: Hitler's troops march into the Rhineland, demilitarized under the Locarno treaty, to which Britain is a party; all that Britain needs to do is to give backing and encouragement to the wavering French, who then can easily reoccupy the Rhineland, thus dealing to Hitler's prestige a possibly decisive blow. The British choose the opposite attitude. Summer of 1938: after the Anschluss, Czechoslovakia is threatened, the French make ready to march on its behalf, the British government invents the Runciman mission which leads to Munich, "peace in our time." The strategic situation is now much deteriorated, but the takeover of Czechoslovakia, which was made helpless by amputation, scandalizes British opinion and Britain waxes militant. No matter that the hoped-for alliance with Russia falls through, it is war; the now reluctant French follow unwillingly, and, as it proves, ineffectively. October 1940: France has been utterly overcome; the only Power left standing in Europe, the Soviet Union, is presently Germany's ally; Hitler offers peace to England, at no cost to her—let her attend to her Empire, which Hitler admires. The offer is not even considered; by now the hearts of the British have been so turned against Hitler that, regardless of relative resources and chances, he must be fought, come what may.

The terrible ordeal was unnecessary; such mistakes will not be repeated: nonsense! Of course they are repeated all the time—though let us hope with no such dramatic consequences—and naturally so: because, at any moment, "the present situation" is appreciated in terms of the present feelings and evaluations. It is not like a chessboard problem which different onlookers can be unequally competent to solve but which they must all see alike; it is a different situation according to the onlooker, not the same to Baldwin or to Chamberlain as to

Churchill. Nor are the policies of a nation the outcome of one man's reading of the situation but of an aggregate of visions. Doubtless the United States could have prevented the Munich capitulation, and Roosevelt saw it should be prevented; but if he expressed it as a private opinion instead of throwing the weight of his nation in the balance, it is presumably because he felt that the nation's mood did not allow him to do so.

What appears as a glaring mistake in a game of strategy may be a natural outcome of a psychological context which "gaming" ignores, and *vice versa*. The last war would have been won by Germany and Japan had the latter Power attacked Russia instead of making the capital blunder of outright aggression against the United States fleet. It was so obviously good strategy for Japan to make sure that Russia was counted out, and so obviously a bad move to bring in the United States, that the unravelling of the psychological motives for such conduct should be very instructive.

There is a political context to strategic situations; situations which are much the same in strategic terms are very different in political terms. An instance is afforded by very recent news. Taking it as a datum that, throughout the period considered, the United States has been interested in precluding the spread of communism in the Indo-Chinese peninsula, we note that, a little more than ten years ago, American aircraft carriers were in the Gulf of Tonkin, available to the American President for an air-strike. In the spring of 1954, great results could be hoped for from an air-strike at Dien-Bien-Phu. Results then likely (not of course certain) were: the French army saved, Giap's army (then offering a concentrated target) crippled, the State of Vietnam (not then partitioned) relieved for a time from communist pressure and communist infiltration in Laos and Cambodia precluded. President Eisenhower decided against making the air-strike which might have had such consequences; an air-strike was made in early August 1964 when it held out no such promises. In terms of strategy, it cannot be explained that it was done in 1964 rather than in 1954. It has to be explained in political terms; not of course in terms of formal politics, for an air-strike in 1954 would have been made at the request of a formally sovereign state on its own territory against those who were formally rebels, while the air-strike of 1964 was made against the territory of a sovereign state. The explanation is not then to be sought in "politics" understood as "public law." The explanation is to be sought rather in terms of a far different emotional context.

Explanation and *a fortiori* prediction are impossible in politics without understanding of affective attitudes. "The springs of politics are the passionate movements of the human heart," says Cournot.[11] Tragedy is meant to display the swiftness and amplitude of such movements, a lesson which statesmen forget to their undoing. It so happens that France in early 1848 had for Prime Minister an eminent political scientist, indeed the restorer of our Academy of Political and Moral Sciences, Guizot. A rare feature in France, the parliamentary opposition acknowledged a leader, Thiers, who was a distinguished historian. Neither of these men had an inkling of the revolution which was to sweep away the regime in a few days of February. What is more, neither of them took seriously the massing of a crowd on February 22d—a crowd which indeed, according to students of those fateful days, showed as yet no signs of violent excitement.

Up to the last moment these eminent men did not foresee the revolution, and had they been told that within a few years Louis Bonaparte would be Emperor, they would have taken it as a joke. Now let me add that the history Thiers had written was that of the Revolution and Empire. He was familiar with such events as were to be repeated, but he must have felt, "It can't happen now"—another version of "It can't happen here." This instance stresses that *the political forecaster must guess how people will come to feel* (my seventh point) and also that this is no easy thing.

To this concern the study of public opinion corresponds, but it may be asked whether adequate attention has been paid to the dynamic of moods.

VIII

Consider "the body politic" as a vast army "making its way" in a literal sense; this raises a variety of problems, to be foreseen by a variety of social scouts, the political scientist a coordinator, wary of mix-ups which would generate excitement and anger. Such is the rough sketch of the picture which has been presented in the preceding sections. This so emphasizes policy expertise as to be possibly shocking, relatively to the established idea that the political scientist is an expert on *institutions*. But far from there being a conflict between the two conceptions, on the contrary the role of the political scientist as detector of problems breathes life into his role as student and designer of institutions.

Institutions are of instrumental value, good in so far as they efficiently cope with problems arising, and operate toward the achievement of social goods. If the machinery of government proves such that no timely action can be taken to ward off some visibly impending harm, a vice in the institutions can be presumed. Of course I do not mean that *any* bad policy is proof of bad institutions; none are so excellent as to exclude the possibility of foolish decisions. What I do mean is that frequency of failure to cope or achieve is a judgment upon what is in essence a coping-and-achieving machinery and nothing else.

Now this is precisely where institutional expertise is needed. Left to itself, public opinion will be apt to reject the whole system, throwing away what is good therein—and thus, for instance, turn from a "government by discussion" regime which is nòt working well, to a more efficient tyranny. It is for the institutions expert to indicate the more modest adjustments required. But, as a forecaster on how people will come to feel (point seven), he must be aware also that by the time public opinion has been aroused against the inefficiency of the system, its disposition will be to repudiate it altogether, so that minor adjustments, however well they might serve, will not be acceptable to it. These therefore must be made before the public has been aroused; and this is no easy thing, as the public does not then demand it and the wielders of the government machinery bask in complacency.

Indeed the political scientist should foresee the deficiencies of the institutional system not only before these have excited popular discontent and brought it into discredit, but even before these deficiencies have been made manifest by faulty performance. For this purpose he will rely to a considerable degree upon the assumed stability of social trends, ask himself how their estimated course will alter the demands made upon the "coping machinery," seek to assess its adequacy to such different demands, and thereupon look for the adjustments which can improve such adequacy.

To be sure, social change by itself has a direct impact upon the institutional machinery and tends to weaken or atrophy some institutions, to strengthen or hypertrophy others. Such direct impact may happen to work toward an improvement of the machinery: but it would be most unwise to take this as a postulate. Quite the reverse can be the case.

I do not propose to develop here my eighth point: *the political scientist should foretell the adjustments suitable to improve the adequacy of the institutional system to cope with changing circumstances.* Of the different points made here, this is the only one which is sure to be accepted by all; therefore the case for it need not be argued. If it comes here as the last point, it is because the institutional preoccupation is made most meaningful when derived from more immediate and concrete preoccupations. The future inflow of public business, its increasing volume, its new varieties, must be vividly pictured by the expert: only thus can he recommend adjustments in the public machinery, adequate to a liberal democratic handling of heavier and shifting burdens.

Any maladjustment enhances attitudes which amount to regarding political and private freedoms as conflicting with progress. It is for rulers who alone are far seeing, to lead their people in the way of progress, untrammelled in their decisions by lengthy discussions, and riding rough-shod over individuals: such is the immanent doctrine sugar-coated in different ideological colors. This nefarious doctrine is rendered plausible thanks to the fact that the ancient bulwarks of liberty are often used as defensive fortifications by the very people who would in previous times have opposed their erection, and the character of such defenders provides an argument for the flattening out of these bulwarks. It seems a most urgent preoccupation for people committed to political forecasting to see what can be done for the progress of liberty in a materially progressing society, the features of which could not be imagined in the seventeenth and eighteenth centuries.

Notes

1. Thucydides I, 83. From Hobbes' version, republished by the University of Michigan Press (Ann Arbor, 1959), vol. I, p. 48.

2. For a more extended discussion of the general topic, *see* my *L'Art de la Conjecture* (Monaco: Editions du Rocher, 1964); eight of the SEDEIS studies in conjecture have been collected, in English, in *Futuribles* (Geneva: Droz, 1963).

3. Royal Institute of International Affairs (London, 1931), pp. 531-36.

4. And not well designed even for that, as commandant Souchon noted in 1929, uttering this prophecy: "our future army will be dissociated, pushed around and cut to

pieces before having struck the least blow." In *Feu L'Armée Française, published without signature* (Paris, 1929).

5. One might elaborate upon the consequences of this inconsistency. First, the discovery of the impotence of the French army was a major cause of the French government's attitude at the time of Munich; but as they could not believe this impotence, the Soviet leaders quite understandably interpreted our shameful desertion of Czechoslovakia as inspired by a machiavellian desire to orient Germany toward an attack upon Russia, which was thought of by no responsible Frenchman. Second, as the Poles trusted the French army–as I found while attending them in the 1939 campaign–they thought it quite unnecessary to agree in the previous Anglo-Franco-Russian negotiations to the entry of Russian troops upon their soil, which the Soviets quite understandably made a condition of their military support. And this increased the Soviet suspicion of our good faith, which may have determined the Ribbentrop-Molotov pact.

6. In his masterly treatment of economic forecasting, H. Theil, *Economic Forecasts and Policy* (Amsterdam, 1961), Pt. V, notes that changes to come are generally underestimated. If our mind tends to underestimate shifts in a continuous course, breaks in this continuity are even less acceptable to it.

7. See the ranking of the different compartments of political science given by Albert Somit and Joseph Tanenhaus, "Trends in American Political Science," *American Political Science Review*, 57 (December 1963), pp. 933, 941. The authors asked political scientists in what compartment of the science the most significant work was being done and "behavioralism" came an easy first.

8. It is here beside the point that "the death of the Great Pan" or depersonalization of natural objects, has implied a great loss of reverence and sensitive enjoyment of them.

9. This mistake gives rise to heated quarrels between those who, being revolted that man should be thought of as a "mere thing," therefore needlessly repudiate the scientific method and those who, addicted to this method, therefore needlessly champion the "mere thing" notion. Justification or condemnation of the method does not rest thereupon but depends upon its efficiency. Here I would like to digress to say that the true danger of a scientific approach, but shared with any other form of intellectual outlook, is that excessive enthusiasm for general statements, however useful, should impair our appreciation of the particular and unique.

10. A. Quételet, *Sur l'homme et le développement de ses facultés ou essai de physique sociale*, 2 vols. (Paris, 1835).

11. A. Cournot, *Traité de l'enchaînement des idées fondamentales dans les sciences et dans l'histoire*, para. 460, p. 525 of the 1911 edition.

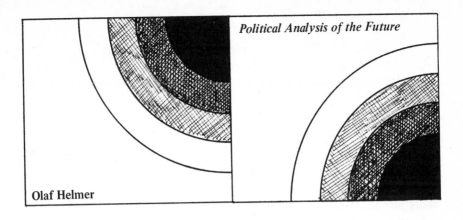

Olaf Helmer

Political Analysis of the Future

The title of this paper is ambiguous—and deliberately so. It could, and indeed is intended to, refer to the analysis of potential future political developments as well as to the future of political analysis as an intellectual endeavor. The remarks I intend to present will have some bearing on both of these subjects; for I shall concern myself, first, with new approaches to forecasting future developments and the role of such forecasts in political analysis, and, second, with the effect that a more deliberate orientation toward the future might have on the future of political science as a professional activity.

I hasten to say at once that my statements are those of an outsider to the profession. I am not a political scientist and consider myself a devout methodologist with a bent toward operations analysis. This makes for a certain detachment, which has obvious advantages and disadvantages. While promising the possibility of a refreshingly novel point of view, it is apt to be afflicted with a good deal of naiveté. I hope, and fear, respectively, that what I have to say will have some of both of these qualities.

Political science, to this outside observer, presents a picture which, in highly oversimplified terms, exhibits two major tendencies. One is that it appears to be oriented primarily toward the past and present and not toward the future, explicit prediction usually being limited to the immediate consequences of present events that historical evidence may suggest. Consideration of the more distant future, five, ten, or fifty years ahead, seems rare, except in rather abstract utopian terms, in which case the time horizon is apt to be quite indefinite. The other notable tendency is that of theory-building, the results of which often provide a profound intuitive understanding of the political scene. But precisely since these are intuitive, the observer is left with the impression that the authors of such theories must have a sense of frustration because their theories lack the intersubjectively testable character of their counterparts in the physical sciences, and consequently do not have the directly predictive quality of physical laws. This perhaps explains the regrettable reluctance to make fuller use of the often enormous intuitive insights derived from subjective theories based on historical consideration, and to apply them to a political analysis of the future.

The standard objection to attempting any analysis of the future, especially in the political sphere, is the claim that prediction is impossible since the state of the future is dominated by the occurrence of unforeseeable events—such as the death of a statesman, the rise in power of a dictator, the irrational behavior of a political negotiator. While it is true that such singular events are largely unpredictable, it is a misconception of the nature of scientific prognostication to conclude that therefore an effective analysis of the future is not feasible.

I cannot but regard such a position—that of rejecting the explorability of the future—as untenable. When placed in its proper perspective, an analysis of the future is both possible and necessary. It is necessary, because—whether we like it or not—whenever long-range plans have to be made, we inevitably do rely, in our choice among alternative actions, on forecasts of their probable consequences. For instance, in the case of such long-term commitments as are involved in the acceptance or rejection of an ABM system or in the selection of a strategy for foreign aid, we clearly anticipate that our actions will affect the future more than randomly, or we would not bother taking them. Since our anticipation of the future, even the long-range future, does indeed enter our decision-making processes, it clearly makes sense to go about the analysis of future potentialities in an orderly and deliberate fashion rather than to rely upon the haphazard and often hurried inclinations of a political decision-making body.

Of course, recognizing the desirability of an orderly analysis of the future does not guarantee its feasibility, which I will consider next. In order to discuss this, we need to have a clearer understanding of what may reasonably be expected of an analysis of the future, and what may not. The first thing to acknowledge is the uncertainty of the future, and hence its unpredictability in principle. There are two main reasons for this uncertainty: one is that our knowledge is insufficient to predict singular yet influential events of the type mentioned earlier. The other, which is the rationale underlying all planning, is the partial dependence of the future on our choice of action.

It is therefore inappropriate to speak of the future (in the singular) as something to be discovered, be it through crystal balls or through analysis. Rather, there are many possible futures, which can be considered in terms of probabilities; and it is through planning decisions and through invention that we may hope to affect these probabilities in the desired direction, raising the probabilities of those potential future states of the world that are preferable and lowering those that are not. An analysis of the future, then, should include the following objectives:

1. It should provide a survey of possible futures in terms of a spectrum of major potential alternatives.
2. It should ascribe to the occurrence of these alternatives some estimates of relative *a priori* probabilities.
3. It should, for given basic policies, identify preferred alternatives.
4. It should identify those decisions which are subject to control as well as

those developments which are not, whose occurrence would be likely to have a major effect on the probabilities of these alternatives.

Once these objectives have been achieved, the groundwork will have been laid for the operational application of political analysis—that is, for its use in the selection of appropriate courses of action toward the implementation of given policies.

The question, now, is whether these objectives are in fact attainable. My contention is that they are, or at least that considerable strides can be taken in the direction of their attainment. However, in order to move in this direction, a reorientation of some of the traditional political science effort will be required. Thus far, there seems to be evidence of a growing recognition of the need for such a reorientation but of only a few relevant pioneering efforts; that by Ivo and Rosalind Feierabend on the correlation between literacy and belligerence is a good example.

What is necessary, I think, and long overdue in political analysis is a deliberate move toward greater acceptance of the attitudes and methods of what has become known as operations analysis. Such a step, however much it may be approved of in principle, is more difficult than it sounds, for the basic attitudes of the operations analyst are in considerable conflict with the work habits of the majority of social scientists. Specifically, operations analysis, as its name implies, is operationally oriented; its practitioners place emphasis on the pragmatic aspects of implementing policies; they are planning-oriented and, therefore, future-oriented. They also tend, of necessity, to take a highly interdisciplinary systems view of things and, primarily because of methodological requirements, to favor quantitative approaches.

Of the methods prevalent in operations analysis, I would like to mention three categories. There is, first of all, the use of so-called mathematical models, including in particular the extrapolation into the future of past time series through correlation analysis. I note in passing that this involves the whole new area of social indicators, in terms of which we can estimate various aspects of the past and present states of affairs and make contingency forecasts of future developments. Other mathematical models include the formulation of so-called behavioral equations (well-known in economics), which attempt to reflect the expected reactions of people to changes in their environment. A special case of a behavioral model that particularly deserves mention in a political science context is one that might be considered an extension of non-zero-sum games. Such an extension would adjoin to the concepts normally included in such games that of the behavioral changes among "players" having to cope with a succession of individual conflict situations, where the behavior in any particular situation is influenced by the behavioral pattern exhibited by other players in previous situations. I shall briefly return later to the rather obvious application of such a model to the international scene.

The second category of operations-analytical tools is concerned with expert opinions. Since many of the inputs into operations analyses derive from the intuitive insights of subject area specialists, methods are needed to extract such expert judgments as effectively as possible. Among these methods are scenario construction, the Delphi technique, and simulation. Scenarios, as I use the term, are descriptions of plausible sequences of events leading from the present to the future; they are in the nature of thought experiments that serve to explore intuitively the realism of an imagined future state of affairs. The Delphi technique, now widely used in government and industry, is a means of extracting group judgments from a panel of experts, using a procedure that involves successive questionnaires and a controlled opinion feedback process. As a third method for the utilization of informed judgment, I mentioned simulation. I meant here specifically manual (or personal, as opposed to computer) simulation, also sometimes referred to as gaming. It requires that a group of experts engage in playing the roles of decision-makers and thus simulate, under assumed conditions, the planning decisions that their real-life counterparts would be expected to make under comparable circumstances.

In the third category of operations-analytical methods, I would like to mention the cross-impact technique, which is still under development and which offers a promising systematic means of examining the mutual effects of a set of potential future developments. Suppose we were interested in a set of potential developments, $D_1, D_2, D_3 \ldots$, with a priori probabilities $p_1, p_2, p_3, \ldots$. Then the method consists in constructing a two-entry table (the "cross-impact matrix") in which these developments are listed as both horizontal and vertical entries. In the cell of this matrix where, for instance, the D_2-row and the D_3-column intersect, information would be entered as to whether the occurrence of D_2 would affect the probability of occurrence of D_3 and, if so, by how much and with what time delay. While, in general, the estimation of the cell entries is a matter of expert judgment, the matrix—once it has been constructed—can be used to follow through the chain reactions of the occurrence of a given development; thus it can be employed for the systematic comparison of alternative policies, and for studies of the sensitivity with which the resultant condition of the world depends on the occurrence or nonoccurrence of specific developments. Therefore, the cross-impact matrix, when applied to potential political developments, may be looked upon as the nearest thing to a model (or theory) of interactions among political events.

An operations-analytical approach then, in summary, implies an interdisciplinary and future-oriented systems view of the subject matter; and it brings to bear such methods as mathematical models of many kinds, simulated planning techniques, the systematic use of expert judgment, and the cross-impact matrix technique for examining the mutual influences of potential future developments.

Having thus sketched the attitudes and methods of operations analysis, it is necessary to describe briefly how the adoption of this approach might in concrete terms affect the pursuits and products of political science research. Can it, in fact, help bridge the gap in comparative progress between the physical and the social sciences?

With respect to the physical sciences and technology, it has been estimated that between now and the end of the century we may expect a tenfold increase in R+D productivity, due to the continuing rise in the number of scientists and engineers and in the number and versatility of computers. The resulting changes in science and technology are bound to be enormous. Nevertheless, precisely because we have already reached such a high level on the scale of scientific and technological development, we may find that further progress in this area will be harder and harder to come by. In the social sciences and in their application to societal problems—that is, in social technology—we have not nearly reached that point where diminishing marginal returns for our efforts have to be expected; and I am firmly convinced that, with the adoption of a more pragmatic and future-oriented viewpoint and some of the methods mentioned earlier, there is an excellent chance that in the next few decades social science research, and political science research especially, will be able to make fundamental contributions to the betterment of the human condition and thus to begin to match the progress that has characterized physical technology in this century.

Specifically, let me list some of the areas where a renewed and redirected effort promises substantial rewards.

1. *International political indicators*: With indicators generally there has been a tendency to prefer those that lend themselves to easy, objective measurement. This can lead to absurd results, as when we measure the status of the cold war against the Soviet bloc in terms of the number of people under Communist domination, an indicator which is a carry-over from an earlier period when population pressure was a political asset rather than a liability. Similarly, we tend to measure our performance in Vietnam in terms of enemy soldiers killed vs U.S. soldiers killed; this accounting not only conveys an inadequate description at best, but it fosters the misconception that the killing per se of as many enemy soldiers as possible is one of our primary goals. What we badly need is an appropriate set of indicators that are in accord with our long-range goals as a nation, in terms of which we can assess how well we are doing on the international scene. Here, the Delphi technique for obtaining a consensus among experts may be very helpful, for it permits us to include indicators which require intuitive appraisal rather than measurement in terms of observable quantities.

2. *National goals*: National goals, just mentioned in connection with political indicators, form a hierarchy. The goals at any given level are merely indicative of the policies chosen to implement the goals at the next higher level. The only absolute goals, at the very top, are probably simply the old cherished ones of life, liberty, and the pursuit of happiness. The President has recently established a National Goals Research Staff that will presumably concern itself with these problems. The work of this group could make notable contributions to the

decision-making processes at the presidential level if it would state this nation's goals and subgoals in relation to appropriate political indicators, so that the degree of attainment of such goals expected from proposed policies could be estimated and stated in terms of these indicators. Aside from again making systematic use of expert opinion for this purpose, the cross-impact technique might be applicable, as it would afford a means of examining the joint effects of a set of measures on a set of indicators.

3. *Capitalism vs. Communism*: As a particular case, a reappraisal of our national goals should include a more future-oriented assessment of our relations with the Communist world. One sometimes wonders whether we have not forgotten what the entire quarrel was about. What started out as a difference in ideology on certain economic principles has inadvertently turned into a power struggle for world domination. Our economies, meanwhile, are converging, each adopting some of the methods of the other; what is more, as affluence steadily increases on both sides of the iron curtain, we will all, before we know it, be entering the age of post-industrial society, where there will be a common search for new principles by which to order our economic processes, and the old quarrel will have become totally meaningless. This suggests that the proper way to a rapprochement with the Soviet Union may well be via futurism, since our long-range goals are much more compatible than our short-range (and often shortsighted) subgoals. There are, in fact, indications that the cultural exchange is already proving the most successful in areas concerned with the long-range future.

4. *Cost-effectiveness analysis of foreign policy*: A well chosen set of international political indicators and a clear statement of national goals in terms of such indicators would eventually put us in a position where we could begin to think of making foreign policy choices on the basis of cost-effectiveness considerations. For our foreign policy to make cost-effectiveness sense, it is essential to attempt the impossible—namely, to take a systems view of our operations in the foreign policy field. This means that we have to create the conceptual as well as the administrative apparatus for across-the-board comparisons of marginal benefits to be derived from investing a million dollars, say, in aid to Indonesia, in our military effort in Vietnam, in military intelligence about China, or in improved cultural relations with Poland. What is more, these estimates of benefits must include comparisons of immediate vs. long-term benefits. To tackle this immense, but I hope not really impossible, task we shall need many of the methods that operations research has to offer—in particular, simulation, the systematic use of expertise in many areas, and the cross-impact technique for studying, in Michael Spicer's words, "the complex ricochet effects of particular policies."

5. *Negotiation*: Two comments seem appropriate on the subject of international negotiation. First, while so-called "crisis gaming" (dealing with antici-

pated cold war crises or with the threat of hot war) has been in vogue for some time and been of some utility to our foreign policy planners, there is little evidence that such simulation is being applied specifically to important forthcoming international conferences. Our negotiators on such occasions might conceivably derive considerable benefit from pre-conference gaming, in which their prospective adversaries are simulated with verisimilitude. The development of appropriate simulation models for this purpose might be a worthwhile undertaking. Second, and perhaps more importantly, in playing the international non-zero-sum game, we do not always seem to be fully aware of the difference between short-term and long-term gains. In theoretic terms, this difference is one between the immediate expected payoff in the game that happens to be going on at the moment and the restructuring of the game into one which promises increased payoffs to both sides; such restructuring can often be achieved by changing the flow of information or by augmenting (or diminishing) the opportunities for negotiation. As I have suggested earlier, the accomodation of such applications may require an extension of traditional non-zero-sum game theory, as we are here no longer dealing with a single game but with the behavior pattern of adversaries engaged in a dynamic sequence of successive conflict situations.

These five very brief examples from the foreign policy field suffice to make my point—that there is some promise in the transfer of operations-analytical techniques to political analysis; it would be easy to give similar examples relating to domestic policy problems.

A reorientation of political analysis toward the future, through the adoption of some such techniques, is likely to make it a more effective tool for policy formation, especially in the area of foreign relations. In analogy to the application of physical science to physical technology, this development may lead to the establishment of "political technology" as an activity explicitly devoted to the pragmatics of the political scene.

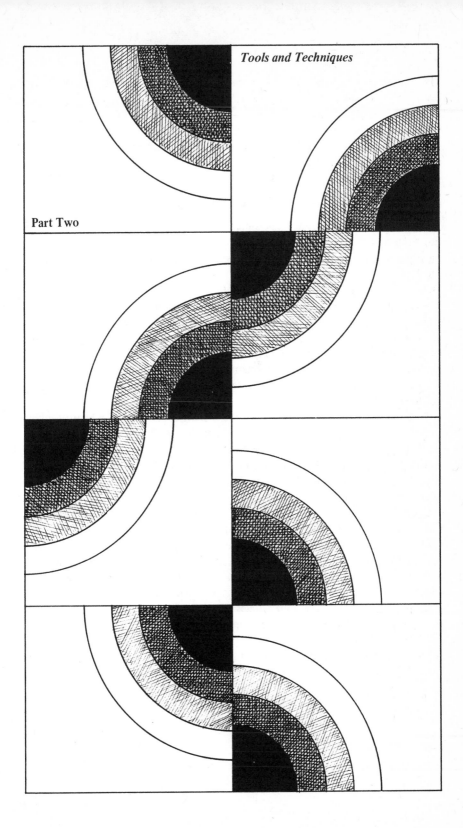

Part Two

Tools and Techniques

The four essays presented in this section were intended to present a coherent overview of the subject, with each author treating it from a particular perspective. While certain anomalies do remain—and I will return to these shortly—I believe that objective was largely achieved.

Daniel Bell's now classic "Twelve Modes of Prediction" describes the diverse approaches available to the futurist. Aware that his twelve categories are neither completely separate from each other nor equal in level of generality, Bell has observed that ". . . the next step would be to order (the twelve modes) in some logical classification."[1]

Denis Johnston's essay undertakes precisely that task. Johnston distinguishes three types of "outlook" statements—prediction, projection, and forecast. The most rigorous of the three is *prediction*, which requires both the application to social phenomena of a "covering" law *and* a resulting deductive conclusion. *Projections* are less rigorous, since they entail only a deductive conclusion without specification of the underlying processes operative. The least scientifically demanding is the *forecast*, which posits "the most likely" outcome in situations not sufficiently deterministic to permit a valid prediction. As might be expected, forecasts (which fall into four general categories—qualitative-exploratory, qualitative-normative, quantitative-exploratory, and quantitative-normative) are the kinds of outlook statements most commonly encountered in political futurism.

T. J. Gordon is more concerned with the *specific tools* which can be utilized in future studies (Delphi, cross-impact matrix analysis, genius forecasting, etc.). With few exceptions, these can be used to operationalize the more general approaches enumerated by Bell and categorized by Johnston. They could readily be applied, following Johnston's terminology, to either quantitative or qualitative forecasting.

Developing a topic treated more briefly by Johnston, Isabel Sawhill examines the role of social indicators, social accounts, and social reports. These three forms of *social intelligence*, she argues, are indispensable to sound governmental decision-making. So far they are available, at best, in rudimentary form; but once perfected, they will permit better evaluation of future policy alternatives and, consequently, more effective methods of social planning.

A careful reading of these four articles reveals some unresolved discrepancies. Bell's "social physics" may be more properly classified as a predictive device rather than, as Johnston would have it, a mode of forecasting. It is not altogether clear whether "social accounting" is "quantitative-exploratory" or "quantitative-normative." Some of Gordon's specific *tools*, to take a last example, seem similar to some of Bell's more general *approaches*. These problems, I would suggest, are essentially definitional; and the resulting classificatory difficulties are hardly unique to political futurism.

Note

1. In a later discussion, Bell identified *three* general methods of social forecasting: (1) analytical identification of future problems, (2) extrapolation of existing social trends "for which we have time series," and (3) construction of a model "in which the relevant independent variables and their dependent functions are identified." Perloff, *op. cit.*, pp. xi-xii.

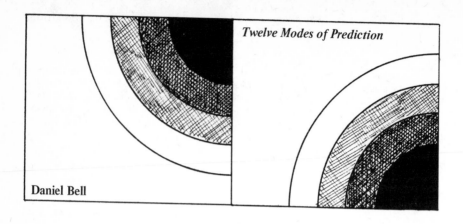

In the *Cours de Philosophie Positive* (1830-1842), perhaps the last individual attempt to write a synoptic account of human knowledge, Auguste Comte cited as an example of the inherently unknowable, the chemical composition of the distant stars and the question of whether there were "organized beings living on their surface."[1] Within two decades, Gustave Kirchoff applied spectrum analysis to the stars and provided that very knowledge which Comte had declared to be impossible. And, as space probes reach Mars and Venus, we shall be in a position to answer the second question of the nature of the forms of life, if any, on the solar planets.

Few persons today would declare with confidence that something is unknowable. So secure is the dominion of science that the obverse attitude rules: today we feel that there are no inherent secrets in the universe, and that all is open; and this is one of the significant changes in the modern moral temper. And yet, every generation now feels that the foundation of its knowledge is inadequate and that the social forms as we know them are bound to change. We expect that science and technology will rework the map of society and no one any longer challenges their claims. One of the hallmarks of "modernity" is the awareness of change and the struggling effort to control the direction and pace of change.

The problem of any science is to understand the sources of change. And in this respect social science is fairly recent. The great intellectual barrier was that men always thought they knew the sources of change, which were also the sources of power, namely the personal will of kings, lawgivers and prophets, those who governed states, drafted laws, and established or reinforced religious beliefs. But only gradually did men realize that behind these visible sets of acts were such intangible nets as customs, institutions, and cultures, which subtly constrained and set the boundaries of social action. At the same time came the slow realization that there were "social forces" which generated change, whether they be impersonal processes such as demographic pressures (increased size and density of populations), technology, and science, or conscious strivings such as the demands of disadvantaged groups for equality or social mobility.

It is the modern *hubris* that we can effect the conscious transformation of society. What stands in our favor is that knowledge is cumulative. And, within the open community of science, it is self-corrective. We know more of economics than the "Political Arithmetick" of Sir William Petty, who started us out with "Number, Weight and Measure." We have clearer conceptual distinctions than Herbert Spencer and his primitive efforts at establishing social differentiation. We have more complex statistical tools than Pearson or Galton. What is more important, perhaps, is that we have a better appreciation of method. For what method allows us to do is to reformulate insight into consistent explanation. More than two thousand years ago, Plato wrote: ". . . it is in sleep that the wild beast in our nature stands up and walks about naked, and there is no conceivable folly or shame or crime, however unnatural, not excepting incest or parricide, of which such a nature may not be guilty. In all of us, even in good men, there is a latent wild beast which peers out in sleep."[2] Yet it was only in *The Interpretation of Dreams* that such wisdom was assimilated into a coherent theory which explained not only the existence of such impulses but the mechanisms of control through the idea of wishes and repressions.

In this emphasis on method, the function of conjecture is not prediction but explanation.[3] Prediction can be derived from experience, such as a farmer's expectation of crop production, without knowledge of the reasons why. Only with adequate explanation—an understanding of the relevant variables—can one seek to control or transform a situation. Conjecture, in this sense, stipulates a set of future predicates whose appearance should be explainable from theory. Prediction without explanation is insight, experience, or luck.

In this sense, too, the function of prediction is to reduce uncertainty. By stipulating, and thus testing, a hypothesis, one is able to verify the relevant factors which account for a predicted or observed change. For this reason, in distinguishing different kinds of prediction in the social sciences, I am ruling out historical theories of rhythms, periodizations and cycles—in most instances, recurrence is not really identity but, at best, analogy—wherein the investigator seeks for the Pythagorean number which rules the wheel of history or imposes a diachronic pattern on the rise and fall of civilization.[4]

In sorting out the different modes of prediction, I shall not be concerned with the relevant methodological tests of adequacy. The sorting is an effort to illustrate the *range* of approaches in the art of conjecture. The different modes are not "equal" to each other in the level of generality or scope of comprehension. Inevitably there are some overlaps, and a stricter reading might show that one mode subsumes some of the others. But to the extent that one can sort out a distinct number of types, the next step would be to order them in some logical classification and specify which mode of conjecture would be appropriate to what kind of problem.

1. Social Physics

The Comtean quest for "social laws" in which some basic regularities of human behavior or some major variables such as mass, pressure, gravitational velocity could be synthesized into a set of formulas akin to Newtonian or the later statistical mechanics of Willard Gibbs finds few serious adherents in the social sciences today. Yet one such model, Marx's "laws of motion" of capitalism, has been one of the most influential ideological doctrines of the past century (in but three years we celebrate the centennial of *Das Kapital*), and to the extent that it is still an element in the Bolshevik belief-system, it is a factor in assessing Communist policy.

Questions of politics apart, the Marxian model is still one of the most comprehensive efforts to create a large-scale system of prediction based on the interaction of a few crucial variables. Granted that the model has not worked, its "logic" is worth explication. Marx began, one may recall, with the components of value as constant capital, variable capital, and surplus value ($c + v + s$), and from these, two ratios become central. One is the rate of surplus value, $s/v = s'$, and the other is the organic composition of capital, the relationship of labor to materials and machinery, $c/c + v = q$. These two are the primary variables from which the crucial variable, the rate of profit, is derived: $p = s'(l - q)$.

The "law of the falling rate of profit," which Marx derives from these equations, is the key to the system. Each capitalist, trying to increase his own profit, substitutes more constant for variable capital and ends by killing off the total of profits. Out of this tendency, Marx derives the corollary social consequences: the reserve army of the unemployed, the impoverishment of labor, the centralization (trustification) of capital, a deepening series of crises, the intensification of exploitation, sharpening class struggle, etc.

One can point out, as Paul Samuelson has,[5] that the model rests on the difficult assumption of fixed coefficients and single techniques, and that modern tools such as linear programming can allow the substitution, analytically, of many alternative techniques in working out adequate production functions (i.e. the combination of units of labor and capital). Or one can argue the empirical point, as Strachey and others have, that the economic system is not autonomous and that a regulating agency, the State, can readjust the "equations" in response to political pressures.

The crucial element in the Marxian model, which defines it as "social physics," is that these actions took place independent of the will of any single individual or, in the long run, of any groups of individuals. The interesting question remains whether such comprehensive, dynamic models are possible, even in the simplified versions such as Marx employed, and what would be the central variables that one would select to describe social and political interaction.

A different kind of "law," which has attracted increasing attention in recent years, is that of "logistics curves," which various authors have fitted to different time-series. The most startling of these are the laws of "exponential growth" or the "doubling rates" of different social phenomena.

The late Louis Ridenour has pointed out that the holdings of university libraries have doubled every eleven years since 1870, that long-distance telephone calls have doubled every seven-and-a-half years, that since Nellie Bly went around the world in 1889 the time for circumventing the globe decreased exponentially between 1889 and 1928 by a factor of two every quarter-century, and since the introduction of aircraft the rate of change has markedly increased. Derek Price has shown that the number of journals in science has increased by a factor of ten every half-century since 1790, and the number of abstracting journals has followed precisely the same law, multiplying by a factor of ten every half-century. At a certain point in these growths, "critical magnitudes" are reached and logistic curves react to "ceiling conditions" in different ways.[6]

Ridenour, in fitting a number of such curves, has argued that the process of growth and saturation in social change follows the so-called "autocatalytic" processes of chemistry and biology. Price has sought to identify more differentiated modes of "reaction." He writes: ". . . growths that have long been exponential seem not to relish the idea of being flattened. Before they reach a midpoint they begin to twist and turn, and, like impost spirits, change their shapes and definitions so as not to be exterminated against that terrible ceiling. Or in less anthropomorphic terms, the cybernetic phenomenon of hunting sets in and the curve begins to oscillate wildly. . . . [One] finds two variants of the traditional logistic curve that are more frequent than the plain S-shaped ogive." One variant is the phenomenon, first recognized by Gerald Holton,[6] of "escalation," in which growth curves "pick up" from earlier, related curves in repeated sequence. The other variant is one of violent fluctuation with a logarithmic decline to a stable maximum or to zero. This leads Price to conclude: "All the apparently exponential laws of growth must ultimately be logistic, and this implies a period of crisis extending on either side of the date of midpoint for about a generation. The outcome of the battle at the point of no return is complete reorganization of violent fluctuation or death of the variable."[7]

If Ridenour's equations hold true and Price's generalizations regarding the "midpoints" of exponential curves are valid, one has here a powerful means of identifying processes of social change and making predictions about the outcomes.

And yet, the history of earlier, similar efforts to find underlying "laws" of variegated social phenomena should give us pause. In the late 1930s, the Harvard philologist George Kingsley Zipf reported remarkable regularities in such diverse phenomena as the distribution of cities by size, the relation of rank order to frequency of word occurrences, the distribution of the frequency of publication of scientists, and many others. Zipf tried to bring all these under the roof of a single mathematical relationship, the harmonic law, and devised a pseudo-explanation which he dubbed the "law of least effort." Fifteen years or so later, Herbert Simon was able to show that the similarity of these statistical distributions was not due to any overriding law but was a consequence of the similarity in the structure of the underlying probability mechanisms.[8]

Yet this corrective effort has given us an interesting tool of prediction. For in the construction of such probability models we encounter stochastic processes,[9] where the sequences of outcomes are uncertain and where we are forced to build "conjecturing" into the structure of the model. The development of stochastic reasoning, using probabilistic models, should allow us to do better estimating in problems involving frequency distributions, as well as those involving future outcomes involving the choice of further information.

Some recent efforts to create a "social physics" devolve from the work of the mathematical biologist Nicholas Rashevsky. One of his students, Anatol Rapoport, has written a book, *Fights, Games and Debates*[10] which sets up mathematical models for mass action and descriptive models for conflict situations. One section of the book deals with arms races, and the equations that are developed seek to describe the development of actual arms races in the same way that the equations of thermodynamics are meant to describe the actual behavior of gases. One intention of the new social physics is to set up general probabilistic laws governing behavior in game-like situations.

One older tradition of social physics is worth mentioning: the efforts, initiated originally by Robert Park, to explain (and predict) the growth of cities and other aspects of social ecology (the spatial distribution of units) as a product of impersonal forces such as competition or technology rather than willed or planned volitional efforts. Among geographers and some sociologists, this effort to create a so-called "biotic" or sub-social framework continues.[11]

2. Trends and Forecasts

The most familiar form of prediction involves some form of extrapolation from time-series either as straight-line projections, cyclical turns, or alternative models based on some definition of upper and lower limits. One can say that this mode of prediction differs from "social physics" in that the latter seeks some general principle, or attempts to create a closed system; trend analysis takes some selected area and seeks to make a more limited prediciton, *ceteris paribus*.

The three major kinds of trend analysis have been economic forecasting, demography, and technological change. The assumptions of economic forecasting itself would require a long paper,[12] so I restrict myself to the other two.

Demographic prediction, in the large, has always been under the long shadow of Thomas Malthus.[13] While the exact relationship between the arithmetical growth rate of food supply and the geometrical tendency of population increase is now suspect, the neo-Malthusians still hold to the general view that the present is in some way an exceptional period and that at some point, either fifty or a hundred years from now, the world "will have begun to go back," as Sir Charles Darwin has put it, "into . . . its normal state, the state in which natural selection operates by producing too many people, so that the excess simply cannot survive."[14]

Sir Charles has made some specific estimates. He feels that by A.D. 2000 the world population will be four billion. He cites the fact that between 1947 and 1953 agriculture production increased by 8 per cent but the world's population by 11 per cent, "so that the world was hungrier at the end than at the beginning. And in fifty years, the four billion will be hungrier than the two and a half billion in 1950."

Leaving aside the question of the definition of hunger, the basic assumptions are threefold: that human population has followed the availability of food supply so consistently that the human animal is responding to biological conditions in no different manner than other animals; that improvements in technology cannot keep pace with the rise of populations; that the voluntary limitations on birth cannot be accepted by the whole of humanity, so that those who limited births would be swallowed up by the others who did not. Each of these is open to question in some manner. As to the first, while this may be true of primitive societies, it is less so of modern industrial countries where the standard of living becomes more controlling of the number of births; the second is still an open question; the third raises vital political questions most notably today about the role of China and secondarily of India in the desires of their governments to control or expand population in these countries and the checks thereon.

What this does point up is that demographic prediction, involving individual and aggregate decisions, the role of custom and the adaptation to standard of living, the influence of education and new class styles, the relationship to economic development and the political role of government, is one of the areas where systematic scrutiny of the conditions of prediction would yield important results.

The area of "technological trends" could lead us very easily, and temptingly, into the alluring field of science fiction. Here one's imagination could quickly climb William James's "faith ladder" and turn possibilities into probabilities and probabilities into certainties. While one would assume that the prediction of invention should be fairly easy, since the antecedent conditions are highly structured, the interesting thing is that a review of such predictions finds them to be singularly inept.[15] Reality, it seems, is more recalcitrant than the imagination.

As S. Lilley writes: "The moral for forecasters is: Do not predict individual inventions in detail—that is usually a waste of time." The correct method, he argues, is twofold: extrapolation of present trends, and predictions in the form of possibilities. "The predictor need not be concerned with how a technical problem is to be solved, but only whether it will be solved or not." This is based on the principle of "equivalent invention" enunciated by S. L. Gilfallen. Gilfallen, writing in 1937, cites the problem of flying in fog. There were twenty-five means suggested of solving it. To predict which means would be the most successful was hazardous; but one could predict that the problem was solvable. "The point is that we are not concerned with the prediction of inventions, only with their effects. And the fact that there are almost always many possible inventions that could lead to the same desired effect enormously increases the chances of successful prediction," Lilley concludes.

The methods of political forecasting—the work of the Gallup organization, the University of Michigan surveys, the Columbia University studies under Paul Lazarsfeld, the work of *Demoskopie* in Germany and *Sondages* in France—would require a separate paper. Strictly speaking, this is not trend analysis, though past trends may be important in such crucial questions as how to allocate "undecided" voters. At bottom the success of the forecast is a function of the accuracy of the sample and the reduction of interviewer bias. Certain presumed disqualifying effects, such as the poll itself creating a "bandwagon," can be discounted. The success of *ex post facto* explanation is a function of the "process analysis" (i.e. the selection of relevant determinants such as the mass media, or personal influence) employed. [16]

One form of trend analysis is beautifully illustrated in the *Futuribles* paper of Colin Clark. It might be described as setting forth the "conditions of fit." [17] Professor Clark takes as a problem the statement of M. Manshold, the vice-president of the European Economic Community, that for economic equilibrium to be attained in Europe, some eight million persons within the Common Market area dependent on agriculture have to be transferred to other sectors. Clark seeks to establish the rates of transfer which might obtain for each country. He does this by computing two formulas; one, on the production side, deals with the number of persons necessary in the agricultural sector to support the food demands in the country (thus in France, in 1957-58 one agricultural worker provided food for ten non-agricultural workers; in New Zealand, the ratio was one to sixty-two); on the demand side, he calculates the rate at which demand per head for any food product may be expected to increase, based on population growth, income rise, and the elasticity of demand for particular products. At the intersects of the two curves one can chart the rates of reduction of agricultural workers for each country.

Since there is a long history of experience on the nature of income elasticities in the demand for products, Clark has been able to work out his formulas with some exactitude. The theoretical foundation, on the demand side, derives from the observations made less than a hundred years ago by the German statistician Christian Engel: as national incomes rise, a smaller proportion of the increment is spent for food. On the production, or supply, side, one can calculate the increased yields per acre on the basis of the amount of fertilizer, and the types of farming used.

In the Common Market countries, the reduction of eight million persons dependent on agriculture means the transfer of *one-third* of the farm population to other areas. Professor Clark computes, on the basis of rates of change obtaining since 1950, this change will be achieved in ten years in Germany, the Netherlands, and Belgium. In Italy, where the size of the agricultural population before 1950 had not changed for more than fifty years, the new methods of farming, combined with the rising national income, and reduced marginal increases for food, the agricultural labor force has been declining at a gross rate of 2 per cent per annum, or, if a reduction of one-third in the labor force is the target, it would take thirty years to reach that figure in Italy.

It is rare to have social change pinpointed over time with the exactness that Clark attempts. Since the politics, as well as the economics, of these countries will be affected by these population transfers, it would be useful to have a sociologist or a political scientist "overlay" Clark's predictions with some similar statement of expected social consequences (e.g. how will the voting patterns in these countries change as a result of the reduction of an agricultural labor force by a third, in ten or thirty years). Clark has set up an "independent variable" (a product, it is true, of more general causes). It would be fascinating to see if the dependent consequences could be charted as well.

3. Structural Certainties

In his *Essai sur l'Art de la Conjecture*, Bertrand de Jouvenel describes an *order of events* that are legally prescribed and traditionally reinforced, which he calls "les certitudes structurelles." This type of ordering differs logically from trends, because it does not describe processes or time-series that are derivable from aggregate behavior, or which may be immanent, but which are based on custom and law.

M. de Jouvenel's example is an interesting one. He describes the problem of a Democrat in 1962 who might like to succeed President Kennedy. He knows that there will be a president of the United States, that elections will take place on the second Tuesday of November in 1964 and 1968, that unless he has a physical accident, John F. Kennedy will be the Democratic candidate, since the party customarily designates the existing office holder. But Kennedy will not be a candidate in 1968 (assuming his re-election in 1964) because a constitutional amendment forbids a third successive term.

Of course M. de Jouvenel, like all of us, had no way of knowing that a physical accident would prevent John F. Kennedy from filling out his term. Yet the "structural certainties" remain. In this instance it is now taken for granted that Lyndon Johnson will be renominated in 1964, and, because he filled out less than half of his predecessor's term, he might well be a candidate for re-election in 1968 as well.

M. de Jouvenel had taken this "prosaic" set of facts to illustrate that much of human behavior can be predicted because of such structural certainties. Yet the concept is useful because it is one of the ways of ranking the stability of different kinds of political and social systems. (What are the structural certainties in the Brazilian political system?) This concept is analogous to what sociologists call "institutionalized behavior," and in any established social system, the chief problem is to define the prescribed norms, the modes of conformity, and the limits of legitimate deviation from such institutional norms which are allowed by the system.[18]

4. The Operational Code (or Les Règles de la Jeu)

Structural certainties (or institutionalized behavior) are based on a known or open mode of conduct, the rules of which are prescribed and reinforced by legal or moral sanction, and this allows one type of prediction. But there is another form of conduct which is usually implicit, rather than explicit, often unrealized even by the actors, and which has to be inferred and explicated by an analyst. This form is the "operational code" or what might be called the "do's and don't's" of conduct, the implicit rules of the game.

In some instances, such as Machiavelli's *The Prince*, these are normative prescriptions for a ruler. But in other cases these are efforts to discern an underlying pattern of behavior, which is either an adaptive mechanism (or rules of strategy) for a political group, or simply a series of adjustments which permit political survival.

One pioneer in this type of analysis, and prediction, is Nathan Leites. In several books on the Soviet Union and on France, he has sought to codify rules.[19] In the case of the Soviet Union, Leites has sought to establish the basic mode of Bolshevik conduct, which he derives from various maxims and precepts of Communist patriotic writings; but he roots this, equally, in some psychoanalytic hypotheses regarding Bolshevik character structure. In his study of France, he has sought to delineate the "rules of the game" as observed in parliamentary behavior.

In an analogous but broader fashion, there have been attempts to establish the "national style" of a country. The national style, or the characteristic way of response, is a compound of the values and national character of a country. It is the distinctive way of meeting the problems of order and adaptation of conflict and consensus, of individual ends and communal welfare, that confront any country. It has been observed, for example, that the American "style" is one that stresses action and achievement, is fundamentally optimistic, believes that life is tractable, the environment manipulable, and that all political problems can be "solved." This does not assume a distribution of such traits among all the persons in the country in any mechanical notion of national character; but it does assume that there is a characteristic way of responding to problems, which is typified in the leadership; and to this extent it can serve as a rough guide to political action.[20]

5. The Operational System

The "operational code" is an attempt to infer styles of conduct derived from psychological hypotheses or the value patterns of social groups or countries. The "operational system," an older form of analysis, is an effort to specify the underlying source of "renewable power" in a society regardless of the momentary fluctuations of office. Here, too, as in the case of "social physics," the most direct effort derives from Marx, and the classic analysis of this "model" in his *The Eighteenth Brumaire of Louis Bonaparte*.[21]

Louis Bonaparte, in Marx's analysis, is an "adventurer" representing no class or social group, although basing himself on the Society of December 10th and the *Lumpenproletariat.*[22] To maintain power, he has to play off one group against another, representing himself at first for the peasantry, and then against them, for the workers, and then against them. Industry and trade prosper in hothouse fashion under the strong government. But the Bonapartist *Lumpen-*

proletariat is to enrich itself. "This contradictory task of the man explains the contradictions of his government, the confused groping hither and thither which seeks now to win, now to humiliate first one class and then another and arrays all of them uniformly against him, whose practical uncertainty forms a highly comical contrast to the imperious categorical style of the government decrees, a style which is copied obsequiously from the Uncle."

The executive authority has made itself an independent power. But underneath there is still a class system. "Bonaparte feels it to be his mission to safeguard 'civil order.' But the strength of this civil order lies in the middle class. He looks on himself, therefore, as the representative of the middle class and issues decrees in this sense. Nevertheless, he is somebody solely due to the fact that he has broken the political power of this middle class and daily breaks it anew. Consequently, he looks on himself as the adversary of the political and literary power of the middle class. *But by protecting its material power, he generates its political power anew.*"[23]

The point here is that a renewable means of power provides continuity for a social system. Whether the specific historical analysis is right or wrong, methodologically, it does sensitize us to look for the institutional sources of power and to specify levels of analysis. Where a system is established (say, property in land), it is "neutral" as to "who" has power. As Schumpeter has said, the rise and fall of social classes is the rise and fall of families, but the *mode of defining classes* may remain a constant. In specifying levels of analysis, we can try to see what kind of political efforts seek to change the system itself, and which are changes *within* a system.

One of the problems of modern political analysis is that *many* "operational systems" coexist as modes of power.[24] In western democratic countries there is property, transferred through inheritance; technical skill, acquired by education; and political entrepreneurship, whose base is a mass mobilization; and each of these systems provides competing or overlapping routes to power. Yet the identification of such systems and the specification of the levels of analysis is a necessary condition for political prediction.

6. Structural Requisites

The idea of structural requisites focuses not on any underlying system but on the minimal set of concerns any government faces and it tries to identify "strains" or problems on the basis of the government's ability to manage those concerns. The list of what constitutes an invariant set of functions for any political system and the kinds of structures necessary to facilitate performance have varied with different authors. But what the approach does seek is a comprehensive typology which, in the words of one of these system-builders, Gabriel Almond, could allow the political analyst to "make precise comparisons relating the elements of the three sets—functions, structures, and styles—in the form of a series of probability statements."[25]

In the formulation by Almond, the product of the three sets would yield a matrix with several hundred cells, and an effort to sample frequencies over time by performances of these three sets would create a stupendous problem. Yet the effort to create a typology is the first necessary step for distinguishing different kinds of political problems.[26]

Au fond, what this approach suggests is what the anthropologist Alexander Goldenweiser once called "the principle of limited possibilities." Goldenweiser was trying to "mediate" the argument between anthropologists on the question of diffusion or independent invention of techniques. Methodologically, he argued that the "relatively fixed features which determined the conditions of effective use" of an object indicated a necessary convergence of forms.[27] (One might say, analogously, that Pareto's *Tratto* of General Sociology is based on the same principle. In it, Pareto disregards the manifest political content of doctrines and seeks to establish a limited number of basic residues, derivations and sentiments, and in the combination of these to establish the basic political forms possible in society.)

Most of these theoretical efforts, if they ever come to fruition, would produce vast sociological "input-out" tables; but a rougher and readier use, implicitly, of the principle of limited possibilities indicates some of its predictive value. Thus, in 1954, Barrington Moore analyzed Soviet society in these terms.[28] According to Moore, the recruitment to a ruling group could be handled through *traditional* (inheritance or nepotism), *rational-technical* (skill), or *political* (party loyalty) criteria. The use of any one criterion limits the range of workable alternatives for the solution of problems requisite to the system. Industrialization requires high technical criteria, but the nature of the power struggle dictates that top jobs should go to trusted individuals, while the traditional modes of clique groups serve to protect individuals from the competition of those selected by the other two criteria. By setting up these three "ideal types" Moore posited a number of alternative combinations as predictors of the future direction of Soviet society. One important consequence of this simplified model was that prediction that terror had gone too far and that some new means of rationalization had to be found.

In a different sense, the principle of limited possibilities, by concentrating on the constraints in a system, indicates the limits of change. Edward F. Denison has argued that the institutional economic arrangements in the United States make it difficult to achieve a 5 or even 4 per cent growth rate as hoped for by both President Kennedy and Governor Rockefeller. By analyzing patterns of investment, sources of capital, tax policies, habits of consumption, etc., Denison argues that an upper limit of 3 per cent a year can be reached. Any other efforts would require some drastic changes in the institutional structure of the society with losses of different kinds of economic choice.[29]

7. The Overriding Problem

Leicester Webb's essay, "Political Future of Pakistan,"[30] provides an interesting illustration of political analysis and prediction which is pitched on the identification of a single overriding problem.

While pointing to the obvious problems of unifying a state whose territorial divisions are a thousand miles apart, whose two units speak different languages, whose population is 85 per cent illiterate and which lacks a viable political system, Webb finds that the chief problem which must be solved, before any efforts can be made to deal with the others, is the problem of a social solidarity which could be the foundation for a national identity.

The question of national identity has been singled out by Lucian Pye, for example, as the overriding problem in the creation of a viable political system in Burma.[31] Where Pye, though, locates the Burmese problem in the general set of cultural ambiguities (e.g. the contradiction of gentleness and violence in the culture), the Webb essay is more focused in that it points to a fundamental dilemma in Pakistan: the effort to use religious sentiments to create a secular state.

The unity of Pakistan lies in its adherence to Islam, yet Islamic thought, and the retrograde attitudes of the sect leaders, hinders the creation of a meaningful political entity. The anomaly, says Webb, is that Pakistan is a "religiously-based state ... at loggerheads with its religious leaders." From the first, President Ayub has been conscious of this dilemma. In his public addresses he returns again and again to the theme: Pakistan needs an ideology; that ideology must be Islamic. But his two roles are in conflict. As the restorer of order and political innovator, he is of necessity a secularizer; as a solidarity maker he must appeal to religious sentiments. The answer, says Webb, is that there has to be a radical readjustment of Muslim religious thought to bring its precepts in line with new secular needs; and for this reason "Ayub is a religious as well as a political reformer."

In his paper, Webb indicates the steps that Ayub has to take to break the power of the local sect leaders and to create his own political institutions. There is a clear set of stipulations by which one can judge whether these steps can be taken, and to this extent the paper serves admirably as a means of predicting the course of Pakistan's political development.

The question whether in any society there is a single overriding problem is largely an empirical one. Yet methodologically it is useful to try to see if such a single problem might emerge, if not in the present, then in the future. In her book *New Nations*, Lucy Mair establishes a proposition that "the world of technology is one of large political units" and thus raises the question whether some of the new states "are big enough to stand on their own feet."[32] In his absorbing study of the breakdown of the Weimar Republic,[33] Professor Karl D. Bracher sets up a model (applicable, he feels, to the political breakdown of a number of democratic states) in which the turning point comes when the established regime confesses that some basic problem seems to be "insoluble." In Weimar Germany, Professor Bracher feels that the insoluble problem was unemployment, giving rise to a sense of despair in the regime and a loss of faith in the political system. One could argue that Algeria was one such problem for France in recent years. Or the failure of the Belgians to create an administrative machinery (as the British did in Pakistan, India, Nigeria, etc.) was the cardinal problem in the Congo.

8. The Prime Mover

In Marxian theory, again, the mode of production was the determinant, directly or indirectly, of the political, legal, and ideological forms of the society. There were always two difficulties with the theory. One was the difficulty of any monistic theory—that in explaining everything, it really explains nothing. The other was the ambiguity of the phrase "mode of production." At various times, Marx would talk of the forces of production, the techniques of production, the social relations, etc., but meanings shifted markedly. A number of writers felt that if the term had any meaning, it could only apply to technology. At one point, I identified fourteen different variables that could be included under "mode of production" if one wanted to use it analytically. Yet the general idea of the mode of production has had a powerful influence as the idea of a prime mover of history or prime determinant of social structure.

For analytical reasons, if not always for historical or empirical ones, there may be situations in which a single powerful force can be taken as the independent variable and a whole series of ancillary changes predicted as a consequence of changes in this independent variable. This is the method, for example, that Herman Kahn has adopted in his book *On Thermonuclear War* and in an unpublished study, "Deterrence and Defense in the Sixties and Seventies."[34]

As Kahn writes: "In a sense we are adopting an almost Marxian view of the world, with military technology replacing the special role that Marx assigned to the means of production as the major determinant of behavior, and with conflicts between nations replacing the class struggle."

It is not, of course, that other elements do not enter; surely political decision is the most decisive and is relatively autonomous, though one can say, after Skybolt, that missile technology has replaced steel production as the indicator of a strength among nations. But for purposes of analysis of future changes in a society, one may want to take a major determinant or prime mover and trace out its effects. The chief point that Kahn is making is that since 1945 there have been three major revolutions in the art of war, with consequent effects on the economy and political strategies of the two major duelists and their allies. By a "revolution" Kahn means a big change, such as the introduction of new sources of energy or a quantum jump in destructive power from a kiloton to a megaton—changes significant enough to render a prevailing strategic doctrine obsolete. "The year 1951," he writes, "is typical of the new era in which there is the introduction, full procurement, obsolescence, and phasing out of complete weapons systems without their ever having been used in war."

In the "mobilized societies" of the West, military technology, in its impact on the economic budget, in its stimulus of research and development, in its absorption of scientists, in the way it constrains certain political decisions (e.g. the need for overseas bases as a consequence of a weapons system), is in many respects a prime mover and can be studied with profit. Kahn has provided one model by setting up three hypothetical technologies for 1965, 1969 and 1973 (he was writing in 1961), and seeking to assess the alternative strategies and problems created by these changes. It is conjecture as a high art.

One can, for example, in examining the emerging states, look to social mobility as a major determinant of the domestic politics of the countries. One may feel that David Apter, for one, has gone too far in saying, "Assuming that no one is ever truly satisfied with the system of social stratification other than conservatives, we find that *the* basic motive of politics then is a striving motive to expand mobility opportunities, either for some special group or for large segments of the society."[35] But one of the most fruitful perspectives adopted by modern sociology is to chart "mobility opportunities" as an index of political change in a society. Modernity, as Edward Shils once remarked, is the entry of masses *into* society. The extension of citizenship rights, the degree of participation, equality of opportunity—the conditions of unhindered social mobility—are a useful framework to organize the problems of political change.[36]

9. Sequential Development

Few persons today believe in a theory of social evolution in which each society passes through defined stages in moving from a simple to a complex state. Yet the phrases "economic development," "political development," and even "social development" do suggest that societies go through some sequential phases as they confront greater tasks and have to create specialized mechanisms to handle them.

Are there some ordered steps that one can identify, at least as an ideal type? In the construction of the theory of industrial society one notices the lineaments of such a theory. One source, clearly, is Emile Durkheim's *The Division of Labor in Society*. In accounting for the change from "mechanical" to "organic" solidarity, Durkheim posited a number of steps. Population increases give rise to certain densities. This leads, under certain conditions, to increased interaction and thereby to competition. Social units in competition (e.g. cities, or occupational guilds) can either engage in a war to the death or begin to differentiate into specialized and complementary units. The distinguishing aspect of modern society for Durkheim is the role of the division of labor in creating a more differentiated society.

Talcott Parsons, the American sociologist, has taken Durkheim's theory and tried to account for western institutional development in terms of a theory of structural differentiation.[37] Economic development is only possible when there is a separation of the household and the firm. Within the firm there goes on a renewed process of differentiation, separating planning from operations, later ownership from control, etc. In the society, functions such as education, recreation, and welfare that were once lodged within the family begin to be taken over by specialized agencies. In the political arena one finds differentiation in the rise of bureaucracy, etc.

To some extent, one can argue, such a theory overlaps the concept of "structural requisites." There are two differences. One is in perspective. The idea of structural requisites is from the viewpoint of the government, i.e. the minimal concerns of any government. The second is that a theory of structural differentiation implies some ordered sequence in the creation of more complex and more specialized agencies for the handling of tasks.

In the new states one has a great laboratory for predicting and testing such hypotheses. In many of these countries, basic functions of the society are concentrated in family and village groups. The onset of industrialization means a transfer of such functions to new and more specialized agencies. Can one say that logically or sociologically such development can be plotted?[38]

10. Accounting Schemes

By accounting schemes, I mean those efforts to sum up in a single case, or nation, or relatively closed social system, a "trial balance" which arrays all the major factors that play a role within that unit.[39]

The *Futuribles* essay of Professor Edmund R. Leach, "The Political Future of Burma," affords an illustration of this method.[40] Leach begins with the proposition that the existing situation in Burma ("or for that matter in any other country") may, in principle, be analyzed as the sum of a series of independent factors, $a, b, c, \ldots n$. Social development is then seen as a series of progressions of a' through a to a'', and b' through b to b'', etc. But not all factors progress at the same pace, and a profile of the country at time II will have some but not all the factors of the country at time I.

In constructing a future profile of the country, some factors which are designated as constant could be predicted with a high degree of certainty; other factors are designated as probable, and still others as pure speculation. If one takes the speculations as a range of alternative possibilities and combines each with the constants, one would have a series of delimited conjectures ordered on some scale of probabilities.

In his empirical analysis, Leach distinguishes four groups of factors:

A. Factors with a high degree of built-in stability which, for any short-run historical period, can be treated as constant. These include, for Burma, climate and topography, language, religion, the bureaucratic structure of the internal administration, and certain culturally-defined expectations.

B. Factors which are subject to more or less linear change, either in increase or decrease. Such rates of change are not immutable, but they do tend to be relatively stable over defined periods. This would include size of population and labor force, the state of communications (roads, railways, waterways), educational level of the population, numbers of trained personnel, capital resources available for investment.

C. Factors which are cyclical. Here the idea of a cycle becomes ambiguous. In business cycle theory one assumes a regularity of peaks and downturns, either long-wave (Kondratieff or Juglar) cycles or short-run cycles, based on an identification of specific determinants (rate of innovations, demand for money, etc.). In politics, the idea of a cycle is more a metaphor. This seems to be the case in Leach's examples: foreign policy ("the allies of yesterday are the enemies of today and the friends of tomorrow"); ruling types (using Pareto's metaphors of the "lions" and the "foxes," Leach assumes an alternation of "the politicians" and "the men of decisions"); age of government ("the longer an administration has been in office, the less vigorous its action"); age in government ("young men are vigorous, radical; old men incline to caution and conservatism"). Is there, here, truly a cycle?

D. Factors which are wholly fortuitous and unpredictable. These include, in Leach's itemization: the short-term objectives of active politicians; the coercive pressures of foreign powers; natural calamities, including international wars.

The historian, says Leach, tends to emphasize factors of the fourth class. But it may be, he says, that these day-to-day actions have only a "superficial and transient influence upon longer-term developmental sequences." Just as Durkheim sought to predict the rates of suicide in various systems, by seeking general causes (e.g. degree of cohesion) which were independent of any individual case in a comparable way, says Leach, "those who seek to make political predictions can and should ignore completely the whole class of short-term political events." And Leach seeks to justify such exclusion on the ground that, seen over a pattern of decades, it is the "long-term developmental sequences" which matter, while the day-to-day events are of minor significance.

Two broad methodological questions can be raised. Can one dismiss so easily the role of decisions, or what historians call turning points? The annexation of upper Burma by the British in 1885 and the consequent destruction of the existing governmental system down to the village level do not fall, as a factor, under the other classes. It was not wholly fortuitous, yet it was external to, and decisively transformed, the system, One can say that such classes of events, because they are outside the system, cannot be taken into account. But if this is so, then a crucial problem in the area of prediction has no place in the accounting scheme. One would have to exclude, therefore, from the possibility of prediction such events as the occurrence of the October Revolution (many people expected February), the rise of Tito, and similar turning points in the history of the countries of Europe.

Secondly, do we want to stop at an "inventory of factors"? Do we not need to specify in some way the skein of relationships so that we know not only classes of factors but their functional dependencies as well? In what way does a joint family system (a constant?) act to constrain certain types of economic development? Under what conditions do the constants change? Is there an ordering principle which can specify the relationship between the groupings as classes of functional relationships?

11. Alternative Futures: the writing of "fictions"

One of the simplest and oldest ways of conceiving, if not predicting, the future was to envisage the possibilities open to man and then create a fiction which in extreme form men call "utopia." (In a somewhat different and systematic sense, the construction of fictions was used by Jeremy Bentham to enlarge the mode of abstractions available to speculative minds, and, quite independently, more than a half-century later, Hans Vahinger was to elaborate this method in his famous book, *The Philosophy of "As If."* The "as if" was a construct, or fiction, which served a heuristic function. It allowed us to simplify our assumptions. [41]

In recent years, the writing of "alternative futures" has been a systematic technique of Rand and former Rand theorists, particularly Herman Kahn. (Curiously, and quite independently, apparently, of Bentham and Vahinger, they have called their fictions "scenarios.") What these theorists do is to sketch a paradigm ("an explicitly structured set of assumptions, definitions, typologies, conjectures, analyses, and questions")[42] and then construct a number of explicitly "alternative futures" which might come into being under stated conditions. Thus the alternative futures become guides to policy makers in sketching their own responses to the possible worlds that may emerge in the next decade.

The writing of a "scenario" is not itself a prediction: it is an explication of possibilities. What it is, in effect, is the step beyond the "accounting scheme" in the construction of a number of plausible profiles, and the explication of the assumptions which underlie each of these alternatives.

Herman Kahn, for example, has sketched a number of alternative world futures for the 1970s.[43] He has constructed what he has called Alpha, Beta, Gamma, Delta worlds and indicated the kinds of international orders or equilibria which might obtain in each. Working from an "accounting scheme" of constants, relatively predictable sequential developments, constraints, and the like, he tries to assess current political factors (e.g. a degree of U.S.-Soviet detente, the strains in NATO, etc.), the present and future military technology, and possible political factors, and then sketch the alternative results.

His Alpha world is one of arms control agreements; the U.S.S.R., Europe, Japan, and the U.S. relaxed and ideologically slack, China maintaining only a defensive military posture, etc. In a variant, Alpha-1, Japan has become the implicit guarantor of South Korea, Formosa, Malaysia and India, and Western Europe is united. In Alpha-2, there is a strong Franco-German Europe, and a rearmed Japan is tending to neutralism. But the basic condition is one of high stability and peace.

The Beta worlds are one of defined structural strains. For example: the U.S.S.R. is losing dominance over the world communist movement; Peking has a low-grade nuclear force; E.E.C. pursues moderately exclusionist trade policies, Japan, Germany and France have independent nuclear deterrents, the *Tiers Monde* develops hysterical and aggressive political movements, etc.

The Gamma worlds, of extensive multipolarity, see the breakup of the old alliances: China, France, Germany, Japan, and India develop or procure nuclear weapons, E.E.C. does not develop into a political community, middle-sized countries are on the verge of becoming nuclear powers because of the development of cheap fission (i.e. atom), though not yet expensive fusion (e.g. hydrogen) bombs.

In these projections, few sophisticated techniques (game theory, systems analysis, cost-effectiveness ratios) are employed to sketch the future worlds. But what we do have is a systematic identification of relevant factors, and the combination of these, to create a coherent fiction or a set of alternative futures. And, to the extent that these alternative futures are realistic possibilities, one has a surer foundation for policy formulations to meet the various contingencies.

A different kind of experiment in conjecture is attempted by the writer in a forthcoming book, *The Post-Industrial Society*. It is, in essence, not a forecast, but a dissection of the recent past—the "prophetic past," in Chesterton's phrase—in order to identify the structural trends and structural possibilities in the society and to create an "as if" about the future. The study deals with the new role of military technology as constitutive of political decisions, the rise of scientists as a new constituency in the political process, the creation of a new "intellectual technology" (a short-hand term I use for cybernetics, decision theory, simulation, and other intellectual techniques that allow us a new way of dealing with the planning process) and other elements of structural change in the society. These changes are then projected forty years as an "as if" in order to see their impact on the composition of the labor force, class structure, elite groups, and the like. Clearly *that* world, forty years hence, will not materialize, for there are many unforeseen and "uncontrollable" variables (particularly the political weights of the new nations and their own commitments) which will shape the reality of that time. But if the "as if," as a rational projection of structural possibilities in the society, does have some heuristic validity, by comparing that model with the reality, one might then be able to gain a clearer sense of the actual agencies of social change that were operative in that time.

12. Decision Theory

One includes in decision theory a wide assortment of new techniques: linear programming, utility preference theory, game theory, simulation, etc. Strictly speaking, decision theory is not predictive because it is normative: it seeks to specify probable outcomes if one or another choice is made. The problem, then, is its adequacy as a tool for the policy-maker. M. de Jouvenel has indicated one of the problems in game theory, the problem of agreement on relative values (the assignment of utilities).[44] Any adequate discussion would have to go far beyond the length of this paper. The singular point to be noted, however, is that any concern with prediction eventually must explore in detail the formalization procedures of decision theory and seek to assess in what way they are useful in the art of conjecture.

In the political realm—where 'one seeks to assess the intentions as well as capabilities of one's opponents—where does one begin? One technique worth exploring—though not strictly within mathematical decision theory—is "political gaming" or "simulation." In effect, these are political mock wars. One can, using the Rand technique, set up actual teams and allow them to work out a political game as armies work out a war game under simulated conditions of diplomatic negotiations, or one can, with a computer, simulate various situations and work out the alternative strategies and likely outcomes under hypothecated conditions. As with any formalization technique, the added knowledge comes from a specification of the likely variables and an awareness of the range of outcomes, rather than from new "wisdom."[45]

Most of the difficulties of politics—unlike probability situations, which are based on repeated experiments—is that decisions often have a "once-in-a-lifetime" consequence. A crucial question, therefore, is whether probabilistic methods can be used for political decision-making. In practice, one does this roughly by asking a number of "experts" and then weighing their advice. Is it possible, as L. J. Savage, for example, believes, that one can take expert opinion as a form of experiment and calculate *a priori* probabilities as a result?

But it is at this point that one runs the risk of the rationalist fallacy of believing that there is a true optimal path for any decision. One of the most heartening developments is the recognition of the "existentialist" element which has entered into modern utility theory, itself the foundation of so much of the work of rational prediction. It used to be that in choosing a strategy in a "game against nature" (i.e. uncontrolled situations), one could follow a maximum path (i.e. go for broke) or a minimax route (i.e. seek to cut one's losses). Now a third strategy has appeared: one can choose, depending on temperament and values, a maximin or a minimax throw, but then, statistically one can hedge one's bet by an added probability which has been termed so neatly, "the criterion of regret." Now clearly, the man who invented that has learned the lessons of love and politics.

II

Why does one seek to predict? This is an era in which society has become "future-oriented" in all dimensions: a government has to anticipate future problems; an enterprise has to plan for future needs; an individual is forced to think of long-range career choices. And all of these are regarded as possible of doing. The government of the United States, for example, makes national estimates in which the intentions and capabilities of opponents are evaluated, and policy is formulated on the basis of these short-run and long-run estimates. Business firms now make regular five-year budgets and even twenty-year projections to anticipate future capital needs, market and product changes, plant location, and the like. Individuals at an early age begin to consider occupational choices and plan for university and later career life. If none of us can wholly predict the future, what we do in these actions, in the felicitous phrase used by Dennis Gabor, is seek to "invent the future."[46]

In the light of all this, what is remarkable is how little effort has been made, intellectually, to deal with the problems of conjecture. In few of the cases are there genuine predictions of the order: these are the changes that I think will take place; these are the reasons why I think these changes will occur, etc. Most of the works analyzed above seek to specify the problems which countries confront, but only rarely is the further effort made such as: if the problems are solved this way, then the following might happen; or: these are the probabilities that the problem will be handled in this fashion. Yet one should not derogate such efforts. The correct identification of relevant problems is obviously the first step in the conjecture about the future; it is easier to make because it tends to be an extrapolation of the present.

I would like to put forth some problem areas for future investigation which, on the basis of the works surveyed, seem most promising. These are simply some suggestions, necessarily brief, of the productive leads derived from the works analyzed. (Necessarily, too, I cannot within the limits of space and competence detail the scope of these proposals; what I can do is to argue briefly their rationale.)

1. The Planning Process

A future-oriented society necessarily commits itself more and more to the idea of planning. This is the chief means of inventing the future. Most of the new states that have come onto the world scene in the last decade have ambitious planning schemes; most of the older societies, to some degree or other, are engaged in planning.

One plans, of course, for different ends; one plans in different ways (from centralized administrative to "indicative" planning); one uses different techniques (input-output schemes, systems analysis, shadow prices, simulation). One plans proportions between economic sectors; one does physical planning, as in the layout of cities; one plans for "guided mobility," i.e. the planned transfer from farms to cities. In all these instances, there is an attempt to direct human actions with different kinds of coercions, manipulations, persuasions and co-operations.

Can we, with full awareness of the problem of choosing between conflicting values, each of which may be cherished, find some way of choosing the *best* planning process that is consonant with our belief in liberty? The function of planning is not only to set forth goals and alternatives and means of achieving these. Equally important, and usually neglected, are the specification of costs and benefits, the reallocation of burdens, and the probable consequences of different kinds of actions. The true function of the planning process is not to designate the most appropriate means for given ends, but to predict the possible consequences to explicate the values of a society and make people aware of the costs of achieving these.[47]

Surprisingly, there are few studies extant of the planning process. There are some theoretical studies of how nations should plan and the principles of city planning,[48] but few critical studies of how nations and groups actually plan and what can be done to improve both methods and procedures.

2. The Standardization of Social Indicators

Over the past decades, economists have developed different series of indicators to anticipate and evaluate trends in the economy. There may be differences in the conclusions drawn from time-series, but by and large there is a consensus of what should be observed.

One need not recapitulate here the obvious difficulties in establishing social and political indicators. Some of the difficulty arises from a failure to agree on what should be observed. Most of the writing on the new states, for example, concentrates on such general concepts as "modernization" or "political development" or "new elites," the dimensions, let alone the indicators, of the concept are still to be formulated.[49] But one of the consistent themes of the recent writings in modern sociology (cf. Aron, Parsons) is that "industrial society" produces a series of common effects, has an "internal logic" in its creation of a new occupational structure, and with the rise of affluence creates new, presumably common attitudes, despite differences in traditional culture. And the work of Inkeles, Lerner, Pye, and others indicates that the break with tradition, the new patterns of urbanization, the exposure to the mass media and education all tend to create common patterns of thought in the new states.

The function of indicators is not to replace analysis or to act as predictors, but to allow comparisons over time within a country, and between countries, and more important, to allow one to *anticipate* certain likely occurrences.[50] It is only when the indicators and the concepts are relatively precise that we could hope that indicators would be predictive of specific events.

In rough ways, we tend to use certain indicators as predictive of events. We say that rising unemployment rates presage a swing to radical groups in voting, that migration rates may be coupled with crime and divorce rates, etc. But clearly the present need is for some coherent effort to create sets of social indicators dealing with social and political change.

Some beginning attempts have already been made. Some studies have shown that in the early stages of economic development demographic indicators (mortality data particularly) are quite predictive of rates of economic growth.[51] Daniel Lerner, in his study of the Middle East, has used such items as literacy, exposure to mass media, and urbanization as indicators of modernization.[52] In an ambitious effort, Karl Deutsch has sought to create an inventory of basic trends in international politics, and to set up some indicators for social mobilization. (By social mobilization, Deutsch specifies a cluster of variables to indicate the entry of persons into a political system.)[53] Almond and his students have sought through opinion polls and other devices to trace the process whereby individuals in a number of countries move from being "subjects" to becoming "citizens," and to chart some rate of absorption.[54] Alex Inkeles and his associates are now engaged in an effort to trace the impact of industrialization on peasants entering the industrial process in a variety of different countries and to set up indicators of attitude change.[55]

Clearly any useful construction of alternative futures will depend upon the success of the compilation of such indicators.

3. Models of Political Structures

The most difficult of all proposals is the heart of the social science enterprise itself, the construction of models of political systems.

The creation of a model allows us to do two (of a large number of) things. It may allow us to understand the "value-relevance" of a statement; it may allow us to see whether a predicted change is one which simply affects the actors in a system (e.g. a shift of power between groups), or affects the nature of a system itself. To illustrate the two points:

1) From the standpoint of a Mohammedan, all Christians are alike. The involved theological disputes between Catholics and Protestants may have little meaning for him because both are "children of Jesus." To a Catholic, the differences between a "hard-shell Baptist" and a Quaker may have little relevance for him since both are "enthusiasts." In a similar fashion, to a confirmed Marxist, the difference between a Democrat and a Republican in the American political system has little meaning since both are capitalists. But to understand any analysis or criticism, one has to identify the standpoint from which it is made. One function of a model, therefore, is to indicate the value-relevance and level of analysis from the standpoint of the observer.

2) The analysis of power in a society can only be carried on adequately if one has a scheme to identify the relevant actors, the arena, the orientations of the actors, and their relationship to the underlying system which defines the politics of the society. By a system, I mean here the basis of renewable power independent of any momentary group of actors. Most of political analysis today, I would argue, concentrates on the "intermediate" sectors (e.g. parties, interest groups, the formal structure) or, as in the case of Soviet politics, through Kremlinology to deal with the "small units" (what I have called only half-jokingly the "small c's") of politics,[56] but rarely is there an attempt to specify, as a Marxist analysis does, the underlying system of renewable power.

There are few operating models of political systems, on the descriptive or the analytical level, extant. Gabriel Almond and his associates have sought to establish a framework of concepts which would lead to the creation of such a model. Many years earlier, Harold Lasswel and Abraham Kaplan set forth comprehensive definitions of power, but they did not seek to combine these into a system. C. Wright Mills created a mechanistic image of a "power elite." Maurice

Duverger, in his book *Political Parties*, at a lesser level has put forth a useful typology. Most recently, Raymond Aron, in his magisterial book, *Paix et Guerre entre les Nations,* has formulated certain models of diplomatic systems. But we still lack any comprehensive analyses of different systems of power.[57]

But here, in this entreaty, one comes full circle. For in the preoccupation with prediction one risks the hubris of the historicist mode of thought which sees the future as "pre-viewed" in some "cunning of reason" or other determinist vision of human affairs. And this is false. One seeks "pre-vision" as much to "halt" a future as help it to come into being, for the function of prediction is not, as often stated, to aid social control, but to widen the spheres of moral choice. Without that normative commitment the social sciences become a mere technology rather than humanistic discipline.

Notes

1. Harriet Martineau (ed.), *The Positive Philosophy of August Comte* (New York: Calvin Blanchard, 1856), pp. 132-33.

2. See *The Republic,* Book IX, No. 571, in *The Dialogues of Plato,* Jowett edition (New York: Random House, 1937), p. 829.

3. As Michael Polanyi has written: "Prediction is not a regular attribute of scientific propositions. Kepler's laws and Darwinian theory predicted nothing. At any rate, successful prediction does not fundamentally change the status of a scientific proposition. It only adds a number of observations, the predicted observations, to our series of measurements. . . ." See *The Logic of Liberty* (London: Routledge, 1951), p. 16.

4. Thus Arnold Toynbee, in tracing western history back to 1494, identifies five great war-and-peace cycles, but one is confounded by the question of what is war (subversion, guerilla forays, rebellions) and what is peace.

5. For one of the most succinct analyses from the basis of modern economic theory, *see* Paul A. Samuelson, "Wages and Interest: A Modern Dissection of Marxian Economic Models," *American Economic Review* (December, 1957), pp. 884-912.

6. Ridenour's discussion, one of the most provocative of recent times, can be found in Ridenour, Shaw and Hill, *Bibliography in an Age of Science* (Urbana: University of Illinois Press, 1951). Derek Price's analyses can be found in two small volumes, *Science Since Babylon* (New Haven: Yale University Press, 1961) and *Little Science, Big Science* (New York: Columbia University Press, 1963). A seminal source for many of these discussions is the work of Gerald Holton, particularly "Scientific Research and Scholarship: Notes Towards the Design of Proper Scales," *Daedalus* (March, 1962), pp. 362-99.

7. These quotations are from *Little Science, Big Science,* pp. 24, 25, 30.

8. *See* Herbert A. Simon, *Models of Man* (New York: Wiley, 1957), pp. 97, 145-64.

9. The following description by Paul Levy explains the concept: "The idea of a stochastic process is, at least for a determinist, tied to that of the existence of hidden parameters which do not intervene in the description of the apparent present state of the system studied and which nevertheless influence its future evolution. Our ignorance of their values forces us to speak for the future only of a set of possible evolutions, and in certain cases we can define in that set a law of probability incessantly modified by the knowledge of new data." Cited in Luciene Félix, *The Modern Aspect of Mathematics* (New York: Science Editions, 1961), pp. 132-33.

10. Published by the University of Michigan Press in 1960.

11. A representative work is Amos Hawley, *Human Ecology* (New York: Ronald Press Co., 1950). For a formal treatment of systems of local communities, regions, and societies, *see* Rutledge Vining, "A Description of Certain Spatial Aspects of an Economic System,"

Economic Development and Cultural Change, III (January, 1955), pp. 147-95. A recent, imaginative effort to use the ecological approach in a holistic way is Clifford Geertz's *Agricultural Involution: The Processes of Ecological Change in Indonesia* (Berkeley: University of California Press, 1963).

12. Recently the U.S. Congressional Committee on the Joint Economic Report conducted hearings on the methods employed by different economic forecasters (e.g. *Fortune,* McGraw-Hill, and others) to make their forecasts.

13. I leave aside here the problem of the failures of short-run predictions or stages theory as involving many complicated considerations. But a study of why many of these predictions went wrong would be fruitful. For example, Frank Notestein posited a stages theory which powerfully influenced David Riesman in the formulation of the theory of character change in the latter's *The Lonely Crowd.* The Notestein theory, metaphorically, is an S-shaped curve. The bottom horizontal line represents traditional societies with high birth rates but also high death rates; a second stage, that of transitional growth (the sigmoid rise), is one of population explosion because of a rapidly declining death rate; the third stage is one of incipient population decline based on a new stabilization of low birth rate and low death rate. Riesman associated the traditional type with the first society, the inner-directed type with the second, and the other-directed type with the third. But the stages theory has been proven wrong. Both France and the United States, for example, have recently resumed a steady population rise, but for how long, it is difficult to say. For the original Notestein formulation, *see* Frank Notestein, "Population—The Long View," in T. W. Schultz (ed.), *Food for the World* (Chicago: University of Chicago Press, 1945). For Riesman's discussion of his abandonment of the Notestein hypothesis as the basis for his own theory *see* "The Lonely Crowd: A Reconsideration in 1960," in S. M. Lipset and Leo Lowenthal (eds.), *Culture and Social Character* (Glencoe: The Free Press, 1961), pp. 419-58.

14. *See* Sir Charles Darwin, "Forecasting the Future," in Edward Hutchings, Jr. (ed.), *Frontiers in Science* (New York: Basic Books, 1958), p. 116. *See,* too, in the same volume, the retort by Fred Hoyle.

15. For a balanced assessment of this problem, *see* S. Lilley, "Can Prediction Become a Science?" in *Discovery* (November, 1946), reprinted in Bernard Barber and Walter Hirsch (eds.), *The Sociology of Science* (Glencoe: The Free Press, 1962). A quick review of different kinds of trend predictions can be found in Hornell Hart, "Predicting Future Trends," in Allen, Hart, et al. (eds.), *Technology and Social Change* (New York: Appleton-Century-Crofts, 1957), ch. 19.

16. Of the vast literature on the subject, two reviews are of use: G. Dupeux, "Electoral Behaviour," *Current Sociology* (1954-1955), pp. 318-44, and S. M. Lipset, P. F. Lazarsfeld, et al., "The Psychology of Voting," in Gardner Lindzey (ed.), *Handbook of Social Psychology* (Cambridge: Addison-Wesley, 1954). The discussion of "bandwagon effects" in relation to election predictions can be found in Simon, *op. cit.,* ch. 5; the discussion of process analysis in Berelson, Lazarsfeld, and McPhee, *Voting* (Chicago: University of Chicago Press, 1954), especially ch. 13.

17. Colin Clark, "Apropos the Eight Million of M. Manshold," *Futuribles* papers, Paris, no. 18.

18. A classic essay in this field is Robert Merton's "Social Structure and Anomie" which seeks to specify under what conditions deviations from such norms or structural certainties obtain. See *Social Theory and Social Structure* (Glencoe: The Free Press, 1957), ch. IV.

19. See *The Operational Code of the Politburo* (New York: McGraw-Hill, 1951); *A Study of Bolshevism* (Glencoe: The Free Press, 1954); also, Nathan Leites with Constantin Melnik, *The House Without Windows: France Selects a President* (Evanston, Row Peterson, 1958), and *On the Game of Politics in France* (Stanford: Stanford, 1959). For a detailed discussion of the validity of this approach, *see* my essay "Ten Theories in Search of Reality: The Prediction of Soviet Behavior," in *The End of Ideology* (Glencoe: The Free Press, 1960).

20. There have been many efforts to identify an American "style." *See,* for example, the essay by W. W. Rostow in Elting Morison (ed.), *The American Style* (New York: Harper, 1958), pp. 246-313; D. W. Brogan, "The Illusion of American Omnipotence," *Harper's* (December, 1952); Daniel Bell, "The National Style and the Radical Right," *Partisan Review* (Fall, 1962); Talcott Parsons and Winston White, "The Link Between Character and. Society," in *Culture and Social Character* (Glencoe: The Free Press, 1961), ch. 6. A fruitful comparison of aspects of British and American patterns can be found in Edward A. Shils, *The Torment of Secrecy* (Glencoe: The Free Press), ch. 2. For a denial of direct links between cultural values and social structure, *see* E. R. Leach, *The Political System of Highland Burma* (London: School of Economics and Political Science, 1954).

21. In Karl Marx, *Selected Work* (Moscow: Foreign Languages Publishing House, 1935) II.

22. It is difficult to resist Marx's description, an extraordinary piece of political analysis and poetic rhetoric: "This society dates from the year 1849. On the pretext of founding a benevolent society, the *Lumpenproletariat* of Paris had been organized into secret sections, each section led by Bonapartist agents, with a Bonapartist general at the head of the whole. Alongside decayed *roués* with doubtful means of subsistence and of doubtful origin, alongside ruined and adventurous offshoots of the bourgeoisie, were vagabonds, discharged soldiers, discharged jail-birds, escaped galley-slaves, swindlers, mountebanks, *lazzaroni,* pickpockets, tricksters, gamblers, *maquereaux,* brothel keepers, porters, *literati,* organ-grinders, rag-pickers, knife-grinders, tinkers, beggars, in short the whole indefinite, disintegrated mass thrown hither and thither which the French term *la Bohème* from this kindred element, Bonaparte formed the basis of the Society of December 10. A 'benevolent society'—in so far as, like Bonaparte, all of its members felt the need of benefiting themselves at the expense of the working nation." And more of the same! *Ibid.,* pp. 369-70.

23. *Ibid.,* p. 423. (Italics added.)

24. The changes in the features of modern capitalist society is the central point of Professor Postan's essay, "The Economic and Social System in 1970," Bertrand de Jouvenel (ed.), *Futuribles,* I (Geneva: Droz, 1963). In concentrating on the changing character of ownership of capital, he is tracing out a major reorganization of the "operational system."

25. *See* Almond and Coleman, *The Politics of the Developing Areas* (Princeton: Princeton University Press, 1960), p. 59. The introduction by Almond, "A Functional Approach to Comparative Politics," proposes a set of definitions for the "common properties of political systems." A more condensed effort, but almost as comprehensive, is the article by David Apter, "A Comparative Method for the Study of Politics," *American Journal of Sociology,* LXIV, 3 (November, 1958), pp. 221-37. One of the earliest and still one of the most interesting efforts to specify the common requisites of any social system is the essay by Aberle, Cohen, et al., "The Functional Prerequisites of a Society," *Ethics,* LX, 2 (January, 1950) 100-111.

26. One such typology, on which Almond bases part of his system, is that of Professor Edward Shils, from *Political Development in the New States* (The Hague: Mouton and Company, 1962).

27. "In many technologically indifferent features the range of variability is unlimited: but the requirements of effective use impose limitations, more or less stringent, on the variability of other features—there is a narrowing of the range if the object is to function as intended. . . . What is so patent in technology applies equally to other aspects of culture, where, however, the operation of the principle is less readily discernible." Alexander Goldenweiser, "The Principle of Limited Possibilities in the Development of Culture," in *History, Psychology and Culture* (New York: Albert A. Knopf, 1933), p. 47.

28. See *Terror and Progress USSR* (Cambridge: Harvard University Press, 1954).

29. Edward F. Denison, *The Sources of Economic Growth in the U.S.,* Committee for Economic Development, 1963.

30. In *Futuribles,* I (Geneva: Droz, 1963), pp. 295-319.

31. Lucien Pye, *Politics, Personality and Nation-Building: Burma's Search for Identity* (Princeton: Princeton University Press, 1961).

32. Lucy Mair, *New Nations* (Chicago: University of Chicago Press, 1963).

33. *See* K. D. Bracher, *Die Auflösung der Weimar Republik* (Stuttgart: Ring Verlag, 1957).

34. Herman Kahn, *On Thermonuclear War* (Princeton: Princeton University Press, 1960), especially chs. IX, X, and "Deterrence and Defense in the Sixties and Seventies," *Progress Report for a Study of Crises and Arms Control,* Hudson Institute (unpublished), ch. II.

35. Apter, *op. cit.,* p. 221.

36. This perspective is central to Professor T. H. Marshall's *Citizenship and Social Class* (Cambridge: Cambridge University Press, 1950). It has been used by S. M. Lipset to account for variations in the degree of radicalism in western societies (see *Political Man,* [New York: Doubleday, 1960] chs. 2, 3) and by Reinhard Bendix and Stein Rokkan to create comparative models of political development in the West. *See* "The Extension of National Citizenship to the Lower Classes: A Comparative Perspective," paper for the Fifth World Congress of Sociology, September, 1962.

37. *See* Talcott Parsons, *Structure and Process in Modern Societies* (Glencoe: The Free Press, 1960), especially chs. 2 and 3.

38. In an unpublished paper, William Kornhauser, a sociologist at Berkeley, has sought to identify four stages of "political development" which new states have to consolidate in order to achieve "political competence" or the achievement of their defined goals. These four are: national identity, integration of authority, participation or mobilization of the population, constitutionalism. Such tags are largely amorphous in themselves, and without a comprehensive description of each of the concepts one risks a disservice to Professor Kornhauser. I call attention to it here to indicate that serious thinking about the nature of "sequential development" is taking place among the students of the "new societies."

One should point out that M. de Jouvenel's essay on "The Evolution of the Forms of Government," though reflecting on past history, does have, in its sketch of the rise and extension of bureaucracy, the basis of a sequential theory. One might say, too, that the concept of "value added," which M. de Jouvenel has called attention to from economic theory, could be the basis of social speculation. One such effort to explain "collective behavior" and particularly revolution is Neil Smelser, *Theory of Collective Behavior* (Glencoe: The Free Press, 1963). Professor Smelser writes: "As the value-added process develops, it allows for progressively fewer outcomes other than the one we wish to explain. This logic of value added can be applied to episodes of collective behavior such as the panic or the reform movement. Many determinants or necessary conditions must be present for any kind of collective episode to occur. These determinants must combine, however, in a definite pattern. Furthermore, as they combine, the determination of the type of episode in question becomes increasingly specific and alternative behaviours are ruled out as possibilities" (p. 14).

39. In using the phrase "accounting scheme," I am following the conventional language of bookkeeping (comptabilité). However, a more restricted use of the phrase is employed by Paul F. Lazarsfeld to deal with causal inferences of single decisions. He is attempting, in effect, a methodology for the historian, the clinical psychologist, or the market researcher, who has to account for the most relevant combination of factors in the making of a single decision. For a short statement of Professor Lazarsfeld's intentions, *see* Lazarsfeld and Rosenberg, *The Language of Social Research* (Glencoe: The Free Press, 1955), pp. 387-91. An elaboration of this mode of "reason analysis" can be found in Hans Zeisel's *Say It With Figures* (New York: Harper, 1957), ch. 6.

40. In *Futuribles,* I., *op. cit.,* pp. 121-54.

41. C. K. Ogden, *Bentham's Theory of Fictions* (London: Kegan, Paul, 1932); Hans Vahinger, *The Philosophy of "As If"* (London: Kegan, Paul, undated).

42. For the role of paradigms in social research, *see* R. K. Merton, *Social Theory and Social Structure* (Glencoe: The Free Press, 1957), pp. 13-16, 50-60.

43. Herman Kahn, "Alternative World Futures," paper HI-342-B IV, Hudson Institute (April, 1964).

44. See *Essai sur l'Art de la Conjecture,* (Paris: SEDEIS), pp. 92-94.

45. On the techniques of political gaming, *see* Herbert Goldhamer and Hans Speier, "Some Observations on Political Gaming," *World Politics* (October, 1959). Harold Guetzkow has edited two volumes on simulation: *Simulation in Social Science: Readings;* and *Simulation in International Relations,* both published by Prentice-Hall, 1962, 1963. A useful volume on decision theory which argues that one can verify ethical judgments is C. West Churchman, *Prediction and Optimal Decision* (Englewood Cliffs; Prentice-Hall, 1961).

46. When individuals and, more particularly, organized movements are committed to rigid invention such as Bolshevik theory, the results can be disastrous. One of the sorriest records of prediction is that of the Bolsheviks. In the 1920s, they predicted that the next struggle would be between Great Britain and the United States (as the two largest imperial powers); in the 1930s, that Hitler could not last and that the Communists would succeed him; in the 1940s, that the West could not go to war against Hitler; in the early 1950s, that the western economies would stagnate, etc.

47. One of the most interesting studies in recent years, in this regard, is Alexander Erlich's *The Soviet Industrialization Debate, 1924-1928* (Cambridge: Harvard University Press, 1960). The reconstruction of this debate makes it clear that the Soviet path was not "inevitable" and that various persons, including those who argued for a course of intensive industrialization, were well aware of the risks and consequences, including the resistance of the peasantry.

48. There is a large and useful literature on planned "organizational change," growing out of the work of such groups as the Tavistock Institute in London, the Institute of Social Research at the University of Michigan, and similar groups.

49. For a useful discussion on the general nature of indicators in relation to concepts, *see* Paul F. Lazarsfeld, "Evidence and Inference in Social Research" in Daniel Lerner (ed.), *Evidence and Inference* (Glencoe: The Free Press, 1959), 31 pp.

50. For an enlightening discussion of the need for indicators and their role in anticipations, *see* the document "Space Efforts and Society," a Document of the Committee on Space Efforts and the Society of the American Academy of Arts and Sciences (Boston, January, 1963).

In this context, the term anticipation is broader than prediction. Say the authors: "The distinction we would make is that between a reasonably precise knowledge of the probability of a given event happening and a sufficient awareness that something of a general sort might happen, that if it does happen we are not caught by surprise. In planning it is often possible to make provision for handling some consequence even though it can be foreseen only in very general terms." There is another distinction worth emphasizing. Prediction places primary emphasis on the probability of something's happening and is less concerned with the importance of events. Anticipation seeks to weigh the relative importance of likely occurrences.

51. For a representative effort along this line, *see* Philip Hauser, "Demographic Indicators of Economic Development," *Economic Development and Cultural Change,* 7 (January, 1959).

52. *See* Daniel Lerner, *The Passing of Traditional Society* (Glencoe: The Free Press, 1958), especially ch. II.

53. *See* Karl Deutsch, "Toward an Inventory of Basic Trends and Patterns in Comparative and International Politics," *American Political Science Review* (March, 1960); and "Social Mobilization and Political Development," *Ibid.* (September, 1961), pp. 463-515.

54. The results of these studies in Germany, Italy, Mexico, Great Britain, and the United States are summed up in the volume *The Civic Culture,* by Gabriel Almond and Sidney Verba (Princeton: Princeton University Press, 1963).

55. This work is going on in Chile, Nigeria and Pakistan. A preliminary statement can be found in Alex Inkeles, "Industrial Man: The Relation of Status to Experience, Perception and Value," *The American Journal of Sociology*, LXVI, I (July, 1960), pp. 1-31.

56. One of the things that has struck me over the years is the way small groups of individuals who have, at an early age, formed a circle or club, move out into the larger political arena. This is a familiar phenomenon in literary or art movements; yet it is equally true in politics. One thinks of the Galileo circle in Hungary in 1919 (for a description, see the essay by Paul Ignotus in the *Essays in Honor of Michael Polayni*), of the Thakins in Burma, of the "young Turks," who have thus given a cognomen to the phenomenon, etc. While the phenomenon is readily understood as important for political analysis, one finds few studies of the process at all. In thinking about these groups, I was struck by the linguistic singularity (in English) that most of the words describing them begin with a small "c." Thus:

clique	club	circle	cabal
cadre	crowd	clan	camarilla
claque	council	curia	church
cortes	cells	caucus	cenacle
condominium	committee	conspiracies	condottieri
college	coteries	cults	

All of which may well be one other illustration of a "Yule distribution" statistically in linguistics.

57. The best effort to create a typology of the new states is the monograph by Edward Shils, *Political Development in the New States*. This study charts the alternative courses of political development (e.g. tutelary democracy, modernizing oligarchies), but does not specify the bases of power, or the social systems of renewable power. The beautiful simplicity of the Marxist scheme is that it took a single variable, wealth in property, or the means of production, as the basis of power. We lack some organizing concepts which will allow us to group the multiple bases of power which now exist in the world into a comprehensive classification, or a system-set.

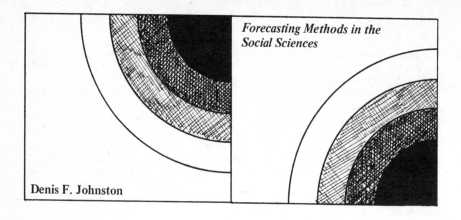

Forecasting Methods in the Social Sciences

Denis F. Johnston

In 1936, an interesting set of "prophecies" relating to 1960 was published.[1] The most dramatic of these was the announcement that by 1960 work would be limited to three hours a day! The author, John Langdon-Davies, went on to present the following picture of life as it would be lived in 1960:

If we are to try and understand life as it will be led in 1960 we must begin by realizing that food, clothing, and shelter will cost as little as air. Science has simply to learn to change cellulose into foodstuffs at a negligible expenditure of human energy and we shall eat as we breathe. Science has only to go a few steps farther in mechanically producing textiles in factories where there is nothing to do but press a button and we shall dress as do the lilies of the field. Society has only to have a strong enough control over the individual to limit population and there will be room for all rent free. . . . I do not say that such a state of affairs will be universal by 1960, but it is the condition towards which we are inevitably trending, a condition wherein our ordinary notions of labour and the rewards of labour will alike be meaningless.

Two years later, the U.S. National Resources Committee published a major study wherein the total population of the United States was projected, under the assumption of "medium" fertility and mortality and 100,000 net immigration per year after 1940, to reach 158 million by 1980, at which time it would have approached a state of equilibrium.[2]

It is hardly necessary to belabor the obvious point that both the prophecies of Langdon-Davies and the projections published by the U.S. National Resources Committee fell wide of the mark. By 1960, millions of workers were spending up to three hours per day merely moving to and from their jobs. As for the notion that food, clothing, and shelter would cost as little as air, we find, by 1970, that breatheable air may soon cost as much as food, clothing, or shelter; and, the valiant efforts of our "flower children" notwithstanding, we are by no means able to dress as do the lilies of the field. Meanwhile, the population of the United States, displaying a lamentable indifference to the laws of logistic growth, passed the 158 million mark less than 15 years after the above projection was issued, is now approaching 210 million, and continues to rise by about 2 million per year.

These two outlook statements may be taken as fairly representative of the polar extremes of forecasting methods available to the social scientist. At the one pole is the reasoned outlook statement, heavily value-laden, whose insights are thinly disguised arguments in support of some particular panacea. At the opposite pole stands the objective and technically sophisticated work of two outstanding demographers, Warren S. Thompson and Pascal K. Whelpton, whose projections of the population of the United States were adopted by the National Resources Committee as representing the most informed and careful investigation of probable future U.S. population growth.[3]

There is much to be learned from these errant forecasts. First of all, neither of them can be criticized as inconsistent with their underlying assumptions. Langdon-Davies perceived in the accelerating growth of science and the enormous potential of its application to the problem of human want an "inevitable trend" toward the conditions he described. When his outlook for 1960 is compared with the current prognostications of a "cybernated world," it is apparent that many of the trends he recognized as nascent causes of a world free of want and labor are still being regarded, a third of a century later, as potential mainsprings of a transformed world. Only the date of the beginning of this millenium keeps being advanced, like a mirage on the horizon.

The case of the Thompson-Whelpton population projections is similarly defensible on the strength of the underlying assumptions. Their analysis of past trends in mortality, fertility, and net migration to the United States, together with their understandable confidence that these trends would continue to manifest themselves, provided a sound logical and empirical base for the projections they prepared. For all the criticisms which have since been expressed of these and similar demographic projections, it is difficult to imagine that any competent demographer, given the same data and objective, could have developed a radically different set of projections.

Secondly, it is sadly evident that neither the reasoned judgment of an insightful observer nor the refined techniques of the objective technician who works with masses of quantitative data can guarantee results which will meet the test of actual historical developments. The events of the past thirty years provide overwhelming evidence that the *least* likely outcome, at least over any period beyond a few years, is precisely the kind of "surprise-free" outcome to which we are led either by imaginative extensions of perceived nascent causes, or by extrapolations of past and current trends. As Nisbet has caustically noted,[4]

What the future-predictors, the change-analysts, and trend-tenders say in effect is that with the aid of institute resources, computers, linear programming, etc. they will deal with the kinds of change that are not *the consequence of the Random Event, the Genius, the Maniac, and the Prophet. To which I can only say: there really aren't any; not any worth looking at anyhow.*

Finally, these two widely different approaches to the task of prognostication illustrate a common difficulty which impedes our efforts to develop improved forecasting methods: our inability to identify and measure the impact of the factor or factors which caused a given forecast to fall wide of the mark. *Ex post facto* analysis readily brings forth a plethora of disturbances—unforeseen consequences of past decisions, chance occurrences, etc.—which may have exerted a decisive influence either in altering the smooth trends on which a forecast may have been based or, indeed, in preserving them. However, the recognition of such "disturbances" is of little help in improving forecasting methods, until and unless their impact can be measured and the likelihood of their occurrence in the future assessed. For this reason, the technician who seeks to improve his procedures by delving into the past to compare earlier forecasts with actual outcomes cannot rest content with the mere discovery of events which were not or could not have been anticipated.

Types of Outlook Statement

Before considering a variety of forecasting methods in the social sciences, it may be useful to introduce certain distinctions with respect to major types of outlook statement. In particular, we wish to distinguish among predictions, projections, and forecasts as a means of indicating both the range of purposes to be served by outlook statements and the technical limitations surrounding their development in the social sciences.

Prediction

To most social scientists, the ability to predict systematically is the ultimate test of the achievement of scientific understanding. Since this kind of prediction, unlike the guess, the hunch, or the inspired intuition, involves the application of a "covering law" to the phenomenon in question, it is essentially similar to explanation. This similarity is well described in a recent study of social science research methods:[5]

...explanation in terms of laws argues that prediction and explanation are simply different uses of the same schema. In prediction we are said to be in possession both of the hypothesis and the statement of initial conditions from which the prediction-claim is derivable. In explanation, on the contrary, the explicandum (that which is being explained) is assumed to hold, and we attempt to find the statements of initial conditions and the hypothesis which jointly entail it. ...According to this view, if we can justifiably predict that an event will occur, then we can also give an explanation of why the event occurred. The explanation and prediction are supported by exactly the same information, i.e., the relevant generalization and the statement of initial conditions.

Hempel has extended this "symmetry" thesis to cover functional analysis as well as nomological explanation. By this extension, the explanations of the functionalists may be used in prediction in precisely the same sense as the conventional explanations in terms of governing laws. In either case, according to Hempel, explanations and predictions are essentially deductive arguments, differing only in their temporal direction with respect to the "explicandum."

It follows from this line of reasoning that the search for covering laws or law-like generalizations must be given first priority in pursuing both explanatory power and predictive ability, and that these goals are inseparable. Unfortunately, the innumerable generalizations which abound in the social science literature offer little basis for the formulation of the kinds of covering laws which have proved useful in the physical sciences. The complex interactions which characterize all but the most trivial instances of social behavior; the interplay of biological, psychological, and cultural determinants of that behavior; our inability to identify, isolate, and measure the effects of even the major factors among these determinants; and the "halo of indeterminacy" surrounding even the most straightforward measures and indices of social behavior or characteristics—all of these limitations effectively guarantee that any generalizations arrived at are either sufficiently abstract as to have little explanatory or predictive significance, or so specific and qualified as to apply only over a highly restricted domain.

This does not mean that the search for "systems" whose functional elements display observable regularity through time is either misguided or hopeless. But it does suggest that the task of developing useful and valid outlook statements should not be too closely identified with the more conventional tasks of scientific research. Furthermore, it is essential to recognize in the diverse purposes to be served by outlook statements a number of important needs which can be met quite apart from the search for scientific generalizations.

Projections

At first glance, projections might simply be described as conditional predictions. They typically display the same format: an assumed system whose governing principles (or covering law), combined with a specified set of initial conditions, provide a framework within which the future state of the phenomenon in question may be deduced. The crucial difference between predictions and projections, however, consists in the factual status of their underlying conditions. The typical "If. . . , then. . ." form in which projections are expressed offers a clue to this difference. The assumed determinants in a projection, unlike those in a prediction, need not reflect known causal relationships or factual governing principles.

In fact, two of the most useful kinds of projections either require no profound understanding of the underlying processes and their determinants or else involve assumptions that are deliberately contrary to current reality. The first and most familiar instance is the extrapolation of observed trends in some periodic measure of the phenomenon in question; and the second is the "heuristic" projection of the consequences (logical or probable) of an assumed set of initial conditions which may be highly improbable, or for which no real-world instance is known. Two brief examples may suffice as illustrations: first, the economic activity rates of a population group (*i.e.,* the percentages of that group who are in the labor force, either working or seeking work) may be projected into the future by extrapolating observed trends in these rates over time, without specifying the covering laws which govern the propensities of the group to work. Second, the future distribution of a country's population among the several provinces, states, or districts of the country may be projected on the improbable assumption of zero-net-migration among these districts. Such a projection, when compared with actual population estimates at a future date, provides an estimate of the impact of migratory streams on population distribution, apart from the effects of natural increase in numbers.

In the first case, the extrapolations are naive in that the technician is working with a "black box" situation. The rates he observes and extrapolates are obviously epiphenomenal, but their determinants are hidden from view and are only partly understood at best. In the second case, a set of initial conditions is chosen for its heuristic value, despite the fact that it is unlikely to be found in the real world.

Forecasts

According to the terminology employed here, a forecast is a projection which has been selected as representing the "most likely outcome" in situations which are not sufficiently deterministic (or whose determinants are insufficiently understood) to permit valid predictions. Forecasts in the social sciences therefore serve as substitutes for the outright predictions of the more "exact" sciences, and must accordingly reflect realistic or plausible combinations of assumed determinants and initial conditions. Where, as is commonly the case, alternative projections cannot be assigned different probabilities of occurrence, the selection of one of them as a forecast may yield an arbitrary "point estimate." In other instances, the alternative projections may represent an attempt to delineate the upper and lower boundaries of an interval estimate reflecting opposite extremes in the values of the assumed determinants. A simple averaging procedure may reduce such an interval to an acceptable "point-estimate" forecast.

Following Jantsch, it is useful to distinguish between two broad subgroups of projections: exploratory and normative.[6] Exploratory (or heuristic) projections are designed to reveal the possible consequences of assumed sets of determinants and initial conditions which need not necessarily reflect the current situation. Normative projections, on the other hand, are designed to delineate an optimal path from current reality toward a specified goal or target. Although these forms of projection have been more thoroughly developed and investigated in the field of technological forecasting, the following section will attempt to illustrate their potential usefulness in relation to the several forecasting methods available to the social scientist.

Methods of Forecasting in the Social Sciences

Strictly speaking, any outlook statement, whether it merits designation as a prediction or merely a projection, forecast, or outright guess, is an extrapolation from our perception of the present. In his provocative criticism of the current generation of outlook statements, scenarios, and the like, Nisbet makes the trenchant observation that these efforts tell us very little about the future, but are quite revealing about the present, as perceived by these experts and social analysts through the filter of their adopted methodologies and values.[7] This is a profound truth, based on the sound epistemological principle that all knowledge of the past, present, and, *a fortiori*, future must take the form of ideal constructs whose components can only reflect the current state of our knowledge, and whose selection and organization reflect current notions of relevance and scientific acceptability.[8]

If, then, all outlook statements are in some sense extrapolations from the present, the remaining task is to outline and discuss the more promising methods whereby such extrapolations may be developed in the social sciences. For expository purposes, these approaches may be classified in four broad groupings: qualitative-exploratory, qualitative-normative, quantitative-exploratory, and quantitative-normative.[9]

Qualitative-exploratory Projections

Three of Bell's modes of prediction would seem to fall into this grouping. Projections derived on the basis of the anticipated impact of a "prime mover," or those reflecting the assumed operation of some "law of sequential development," or those which take the form of "scenarios of possible futures" commonly share a concern with the possible consequences of an assumed set of determinants and initial conditions which cannot be fully expressed in quantitative terms. As Massenet observes, the search for nascent causes is a key feature of this type of exploratory exercise, since the coherence of the resultant projection is heavily dependent upon the through-time evolution of the key factors which are assumed largely to determine the character of the society in question.[10]

The only research method which seems appropriate for this type of projection involves some combination of arm-chair theorizing and a capacity to absorb large amounts of "hard" and "soft" data. Most efforts in this direction have been the work of individual scholars; only recently have such enterprises been carried out by small groups of researchers.[11] Since this kind of research activity obviously places a high premium on both the expertise and the credibility of the individual researchers, it is likely that qualified researchers will remain in short supply. For this reason among others, some adaptation of the Delphi technique merits serious consideration.

The Delphi technique was developed initially for the purpose of pooling the informed opinions of selected panels of experts with respect to the likelihood and timing of the appearance of different technological items or developments currently envisioned but not yet realized.[12] In its original form, this procedure involves, first, the preparation of a questionnaire relating to the subject-area of concern. The questionnaire items may consist of any combination of codable materials—statements with which the panel experts may agree or disagree, or questions which they can answer by choosing the most appropriate of the responses provided, as in multiple-choice examinations. Some allowance for lengthier expressions of opinion may of course be made as well. Next, an appropriate panel of experts in the particular area of concern must be selected. When the panel has received, filled, and returned their questionnaires, the first phase of the operation has been completed. In the second phase, the returns of the first round are pooled, coded, and averaged, and these results are circulated among the panel members. In this phase, panelists whose initial responses differed markedly from the group norm are asked either to modify their response or to provide a more elaborate defense of their position. These responses are again pooled, averaged, and redistributed. The cycle can be repeated as long as the process appears to yield significant changes in the expressed views.

Two features of this technique would appear to warrant its adoption in social forecasting. First, it avoids the need to bring the experts together in a committee setting. Second, its reliance upon a readily coded schedule of items permits a rapid and objective measure of the range and central tendency of the responses obtained. Experience with the Delphi technique is rapidly accumulating, particularly in connection with technological forecasting efforts, where its chief value consists in what Hacke aptly terms "delineating the boundaries of the possible."[13] The advantages of the technique, in addition to the welcome avoidance of time-consuming committee meetings, include the avoidance of some of the distortions commonly associated with committee settings, such as the spurious consensus obtained via the "bandwagon" effect, or the tendencies to support the opinions of the more "authoritative" individuals or to adhere rigidly to previously expressed opinions because their later modification is thought to imply a lack of conviction or competence. This technique may also reduce the distortions induced by the pressures of time, which so often results in a last-minute profusion of hasty decisions.

The Delphi technique is not, however, free of dangers and limitations. The initial selection of the panel of "experts" is both crucial and difficult. Persons who enjoy the highest professional status in a given field may be fully in tune with the present, since they have probably influenced its evolution in some small measure; but they are not necessarily harbingers of the future. A more serious problem is the design of the questionnaires to be employed. If the items on the schedule are to be objectively coded, they must be presented in a rigid format—either as statements with which the respondent may agree or disagree, or as a set of alternative answers among which a choice must be made. Such techniques suffer from a twofold weakness: first, they force the expert to adopt one of the alternatives presented, so that the very subtleties of judgment which qualify the individual as an expert may be lost to view. Second, overly facile "box-checking" techniques invite rapid, off-the-cuff responses which may not reflect the careful consideration which is needed.

Finally, the Delphi technique suffers from the loss of certain features which are unique to the committee setting. The interplay of judgments and influences that occurs in face-to-face association may be of great importance in the development of reasoned views on a given subject. Only through such contact can the participants perceive the nuances of meaning and intensity of convictions so essential in assessing the true significance of expressed views. Much of this contextual matter is lost when we resort to written communication. All of it is lost when that communication takes the form of statistical measures of coded responses.

Qualitative-normative Projections

Several of Bell's modes of prediction can be placed under this heading. Reliance upon "structural certainties" to provide benchmarks in the future implies that these perceived certainties will continue to operate as norms in regulating significant areas of activity in a given society. Similarly, the assumption that "operational codes or rules" will continue to exert directional guidance in the future implies that a society's relatively stable sub-strata of folkways and mores can be relied upon to provide some coherent framework within which future potentialities will find expression. The attempt to develop projections which satisfy the "structural-functional requisites" of a society also belongs in this grouping, inasmuch as these requisites may be recognized as delineating ultimate constraints on the evolution of any society.[14]

Two additional modes might be classified here: "operational systems of power" and "the overriding problem." In the former approach, the basic interests of the major power blocs in a given society are assumed to operate as norms which will continue to determine the ways in which that society adjusts or responds to changing circumstances, and to strongly influence the formulation of societal goals in the future. Similarly, the development of a projection which reflects the possible resolution of what is postulated as a society's "overriding problem" imposes that solution as an ultimate goal or target. Numerous elaborations of this type of approach are familiar to social scientists in the form of the classical theories of class conflict and the working out of the Hegelian dialectic of "thesis, antithesis, and synthesis."

The basic feature of all these approaches to the development of qualitative-normative projections is their attempt to shift from what Massenet refers to as the "principle of extrapolation" to the "principle of causality." As Massenet observes, this shift of focus should not be misconstrued as an attempt to predict within a framework of causal determinism in the usual scientific sense. He expresses the distinction between scientific prediction and projection by means of postulated causal principles as follows:[15]

We must avoid establishing too close a relationship between science and social forecasting. The first seeks to abstract out a causal relationship in all its purity; the second operation, in which the mind tries to imagine the future effects of presently existing causes, is purely empirical. In a word, forecasting tries to enlarge the horizon of our knowledge of the concrete reality; it does not tend to deepen our explicative knowledge of the structures of the world.

Insofar as the above approaches are distinguished from the first group by virtue of their explicit concern with norms, it would appear that social scientists would find a rich source of insight into the implications of alternative values and value hierarchies in undertaking the systematic development of normative projections. Here also, the Delphi technique offers some promise, in view of its demonstrated utility in the development of normative forecasts in technological areas.

Before turning to a consideration of quantitative forecasting methods, it may be appropriate to summarize our argument with respect to qualitative forecasting in general. First, qualitative forecasting cannot be adequately described as the application of any particular method, nor can it be usefully evaluated purely in terms of its underlying procedures. One can only repeat Georgescu-Roegen's advice to economists in dealing with uncertainty: "Get all the facts and use good judgment."[16] Although social scientists are amply equipped with tools for the collection and processing of data, they are much less informed as to the ingredients of "good judgment." Second, qualitative projections allow us both to appraise our present condition in the light of our values and aspirations and, conversely, to estimate the ultimate impact of our current values and behavior patterns upon our future condition. Even if they fail to foretell the future, they offer a unique perspective in our attempt to understand the present. Finally, the Delphi technique may be utilized to provide more systematic inputs of information which might improve the judgments underlying the projections; it cannot be relied upon to produce those judgments.

Quantitative-exploratory Projections

"Trend extrapolation" and projection by means of "social accounting schemes" are the two major techniques listed by Bell which may be considered in this grouping. Hacke distinguishes further among extrapolative techniques by recognizing projection on the basis of an assumed periodicity or in conformity to an assumed growth curve as separate from ordinary extrapolation in that these techniques impose external constraints upon the extrapolation that is produced.[17]

From the viewpoint of the social scientist, the chief difficulty in extrapolating a trend consists in the need to accept some numerical measure as an index of the phenomenon with which he or she is concerned. The problem is not that such indices are unavailable, but rather that they are commonly misinterpreted as reflecting more of the underlying phenomenon than they, in fact, do. For example, labor force projections are commonly prepared by extrapolating observed trends in the activity rates of the several age-sex groups of the population. Obviously, the rates observed do not reveal the intensity of labor force participation (*i.e.,* hours worked per week or weeks per year), nor do they reflect the work commitment of the individual worker (*i.e.,* whether he is working temporarily or permanently). Similarly, projections of the educational attainment of the adult population and labor force are prepared by extrapolating the reported years of school completed by successive age-sex cohorts, with an allowance for current school enrollment rates. Equally obviously, these data reveal nothing whatsoever in regard to what was learned in school or out of school, or what has since been forgotten.[18] Insofar as we are willing to accept a labor force participation rate as an index of the economic activity of a population group, or a percentage distribution by years of school completed as an index of educational attainment, extrapolations of trends in these indices provide valid and useful descriptions of future prospects in these areas. These indices can hardly be criticized for failing to do something for which they were not designed. But the interests of social scientists in the phenomena they purport to reflect cannot be met fully by this kind of convenient measure alone.

A further limitation of trend extrapolation is familiar to all practitioners of the art: except for arithmetical errors, such projections are likely to be reasonably accurate so long as the underlying trend is maintained; but they quickly become disastrously inaccurate as soon as the trend is disrupted for any reason. Thus, they "fail" at precisely the point where foresight would be most helpful—where the assumed continuity is broken at a turning point.

The attempts of economists to project on the basis of observed periodic fluctuations in a time-series, and those of demographers in applying growth (logistic) curves to observed trends in total population do not offer great hope for the applicability of these techniques in other areas of human behavior. While many forms of behavior display periodic fluctuations, the recognition and measurement of this periodicity is useful mainly in establishing the existence of a trend when the effect of the periodicity has been statistically controlled. The fluctuations by themselves cannot provide a basis for useful forecasts beyond the period required for the manifestation of one or two cycles at best. The problem with the logistic curve is the need to specify both its upper asymptote and the time period required for its attainment. Furthermore, unless the curve is postulated as symmetrical, there remains the problem of establishing the locus on the curve of the "present status." It is well established that the growth cycle of many forms of life conforms to this kind of curve, given a fixed ecological environment and a constant mode of adaptation thereto. Insofar as human populations are concerned, it is equally obvious that the mode of adaptation to the ecological environment is continuously modified by both social and technological developments.

Despite the above limitations, three arguments may be raised in support of the technique of trend extrapolation. First, such projections are simple to develop, and the underlying assumptions and procedure can usually be described in a straightforward manner. Such simplicity should not be confused with naiveté. When dealing with social phenomena whose inner dynamics are only partly understood, the simplest procedure may well be the most defensible. Second, the technique is highly flexible, particularly when the mechanics are carried out by computer. Such extrapolations can be quickly updated by the insertion of the most recent observed values. More importantly, the observed time-series can be reassessed periodically with the aim of removing or reweighting data which are deemed to be obsolescent, irrelevant, or aberrant. Finally, this technique, by its very simplicity, minimizes the danger that the resultant projections will be misconstrued as predictions reflecting the inexorable movement of some causal force within a deterministic framework. Given the strong pragmatic arguments in favor of this technique, it is likely that social scientists will continue to use it. Therefore, it may be appropriate to conclude by quoting Winkler's admonishment to those economists who rely so heavily upon quantitative time-series analysis:[19]

. . . .we seem to have forgotten that every time series is in the first place quantitative history of a situation and its analysis, historical analysis. This predominantly historical nature of time series has two aspects: first, in every series the definitions, survey and computing techniques have their own development. They are part of the data and must be considered when analyzing the series. Second, each series is embedded in a complete historical landscape of other events, most of which cannot be quantified. The data in a time series therefore are not a simple sequence of pure algebraic numbers, but history presented in statistical terms.

This reminder is a plea for the social scientist to retain a critical awareness of what is involved in attempting to deal exclusively with those aspects of historical reality which can be readily quantified. It is also an argument for the continued development of qualitative projections wherein our interpretations of historical processes may find expression.

Quantitative-normative Projections

What Bell (and earlier, Sorokin) has aptly termed "social physics" may be classified here, together with the several techniques he refers to as "decision theory." The several projective techniques which can be grouped in this category have in common the attempt to construct some kind of representation of the actual functional relationships which characterize some segment of human behavior. This representation (or model) is essentially quantitative, although it is of course possible to include unmeasured factors in the form of two-valued dummy variables. The resultant model can then be used to generate "predictions" by the insertion of given or assumed values for the independent variables.

The difficulties to be faced in the development of such forecasting models in the social sciences can readily be appreciated by considering the fundamental requirements of such model construction. The first requirement is a theoretical grasp of the relevant processes and relationships in the system—a requirement which presupposes the identification of such a system and its boundaries. Second, a body of quantitative data must be available which reflects the observed operation and mutual influences of the key elements in the system. Finally, there is need of appropriate statistical techniques whereby the postulated processes and relationships can be expressed in testable form—*i.e.*, as a system of equations permitting separate identification of the influence of each major variable in the system.

For purposes of forecasting, such an equation system must satisfy a further requirement. Either the key independent variables must exert a measurable lagged effect upon the variable to be predicted, or else their future values must themselves be predictable. In the first instance, it is possible to "predict" the future value of the dependent variable from the present values of the independent variables. In the second case, it is necessary to develop independent forecasts of the independent variables first. In practice, these values may be assumed, so that the resultant "prediction" is, in effect, a prediction of the future values of every variable in the system. In rare instances, the independent variables may represent factors which are in some sense subject to control, and can therefore be assigned desired or prescribed values.

Finally, the need to assume stability in the underlying structure of postulated relationships over the period of the projection introduces a strong flavor of hypothetical "as if" reasoning to such constructs. Granting the availability of the necessary statistical techniques, it remains an open question whether the behavioral sciences, including economics, can be expected to attain the requisite levels of theoretical sophistication together with the essential data base. At present, these procedures can only provide, at best, heavily qualified "predictions" of narrowly defined segments of behavior under restrictive assumptions that are typically artificial and greatly simplified.[20]

The prospects for the development of "social accounting schemes" as a tool for projective purposes may be more hopeful. In manpower analysis, for example, the distribution of employed workers by occupation and industry as observed at a given census date can be utilized to distribute a projected employed labor force total for a future date so as to yield an estimate of the future occupational and industrial distribution of workers.[21] In addition, such an approach can be given a greater degree of verisimilitude by incorporating information on past trends in the occupational mix of the several industries. It is also feasible, in principle, to incorporate information on the changing educational or training qualifications of workers in the future, and thus to assess the probabilities of an emerging imbalance between anticipated work requirements and available personnel possessing the requisite skills. Where these job requirements, in turn, are prescribed by the expected manpower needed to attain specified social goals, the resultant matrix can be viewed both as a "target" for appropriate social and economic programs and as a prescription of the intermediate objectives which must be reached in order to achieve the primary goal.[22]

Similar input-output matrices might be useful in forecasting the need for teachers and facilities in the area of education, particularly in those fields where the attainment of specified social objectives entails the supply of certain numbers of qualified persons. More challenging, perhaps, is the possibility that input-output analysis could provide social scientists with a powerful tool for estimating and objectively demonstrating the probable spread of consequences stemming from particular inputs within the framework of human ecology. If, as is currently being suggested, concern for the ecological consequences of our continuing industrial development is to become a major issue in the coming decades, the possibilities for interdisciplinary research in combining ecological theory with input-output analysis merit serious consideration.

The exploratory work with "cross correlation" techniques in forecasting the implications of given or assumed technological breakthroughs is a highly promising start in this direction. As Gordon points out, a major criticism of the conventional Delphi technique is that it yields "linearly independent" forecasts whose possible interrelations may be overlooked.[23] Placing these alternative developments into an "input-output" matrix provides a framework for assessing the probable impact of a given development or event on the probabilities of occurrence of the other elements in the matrix. At present, these assessments involve nothing more than the crude judgment that the occurrence of event X may be expected to increase, lower, or have no significant impact upon the probabilities of occurrence of the remaining events in the matrix. But this approach at least introduces the notion of interdependence of outcomes into our reflections on future prospects.

Forecasting and Planning: The Need for Social Indicators

In a recent science fiction novel, the conditions under which accurate social prediction might be made are described rather neatly:[24]

Well, what can heighten the predictability of human behavior? Two opposite conditions: either the human goes mindless and becomes a purely physical victim of physical events; or, the human can form a purpose and persevere in it. And what can heighten the prediction possibilities of social action? Two not quite opposite conditions: there can be fulcrum events and forces which for a while dictate automatically and inescapably which way a society will go, or, there can be concerted long-range planned programs by a society or its power structure. . . .

This quotation helps to illustrate the dual function of social projections: advance warnings and explorations of the possible. In providing advance warnings of potential imbalances or impending crises, they may serve to generate appropriate policies or programs whereby we can avoid the pitfalls which would otherwise reduce or eliminate our freedom of action. In providing descriptions of the probable consequences of ongoing or proposed programs or practices, they may generate a better understanding of their true costs and benefits, together with a fuller awareness of the possible alternatives open to us. In short, social projections may help us to escape both the determinism resulting from problems left too long untended, and that resulting from a failure to recognize the degrees of freedom we may in fact possess.

The requirements which must be satisfied if social projections are to fulfill this dual function suggest the directions to be followed in developing an improved methodology for projections in the social sciences. In the first place, quantitative procedures alone cannot be relied upon to produce an adequate awareness of alternative goals we might pursue, or of the arrangements of our values whereby our social priorities might be more rationally determined. Qualitative procedures, on the other hand, cannot possibly incorporate in a systematic manner the number and complex interrelatedness of the factors influencing social be-havior. Although the importance of qualitative or judgmental elements may be greater in developing scenarios of alternative futures than in extrapolation of trends or computer simulations, these elements cannot be eliminated from any exercise in social projection.

Three streams of current thought and practice point toward an eventual con-vergence in the so-called "qualitative" and "quantitative" approaches to social projection. First, there is growing recognition by practitioners of the arts of model building, systems analysis, computer simulation, and the like that their constructs and data manipulations are infused with qualitative judgments—an infusion which is dictated both by their research objectives and by the limita-tions of the data with which they must operate.[25] Second, there is the dis-covery, shared with equal dismay by numbers of pure and applied scientists alike, that typical social problems, as presently conceived, cannot readily be solved merely by applying the techniques which have proven so effective in physical science and its technological extensions.[26] Finally, there is the insight shared by such scholars as Emery and Klages, to the effect that de Jouvenel's proposed "surmising forum" cannot produce useful results until and unless these disparate methodologies are somehow combined.[27]

A key element in achieving such a convergence is the development of im-proved social indicators. Resort to such indicators in ascertaining our current status as well as our progress toward agreed-upon goals is no guarantee that controversy can be avoided, particularly with respect to basic values; but the availability of such indicators offers some hope for the eventual development of a viable alternative to the endless and often fruitless confrontations between what Klages terms the "imperatives of social stability" and the "demands for social innovation." A recent study of the current status and the prospects for improvement of social indicators suggests both the directions to be followed and the distance to be covered in this enterprise.[28]

To begin with, Sheldon and Freeman offer a needed corrective to the excessive enthusiasm with which "social indicators" (consisting largely of old wine in new bottles) have been greeted by technicians and policy-makers alike. They argue that social indicators cannot be expected to increase the objectivity of socio-political policies, because the social goals and values whereby policies are deter-mined cannot be validated by an appeal to statistical descriptions of past and current status. What we are and have been may tell us what we are likely to be in the future, but not what we *should* be or *should* aspire to being. Further, indicators cannot be relied upon in evaluating social programs. This limitation stems from our inability to develop reliable and valid measures of the effective-ness of given programs by statistical manipulations alone, in the absence of experimentation under controlled conditions. Finally, social indicators, they argue, cannot be neatly organized into a "social accounting scheme," because of our inability to rank the wide range of social phenomena to be indexed by means of a common interval scale, such as monetary valuation.[29]

Given these constraints, Sheldon and Freeman suggest instead that social indicators should be developed with the more modest but attainable aim of providing a more adequate monitoring of the changing status and characteristics of society, to which might be added a more challenging objective: the construction of social indicators designed to provide new perspectives on both our accepted institutions and practices and the new modes of action and organization which challenge these traditions.

In pursuing these objectives, our desire to acquire convenient and objective indices of the phenomena of interest must be tempered by an awareness of the complexity of these phenomena. In addition to the temptations of the "new Philistinism" Gross has warned against, there is a danger that quantitative measures may be regarded as adequate reflectors of the phenomena they purport to represent, purely because of their definitional explicitness. Any quantitative measure or index is believed to enjoy the advantage that it can be defined in seemingly unambiguous, "operational" terms. Unfortunately, the explicitness with which a given measure may be defined enhances its reliability by permitting its accurate reproduction, but it does not necessarily guarantee its validity.[30] Furthermore, resort to quantitative measures or indices, at least in the behavioral sciences, does not necessarily imply freedom from ambiguity; it merely transfers the locus of possible ambiguity from the terms employed in qualitative discourse to those employed in executing the operational instructions whereby values for the index in question are in fact obtained. An examination of these procedures quickly reveals that many widely accepted quantitative indices are based upon responses to questions; that both the questions and the responses they elicit are expressed in ordinary language; and that these responses are subject to possible distortions resulting from misunderstanding of the terms employed in asking the questions, from faulty recollection, from various kinds of rationalization, or from deliberate falsification.

But these limitations are well known to social scientists and statisticians alike. What is more pertinent, perhaps, is de Jouvenel's reminder, which appears to be addressed not to the technicians but to the decision makers and their informed publics—to those who are expected to utilize the outputs of the technicians in developing viable and rational courses of action in a world of uncertainty. De Jouvenel reminds these potential users that:[31]

Designers of statistics are indeed philosophers, however unwilling to claim the name, and are fully aware that different aspects of reality can be lit up if alternative sets of concepts are used.

Those who must decide on a course of action need more than a statistical model of the workings of selected aspects of the social system, however elegant and intricate its construction. To be sure, such models should eventually facilitate our estimation of the probable consequences of alternative policies and assumed conditions, but they cannot provide a deeper sense of social values and derived goals which alone lend meaning to any course of action. By the same token, social indicators must not only serve as benchmarks in our efforts to ascertain our current status and direction of change; they must also specify for the decision makers the timing, location, and requisite conditions for effective decisions—*i.e.,* where decisions may be expected to introduce new causal influences which can alter the course of events in a desired direction. Insofar as social indicators can fulfill these needs in the context of public information, they may ultimately provide the informational underpinning for the kind of rational and democratic decision-making so eloquently described by Shackle:[32]

In a predestinate world, decision would be illusory; in a world of perfect knowledge, empty; in a world without natural order, powerless. Our intuitive attitude to life implies non-illusory, non-empty, non-powerless decision.

Conclusion

Bertrand de Jouvenel has managed to express in a single sentence the essential nature and significance of social forecasting:[33]

It is necessary to struggle to achieve in reality what we are decided upon in our mind.

It is this necessity which most clearly reveals the extra-scientific purpose of such endeavors, and which differentiates the task of social forecasting from the conventional scientific search for regularities and associations in human behavior. Furthermore, this insight implies that social forecasting must be rooted in explicit values if it is to provide a basis for rational decision and action. As Louch states:[34]

For the study of action does not require new and hidden events and processes, but reflection upon and reordering of what we see men doing. Its object is not to make more certain the basis for prediction, but to enlarge the grounds for rational decision and appraisal. Psychology and social science are moral sciences; ethics and the study of human action are one.

The problem of values, both as objects of study and as factors influencing the scientists in his perception of reality, remains a controversial issue in the behavioral sciences. The problem becomes even more critical in social forecasting, particularly when these forecasting efforts are viewed as vital inputs to the process of policy formulation and decision-making in society. In her brief summary of alternative approaches to the study of prospective value changes, Taviss argues persuasively that social forecasts cannot satisfactorily handle the "values" variables as "dependent" upon emerging technological or environmental processes. Neither the Kahn-Wiener approach, which assumes that technologically produced social changes may be expected to produce corresponding value changes, nor Rescher's proposed approach, whereby future changes in values are to be predicted on the basis of a "cost-benefit" analysis of their consequences under current or anticipated future sets of situational constraints, offer adequate solutions to the problem. The first approach ignores the possibility that a society may prefer, or be forced, to adapt its growth potential to the service of more fundamental values. The second ignores the problem that both costs and benefits can only be calculated on the basis of values which are granted *a priori* acceptance.[35]

In other words, the attempt to "predict" value changes implies that they be viewed as dependent variables. Predictions so devised may be expected to yield useful information as to the likely consequences of social commitment to particular sets or hierarchies of values, and they may even turn out to be accurate in foretelling the rise or decline of particular values; but they cannot in themselves provide the guidance needed in arriving at critical decisions in regard to the course to be followed or the goals to be pursued. The essential problem for the policymaker is the selection of values as independent variables and their use in establishing goals and priorities, and in validating courses of action.[36]

In his recent series of papers concerned with policy-oriented future studies, Dror has provided a detailed set of guiding principles to be followed in ensuring a fruitful marriage between the technical-scientific efforts of the experts who seek to improve the accuracy of their forecasts in particular subject-matter areas and the politically sensitive activities of those individuals and groups who find themselves in key decision-making positions in various sectors of the society. His overview of the directions to be pursued in such studies recognizes the need to elaborate the implications of alternative sets of values or value hierarchies by developing future-oriented "scenarios" which attempt to describe their consequences under assumed conditions.[37]

These new directions for the study of the future have profound implications for the methodology of social forecasting. First, the methods employed must be appropriate to the task. Analytic schemes whose "predictions" assume the operation of some set of governing laws, or extrapolations based on the assumption of continued stability in underlying structural relationships need to be supplemented by social forecasts which are explicitly normative. Second, the normative forecasts themselves should not be restricted to the type commonly recognized by technological forecasters, in which a desired goal is the starting point for the elaboration of alternative paths toward its attainment. Of far greater importance are normative forecasts which seek to describe the likely implications of given sets of values under alternative sets of assumed situational or environmental constraints. Finally, a strong sense of urgency emerges from much of the current literature on this subject. Here again, de Jouvenel has captured this feeling with a few well chosen words:[38]

How urgent it is for the moral sciences to engage in forecasting is seen more clearly if one considers that otherwise the social need in this area will be satisfied by an extension of technology; that is to say, a way of seeing developed for "objects" will be extended to "subjects," who, it will be thought, are to be manipulated in the same way as things.

Notes

1. John Langdon-Davies, *A Short History of the Future* (London: Routledge, 1936), pp. 221f. (Italics added.)

2. U.S. National Resources Committee, *The Problems of a Changing Population* (Washington: U.S. Government Printing Office, May, 1938), pp. 22-27.

3. The projected population totals of Thompson and Whelpton, if plotted against time together with the recorded totals in the several decennial censuses since 1790, described an excellent "S-shaped" or logistic curve—a fact which may have added to the credibility of the projections at the time. However, these projections were actually developed by the separate analysis of trends in mortality, fertility, and migration, a method known as the "component" method, and still employed by the Bureau of the Census.

4. Robert A. Nisbet, "The Year 2000 and All That," *infra,* pp. 257-267. For a much fuller development of Nisbet's critical insights, *see* his *Social Change and History* (New York: Oxford University Press, 1969). An equally strong expression of skepticism in regard to the prospects for the development of useful forecasts in technological fields is provided by Peter F. Drucker, "Is Technology Predictable?" in *Technology and Culture,* 10, 4 (October, 1969), pp. 522-27.

5. Robert Brown, *Explanation in Social Science* (Chicago: Aldine, 1963), pp. 158ff. Compare Felix Kaufmann, *Methodology of the Social Sciences* (New York: Oxford University Press, 1944), chapter V. The view that prediction and explanation are "symmetrical" processes is developed by Carl G. Hempel in "The Logic of Functional Analysis," in Llewellyn Gross (ed.), *Symposium on Sociological Theory* (New York: Row, Peterson & Son, 1959), pp. 271-307, and in Hempel and Paul Oppenheim, "Studies in the Logic of Explanation," *Philosophy of Science,* 18 (1948), pp. 135-75, reprinted in Herbert Feigl and May Brodbeck (eds.), *Readings in the Philosophy of Science* (New York: Appleton-Century-Crofts, 1953), pp. 319-52. *Also see* his more recent work, *Aspects of Scientific Explanation* (New York: The Free Press, 1965), especially chapter 10, pp. 291-95. The applicability of "covering law" theory and its implied methodological rules in the behavioral sciences is by no means agreed upon. For profound criticisms and alternative theories, *see* T. S, Simey, *Social Science and Social Purpose* (New York: Schocken Books, 1969), and A. R. Louch, *Explanation and Human Action* (Berkeley: University of California Press, 1966), especially chapters 3 and 4.

6. Erich Jantsch, *Technological Forecasting in Perspective* (Paris: Organization for Economic Cooperation and Development, 1967), chapter 1.2. Compare Robert U. Ayres, *Technological Forecasting and Long-Range Planning* (New York: McGraw-Hill, 1969), chapter 3.

7. Nisbet, *infra, op. cit.*

8. This position is commonly attributed to David Hume. For profound insight into the many "extra-scientific" influences affecting the criteria of scientific acceptability and relevance, *see* Philipp G. Frank (ed.), *The Validation of Scientific Theories* (Boston: Beacon Press, 1954), and Thomas S. Kuhn, The Structure of Scientific Revolutions (Chicago: University of Chicago Press, 1962).

9. The discussion which follows draws upon both Daniel Bell, "Twelve Modes of Prediction—A Preliminary Sorting of Approaches in the Social Sciences," *infra,* pp. 40-67 and James E. Hacke, Jr., "Anticipating Socioeconomic Consequences of a Major Technological Innovation," in the U.S. Air Force, Office of Aerospace Research, *Long Range Forecasting Methodology* (Springfield, Virginia: Clearinghouse for Scientific and Technical Information, 1968), pp. 131-46.

10. Michel Massenet, "Methods of Forecasting in the Social Sciences," an unpublished paper prepared for the members of the Commission on the Year 2000 of the American Academy of Arts and Sciences, (no date). Informative examples of political forecasting methodology are provided by Saul Friedlander, "Forecasting in International Relations," and Michel Massenet, "The Foreign Policy of a United Europe," in Bertrand de Jouvenel (ed.), *Futuribles II* (Geneva: Droz, 1965). *See* especially pp. 14-26 and 273-85, respectively.

11. Probably the best-known example of team research in this area is Herman Kahn and Anthony J. Wiener (eds.), *The Year 2000* (New York: Macmillan, 1967). On the need for the establishment of new forms of forecasting institutes (of which the Institute for the

Future in the United States is an example), *see* Erich Jantsch, "From Forecasting and Planning to Policy Sciences," *Policy Sciences,* I, 1 (Spring, 1970), pp. 31-47, and his "New Organizational Forms for Forecasting," *Technological Forecasting,* I, 1 (Fall, 1969), pp. 151-61.

12. The underlying theory for this technique is presented in Olaf Helmer and Nicholas Rescher, *On the Epistemology of the Inexact Sciences* (Santa Monica: The Rand Corporation, February, 1960). Its large-scale use and the results obtained are described in T. J. Gordon and Olaf Helmer, *Report on a Long-Range Forecasting Study* (Santa Monica: The Rand Corporation, September, 1964). For a recent summary of the technique, *see* Olaf Helmer, "Analysis of the Future: The Delphi Method," in James R. Bright (ed.), *Technological Forecasting for Industry and Government* (Englewood Cliffs: Prentice-Hall, 1968), pp. 116-33.

13. Hacke, *op. cit.*

14. For an example of effort toward delineating these societal requisites, *see* Aberle, et al., "The Functional Prerequisites of a Society," *Ethics,* LX (January, 1950), pp. 100-111.

15. Massenet, *op. cit.*

16. Nicholas Georgescu-Roegen, "The Nature of Expectation and Uncertainty," in Mary Jean Bowman (ed.), *Expectation, Uncertainty, and Business Behavior* (New York: Social Science Research Council, 1958), pp. 11-29. Also reprinted in Georgescu-Roegen, *Analytical Economics* (Cambridge: Harvard University Press, 1966), pp. 241-75.

17. Hacke, *op cit.*; also Ayres, *op. cit.*, chapter 6.

18. For recent projections of population and labor force in the United States, including brief summaries of the methodology employed, *see* U.S. Bureau of the Census, Current Population Reports, Series P-25, No. 448, "Projections of the Population of the United States, by Age and Sex (interim revisions): 1970 to 2020"; Sophia C. Travis, "The U.S. Labor Force: Projections to 1985," and Denis F. Johnston, "Education of Adult Workers: Projections to 1985," in *Monthly Labor Review,* 93, 5 and 8 (May and August, 1969) pp. 3-12 and 43-56, respectively.

19. Othmar W. Winkler, "A Critical View of Time Series Analysis in Business and Economics," 1966 Proceedings of the Business and Economic Statistics Section of the American Statistical Association, pp. 352-70. (Italics added.)

20. For a general account of the requirements of econometric model building, *see* Carl F. Christ, *Econometric Models and Methods* (New York: Wiley, 1966). For trenchant criticisms of earlier efforts at econometric model building, *see* Sidney Schoeffler, *The Failures of Economics: A Diagnostic Study* (Cambridge: Harvard University Press, 1955).

21. For example, *see* U.S. Department of Labor, Bureau of Labor Statistics, Bulletin No. 1599, *Occupational Employment Patterns for 1960 and 1975,* and Bulletin No. 1606, *Tomorrow's Manpower Needs,* in four volumes (Washington: U.S. Government Printing Office, 1968 and 1969, respectively).

22. For an excellent example of this kind of research undertaking, *see* Leonard A. Lecht, *Manpower Needs for National Goals in the 1970's* (New York: Frederick A. Praeger, 1969).

23. T. J. Gordon, "New Approaches to Delphi," in James R. Bright, (ed.), *op. cit.*, pp. 134-43. The assumption of "independence" is a limitation characteristic of any simple forecasting technique.

24. Ian Wallace, *Dr. Orpheus* (New York: G. P. Putnam's Sons, 1968; Putnam-Berkley Medallion edition, November, 1969), p. 119.

25. Oskar Morgenstern, *On the Accuracy of Economic Observations,* 2nd edition (Princeton: Princeton University Press, 1963). Compare Adolph Lowe, "Comment on Hans Jonas, 'The Practical Uses of Theory,' " *Social Research,* XXVI, 2, pp. 127-66, reprinted in Maurice Natanson (ed.), *Philosophy of the Social Sciences* (New York: Random House, 1963), pp. 152-57.

26. For a strikingly effective recent example, *see* Garrett Hardin, "The Tragedy of the Commons," *Science,* 162, 3859 (13 December 68), pp. 1243-48, and a further elaboration

by Beryl L. Crowe, "The Tragedy of the Commons Revisited," *Science,* 166, 3909 (28 November 69), pp. 1103-7. The "commons" is publicly owned, centrally located grazing land whose continued utilization by all members of the surrounding community requires that each user limit the size of his personal herd. The "tragedy" stems from the recognition by individual users that incremental increases in the size of their own herds offer significant personal advantages while presenting insignificant disadvantages to the totality of other users of the commons. In the long run, therefore, the rational pursuit of personal advantage leads to the destruction of the commons itself.

Hardin extends this example to cover a multitude of contemporary social problems, including traffic congestion, air and water pollution, and overpopulation, arguing that these problems belong to a class for which there are no technical solutions, at least unless accompanied by an "extension of morality." Crowe argues even more pessimistically that neither technical nor moral solutions to these problems are likely at present, and that the continued growth of science is itself endangered by the societal collapse that is threatened by our continued failure to cope with these social problems. He concludes with a plea for a concerted redirection of both social and natural science toward an active public information program in support of the changes in values and behavior which are required in solving these problems.

27. Fred E. Emery, "The Next Thirty Years: Concepts, Methods, and Anticipations," *Human Relations,* 20, 3 (August, 1967), pp. 199-237, reprinted, in part, in Michael Young (ed.), *Forecasting and the Social Sciences* (London: Heinemann Educational Books, Ltd., 1968), pp. 41-70. Helmut Klages, *Soziologie zwischen Wirklichkeit and Moglichkeit— Pladoyer fur eine projektive Soziologie* (Koln und Opladen: Westdeutscher Verlag, 1968).

28. ". . . . Promises and Potential," *Policy Sciences,* I, 1 (Spring, 1970), pp. 97-111. For a number of practical proposals regarding the directions to be pursued both in developing social indicators and in their use in gauging the impact of social programs and policies, *see* Otis Dudley Duncan, *Towards Social Reporting: Next Steps* (New York: Russell Sage Foundation, 1969), and Mancur Olson, "An Analytic Framework for Social Reporting and Policy Analysis," *Annals,* 388 (March, 1970), pp. 112-26. For examples of recent exploratory efforts within the federal government in this direction, *see* the U.S. Department of Health, Education and Welfare, *Toward a Social Report* (Washington: U.S. Government Printing Office, 1969), which was prepared under the direction of Professor Olson; and the National Goals Research Staff report, *Toward Balanced Growth: Quantity with Quality* (Washington: U.S. Government Printing Office, 1970).

29. Compare Gross, who criticizes the "new Philistinism" of attempting to use monetary units as universal measures of value, whether in the form of "cost/benefit" analysis recognizing only those costs and benefits that can be expressed in monetary units, or in the form of econometric approaches which assume the existence of a "single-valued, objective welfare function," or, finally, in the form of a depression-rooted concept of the quality of life which reflects only the material requirements for minimal subsistence. *See* Bertram M. Gross, "The State of the Nation: Social Systems Accounting," in Raymond A. Bauer (ed.), *Social Indicators* (Cambridge: M.I.T. Press, 1966), pp. 154-271, reprinted by the Tavistock Press, London, 1966. The pitfalls of excessive reliance upon quantitative measures in the social sciences are well summarized in Amitai Etzioni and Edward W. Lehman, "Some Dangers in 'Valid' Social Measurement," in Bertram M. Gross (ed.), *Social Intelligence for America's Future* (Boston: Allyn and Bacon, 1969), pp. 45-62. *Also see* the criticisms of "systems analysis" in Yehezkel Dror, *Analytical Approaches and Applied Social Sciences* (Santa Monica: The Rand Corporation, November, 1969), pp. 7ff.

30. Compare Baumol's distinction between "explicit" assumptions and "transparent" ones. William J. Baumol, "Economic Models and Mathematics," in Sherman Roy Krupp (ed.), *The Structure of Economic Science* (Englewood Cliffs: Prentice-Hall, 1966), pp. 88-101.

31. Bertrand de Jouvenel, *The Art of Conjecture,* translated from the French by Nikita Lary (New York: Basic Books, 1967), p. 174.

32. George L. S. Shackle, *Decision, Order and Time in Human Affairs* (Cambridge: Cambridge University Press, 1961), p. 43.

33. De Jouvenel, *op. cit.*, p. 30. He has chosen to express this idea in Latin: "Certo ut certum fiat in re quod certum in mente."

34. Louch, *op. cit.*, p. 235.

35. Irene Taviss, "Futurology and the Problem of Values," *International Social Science Journal*, XXI, 4 (1969), pp. 574-84. It may be comforting to bear in mind that value choices, once made, tend to be "self-supporting" in the sense that the chooser is more likely to perceive or give greater weight to evidence which justifies his prior choice. On this point among others, *see* the penetrating analysis of Fred Charles Iklé, "Can Social Predictions be Evaluated?" *Daedalus* (Summer, 1967), pp. 733-58.

36. For an insightful summary of the requirements to be met in the analysis of the processes of social change in the manifold aspects, *see* Henri Bianchi, "For a Prospective Conflictology," a paper presented at the International Future Research Conference, Kyoto, Japan, April, 1970.

37. Yehezkel Dror, "Prolegomena to the Policy Sciences," *Policy Sciences*, I, 1 (Spring, 1970), pp. 31-47, and his "A Policy Sciences View of Future Studies: Alternative Futures and Present Action," a paper presented at the International Future Research Conference, Kyoto, Japan, April, 1970.

38. De Jouvenel, *op. cit.*, p. 278.

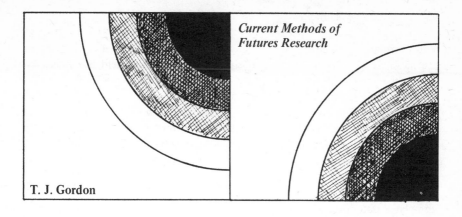

**Current Methods of
Futures Research**

T. J. Gordon

This is a paper about the methods of futures research. These methods grew from operations research and systems analysis, which essentially involve the conceptual fabrication of an intellectual, analytical, or physical model that resembles the performance of its real-life counterpart. The model is tested against possible alternative actions. Then the actions which produce the consequences most resembling those desired at least cost are recommended. The techniques lack the precision of the laws of natural science, but substitute judgment and probability instead. Futures research is not science, but it does bring some order to disciplines not amenable to the scientific method.

In the late fifties and early sixties, there was a great deal of enthusiasm about the possibility of applying systems-analysis techniques to solution of large-scale social problems. Previously, the methods had been applied primarily to problems of military effectiveness, business system optimization, and certain design problems. For social issues, however, costs were soon found to be multidimensional. Benefits to one group were perceived as costs to another: and, in any event, both costs and benefits were extremely difficult to quantify. Clearly more methodological research was needed.

Not only were there methodological difficulties in applying systems analysis to social issues, but there seemed to be no client for such work. Rand had developed its military analysis capacity for the Air Force, but who could sponsor such an enterprise for society? Probably not existing "think tanks"; they had their own biases, customers, and problems. Probably not universities, for the research indicated was truly interdisciplinary; and, despite protestations to the contrary, interdisciplinary work was very rare at universities. The only reality was the need.

Now, there are institutions designed to study the future in a dozen countries. Their staffs are dedicated to the development of systematic methods for understanding how current actions might affect the course of man's future history. There are at least three journals which are devoted solely to this field, and many others publish occasional articles on the future. There have been international conferences and symposia devoted to the topic of futures, substantive and methodological. Universities in the United States and elsewhere are designing and offering courses on technological, environmental, and social forecasting, or the mesh between them.[1] The published literature in the field is now so extensive that no single person could follow it all. In short, it appears that futures research, ready or not, has assumed many of the attributes of a protodiscipline.

Following de Jouvenel, most people in this field view the future as composed of a large set of alternatives.[2] Policies steer us through the maze of interlocking possibilities. Futures research is a means of discovering and articulating the more important of the alternative futures and estimating the trajectory likely to be produced by contemplated policies. Thus forecasting is perceived as an aid to decision-making in the present, and not as a means of producing a list of chromium-plated potential mousetraps.

Forecasts indicate what might be. They speak of a process of selection from among possible worlds. They indicate that man has at least some control over his destiny. The concept is anti-nihilistic, anit-deterministic. If the discipline develops, it may provide a new orientation to education, a new means of communication between age groups, individuals, and nations, and a new method of conflict resolution. But the protodiscipline stands in danger of raising aspirations for rationality that cannot be fulfilled; its techniques are provocative and suggestive, but unproven; its practitioners are learning as they go. The future is a new intellectual frontier; the rewards there may be real or yet prove a chimera.

There are some important caveats about forecasting the future that must be noted. First, there is no way to state what the future will be. Regardless of the sophistication of the methods, all rely on judgment, not fact.

Second, there will always be blind spots in forecasts. If we try to guess what will happen in the future, we will likely omit events for which there are no existing paradigms (forecasts made in 1964 didn't contain pulsars or quasars); events which seem trivial, but through secondary or tertiary effects become important (the Gulf of Tonkin resolution); events based on whim, chance or unexpected coincidence (an assassination).

Finally, potential futures are posed to serve as a backdrop for policy-making. If enacted, policies will change the forecasts, hopefully. Therefore, accuracy is a term which involves some paradoxical considerations.

Methods of Forecasting

The methods of futures research described herein are: genius forecasting, trend extrapolation, consensus methods, simulation methods, cross-impact methods, scenarios, decision trees, and input-output matrices. This taxonomy is personal, but most other practitioners would recognize similar divisions.

Genius Forecasting

The category of genius forecasting includes a myriad of intuitive methods which an individual uses to estimate, assess, or predict some aspect of the future. Since the methods are internal rather than explicit, the quality of his forecasts depends almost entirely on the "inspiration" processes of the forecaster. The method is thus embroiled in the psychology of insight; somehow an individual engaged in genius forecasting integrates possibilities which he considers important, draws from his relevant experience, and states what he thinks might be.

Until relatively recently, most forecasts were of this sort. A chronology of the history of forecasting might show genius forecasting beginning at about the time of the French Revolution (although earlier examples can be cited—e.g., Grecian utopias and some of the writings of Francis Bacon). S. C. Gilfillan, a sociologist, technological forecaster, and historian of forecasting, mentions in particular: d'Argenson, who in the 1750s wrote of future political arrangements; Turgot, who at about the same time articulated principles of the accumulation of scientific knowledge, technological diffusion, and the future state of items such as the phonograph, cross-breeding, the swivel chair, the future role of hospitals, and waste purification; Condorcet, who wrote of census taking, meteorology, eugenics, and the political role of women.[3]

Genius forecasting in fictional form has also had its share of spectacular successes. Swift, Verne, Wells, Huxley, Orwell, and Clarke are a few fiction authors who come to mind. Swift, in his satire, *A Voyage to Laputa*, published in 1726, told of the two satellites of Mars, with the uncommonly short orbital periods of 10 and 21.5 hours. Mars was not known to have satellites until 1877 when two were discovered; their orbital periods were 7.6 and 30.4 hours. Wells, of course, wrote about trips to the moon, biological warfare, sex in society, and the possibility of self-annihilation of the race by warfare. As for Huxley, we are uncomfortably close to his "brave new world."

Genius forecasting has not been completely contained in science fiction. In 1946, Rand forecasted with some accuracy the implications of the launching of an orbital satellite. Herman Kahn, one of the foremost practitioners, uses the method with consummate skill in *On Thermonuclear War* and *The Year 2000*.

But, as one might expect, the method fails more often than it succeeds; and its failures have been spectacular. The Library of Congress has compiled a list of faulty forecasts through history which reminds one somehow of slapstick comedy or the vintage movies showing intrepid would-be pilots sitting amidst collapsed wings.[4]

In 1902, *Harper's Weekly* stated, "The actual building of roads devoted to motor cars is not for the near future, in spite of many rumors to that effect." Henry Ford said the Edison Company once offered him a job on the condition he would "give up my gas engine and devote myself to something really useful." Vannevar Bush told the President in 1945: "The Bomb will never go off, and I speak as an expert in explosives." He also said to the Senate, "A 3,000 mile high angle rocket is impossible for many years." (The United States decided not to pursue the ballistic rocket to deliver the bomb; the Russians developed it, and this resulted in their early lead in space.) Terman, the great electrical engineer, said FM radio was "not particularly satisfactory for transmitting intelligence"; and Millikan, the famous physicist, said in 1930, "There is no appreciable energy available to man through atomic disintegration."

In the end, genius forecasting depends on more than the genius of the forecaster; it depends on luck and insight. There may be many geniuses whose forecasts are made with a full measure of both, but it is nearly impossible to recognize them *a priori*; this, of course, is the weakness of the method.

Trend Extrapolation

Forecasts of potential developments may be made by assuming that trends established in history will continue into the future. This extrapolative method assumes, implicitly, that the forces which were at work to shape the trend in the past will continue to work in the future. Thus, for example, if world population doubled in the last forty years, we might expect, as a first approximation at least, that population would double again in a similar period in the future.

Trend extrapolation is most often accomplished in graphical form. Figure 1 shows a characteristic S-shaped or logistics trend curve, starting its slow increase shortly after a triggering discovery or technological invention, going through a period of more rapid growth which reflects technological refinement and improvements in efficiency, and then slowing in growth as functional limits are approached. These limitations might be in the form of physical bounds (for example, who wants to fly the Atlantic in five minutes when baggage still takes an hour?); or operational bounds (efficiency being limited to 100 percent). A graph of speeds attainable at various periods in history is bounded by orbital velocity; at speeds higher than this, energy is required to hold the vehicle in its

Figure 1
Example of S-Curve

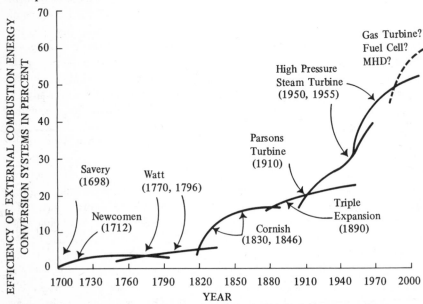

Source: Robert V. Ayres, "Envelope Curve Forecasting," in James Bright (ed.), *Technological Forecasting for Industry and Government* (Englewood Cliffs, New Jersey: Prentice Hall, 1968).

path around the earth. Without such a push, the vehicle would spiral out to an elliptical orbit or escape the earth entirely; and both eventualities would add considerably to transmit time.

If such boundaries are neglected, extension of historical trends into the future can result in naive forecasts. For example, at the rate of growth experienced in crime risk in 1968, all people in the United States might expect to be victims of crime once per year shortly after the turn of the century.

Figure 2 shows that the boundary curve defined by plotting successively developed technologies in the same field is often an S-curve itself. Where the demand for progress continues and physical limits are not exceeded, such technology-on-technology growth seems typical.

Over short periods of time, any section of the S-curve may appear as linear (increasing arithmetically) or as exponential (increasing geometrically). This makes it impossible to discern which part of a growth curve is actually being described. For example, Colonel Joseph Martino has presented the curve shown in Figure 3; this is an exponentially increasing curve.[5]

Trend forecasting need not be confined to demographic or technological performance data. In a recent study conducted by the Institute for the Future, forecasts were to be made about the likelihood of government-sponsored social welfare programs.[6] Past performance in rate of adoption of such programs by twenty-four countries throughout the world leads to the curve shown in Figure 4. The following generalizations could be made from such a curve:

1. The rate of spread of social welfare programs among the countries studied has not varied much over the last hundred years.
2. The United States has never been an innovator in such programs.
3. Certain programs are now in existence in other countries in the group which the United States might expect to have within the next ten to twenty years.

Such a trend forecast exhibits the major weakness of this method: it assumes that forces which have been at work in the past will continue to be at work in the future. Such an assumption is probably warranted for the near term, but grows less satisfying the further the time horizon is stretched. Recognizing that this premise underlies all trend forecasting leads to the concept of "development inertia"; some systems are more easily changed as a result of external influences than others. Slow changes are symptomatic of high inertia systems. The wheeled automobile is imbedded in our economy and probably could not be replaced by another form of personal transportation (for example, hovercraft) very rapidly. On the other hand, there is little inertia to womens' clothing styles.

Techniques for trend extrapolation have been devised which are somewhat more sophisticated than the "eyeball" extension of historical data. Curve-fitting methods, for example, allow more complex curves (curves with exponents of two, three, or above) to be matched to the available data points with least error. Factor analysis can be used to isolate parameters which correlate with one another, and the resulting curves provide a basis for trend forecasting. Some

Figure 2
Example of Envelope Curve

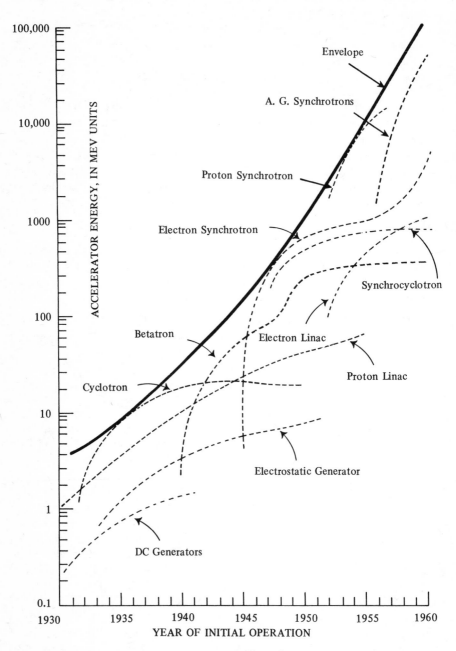

Source: M. Stanley Livingston, *Introduction to the Development of High Energy Accelerators* (New York: Dover Publications, 1966), reprinted by permission.

Figure 3
Top Speed of U.S. Combat Aircraft

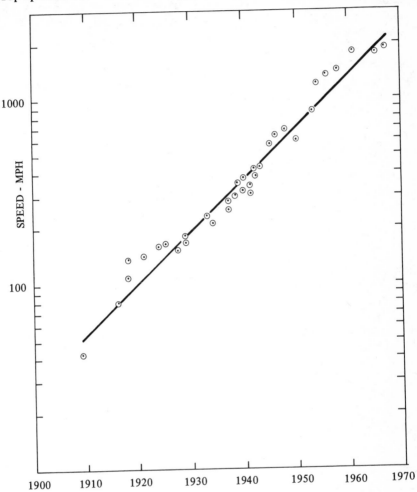

Source: Colonel J. P. Martino, "Trend Extrapolation," a paper presented at the Environmental Forecasting Conference, University of Texas, January 19, 1970.

econometric modeling (through which future labor force and economic conditions may be forecast) employs factor analysis and multiple correlation techniques to establish the basic regression equations.

But regardless of the sophistication of the application, trend forecasting assumes that the present is but a point on a continuum and that discontinuities in the flow of history are rare.

Consensus Methods

In areas of inquiry which are devoid of laws of causality, recourse to expert opinion is admissible.[7] An expert, after all, is defined as a person who is often correct in his judgment about the likely outcome of events in inexact fields.

If the services of more than a single expert are required (when several disciplines are involved, or when opinions of equally competent experts differ), methods of synthesizing opinion are required. One approach is to place the potential contributors in face-to-face confrontation and let them argue it out. This situation has several potential hazards: dominant individuals may carry the discussion by weight of their personality rather than by force of argument; the psychology of the group may lead to consensus through "bandwagon" dynamics; time may be lost in the establishment of intellectual "pecking orders." Nevertheless, as Dalkey points out, given no other information, a group estimate is at least as reliable as that of a randomly chosen expert.[8] Furthermore, if the range of answers contributed by the individuals of the group contains the true answer, then the median of the group is a closer approximation to the true answer than the answer provided by more than half the group.

The Delphi technique is a method of seeking a group consensus which avoids some of the problems of face-to-face confrontation. Generally a Delphi exercise engages experts in an anonymous debate, their opinions being exchanged through an intermediary. Anonymity exists at two levels: participants are unknown to each other, and individual responses are never attributed to particular respondents. In the first round of a typical Delphi study, the participants might

Figure 4
Historical Growth of Social Benefit Programs

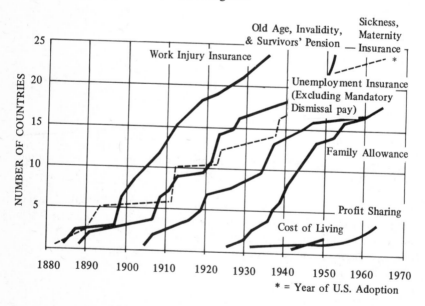

Source: T. J. Gordon, *A Study of Potential Changes in Employee Benefits*, Reports R-1, R-2, R-3, The Institute for the Future (April, 1969).

be asked when a future event might take place. Their answers are collated by the experimenters and fed back to them in a second round. The second round questionnaire seeks justification of extreme views expressed in round one. The responses are again collated by the experimenters and furnished to the participants in a third (and usually final) round. This questionnaire asks that the experts reassess their previous positions in view of those taken by the other participants.

Probably more than two hundred studies using this general technique have been conducted in the past five years covering a diversity of subjects which included: scientific breakthroughs;[9] economic forecasts;[10] medical developments;[11] automation developments;[12] societal trends;[13] employee benefits;[14] physical and biomedical technologies;[15] education developments;[16] corporate forecasting.[17]

The Delphi technique generally produces a narrowing of the initial spread of opinions and a shifting of the median as the questioning proceeds. If no consensus emerges, at least a crystallizing of the disparate positions usually becomes apparent.

Norman Dalkey at Rand recently performed a series of detailed experiments using the Delphi method. A relatively large number of UCLA students were given a questionnaire pertaining to issues with known answers against which the group consensus could be checked for accuracy.[18] Admittedly, questions of this sort differ from questions about the future, but they afforded an opportunity to observe some of the characteristics of group interactions and behavior under controlled conditions. The six major findings of the study were:

1. The spread of opinions narrows from the first to the second questionnaire, and the median, more often than not, shifts toward the true answer.
2. Delphi interactions generally produce more accurate estimates than do face to face confrontations. If face-to-face discussions follow Delphi interactions, the results are generally degraded.
3. The error of the group is a function of the standard deviation.
4. Feeding back reasons for extreme opinions does not improve group accuracy.
5. Group self-appraised expertise is a powerful determinant of accuracy; if the group believes it is expert, it probably is.
6. Accuracy of the respondents improves when they are allowed one-half minute for answering; shorter or longer intervals (at least up to four minutes) lead to increased error.

Some of these results are surprising (for example, the extremely short time required for highest accuracy and the failure to improve accuracy with the feedback of reasons); but the overall findings of the study are encouraging.

Do these results reflect the performance of the Delphi method when the questions under study relate to the future? Campbell's short-range forecast of future economic conditions was made by Delphi and "normal" methods.[19] The Delphi forecasts proved to be more accurate. Dalkey found that the responses obtained by Campbell followed the same kind of distribution as answers given to his encyclopedic questions. Martino has analyzed the data obtained in the responses to the study conducted by North and Pike of TRW. He found a similar distribution.[20]

Six years have passed since the 1964 long-range forecasts were made by the panels under Gordon and Helmer at Rand.[21] Ament at the Institute for the Future has compared these forecasts to actuality and has found that of the twenty events forecast to occur by 1970, fifteen have occurred, five have not, and two are uncertain.[22] His analysis is summarized in Table 1.

One of the interesting sidelights of Ament's review is the difficulty he encountered in determining whether or not an event had in fact actually occurred. For example the original forecast was: "Direct link from stores to bank to check credit and to record transactions." Such links exist now but are not pervasive.

Table 1
Near Term Forecasts of 1964 Rand Report

	50% occurrence probability			Has the development occurred?		
	Lower Quartile	Median	Upper Quartile	Yes	No	Partly or uncertain
Scientific Breakthroughs						
Economically useful desalination of sea water	1964	1970				0
Feasibility of effective large-scale fertility control by oral contraceptive or other simple and inexpensive means	1970	1970	1983	0		
Progress in space						
USSR orbital rendezvous	1964	1964	1966	0		
USA orbital rendezvous	1965	1967	1967	0		
Increased use of near-Earth satellites for weather prediction and control	1967	1967	1970	0		
Unmanned inspections and capability for destruction of satellites	1967	1967	1970		0	
USSR manned lunar fly-by	1967	1967	1970		0	
Establishment of global communications system	1967	1968	1970	0		
USA manned lunar fly-by	1967	1970	1970	0		
Manned lunar landing and return	1969	1969	1970	0		
Rescue of astronauts stranded in orbit	1968	1970	1975		0	
Operational readiness of laser for space communications	1968	1970	1975			0

Table 1 Cont.
Near Term Forecasts of 1964 Rand Report

	50% occurrence probability			Has the development occurred?		
	Lower Quartile	Median	Upper Quartile	Yes	No	Partly or uncertain
Manned co-orbital inspection of satellites	1970	1970	1974		0	
Manned scientific orbital station—ten men	1970	1970	1975		0	
Future weapon systems						
Tactical kiloton nuclear weapons for use by ground troops	1964	1965	1967	0		
Extensive uses of devices that persuade without killing (water cannons, tear gas, etc.)	1968	1968	1970	0		
Miniature improved sensors and transmitters for snooping, reconnaissance, arms control	1968	1968	1970	0		
Rapid mobility of men and light weapons to any point on Earth for police action	1966	1969	1973	0		
Incapacitating chemical (as opposed to biological) agents	1965	1970	1975	0		
Use of lasers for radar-type sensors, illuminators, communications	1968	1970	1975	0		
Incapacitating biological agents	1968	1970	1976	0		
Lethal biological agents	1967	1970	1980	0		

Source: R. Ament, "Comparison of Delphi Forecasting Studies in 1964 and 1969," *Futures* (March, 1970).

In the end, Ament resorted to a brief opinion poll among the IFF staff to determine whether or not the events forecast in 1964 had occurred yet. One reason for the difficulty is that many of the events, in retrospect, were not specific enough, and defined trends rather than "happenings." Furthermore, the occurrence of highly specialized events is noted by specialists and is not systematically recorded or generally accessible.

Delphi studies do not produce "truth" about the future; under the best of circumstances, they yield only consensus opinion about what might be. If the participants are experts, perhaps their opinion represents a possible future which deserves consideration in planning.

Some interesting variations on the Delphi method have been devised. The method has been used with graphical data. In this application, the respondents are given historical data in graphical form and are asked to extend them in time. The range of responses are fed back graphically in the second round and those holding extreme opinions are asked to justify their positions. The reasons given are furnished to all respondents, who are asked to reconsider their own curves. In several studies using this technique, it was found that the range of opinions converges in later questionnaires and the median curve shifts. Figure 5 shows examples of the type of data which have been produced this way.

The Delphi technique has also been used to collect opinions about social changes. In one case, the group was asked to forecast the likely impact on society of various technological changes and the desirability of those impacts. Figure 6 shows an example of the results of this inquiry. [23] In another study, the panel was asked to provide its judgment on the likely course of social trends. [24] Some of the data produced in the portion of the study dealing with education is shown in Figure 7.

Figure 5
Convergence of Opinion

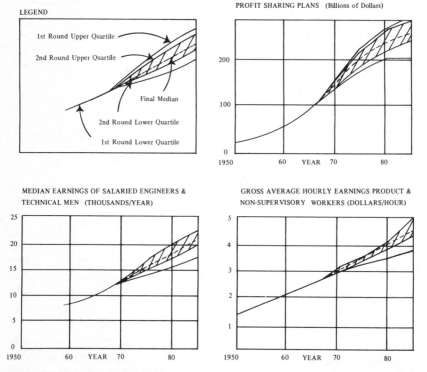

Source: R. deBrigard and Olaf Helmer, *Some Potential Societal Developments*, Report R-7, Institute for the Future (December, 1969).

Figure 6
Display of Judgments of Consequences of Technology

NEW MEDICAL TECHNIQUES		HOW LIKELY IS IS THAT THE RESULT WILL BE A CONSEQUENCE OF THE DEVELOPMENT?				WHAT WILL THE EFFECT OF THE CONSEQUENCE BE?				
IF THESE DEVELOPMENTS WERE TO OCCUR·	THEY MIGHT RESULT IN:	VIRTUALLY CERTAIN	PROBABLE	POSSIBLE	ALMOST IMPOSSIBLE	VERY FAVORABLE	FAVORABLE	LITTLE OR NO IMPORTANCE	DETRIMENTAL	VERY DETRIMENTAL
2. Demonstration of implantable artificial hearts with power sources capable of lasting five years.	M. Change in emphasis of medicine from repair to replacement.									
	N. Rise of new industries, technologies and technicians devoted to production and installation of artificial organs.									
6. Practicial use of general "immunizing" agents (such as interferon) which can protect against most bacterial and viral diseases.	O. End to the common cold.									
	P. Increased productivity (fewer sick days).									
8. Laboratory demonstration of bio-chemical processes which stimulate growth of new organs and limbs in human beings.	Q. Severe addition to medical cost burden of the poor.									
	R. Economic improvements resulting from making disabled persons more self-sufficient.									
11. Demonstration of chemical control of the human aging process, permitting extension of life span by fifty years, with commensurate increase in number of years of vigor.	S. Used as reward for small groups, perhaps "high-ranking officials."									
	T. Changes in values regarding death and punishment.									
	U. Sociological chaos, if developed quickly.									
19. Demonstration of capability to repair the central nervous system including regeneration or repairs to individual neurons.	V. Reduction of the number of insane.									
	W. Decreased suffering through the repair of congenital defects, stroke damage, certain types of polio, and certain head injuries resulting from accidents or warfare, to restore functional capability but probably not learning and experience.									

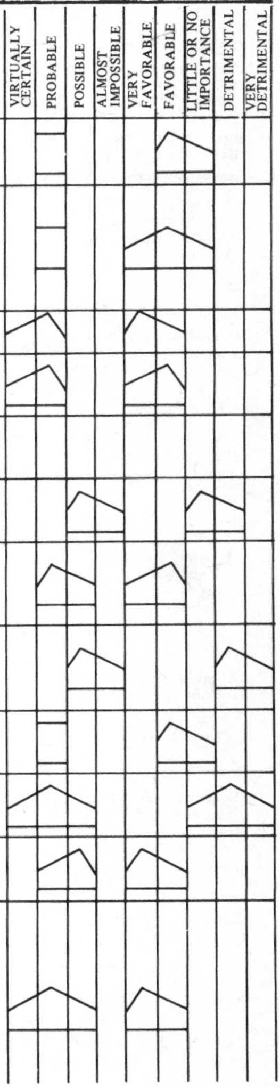

Source: T. J. Gordon and R. Ament, *Forecasts of Some Technological and Scientific Developments and Their Societal Consequences*, Report R-6, The Institute for the Future (September, 1969).

Social forecasting proved to be much more difficult than scientific and technological forecasting. In a sense, scientific and technological forecasts have their roots in the research and development in progress in laboratories throughout the world; experts can base their forecasts on their knowledge of this work. But in the societal domain, there is no analogous research-in-progress on which to base forecasts. As a result, there tends to be less agreement and less inclination to

Figure 7
Judgments of Trends in Education

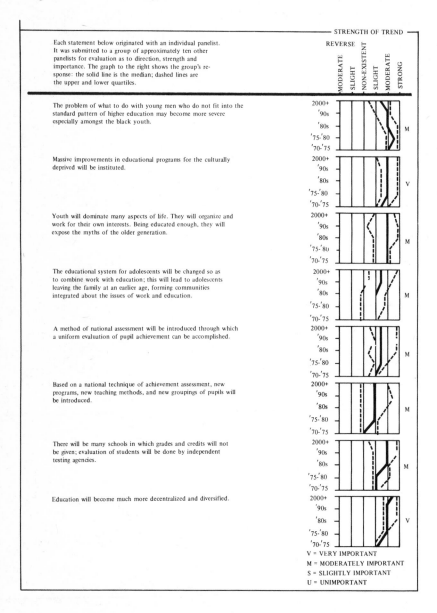

Source: R. deBrigard and O. Helmer, *Some Potential Societal Developments*, Report R-7, The Institute for the Future (December, 1969).

change opinion. Nevertheless, interesting results can be achieved which may also prove to be useful in planning.

Delphi techniques are benefiting from automated data processing. North at TRW has processed his inter-round data automatically.[25] At the Institute, specific questions are being matched to respondents according to their skill profiles. Also planned is a system known as the D-Net, which, through the utilization of computers and modern communications systems, will permit rapid exchanges between participants on a routine basis.

The Institute for the Future has experimented with "mini-Delphi" interactions in which only a portion of the anonymity of Delphi interactions is preserved. Participants, in a face-to-face conference, are asked to write their opinions about the subject under discussion and give them to the moderator. These opinions are collated rapidly and fed back to the group. Re-estimates are requested without divulging which members of the group held divergent views. This type of interaction has been found to produce the characteristic narrowing of opinions and median shifts found in the more elaborate studies.

Simulation Methods

Simulation is the approximation of complex systems by dynamic models. These models may exist in several forms:

—mechanical analogs
(for example, a wind tunnel model of an SST)
—mathematical analogs
(a set of equations describing the economic situation of a country)
—metaphorical analogs
(the growth of a bacteria colony taken to depict human population growth)
—game analogs
(interactions between "players" taken to represent social interactions)

These models can change with time and are useful where experimentation with actual systems is too costly, is morally impossible, or involves the study of problems so complex that more precise analytic solutions appear impractical. Mathematical and game analogs are of particular importance to futures research.

Mathematical models of physical systems have been used successfully in many applications. For example, computer simulations of the smog conditions in the Los Angeles basin have yielded insight into the relative contributions of automobiles and power stations to atmospheric pollution and the expected effect of varying either input. If the performance of a system can be approximated by an equation, then the mathematical relationship is a forecasting device which predicts the response of the system to anticipated external stimulation.

When one considers techno-social systems, the situation becomes enormously more complex. Attempts at modeling aspects of social behavior can be found in various economic and social science publications. The economics literature, for example, now encompasses general economic theory relating not only to development growth in planning, but also to the economics of health, education, poverty, crime, discrimination, and technological change.

For example, J. W. Forrester of M.I.T. has attempted in a recent book to model various aspects of the city and the people who use it.[26] His model involves descriptions of the dynamic interactions between the availability of housing, employment levels, and certain demographic descriptors of the various socio-economic classes that inhabit the city. The model design is similar to that employed in a control system in that the behavior of various aspects of the model are described in terms of feedback loops, system gains, and so on. Forrester's model has produced some counter-intuitive results. For example, his work suggests that the construction of low-cost housing within an urban area will cause conditions of the city to deteriorate even further.

The difficulty with such mathematical models is that they necessarily imply certain values and attitudes on the part of the society they describe. These values and attitudes are probably a complicated function of other social and technological changes. One solution to this difficulty is to substitute real people for mathematical constructions depicting their supposed behavior—that is, to use game analogies rather than mathematical analogies.

Simulation gaming involves the creation of an artificial game environment in which players (real people acting out assigned roles) are asked to interact. A simulation game generally has the following five elements:

1. Rules of play to govern the "moves" and interactions between players, and other variables of the game.
2. Objectives or goals; players may work cooperatively toward a joint goal or competitively toward goals which cannot be shared. (A single game may incorporate both modes, as in *Monopoly* when players decide to "gang up" on the "apartment house owner.")
3. A method of translating the moves of the players into indicators which measure the degree of attainment of goals. This device may be a game board, mathematical model, or another group of participants charged with responsiblity of judging the effect of the players' moves.
4. A display system to illustrate the progress of the game.
5. A set of exogenous variables to introduce "outside events" into the play.

While simulation gaming has not yet demonstrated forecasting precision, it serves other ends. First, it can teach players and experimenters about the issue under study. A well designed simulation game includes descriptive elements which acquaint the players with definitions of, and interrelationships among, some of the variables, at least as perceived by the experimenters. In designing the game, the experimenters learn to define the parameters thought to be relevant to the issues being simulated and to describe their mode of interaction. Tolerance (or at least sensitivity) to various points of view is usually a part of the player's game experience.

Second, simulation gaming can provide a framework for systematic review of the issue being studied. In constructing a game, it is usually necessary to define the constituent elements of the issues being simulated and consider how these elements are likely to interact. Because games generally require a structure of sorts, these considerations are usually orderly and may thus replace haphazard and sporadic probes into issues. The game structure often forces the role players to consider the issues surrounding the simulation from attitudes unfamiliar to them—usually in a systematic fashion.

Third, a simulation game can allow role players to exhibit emotions and make decisions normally excluded in real life but permitted in the game environment. In effect, the game may become a psychological device—a means of experimenting with and exerting power in circumstances not likely to be detrimental to society at large.

Finally, it can improve communications between players. The cooperation or competition engendered by the roles of a game may promote relationships between the players which last long after the game is over. By exposing concerns in the game environment, players may build new sensitivities to each other's personalities and behavior patterns in real life.

Simulation gaming has been used in diverse applications, including the derivation and testing of military strategies and the teaching of certain aspects of political science. The method may eventually be useful in resolving conflicts between individuals, groups, or nations. With more experience and data, the tool might also be developed into a more precise forecasting instrument.

Cross-Impact Matrix Methods [27]

The various forecasting techniques already described often produce lists of potential future events and their likely dates of occurrence. Yet potential relationships may exist between the forecasted events; that is, forecasted sets might well contain mutually reinforcing or mutually exclusive items. The cross-impact matrix method is an experimental approach by which the probabilities of an item in a forecasted set can be adjusted in view of judgments relating to potential interactions of the forecasted items. Most events and developments are in some way connected with other events and developments. A single event, such as the production of power from the first atomic reactor, was made possible by a complex history of antecedent scientific, technological, political and economic "happenings."

In its turn, the production of energy from the first atomic reactor provided an intellectual conception which influenced or shaped many of the events and developments which followed. In a sense, history is a focusing of many apparently diverse and unrelated occurrences which permit or cause singular events and developments. From these flows an ever-widening tree of downstream effects which interact with other events and developments. It is hard to imagine an event without a predecessor which made it more or less likely or influenced its form—or one which, after occurring, left no mark. This interrelationship between events and developments is called "cross impact."

The systematic description of all potential modes of interaction and the assessment of the possible strength of these interactions is vastly complex but methodologically important, since these descriptions and metrics may provide new insight into historical analysis and permit greater accuracy and precision in forecasting. A general theory of such cross impact, which is not available, would almost certainly permit the exploration of the side-effects of decisions under consideration. It might also be useful in illuminating less expensive means of attaining goals through investment in high payoff areas which initially seem to be unrelated or only weakly linked to the decision.

Although the computational techniques used in a cross-impact analysis are somewhat complicated, the basic concepts underlying the techniques are straightforward. Suppose that a set of developments had been forecast to occur prior to some year in the future, with varying levels of probability. If these developments are designated D_i (i = 1, 2 ..., n), with associated probabilities P_i, then the question can be posed: "If $P_m = 1$ (that is, if D_m happens), how do the other P_i change?" In other words, we speak of a cross-impact effect if the probability that one event occurs varies either positively or negatively with the occurrence or nonoccurrence of other events.

By way of illustration, if the following developments and probabilities were forecast for a given year:[28]

Development D_i	Probability P_i
1. One-month reliable weather forecasts	.4
2. Feasibility of limited weather control	.2
3. General biochemical immunization	.5
4. Elimination of crop damage from adverse weather	.5

These events might then be arranged in matrix form:

	Then the probability of			
If this development were to occur:	D_1	D_2	D_3	D_4
D_1	▨	—	—	⬆
D_2	⬆	▨	—	⬆
D_3	—	—	▨	—
D_4	—	—	—	▨

The upward arrows indicate an increase in probability. Thus if D_2 (the feasibility of limited weather control) were to occur, D_1 (one-month reliable weather forecast) and D_4 (elimination of crop damage from adverse weather) would become more probable as noted by the upward arrows.

This kind of array is called a "cross-impact matrix." Interactions between events are much more complex, of course, than those that can be indicated by an arrow. The arrow denotes only a linkage between events and the direction of the influence one event has on another. In addition, it is necessary to identify the linkage strength (how strongly the occurrence or non-occurrence of one event before another event is influenced).

Once the arrows have been replaced by the requisite numerical data and the relevant formulas have been developed for calculating the changes in probabilities, such a matrix can be analyzed on a computer. Briefly, the following seven steps are involved:

1. Assessing the potential interactions (cross impacts) among individual events in a set of forecasts in terms of:

     – Direction, or mode, of the interaction
     – Strength of the interaction
     – Time delay of the effect of one event on another

2. Selecting an event at random and "deciding" its occurrence or nonoccurrence on the basis of its assigned probability.
3. Adjusting the probability of the remaining events according to the interactions assessed as likely in step 1.
4. Selecting another event from among those remaining and deciding it (using its new probability) as before.
5. Continuing this process until all events in the set have been decided.
6. "Playing" the matrix in this way many times, so that the probabilities can be computed on the basis of the percentage of times that an event occurs during these plays.
7. Changing the initial probability of one or more events and repeating steps 2 to 6.

By comparing the initial probabilities to those generated in step 6, it is possible to determine how the initial probabilities might be modified to reflect the cross impacts of other events on the list. By comparing the results of step 6 and step 7, it is possible to determine how a change in the probability of occurrence of one or more events would, through the cross impacts, affect the probability of the other events.

The cross-impact method has been used experimentally in several situations. The first examples, which were completed in early 1968, related to the decision to deploy the Minuteman missile and the future of transportation services. Since then, numerous other cross-impact analyses have been completed, including techno-socio situations, corporate investment strategies, technological assessments, and political interactions. Otto Sulc has experimented with a similar method for relating forecasted technological and social changes.[29]

Of particular interest is the possibility of evaluating alternative policy decisions through cross-impact methods. An illustration of this policy-test capability is provided by a simple cross-impact analysis undertaken in connection with an

Institute for the Future study of alternative future environments for education. Five specific future developments were postulated:

1. Initiation of laws requiring negotiation between primary and secondary public school teachers and school boards in the United States.
2. Most teachers belonging to negotiation unions.
3. Most students in secondary public schools belonging to recognized unions.
4. Increase in parent-teacher conflict (triple present levels).
5. Initiation of ethnic study programs in most secondary schools.

These developments were reviewed independently by several experts engaged in educational policy research, who assessed the probability of the developments' occurrence prior to the year 1985. The potential cross impacts among pairs of these developments were evaluated in terms of expected mode and strength of interaction.

The matrix was "played out" in accordance with techniques described earlier. The play suggested that several of the items were more probable than had been believed previously, based on the judgments about the linkages between individual items.

Next, the initial probability of each item in turn was artificially increased, and the time of 10 percent probability reduced, to observe the effects of simulated policy action. For example, in the next set of 1,000 runs, the initial probability of "most students in secondary public schools belonging to recognized unions" was increased from 0.30 to 0.60, and the estimated time of its earliest occurrence changed from 1976 to 1972. The resulting probabilities of this set (after 1,000 repeats) were somewhat different than the first set. Item 5 (ethnic programs) had changed by a significant amount. Thus, one might say that the subjective judgments about interactions contained in the cross-impact matrix led to the conclusion that policy action which increases the probability of "student unions" will also increase the probability of "ethnic study programs."

This discussion illustrates the use of cross-impact matrices to test the expected effects of potential policy actions. Clearly, the results are an artifact of the judgments originally supplied when constructing the matrix cells. Nevertheless, the method permits systematic collation of judgment and makes explicit the sometimes hidden effect of multiple linkages between events under consideration in assessing potential outcomes of proposed action.

The cross-impact method raises a logical puzzle: if the initial probabilities are derived by a method which only loosely constrains the reasoning of the forecasters, then these initial probabilities themselves may already reflect some of the cross impacts described in the matrix. This would introduce a kind of "double accounting" that would be quite difficult to anticipate explicitly.

On the other hand, it might be assumed that the initial probability estimates are fully impacted, in the sense that the impact effect of the occurrence or nonoccurrence of other developments has been taken into account. This would mean that, ideally, the initial probabilities would coincide with the terminal probabilities resulting from the cross-impact analysis. If in fact they did not, the error would be the estimator's and stem from his inability to handle the complexity of the situation, which the cross-impact process helps to identify and to correct.

The discipline involved in the selection of items, and particularly the systematic questioning necessary to the establishment of cross impacts, is often enlightening. One is faced with deciding what events may be important and how they may affect one another. This confrontation often illustrates that issues once believed to be simple and independent are, in reality, interrelated. Just completing a matrix can force a level of introspection helpful in some planning situations. The mathematical play of the basic matrix using new initial conditions to simulate policies can show unexpected secondary and tertiary consequences of the potential actions.

Other Methods

A "scenario" is a narrative description of some future state of affairs, and a "future history" is a narrative description of a potential course of development which might lead to that state of affairs. Both techniques can be very powerful if constructed under the hand of an experienced and talented author, since they can carry the force of eloquent narrative prose. Herman Kahn, Anthony Weiner, and Paul Ehrlich are masters of the technique. Some brief excerpts from their work will serve to illustrate the methods.

In their book, *The Year 2000*, Kahn and Weiner wrote a scenario depicting social controls:

... Perhaps many (most) men would be kept in a permanently drugged state (pacified?) and adapted to the ecology to which they are assigned according to some computerized calculation. As always the central government would so likely be swamped by the problem of keeping the system functioning properly that it would be concerned only with marginal and immediate problems rather than with the increasing repulsiveness of the entire system or with other basic issues. In any event there may be no rational or moral (whatever these terms mean in the twenty-first century) feasible solution that does not reject the modern technology or condemn billions of surplus humans to death or deprivation. [30]

In *Ramparts*, Ehrlich described a future history of pollution:

The end of the ocean came late in the summer of 1979, and it came even more rapidly than the biologists had expected. There had been signs for more than a decade, commencing with the discovery in 1968 that DDT slows down photosynthesis in marine plant life. It was announced in a short paper in the technical journal, Science, *but to ecologists it smacked of doomsday. They knew that all life in the sea depends on photosynthesis, the chemical process by which green plants bind the sun's energy and make it available to living things. And they knew that DDT and similar chlorinated hydrocarbons had polluted the entire surface of the earth, including the sea.* [31]

Kahn and Weiner have attempted to categorize types of scenarios. They recognize "surprise-free" projections, which define a "standard world." They point out that such a world is highly unlikely, since the future undoubtedly will contain surprises. "Canonical variations" can be derived from the surprise-free projections by asking, "What would happen to my surprise-free world if all things stayed as I expected except that . . . ."

The strength of the method is also its weakness. It is extremely dependent on the capability of the storyteller. It is easily dismissed as politically biased, since it represents a single point of view. Nevertheless, it can be powerfully persuasive.

"Decision trees" are graphic devices which display the potential results of alternative approaches to crucial decisions. Figure 8 illustrates a portion of a very simplified decision tree which might describe some of the futures connected with establishing a base on Mars. There are sixteen future histories implicit in this diagram; they range from: "no public, Presidential, or Congressional support" to "the establishment of a Mars base after the accomplishment of a scientifically interesting mission, supported enthusiastically by the public and the government." Of course, no path into the future is this clear-cut; every branch point has gradations of decisions, and decisions at one level might well feed back to decisions at other levels. These considerations lead to the construction of very complex maps. Such large trees can be contained on computers, and various scenarios and future histories generated automatically. Subjective probabilities of the various paths also can be introduced, so that the overall probability of following a particular path into the future may be computed.

"Input-output matrices" are used by economists to detail inter-industrial transactions. Typically, an input-output matrix is a kind of balance sheet; the row entries depict input sectors, and the columns depict the sectors which utilize these inputs. The cells of the matrix contain coefficients which express conversion by which the products of the various listed input sectors are transformed into the various listed outputs. These coefficients are generally constructed from historical data; and, of course, any such matrix presents only a static picture at a particular point in time. Since time histories of the coefficients are computable, it is possible to forecast changing values of the coefficients through any of the methods mentioned earlier. Forecasting of input-output coefficients under various projected economic circumstances has been attempted by researchers at Battelle Memorial Institute, Arthur D. Little, and Harvard. If such efforts prove successful, economists may be able to build projections of technological and social change into some of the models. Such a goal is well worth pursuing.

Uncertainties and Research

As indicated at the beginning of this paper, futures research is an embryonic discipline, a collection of techniques and estimates, with partially unifying philosophy. Its research agenda is immense. Some of the questions currently facing futures researchers are:

To what extent will these techniques actually prove useful in decision-making?

Putting questions of accuracy aside, will the techniques lead to more effective teaching methods, approaches to conflict solution, or beneficial public attitudes?

Figure 8
Decision Tree

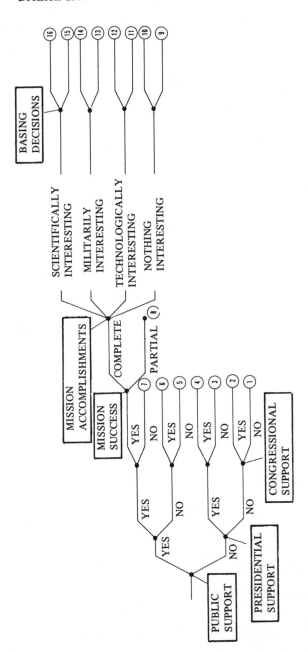

Under what conditions will simulation accuracy be improved? How can good simulations and simulators be recognized?

How can a good forecaster be recognized? Can he be trained?

What kinds of events and developments are, by their nature, unanticipated?

How can potentially important events be recognized?

What are the attributes of plausibility (as opposed to probability)?

The systematic methods may sometimes lend more credibility to results than they may warrant. How can technique be subordinated to content?

Among the pressing problems facing the protodiscipline is that of value forecasting. Psychologists have not produced general models of value change, yet it is clear that values do change. They are shaped by pressures of technology (the effect of the automobile on sexual mores); advertising (the anti-cancer ads on TV); peer groups (long hair, short skirts, drugs); institutions (chauvinism); economic conditions (affluence permitting youth to look with disdain on the profit motive); and probably many other social interactions. Without some knowledge as to how values might change in the future, planners must work with the value set they have at hand: their own as of the moment of planning. Suppose a planner were to design a transportation system to provide economical and safe travel. Economy and safety are current values; and his transportation system, which might happen to cut through a mountain, would satisfy those values. If, however, in some future society, the integrity of the countryside were more valued than cheap travel or safety, the planner would not only have been wrong, he would have been delinquent.

How can a planner anticipate what values will be "good" and "right" and "proper" tomorrow? Even if he could, should he attempt to change their evolution so that our values can prevail?

The implications for futures research are important: forecasts raise value questions. Which future do we value the most, do we find in closest agreement with our own values? Planners answer this question implicitly by making choices among alternative plans.

But their values may be narrow. They are probably not values held by society as a whole. Perhaps worse, their values are today's values, not those which will be held by people in the future. This is a form of tyranny—the tyranny of the present.

If you make forecasts, be aware of this possibility.

Notes

1. H. Wentworth Eldridge, "Teaching Futurism in American Colleges and Universities," a paper presented at the Environmental Forecasting Conference, University of Texas at Austin, January, 1970. According to Dr. Eldridge, forty courses are now being offered at various institutions (half at the graduate level), and forty-one other schools are considering such courses.

2. B. de Jouvenel, *The Art of Conjecture*, translated from the French by Nikita Lary (New York: Basic Books, 1967).

3. S. C. Gilfillan, "A Sociologist Looks at Technical Prediction," in J. Bright (ed.), *Technological Forecasting in Government and Industry* (Englewood Cliffs: Prentice Hall, 1968).

4. N. T. Gamarra, *Erroneous Predictions and Negative Comments Concerning Exploration, Territorial Expansion, Scientific and Technological Development*, Legislative Reference Service, Library of Congress (April, 1967).

5. Colonel J. P. Martino, "Trend Extrapolation," a paper presented at the Environmental Forecasting Conference, University of Texas, January 19, 1970.

6. T. J. Gordon, *A Study of Potential Changes in Employee Benefits*, Reports R-1, R-2, R-3, The Institute for the Future (April, 1969).

7. O. Helmer and N. Rescher, " The Epistemology of the Inexact Sciences," *Management Science*, 6, 1 (October, 1959).

8. N. Dalkey, *The Delphi Method: An Experimental Study of Group Opinion*, Memorandum RM-5888-PR, The Rand Corporation (June, 1969).

9. T. J. Gordon and O. Helmer, "A Report on a Long-Range Forecasting Study," *Societal Technology* (New York: Basic Books, 1966), pp. 44-96.

10. R. M. Campbell, *Methodological Study of the Utilization of Experts in Business Forecasting*, unpublished Ph.D. dissertation, University of California, Los Angeles (September, 1966).

11. A. D. Bender, *et al., A Delphic Study of the Future of Medicine*, Philadelphia: Smith Kline French Laboratories, January, 1969.

12. C. Bjerrum, "Forecast of Computer Developments and Applications 1968-2000," *Futures* 1, 4 (June, 1969).

13. R. de Brigard and O. Helmer, *Some Potential Societal Developments*, Report R-7, The Institute for the Future (December, 1969).

14. T. J. Gordon, *A Study of Potential Changes in Employee Benefits, op. cit.*

15. T. J. Gordon and R. Ament, *Forecasts of Some Technological and Scientific Developments and Their Societal Consequences*, Report R-6, The Institute for the Future (September, 1969).

16. M. Adelson, "The Education Innovation Study," *American Behavioral Scientist*, 10, 7 (March, 1967), pp. 8-12.

17. H.Q. North and L. Pike, "Technological Forecasting in Planning for Company Growth," Institute of Electrical and Electronics Engineers *Spectrum*, 6, 1 (January, 1969).

18. Dalkey, *op. cit.*

19. Campbell, *op. cit.*

20. Martino, *op. cit.*

21. Gordon and Helmer, *op. cit.*

22. R. Ament, "Comparison of Delphi Forecasting Studies in 1964 and 1969," *Futures* (March, 1970).

23. Gordon and Ament, *op. cit.*

24. deBrigard and Helmer, *op. cit.*

25. North and Pike, *op. cit.*

26. J. W. Forrester, *Urban Dynamics* (Cambridge: M.I.T. Press, 1969).

27. Portions of this section are drawn from T. J. Gordon and H. Hayward, "Initial Experiment with Cross-Impact Matrix Method of Forecasting," *Futures* (December, 1968); T. J. Gordon, "Cross-Impact Matrices: An Illustration of Their Use for Policy Analysis," *Futures* (December, 1969); and R. Rochberg, T. J. Gordon, and O. Helmer, *The Use of Cross-Impact Matrices for Forecasting and Planning*, Report R-10, The Institute for the Future (April, 1970).

28. Rochberg, Gordon, and Helmer, *op. cit.*

29. O. Sulc, "Interactions between Technological and Social Changes," *Futures* (September, 1969).

30. H. Kahn and A. Weiner, (eds.) *The Year 2000* (New York: Macmillan, 1967), p. 351.

31. P. Ehrlich, "Eco-Catastrophe!" *Ramparts* (September, 1969).

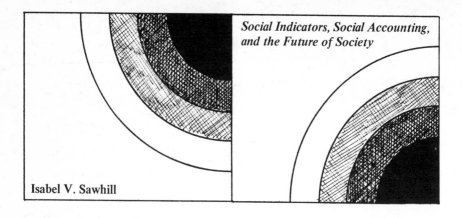

Social Indicators, Social Accounting, and the Future of Society

Isabel V. Sawhill

Crime, poverty, pollution ... these are the domestic issues of the day, perhaps of the decade and beyond. They are *social* issues in the sense that no individual working alone in his capacity as a private citizen can solve these problems, no matter how dedicated he might be to securing their elimination. Some form of collective action is required; and, in a modern democracy, the task is commonly delegated to government. But can governments rise to the challenge? To date, the problems have largely defied solution, and the effectiveness of collective action is increasingly in question, particularly among the young.

Social reporting and social indicators are designed to improve, in a modest way, the effectiveness of government decision-making. Just how this might be accomplished and what its political consequences might be are still open to debate. The purpose here is to enliven this debate by providing a review of some of the pertinent work in this field, as well as some further thoughts on the significance of these efforts for policy formulation in general and futures-oriented policy in particular.

As a preliminary and somewhat oversimplified guide, a social indicator may be defined as a quantitative measure of the condition of one aspect of society, a social account as a framework for organizing social indicators in a meaningful way, and a social report as a document which uses these and/or other types of information to assess the social state of the nation. Social indicators include economic indicators such as the GNP, but they also include attempts to measure such noneconomic variables as the quality of the environment, the degree of social mobility, or the health status of the population.

The above concepts have been extensively discussed of late by those in both the academic world and the government.[1] Major contributors to the field have included Bertram Gross, Raymond Bauer, and Mancur Olson, all of whom have written extensively on the need for more highly developed information systems for measuring social change.[2] The task of actually constructing indicators is still in its infancy, but ongoing work at the Urban Institute, the Russell Sage foundation, and the Office of Management and Budget may help to fill the gap.[3] In the meantime, economists at both the National Bureau of Economic Research and Yale University have been looking into possible modifications of our existing national income statistics in the hopes of turning them into more accurate measures of social welfare.[4] Although some would argue that such efforts are doomed to failure because of their essentially normative content, others contend that the GNP is an increasingly misleading statistic and that some improvements are both desirable and possible.

Perhaps even more significant are recent attempts within the government to introduce these ideas in a tentative way into the decision-making process. In 1966, President Johnson directed the Secretary of Health, Education, and Welfare to develop a series of social indicators in order that the nation might "better measure the distance we have come and plan for the way ahead." In response to this directive, a "panel on social indicators," consisting of leading social scientists, was assembled to gather and develop what information they could on health, social mobility, the environment, income and poverty, public order and safety, learning, science, and art. With the help of a staff within the department, headed by Mancur Olson, this resulted in the publication of *Toward a Social Report,*[5] which was released the last day of the Johnson Administration.

Support for such a document has also come from Senator Walter Mondale and a group of other senators who have introduced pertinent legislation in the last three Congresses. The most recent bill, entitled "The Full Opportunity and National Goals and Priorities Act" (S.5), calls for the establishment of a council of social advisors which would be responsible for reporting to the President and the nation about social conditions in the same way that the Council of Economic Advisors reports on economic progress.

Although the Nixon Administration has expressed reservations about the desirability of such legislation,[6] it has not abandoned the idea of social reporting entirely. Although short-lived, a National Goals Research Staff was established within the White House in 1969, issued its report, "Toward Balanced Growth: Quantity with Quality," on July 4, 1970, and then disappeared from the scene. In the meantime, the Office of Statistical Policy within the Office of Management and Budget continues to gather existing statistics with a view to publishing a list of indicators in nine major areas of social concern.

What is the significance of these varied activities? To answer this question, we need to trace the intellectual foundations of social reporting and probe more deeply into its possible contribution to public policy-making.

Origins of an Idea

Although social reporting has many historical roots which have been extensively chronicled elsewhere,[7] the present interest in the topic seems to emanate from two broad developments—one substantive and one methodological in nature. On the substantive side, there has been a shift in the kinds of concerns which have absorbed our moral energies as a nation. We have become more concerned with the quality of life and less with the quantity of goods and services available, more with equity and less with efficiency, more with the uses to which existing resources are put and less with the overall rate of economic growth. As a result, the GNP as a measure of national welfare has fallen into disrepute, and charges of "economic Philistinism" are common.

Paradoxically, from a methodological point of view, social reporting is to a large extent the brainchild of the economists—or perhaps more accurately, of "the new political economists," to use William Mitchell's phrase. These include some political scientists who wish to make the study of politics more "scientific" by borrowing some methodological principles from their colleagues in economics and some economists who have a strong interest in applying the tools of their discipline to public policy problems. The latter usually have a background in public finance or welfare economics, and view social accounting as being a useful addition to the planning-programming-budgeting system. This group believes that the economist's traditional concern with finding the most efficient way to use scarce resources to achieve a variety of objectives can be fruitfully applied to a whole spectrum of noneconomic problems once very broad definitions of both resources (costs) and objectives (output) are adopted. Cost-benefit analyses, for example, can be better used to evaluate social programs once social indicators have been developed as benefit measures and the concept of cost has been expanded to include nonmonetary sacrifices, opportunities foregone, and the like.[8] In general, the economist emphasizes that wherever decisions are required, it is because there is more than one way of accomplishing a particular task. And, as Arthur Okun writes, "the analytical approach to choice is the hallmark of the profession. It is the essence of the discipline to focus on, and especially to quantify, the dimensions of choice—the costs, the benefits, and the alternative ways to achieve a given result."[9]

In addition, there seems to be a feeling that economic indicators (of production, employment, prices, etc.) and national income accounting have played a significant role in enabling us to achieve a measure of affluence and reasonably full employment, and that a similar commitment and development of information in some of the noneconomic areas of life would be beneficial. Thus, social indicators, social accounts, and social reports, as well as proposals to create a council of social advisors and to establish "full opportunity" as a national goal, all have their parallels in the economic realm.

It would be a mistake, however, to carry the analogy between economic indicators and social indicators too far. In the first place, there is no unified body of social theory comparable to that which exists in the field of economics. Economic theory permits economists to trace the effects of a change in tax rates or a shift in monetary policy on such variables as income, prices, and employment with *some* success. It is much more difficult to predict the effect of, say, a change in police practices on crime rates. Secondly, there is little agreement about goals where social policy is concerned, whereas the goals of economic policy are rather clearly set forth in the Employment Act of 1946. However, the fact that there are gaps in social theory and little consensus about social goals does not imply that better measurement of social conditions can serve no purpose. In fact, one of the benefits of such measurement would be to assist both the development of better theory and the establishment of national goals or priorities in the social field.

My own view is that this is an intellectual movement of some consequence and one deserving of careful consideration by all those with an interest in policy-making in the public sector. At this point, it may be helpful to spell out in somewhat greater detail the specific role envisaged for social reporting and social accounting by some of its proponents.

Approaches to Social Reporting, Social Indicators, and Social Accounts

The most fully articulated concept of social reporting and social indicators is the one which was developed by Mancur Olson [10] and used in the preparation of *Toward a Social Report*. The following is my own understanding and further interpretation of these ideas.

Social Goals

Social goals and values need to be made explicit. Only when objectives are clear can the development of solutions proceed in an unambiguous fashion. Although the formulation of goals ultimately remains the province of the citizen or his elected representatives, the social scientist may influence preferences by making more social intelligence available. A well-developed set of social indicators and periodic social reporting on the condition of society could, for example, give greater visibility to social problems and make the trade-offs and interrelationships between one social value and another clearer. As Galbraith has argued, [11] in a large, technologically complex society, preferences are not bred in a vacuum, but are in part determined by the very technology which satisfies them; and this observation holds true for public as well as private goods. Just as people must be informed that a new, improved detergent is available for eliminating stains, so they may need to be told that a negative income tax can be used to eliminate poverty. Thus, as Boulding notes, [12] Galbraith's "revised sequence" may be applicable to the public as well as the private sector. But, as he also points out, this does not mean that the "accepted sequence," whereby individuals communicate their relatively independent preferences to decision-makers, will or should cease to operate. The public sector has its Edsels, too, the most notable example being the Vietnam War.

Social Indicators

Given a set of goals or social values—and realistically there may only be (and may only need to be) a modicum of agreement as to their content—a set of social indicators could be developed which would serve as measures of the nation's performance in various areas. There are already any number of commonly reported statistics which, although they are far from perfect, could be used as social indicators. As examples, Table 1 provides a list of the indicators which were used in *Toward a Social Report*. As mentioned above, ongoing work within the Office of Management and Budget is directed toward better utilization of other existing statistics. Eventually, however, new statistics will need to be collected as information gaps are identified.

Table 1
Some Social Indicators Used in *Toward a Social Report*
to Measure Major Social Conditions

Aspect of Life To Be Measured	*Some Social Indicators**
Social Mobility	Correlation coefficient between father's occupational status and son's occupational status
Health	Expectancy of healthy life (free of bed disability and institutionalization)
The Physical Environment	Ratio of a city's actual level of pollution to an acceptable standard
	Proportion of housing that is substandard or overcrowded
Income and Poverty	Personal income per capita
	Number in poverty
Public Order and Security	FBI Uniform Crime Reports Index of crimes
	Value of property involved in theft per $1,000 of appropriable property
Learning, Science, and Art	Performance on selected achievement tests
	Technological balance of payments
	Attendance at theaters, operas, ballet

*These are not necessarily the best indicators but rather what was currently available.

This leads us to the question of what criteria should guide the choice of indicators; not every statistic is equally useful. One view is that an indicator should be a link between program outputs on the one hand and social goals on the other. In the words of *Toward a Social Report*, "a social indicator is a statistic of direct normative interest which facilitates concise, comprehensive and balanced judgments about the condition of major aspects of a society. It is in all cases a direct measure of welfare and is subject to the interpretation that, if it changes in the 'right' direction, while other things remain equal, things have gotten better, or people are 'better off.' "[13] Thus, statistics on the number of teachers employed in the school system would not be a good social indicator, because teachers are only an input to the educational system; there could be an increase in the number of teachers with no corresponding increase in the quality or quantity of what children learn. In other words, there is no one to one relationship between the amount of money spent on social programs and the benefits to society. Sometimes they even change in opposite directions as the result of changes in the efficiency with which resources are used. Yet, since many of our existing statistics are the by-product of administrative accounting practices, they focus on inputs (dollars spent, personnel involved, equipment used) rather than on program outputs or achievements.

Very little work has been done on the actual construction of new social indicators in areas where they are now lacking. Yet the possibilities are almost unlimited. From a technical standpoint, social phenomena are not as difficult to quantify as has often been assumed. If one can define social goals fairly carefully, one can usually measure social conditions. The principal barrier to quantification, in the long run at least, is not a lack of meaningful data but a failure to define what is meaningful, to have a clear idea of what is wanted in various areas of social concern, or to give operational content to national goals. For example, there is nothing difficult about measuring poverty once there is some agreement about what poverty is. Can it be defined in terms of income alone, or is there a culture of poverty which is partially independent of an individual's financial condition? If income can be used as an indicator of poverty, where should one draw the line between poor and nonpoor? And should this line be changed from time to time to reflect not only changes in the cost of living but also changes in the general level of affluence within the nation?

These are questions which have already been asked and for which some partial answers exist. [14] One should not insist that these answers be incontrovertible. Definitions of unemployment, for example, are not beyond debate, yet they have been used for a long time now to count the unemployed; and any conceptual error which may be hidden in such definitions is far outweighed by the convenience of having these statistics. Although great care must be exercised when the definitions and guidelines for new social statistics are formulated, we should not let the mumblings and grumblings of the experts about relatively minor problems of measurement deter us from benefiting from the potential usefulness of these statistics. The hope is that a social report which makes judicious use of such indicators will help to monitor the nation's performance in various areas of public concern and perhaps even serve to identify emerging needs and the issues of the future.

Social Accounts

Finally, there is an even more ambitious role for social accounting to fulfill, and that is in the choice of program strategies for dealing with social problems. Here, what is needed are "social production functions" or social accounts [15] which will link program inputs (conventionally measured in dollar terms) and program outputs or social indicators. It is fashionable for social scientists to pessimistically despair of ever establishing such links: the causes of poverty, violence, or decay in the cities are not easy to untangle and are hardly quantifiable at the present time. But the alternatives—to do nothing or to proceed on an *ad hoc*, trial and error basis—may be even more unsatisfactory. Moreover, even crude, qualitative notions about the relationships involved may be all that is necessary to make a quantum jump in providing more effective solutions to social problems. In other words, it may be the discipline of thinking in social accounting terms which is the key to good analysis.

Figure 1 attempts to schematize the role of social reporting, social indicators, and social accounts in the decision-making process. For the most part, it is self-explanatory; however, the following points are worth emphasizing.

First, final decisions or legislative action ultimately depend on both the policy-maker's view of his constituents' needs and desires and the social technicians' evaluation of the best way to achieve desired ends. The political feasibility of various types of action, in turn, affects the range of alternatives considered by the technicians and thus, to some extent, their final recommendations. As Charles Schultze has aptly suggested,[16] however, their major function is as partisan efficiency advocates in the political process. It is in the establishment of social accounts and the design of programs that the analyst plays the greatest role. The policy-maker continues to decide what public goods and services are desirable; but, given the complexity of the problems, he must rely increasingly on advice from the analyst on how best to provide them. The line between "what" and "how" will inevitably be somewhat fuzzy, but not impossible to draw, in a specific case.

Secondly, social goals or issues emerge as the expressed interest of special groups or the general public, but these interests are often stimulated or awakened by the institution of social reporting itself. (At present, this function may be partly filled by the news media.) Thus, there is what might be called a "combined sequence" at work.

Finally, social accounting should help to clarify the interrelationships between various aspects of life and the multipurpose nature of many government programs. In the diagram, the links between program inputs and social indicators should be thought of as complex and multifarious. Each program affects more than one social indicator; and each social indicator, in turn, may respond to a variety of influences, both public and private, which need to be sorted out. The ultimate goal is to produce a framework which will specify the more important relationships involved.

Not everyone would accept the particular approach to social reporting and the use of social indicators outlined above. In a recent paper,[17] Michael Springer contrasts the two different views of social accounting held by Bertram Gross and Mancur Olson. Olson's approach, which has been described in some detail, emphasizes the possibility of developing social production functions or accounts whose parameters would serve to guide policy choices. Gross would concentrate on the description of social systems rather than on either explanation or the use of social accounting for policy-making purposes. His approach consists of examining the structure of a social unit (a family, a firm, or possibly even a nation) and then judging how well it performs by a variety of criteria (satisfying interests, producing output, behaving rationally, etc.).

Figure 1
Schematic Representation of the Role of Social Reporting,
Social Indicators, and Social Accounts in the Decision-Making Process

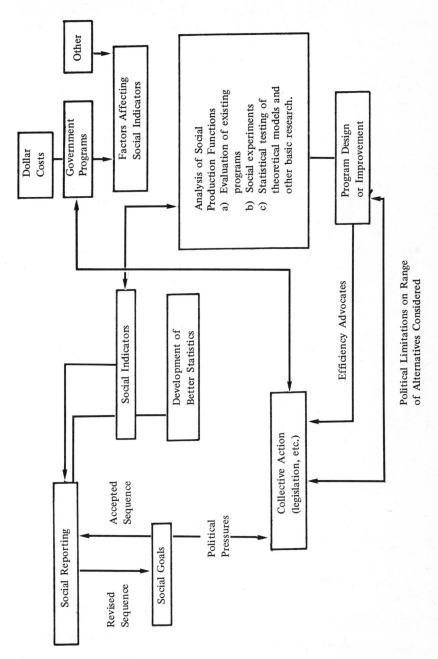

Olson has provocatively suggested that such differences in approach to social accounting reflect differences in the methodological training provided by the various academic disciplines involved.[18] Specifically, he contrasts the "problem-solving" approach of the economist or operations researcher to "structural-functionalism"—the latter being the prevailing *modus operandi*, crudely described, of some sociologists and some political scientists. The structural-functional analyst begins by studying existing structures (organizations, institutions, patterns of behavior) in an effort to determine whether they are functional or dysfunctional. The problem-solver, in contrast, starts with desired goals (a social welfare function) and looks for the most efficient way of organizing to reach those goals. The structural-functionalist tends to be a satisfier rather than a maximizer; he doesn't search for the most efficient way of achieving societal goals, but merely asks whether existing institutions are doing the job. Methodologically, he is more conservative than the problem-solver because he does not explicitly search out every possible means of achieving a given objective, but rather is content to analyze those institutions already in use. His approach is ill-suited for decision-makers or social planners. The latter are often faced with the task of actually creating new structures and new strategies to deal with existing problems. For this purpose, they need to know not only the advantages and disadvantages of existing arrangements but also what other choices are available.

On the other hand, the structural-functional analyst may provide a more richly detailed description of existing institutions and possess a capability for making more sophisticated judgments about what these institutions contribute to society's well-being. Moreover, he is less likely to optimize over too narrow a range of phenomena (although more likely to optimize the wrong things) or to neglect the diversity of goals. As Olson concludes, "the task is to combine the better logic and the policy orientation of the problem solving approach with the broader perspective and sensitivity to softer variables of structural functional analysis."[19]

Personally, I would question whether or not the different proponents of social intelligence systems would disagree on either the fundamental usefulness of building such systems or on their *ultimate* value as a policy-oriented tool. What disagreements there are tend to center around the most fruitful way to proceed in the *immediate* future. Some would emphasize the need for basic research on causal links; others, such as Gross, feel that this is premature, and would limit themselves to building better frameworks for descriptively arraying social information; still others are of the opinion that too much time has been spent on developing concepts and too little on putting these concepts into practice, and thus might devote their efforts to compiling better statistics to be used as indicators or to studying national goals.

More fundamental, perhaps, than these different approaches to social reporting is the question of the political implications of these innovations, a question to which I now turn.

Some Political Consequences

How would a more rational and complete use of social intelligence as envisaged here affect the distribution of power within society? This is a topic which I would prefer to leave to political scientists to discuss, but perhaps a few rather uninformed comments will serve to stimulate the discussion.

Basically, social reporting is a tool for publicizing and analyzing social issues. As I have tried to indicate, this does not mean turning a group of social scientists or government bureaucrats into philosopher kings who would dictate to society its ultimate goals; it does mean providing more scope than presently exists for the use of rational decision-making and systematic planning. However, as Aaron Wildavsky has pointed out,[20] such reforms are not likly to be neutral in their political impact. They may well affect the content as well as the methodology of decision-making. Moreover, they may even entail a radical restructuring of the political system.

The Wildavskys of the world question whether there are any agreed-upon goals which the social scientist can take as "givens" in his analysis. They argue that, because individual and group preferences differ, conflict is inevitable; and that only the give and take of the political process can resolve this conflict and achieve consensus. In addition, many policies and programs have multiple goals, and by not focusing on specific goals a greater measure of support from a variety of groups can be engendered for any particular program.

In response to this line of argument, I would like to make several points. First, social intelligence does not remove the necessity for compromise; it simply places the debate and thus the conflict which needs to be resolved on a higher level. If successful, it can turn what now appear to be normative (*i.e.*, political) issues into rather neutral means of achieving higher-order priorities.

Secondly, conflict emanates largely from the increasing complexity and inter-dependence of society, which thus far has required that more decision-making be transferred to governments and that the people accept the collective decisions which are made regardless of their individual preferences. If these decisions are to be made palatable to those who disagree with them, the dissenters must at least be convinced that they rest as far as possible on a solid analysis of the objective facts. The latter, along with the usual appeal to democratic principles, can help to legitimize the action taken. A government must not only be re-sponsive to society's needs but also *intelligently* responsive. Thus, the "wrong" programs in pursuit of the "right" goals lead to disappointed expectations and a discrediting of collective action, in general. If governments continue to spend more and more while achieving less and less, the entire system may well be in jeopardy. As Peter Drucker has suggested,[21] if "consensus" means doing a little bit of everything and thus nothing very well, we may end up sacrificing effective government for political agreement.

At a more practical level, it has been suggested that the spread of the Planning-Programming-Budgeting System within the federal establishment has tended to give greater power to department and agency heads vis-à-vis their subordi-nates.[22] Similarly, social reporting or a council of social advisors could place greater control in the hands of the President, and provide a still broader perspec-tive on the issues. There is already a small, understaffed office within the Budget

Bureau where interagency analyses of strategic issues are attempted, and where "overviews" and even "superviews" of federal programs are provided. But considering the magnitude of the programs and the issues, the resources devoted to such efforts are small indeed.

What is needed here is a reassertion of control over the bureaucracy. To the extent that presidents, cabinet heads, and legislators are more responsive to national needs than lower level administrators, who are often captivated by their own entrenched interests and myopic views, this shift is, in my opinion, desirable. It must be remembered that it was McNamara's rationalization of decision-making within the Pentagon which in part began the trend toward closer scrutiny of defense expenditures within both the Congress and the Budget Bureau.

In conclusion, I might reassert what seems to be fundamentally at issue here— *i.e.*, the responsiveness of government not as a political entity but as an organization charged with the responsibility of managing large portions of our national life. It matters little that the wheels of social progress are headed in the right direction if they turn so slowly that goals are never achieved.

Social Intelligence and the Study of the Future

Writing in 1933, John Maynard Keynes predicted that within a hundred years the economic problem would be solved.[23] What he had in mind was a level of affluence, wrought by the miracle of compound interest, which would provide all of the economic necessities of life. Although Keynes may have underestimated the ability of technology to create new economic wants, it is clear that, in the United States and other industrialized nations at least, we have achieved a measure of economic well-being unknown in the past or in other parts of the world. What we have also learned is that economic success brings whole new sets of problems and opportunities. Some problems like traffic congestion, pollution, and urban sprawl are the direct result of rising levels of income and technology. Others, like poverty and racism, have been around for a long time, but were not as visible or as shocking in a less affluent society. Similarly wealth brings new opportunities: for leisure, for education, perhaps even for contemplating the future. In this evolving environment, social reporting and social indicators have an increasingly significant contribution to make. This contribution has at least four dimensions.

First, the development of social indicators and social accounts could make some small contribution to more intelligent prediction or at least make us more aware of emerging trends. At the crudest level, the simple extrapolation of carefully constructed time-series may raise some interesting questions about the future. In addition, where social accounts or macrosocial models have been partially specified, an evaluation of the consequences of an assumed secular change in one variable on other variables in the system might be possible. To take a very simple example, one might predict that crime will become more prevalent as the composition of the population becomes younger, since most crimes are committed by juveniles. (Since youth is a correlate of, and not necessarily a cause of, crime, such a prediction might prove hazardous because the underlying factors responsible for the correlation might change.)

Prediction of the future has little value if the knowledge gained is not used to alter or plan for the future. If extrapolation of a trend or other predictive techniques reveal a dismal outcome, steps can be taken either to modify the trend or to develop new institutions or strategies for coping with the outcome. Some forecasting capability is particularly essential where (1) change is rapid and (2) strategies for dealing with the change can only be designed and put into effect over a substantial period of time. For example, the impact of many human resource programs does not occur for a generation or more.

Second, as economic problems decline and social problems grow in relative importance, collective decisions and social investments may increasingly supplement or replace private decisions and expenditures in the market place. Many important "inventions" may well come from the social scientists in academic and other research institutions rather than from engineers and others in the physical sciences. Social reporting would provide one link between such invention (the creation of knowledge) and innovation (the use of knowledge). It could publicize the gaps in social theory and help to insure that research findings were used to improve public policy. In this way, it could hasten the creation of relevant new knowledge, shorten the lag between creation and use, and thus contribute to social progress.

Thirdly, social reporting could emphasize the longer-term consequences of whatever collective action is taken. One of the criticisms of the existing process of policy formulation within government is that its time horizon is too short. The future implications of present decisions are often ignored, particularly where costs are involved. Thus, it is common for political leaders to propose programs, present estimates of their *first*-year costs, and then justify them on the basis of their long-term anticipated benefits. The average citizen is sometimes left with the erroneous impression that a particular social problem can be largely eradicated at the level of expenditures budgeted for the first year, and gives little thought to the year-to-year increases which will probably be necessary or to the number of years it will take to achieve significant progress. These shortcomings in the existing system have long been recognized, and some improvements have been instituted in recent years. Various tools of the Planned-Programming-Budgeting System emphasize the long-run costs and benefits of various programs, and analysts are using increasingly sophisticated methods of discounting to compare the worth of different social investments. Social reporting could move analysis further in this direction, providing estimates of different combinations of *time* and *money* (at a given level of knowledge) needed to "solve" a major public problem.

Finally, at a more global level, the social planner realizes that the economic constraint of scarce resources continues to operate and that there is too little attention paid to the long-run limitations on the total amount of resources available for solving national problems. He will insist on a realistic appraisal of how much can be accomplished *in the aggregate* (which depends not only on total resources available, but also on the efficiency with which they are used) and will emphasize the kinds of trade-offs between one type of social achievement and another which will be required.

The budget for fiscal year 1971 included for the first time a five-year projection of the fiscal dividend—the automatic increase in federal revenues which will become available as the result of economic growth minus already existing claims against these additional revenues. It is these discretionary funds which can be used to create new programs, expand older ones, cut taxes, or reduce the federal debt. Interestingly enough, present projections of the fiscal dividend show that existing claims will absorb all available resources during the next few years, and that there will be no fiscal dividend of much significance until 1977. In this environment, new programs can be created only if old ones are scrapped, taxes increased, or inflationary deficits incurred. This necessitates that some hard choices be made. In a modest way, a social report could attempt to provide an inventory of the choices in a few critical areas, rough estimates of their relative costs, and an analysis of the social consequences of various decisions.

Conclusion

Social reporting is still very much of an idea, not a reality; but it may be "an idea whose time has come." Some will criticize it as being utopian and impractical, others as being conceptually self-evident, and still others as being politically naive. Although I believe such criticisms are valid, I also believe that they do not strike at the *roots* of the idea. These roots grow deep. They are nurtured by the optimistic thought that man can control his destiny and improve upon his inheritance, and that no information, no rational process, and no intellectual framework should be left unturned in the effort. The future will perhaps reveal whether such idealism was misdirected.

Notes

1. *See* for example, *Annals of the American Academy of Political and Social Science*, 371, 372, 388, and 393 (May and September, 1967; March, 1970; and January, 1971).

2. Raymond A. Bauer (ed.), *Social Indicators* (Cambridge: M.I.T. Press, 1966); Bertram M. Gross, *The State of the Nation: Social Systems Accounting* (London: Tavistock, 1966). Mancur Olson, "The Plan and Purpose of a Social Report," *Public Interest*, 15 (Spring, 1969), pp. 86-97; "An Analytic Framework for Social Reporting and Policy Analysis," *Annals of the American Academy of Political and Social Science*, 388 (March, 1970), pp. 112-26); and "Social Indicators and Social Accounts," *Socioeconomic Planning Sciences* (1969), pp. 335-46.

3. *See* Michael J. Flax, *Blacks and Whites: An Experiment in Racial Indicators* (Urban Institute, 1971) and *A Study in Comparative Urban Indicators* (1972); Eleanor Sheldon and Wilbert Moore, *Indicators of a Social Change* (New York: Russell Sage Foundation, 1968); Daniel B. Tunstall, "Developing A Social Statistics Publication," a paper presented at the 1970 annual meeting of the American Statistical Association, Detroit, December 27, 1970.

4. William Nordhaus and James Tobin, "Is Growth Obsolete?" Cowles Foundation Discussion Paper No. 319, October 7, 1971; F. Thomas Juster, "On the Measurement of

Social and Economic Performance," in *Economics—A Half Century of Research, 1920-1970*, National Bureau of Economic Research, 50th Annual Report, pp. 8-24.

5. U.S. Department of Health, Education and Welfare, *Toward a Social Report* (Washington: U.S. Government Printing Office, January, 1969).

6. *See* statement of Mr. Lewis Butler, Assistant Secretary for Planning and Evaluation, Department of Health, Education, and Welfare, before the Special Subcommittee on Evaluation and Planning of Social Programs of the Senate Committee on Labor and Public Welfare, July 10, 1969. Also, statement of Mr. Dwight A. Ink, Assistant Director for Office of Management and Budget, before the Special Subcommittee on Evaluation and Planning of Social Programs of the Senate Committee on Labor and Public Welfare, July 13, 1971.

7. *See*, for example, Daniel Bell, "The Idea of a Social Report," *The Public Interest*, 15 (Spring, 1969), pp. 72-84.

8. For an expanded discussion of the topic, *see* my paper on "The Role of Social Indicators and Social Reporting in Public Expenditure Decisions," in *The Analysis and Evaluation of Public Expenditures: The PPB System* (Washington: U.S. Government Printing Office, 1969).

9. Arthur M. Okun, *The Political Economy of Prosperity* (Washington: Brookings Institution, 1969), p. 3.

10. Mancur Olson, *Public Interest, op. cit.*

11. John K. Galbraith, *The Affluent Society* (Boston: Houghton Mifflin, 1958), Chapter XI.

12. Kenneth E. Boulding, *Economics As a Science* (New York: McGraw Hill, 1970), pp. 89-90.

13. *Toward a Social Report, op. cit.*, p. 188.

14. Many of the conceptual and technical problems which need to be faced in developing indicators are discussed in the September, 1967 issue of the *Annals, op. cit.*

15. In *Toward a Social Report*, social accounts were called "policy accounts" to avoid confusion, since the word "social account" is sometimes used to mean any body of aggregative statistics.

16. Charles L. Schultze, *The Politics and Economics of Public Spending* (Washington: Brookings Institution, 1968).

17. Michael Springer, "Social Indicators, Reports, and Accounts: Toward the Management of Society," *Annals of the American Academy of Political and Social Science*, 388 (March, 1970), pp. 1-13.

18. Mancur Olson, *Annals, op. cit.*

19. *Ibid.*, p. 126.

20. Aaron Wildavsky, "Political Implications of Budgetary Reform" *Public Administration Review*, 21, 4 (Autumn, 1961).

21. Peter F. Drucker, *The Age of Discontinuity* (New York: Harper and Row, 1969), p. 195.

22. Schultze, *op. cit.*

23. John Maynard Keynes, "The Economic Possibilities of Our Grandchildren," *Essays in Persuasion* (London: Macmillan, 1933).

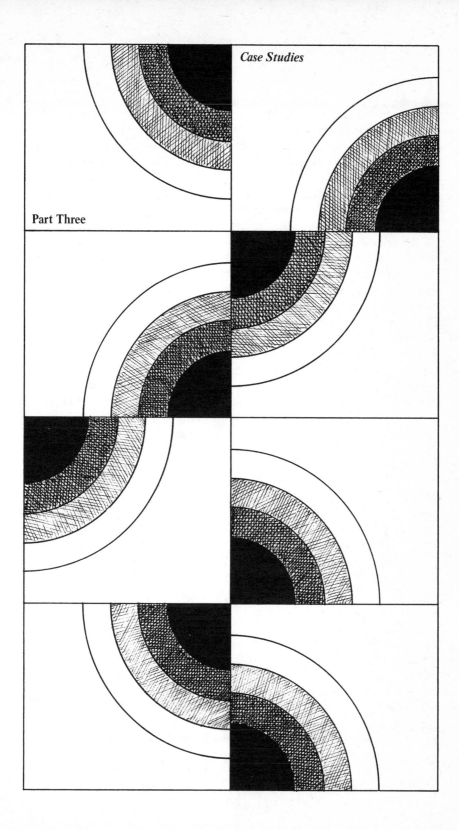

Part Three

Case Studies

In the final analysis, the success or failure of futurism will not turn on the persuasiveness of the theoretical case made for it or on the elegance and sophistication of the techniques available to its practitioners. The outcome will hinge, instead, on what the futurists have, or have not, been able to accomplish. While it is still too soon to expect anything definitive in this respect, there have been numerous attempts at what we might call "applied futuristics." Eight such "case studies" are presented in the following pages. As even a casual reading of the titles evidences, the authors move in diverse directions; and the eight enterprises range across the broad spectrum of political science. They also differ strikingly in approach, objective, and tone.

Cable television already exists as a commercial reality with a steadily swelling body of subscribers. The technology for two-way transmission in cable television (*i.e.*, from station to subscriber, and from subscriber to station) is in the immediate offing. The utilization of this two-way capacity, Norman Nie points out, will make available, *inter alia*, almost immediate readings of public opinion. What might be the impact of such a development on the American political system? Nie's exploration of this question provides one of the most engrossing contributions to the literature of political futurism.

In an earlier discussion, I suggested that the post-1945 interest in political development was a factor in the emergence of political futurism. Focusing on this field, Franklin Tugwell notes that students of political development have continually been disappointed by the failure of many "emerging" nations to make satisfactory progress. He then seeks to explain why this has occurred and, by applying the standard forecast technique, to anticipate what is likely to occur in the future. Although he arrives at some rather dismal conclusions, he leaves open the possibility that the likely course of events might yet be altered.

To the extent that we accept a given (futures) prediction, that prediction may become self-fulfilling. David Porter examines that aspect of futuristics which is intended not only to predict the future but, by mobilizing the resources necessary to fulfill the forecast, to control it. Porter looks at the environmental and organizational factors influencing resource mobilization, stressing the fact that translating a forecast into reality is actually an exercise of power. These same organizational and environmental factors, he emphasizes, affect the perceptions of the forecasters and their estimates of the future.

Hawaii is one of the few states which, according to James Dator, has attempted to get "a running start on its future." Beginning with the 1970 Governor's Conference on Hawaii 2000, state policy has sought to embody the concept of participatory futuristics or, to use Toffler's term, "anticipatory democracy." Dator's discussion elaborates both the necessary elements of futuristics, as he understands it, and the manner in which these requisites have been, or are being achieved in Hawaiian futurism.

On the premise that "every age develops a form of organization most appropriate to its genius," Warren Bennis predicted in 1964 that we were entering a "post-bureaucratic world." He then went on to describe how the new bureaucracies would differ drastically from their predecessors. Several years later, looking back over the intervening chaos of Vietnam, urban riots, and campus disorders, Bennis reassesses his earlier sanguine forecasts. In characteristically forthright fashion, he addresses three questions: Where did the earlier predictions go wrong? Why did they go wrong? What does this imply for the nature of organizations and bureaucracies in the future?

A similar reassessment of an earlier prediction, and an updated version thereof, is offered by Max Beloff. In 1963, Beloff described the Constitution of the United States as he foresaw it in 1970. That date having arrived, Beloff draws a balance sheet for his early effort in futuristics and then casts another look ahead, this time in 1980.

Science fiction reflects, consciously or otherwise, an author's understanding of how society will be organized in coming decades or centuries. At the same time, the same author may *influence* the future by adding to the "stock of futuristic images"—*i.e.*, conscious options—presently available to his readers. Selecting some "major" science fiction works, Dennis Livingston attempts to ascertain whether there emerges from this literature any consistent "understanding" of what a future world system(s) may be like. In this essay, we have an example of a futurist presenting not so much his own forecast but, rather, his analysis of those made by other futurists.

The concluding piece in this section is by Harold Lasswell, one of the most distinguished—and certainly the most imaginative—of American political scientists. Lasswell, who might well be called the father of political futurism, here serves as futurist for his own discipline. Adopting the "convention of treating 1990 in the present tense," he describes, in characteristic fashion, what he believes will be the political science of that era. Those familiar with Lasswell's writings will not be surprised to discover that he envisages a policy science orientation. They may, however, be surprised by other elements of his forecast.

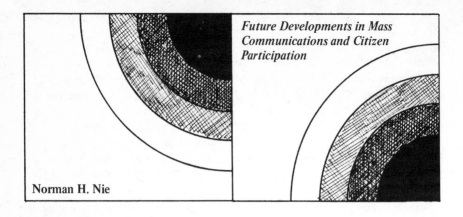

Future Developments in Mass Communications and Citizen Participation

Norman H. Nie

Communications media have always been central to political participation in democratic societies. The media, written and electronic, are the major means available to the ordinary citizen for monitoring the activities and actions of government and, as such, are of primary importance to the process of democratic accountability and popular control. Furthermore, political participation itself, at least for the ordinary citizen, is basically a process of communication, only in the reverse direction. Some of these communications already flow through the mass media, such as when citizens write letters to the editor or participate in the multitude of talk, telephone, and public affairs programs so prevalent on both radio and television.

The participatory process in democratic societies is thus closely related to the nature of the mass media: First, because the mass media provide the citizenry with information about governmental activity; secondly, because the media often carry important political messages from the citizenry to the government. The new communications systems may have important consequences for citizen participation in the future, for they may alter the role of the mass media as a communicator of both types of message—those which flow from the government to the citizenry and those which go in the other direction.

In this paper, we will attempt to examine various aspects of these new communications systems to see how they might affect political participation in the future. Might they, for example, create new forms of citizen participation or alter the meaning of existing types? Will they affect rates of citizen participation and the number of citizens who become politically active? And might they have some impact on the types of citizens who participate or on the ways in which different kinds of citizens engage in our political processes? Before we can answer these questions, we must, however, carefully spell out the structure and configuration of these new systems, for only when we know what they are will we be able to discuss what they might do to our participatory processes.

Unfortunately, this is easier said than done, for the technology on which these systems will be based is just beginning to emerge, and much of what has been developed remains cloaked in corporate secrecy. Furthermore, much will depend on the economics of these systems, for the private sector will no doubt play the predominant role in their development. What will actually emerge is much less likely to be determined by what is technically feasible than by what is economically profitable. Based on my admittedly limited understanding of both the economic and the technical factors, I see a relatively clear picture of what will develop in the near future and a somewhat less certain set of possibilities for the long run.

The next ten years are likely to bring the beginnings of a series of cable television networks which in all probability will form the base for the coming generation of communications systems. Cable television networks will be the forerunners of what I will refer to in this paper as an "Individualized Home Entertainment and Information System." The central feature of this system from its very inception (which differentiates it from current television broadcasting networks) will be greater variety of entertainment and information. The individual will, therefore, have increased control over what he views. Cable television may initially produce a several-fold increase in the number of programs which are available. This quantum jump will hopefully produce a qualitative shift in the strategy of program production—from a production strategy in which all networks compete for the center in a unidimensional spatial market to one where successful competition is based on catering to specialized interests and tastes. As regional cable networks develop and integrate, the larger numbers of potential viewers should continue to increase the variety of entertainment and information so that the individual viewer will have a better chance to select programs which relate to his personal interests and tastes. This much of the future seems quite certain.

If and when these cable networks are wedded to a computerized switching system as well as to a highly efficient means of audio-visual storage, a completely individualized system for entertainment and information will be likely to emerge. If the storage media are truly efficient, the contents of this system would be unlimited. Everything which has been or will be recorded on some type of audio-visual medium could, under these conditions, be available for consumption. In addition, a complete information service for written material could be very easily integrated into this system. The computerized switching system would allow the user to have access to any of these materials on demand. In other words, the viewer sees what he wants to see when he wants to see it. This much, I believe, is highly probable.

If dual cables are provided (as Likelitter and others have urged) and significant improvements in the speed and organization of large computers continue to be made, some interactive ability might emerge. This would turn unidirectional information and entertainment systems into an "Interactive Home Services System." Such systems could be used to provide a variety of conveniences: home purchasing and, in fact, all financial transactions; interactive educational television; appointment scheduling; as well as a variety of types of participatory entertainment. This, I believe, is entirely feasible, and whether it happens will depend upon the uses to which such a system could be put. If it has potential for large revenues, it is likely to develop; if not, it probably won't.

There seem to be at least two major aspects of these communications systems (both short and long run) which have potential for altering citizen participation. For the lack of a better terminology, let us call the first "specific participatory applications" and the second "indirect consequences." Specific participatory applications refer to the direct capabilities that the "interactive home services system" with its two-way capacity—might have as a conduit of various types of political messages *from* the citizen *to* the government. Indirect consequences, on the other hand, refer to the more diffuse impact that such systems (particularly the Individualized Home Entertainment and Information System) might have on the distribution of interest, activity patterns, and available time among the citizenry that, in turn, may alter rates and patterns of participation.

The specific participatory applications and the more indirect or diffuse consequences may push in the same direction to increase or decrease participation; alternatively, they may push in opposite directions so that one aspect of these new communications developments acts to generate participation while the other acts to inhibit it. In either event, they are separate and should be looked at individually. We begin with the direct participatory applications of the interactive home services system of the distant and uncertain future.

Direct Participatory Applications of Interactive Communication Systems

Any communications system which provides citizens with the capacity to send messages as well as receive them inevitably raises the prospect of instant participatory democracy and citizen decision-making from the living rooms of the nation. From a technical point of view, there is no reason why a home services system designed to convey two-way communications could not be used to carry political messages from the citizenry to the government. Actually such systems might be well suited for instant referenda or even for nationwide electronic "town meetings." However, technical feasibility does not necessarily imply social feasibility and says nothing about the desirability of such procedures. The idea of direct popular democracy is, I suppose, attractive to some, for it represents the ultimate in popular control. Unfortunately, such notions bear no relationship to social realities. As Professors Eulau and MacRae have indicated, all that we know about the policy-making process itself and the capacities, interests, and behavior of the citizenry suggest that systems of direct democracy for large collectivities are both totally infeasible and highly undesirable.

If mass interactive communications systems will not be used for direct democracy, what types of more reasonable participatory applications might they have? Probably, not many. Most forms of participation do not lend themselves to an electronic format and many of those that do would not be greatly enhanced or altered if they were incorporated into such a system. Voting, I suppose, could be moved from the polling booth to the living room if ownership of the communications device were mandatory, and such a system might yield some marginal increase in turnout. Citizens could contact congressmen or other officials (or rather, their computer files) via these devices, but the telephone and the mails already serve these purposes and may be more desirable because they are more personalized. Organizations and pressure groups, as Professor Ziegler has observed, might utilize such devices to contact and mobilize their membership, but here again the advantages over mailing lists must be considered somewhat marginal.

There is, however, one area where the speed, organization and economics of the home services system might have important implications for the quantity and quality of messages that flow from the citizenry to the government. That, of course, is in polling and information gathering.

The responsiveness of government and the quality of its policies are, to some extent, dependent upon the amount of accurate information it has on the needs, problems, and preferences of various segments of the citizenry. While representatives, government agencies, and private opinion organizations currently do attempt to collect this type of information, our achievements in this area (with perhaps the exception of economic indicators) have been limited by the great effort and expense involved. Recent interest in the regular collection of a variety of "social indicators" suggests just how important this problem has become in a large, technically complex, and heterogeneous nation.[1] The home services system could drastically reduce the costs of gathering this type of information and therefore create the possibility of a better fit between governmental policy and the needs and desires of the citizenry.[2]

Senators and congressmen as well as local and state representatives could quickly and inexpensively generate information on any issue or problem area. They could target their surveys toward special segments of their constituencies—the poor, black, women, homeowners, doctors, and the like. Government agencies, again at any level, could on a continuing basis evaluate the impact of governmental programs or administrative practices. A system in which citizens could voluntarily register their opinions on a variety of types of public issues and problems could also be cheaply instituted by either government itself or polling agencies.

There are no doubt dangers in increasing the amount of information which flows from the citizenry to government; but information, unlike referenda, is not binding, and if correctly utilized can add to, rather than detract from, the representational process. In the current context, information on the needs and wishes of the citizens flows solely through the participatory mechanisms, and those social groups who participate most have the loudest voices while those who participate little or not at all may never be heard.[3] Supplementing the participatory channels with regularized sets of mechanisms for the collection of information may produce more equitable voices for those who are currently politically underrepresented. This may be particularly important, for these are often the same groups who are socially and economically deprived.

At the same time, however, we must realize that preferences reported in sample surveys, electronic or otherwise, are often very different in nature than those actively volunteered when citizens participate. The opinions expressed in polls are frequently shallow responses to problems to which the respondent has never given much thought. The saliency of the issue to him may be low, and the opinion is likely to be based on little or no information. Preferences communicated by acts of participation, on the other hand, are more likely to be well thought out and deeply held convictions on an issue about which the citizen is deeply concerned. Giving these two types of opinions equal weight may constitute as much of a distortion as those produced by the current stratification of the population into participants and nonparticipants.

In short, two-way communications systems may directly increase the flow of information and messages to government, not by increasing direct participation but by inviting or requesting more information from the citizenry. In this sense, our term direct participatory applications is somewhat of a misnomer, for participation at least as students of politics have come to use it implies the notion of "citizen initiation." When we employ the term participation in the remainder of this paper, we will be using it in this latter, more accepted definition.

Indirect Effects of the Home Entertainment and Information System

The specific participatory applications of the home services system are but one of the ways in which new communications systems may affect rates of citizen-to-government communication. In fact, the most important consequence of these systems, like so many previous technological developments, may not lie in their direct applications but rather in the very indirect ways in which they alter the interests, life circumstances, and activity patterns of the citizenry. Participation in politics, after all, competes with many other interests and activities for the time, energy, and attention of citizens—it is only one of many sideshows to which they may occasionally turn. Any development, therefore, which modifies the distribution of interests, changes the foci of attention, or alters the amount of available leisure time in the society may, in turn, have important consequences for rates of citizen participation and the size of the participating strata.

Several aspects of the individualized home entertainment and information system may have considerable potential for this type of change. First, the type of entertainment and information to which a citizen is exposed may have an effect on the type of interests and activities he is likely to pursue. If, as we have suggested, new home entertainment and information systems give the individual virtually complete control over the type of material he views, he may then choose programming which has either more or less relevance to politics and public affairs. A heavier concentration of a variety of types of public information and political messages may increase the citizen's appetite for political involvement, and a systematic avoidance of such material may have the opposite results. Second, these new entertainment systems may be very attractive devices and as such may represent a considerable drain on the average citizen's available leisure time. Most forms of political participation (with the exception of voting) require considerable amounts of time and energy, and thus there may be a basic conflict between large amounts of home viewing and political participation.

What types of entertainment and information will citizens choose when they have virtual control over what they view? How much time will they spend in front of these new and more attractive communication devices? And what types of effect will these factors have on rates and patterns of citizen participation? One of the ways to approach these questions is to examine some of the available evidence on existing media (particularly television, which is our present home entertainment and information system) and its impact on political participation to see if these data provide us with any useful information for projecting future patterns of political activity.

Such a method of forecasting is in essence "prediction by analogy," for it projects current patterns and relationships among variables into a future which is composed of analogous ones. This type of technique has many pitfalls, and predictions based on it must be considered highly speculative. This is true first because new communications systems may simply not be analogous (in terms of their effect on the individual) to existing systems. Second, new variables which can be neither foreseen nor taken into account may emerge to modify, nullify, or even reverse patterns and relationships which today seem basic and enduring. We are simply not in a position to know all of the significant components of the future social matrix. Nevertheless, if we are to attempt to make any reasonable predictions, it would seem more desirable to ground them in the current social reality rather than in no reality at all.

As new entertainment systems become more attractive by more closely paralleling individual interests and tastes, the amount of home viewing is likely to increase and to increase substantially—for when citizens can view precisely what they want when they want it, they are likely to find more worth viewing. I believe as Dwaine Marvick does that it is this aspect of new home entertainment and information systems which has the greatest potential to affect rates of participation as well as all other forms of voluntary social activity.[4] And unfortunate though it may seem, this potential is all in the negative direction. The logic implicit in Marvick's argument and explicit in my own is simple—if citizens are home watching television or its future counterpart, they cannot be out participating in politics or, for that matter, in anything else. In short, if home viewing becomes increasingly attractive, a greater number of citizens will simply choose it over other forms of social participation.[5]

This basic conflict between home viewing and other forms of social activity can be substantiated to a large degree with current data on television viewing and participation. The severity of the existing conflict between home viewing and political participation is quite clearly indicated in Figure 1, which reports data from a large national sample of American citizens conducted early in 1967. This figure presents a plot of the average number of political activities performed by those in the population who watch varying amounts of television each day.[6]

While those who have no daily exposure to television have relatively low rates of participation,[7] those who are exposed *for less than one hour a day* have the highest. From this point on, as the number of hours of television viewing increases, the level of political participation declines, and the rate of decline seems to increase. Actually this relationship makes a great deal of sense—those who

Figure 1
Average Number of Political Activities Performed by Those
Who Watch Different Amounts of Television Each Day

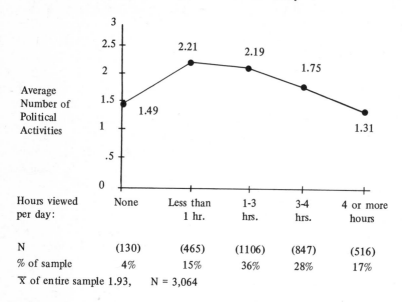

	None	Less than 1 hr.	1-3 hrs.	3-4 hrs.	4 or more hours
N	(130)	(465)	(1106)	(847)	(516)
% of sample	4%	15%	36%	28%	17%

X̄ of entire sample 1.93,   N = 3,064

have absolutely no exposure to what may be the single most important common national stimuli also participate at low levels in other aspects of our social life, while those who gorge themselves on it have no time for participation in politics. Further, it is clear that the vast majority of low participators are to be found among those whose television viewing is in excess of three hours a day. Non-viewers, though low participators, constitute only 4 percent of the population, while those who watch three or more hours a day comprise over 45 percent of the population and those who watch in excess of four hours, 17 percent.

In addition, levels of political participation are but one of the many forms of social activity which display this relationship to television viewing. Our data indicate that membership and activity in voluntary associations, frequency of travel, and consumption of periodicals all have virtually an identical curvilinear relationship with television viewing. Once viewing exceeds an hour a day, most other forms of social activity seem to decline.

The conflict between television viewing and political participation is a genuine and direct one which affects all segments of the population, whether they are defined socially or attitudinally. To demonstrate the severity and nature of this conflict, let us look more closely at the relationship between television viewing and political participation among different educational groups. This is a particu-larly good example, because education has a strong and well-documented influ-ence on citizen participation. The data presented in Figure 2 make it abundantly clear that long hours of television viewing are associated with low rates of political activity among those at all educational levels. Here again we see that limited amounts of viewing are associated with high rates of participation; but as the number of viewing hours increase, the amounts of participation decline. While the basic pattern is consistent for all educational groups, it is interesting to note that television viewing seems to have its most dramatic impact on those of high education, where participation is also highest.

The same pattern is evident for racial, economic, religious, and virtually all other social groupings. Beyond a minimal amount, the more hours a citizen spends in front of his television, the lower are his rates of participation. This remains true even when all other social characteristics are held constant, and

Figure 2
Average Number of Political Activities Performed by Those
Who Watch Varying Amounts of Television Within Educational Groups

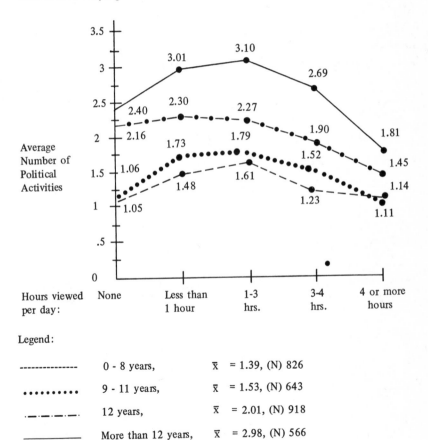

Legend:

-----------------	0 - 8 years,	$\bar{x}$	= 1.39, (N) 826
••••••••••	9 - 11 years,	$\bar{x}$	= 1.53, (N) 643
.—..—..—.	12 years,	$\bar{x}$	= 2.01, (N) 918
_____	More than 12 years,	$\bar{x}$	= 2.98, (N) 566

Entire sample $\bar{x}$ = 1.93, (N) 2,953*

*N varies slightly from one figure to another due to missing data.

seems particularly pronounced among those groups who tend, based on their other characteristics, to participate most.[8]

When we shift our attention from social characteristics to attitudinal ones, the situation remains very much the same. For example, television viewing affects rates of participation for all citizens, irrespective of their level of interest or involvement in politics. Figure 3 presents these data. Here citizens have been divided into three groups, depending upon whether they report a great deal of interest, some interest, or no interest in politics and national affairs.

While interest in politics and national affairs (like education) increases participation irrespective of the amount of viewing, participation is least among those who watch television most; and this is true at each level of interest. Once again we see that minimal amounts of viewing are associated with relatively high rates of participation, but participation declines from that point on. The impact of

Figure 3
Average Number of Political Activities Performed
By Those Who Watch Varying Amounts of Television
By Difference in Interest in Politics and National Affairs

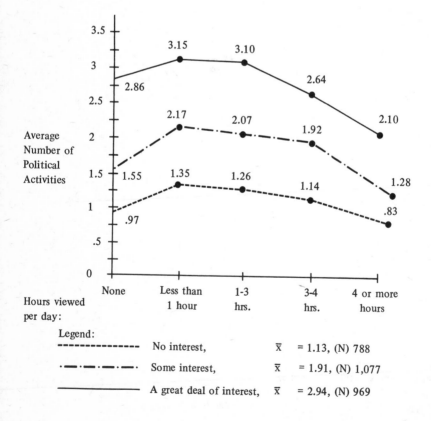

Legend:

- - - - - - - - - -	No interest,	$\bar{x}$ = 1.13, (N) 788
· — · — · — · — ·	Some interest,	$\bar{x}$ = 1.91, (N) 1,077
—————————	A great deal of interest,	$\bar{x}$ = 2.94, (N) 969

viewing is most dramatic, however, among those citizens who report the greatest amounts of interest. In this case, even more clearly than with education, this finding suggests that large amounts of television viewing are associated with the largest differences in rates of participation among those who, by their other characteristics, are likely to participate most.[9]

There is, in addition to this cross-sectional data, some very indirect evidence to suggest that television viewing may already be affecting rates of citizen participation in this country. Time-series data for a number of measures of citizen participation in presidential campaigns indicate that there have been no statistically significant increases in this type of participation from 1952 through 1968.[10] During this same period, however, many of the variables which we know to be highly correlated with levels of political participation have been rising, and rising rapidly. Median years of education has risen in this sixteen-year period from 9.5 to above 12.1, and the proportion of the population who have completed college has just about doubled. Income, which opens the way for a greater variety of leisure activities, has risen dramatically, and the proportion of the population in white-collar occupations has increased by almost 10 percent.[11] Yet levels of participation which are so highly correlated with these factors (income, occupation, and education jointly explain as much as 20 percent of the variance in rates of participation in the United States)[12] have not been substantially altered. Clearly much has been happening in our society during this period other than the growth of television, and a detailed analysis would be required in order even to begin to demonstrate that television is the main causal factor in what seems to be a relative decline in political participation.[13] Nevertheless, this finding, when placed alongside of the dramatic cross-sectional relationships between television viewing and participation, is suggestive of what might happen in the future if the amounts of television viewing were to increase dramatically.

The average American citizen currently performs slightly less than two political acts, according to the index of participation employed here, while heavy television viewers average only one and a third political acts. If new home information systems add, let us say, an hour a day to the viewing time of the average person, the mean rate of participation for the average citizen could (measured by this index) be reduced to one and one-half acts. An addition of an average of two hours of viewing a day could reduce the mean number of acts to well below one. There are, of course, great dangers in simplistic linear projections of this sort, and the numbers may therefore be no more than statistical fantasy; but the strength of the underlying relationship they signify is alarmingly real. The laws of time budgeting simply demand that an additional hour of home viewing must come from somewhere. Given what we know about the priorities of life and the low salience of politics and public affairs within the citizenry, there is little doubt in my mind concerning the kinds of activities which will be sacrificed.

The really significant questions about the effects of future home viewing, therefore, hinge around how much viewing will increase and among what types of citizens. Unfortunately, there is no way of knowing how much these new systems will increase viewing, for much will depend upon the type of entertainment and information offered and its quality. Some students of the mass media feel that television viewing has already reached its potential maximum, yet the best available data indicate a 33 percent increase in the average number of viewing hours per *Television Household*[14] from 1950 to 1965, and the largest portion of that increase came after 1962.[15] While the variety of programming, if not its quality, has improved significantly from the early fifties, such differences may be minor when compared to the potential improvement of an individualized home entertainment system where the viewer may have virtual control over what he views.

While the overall amounts of increase in home viewing are difficult to determine, the effects that such systems might have on the viewing habits of different types of citizens are clearer, as are their potential implications on rates of participation.

First, while television viewing is pervasive throughout our society, the more educated and politically motivated citizens are currently somewhat less likely to be among those who watch the largest amounts of television.[16] However, a completely individualized home entertainment and information system would seem to have its greatest appeal to these more discriminating viewers who would, in this situation, have the ability to pursue within the media itself their many and varied interests.[17] Second, as we have already suggested, the data indicate that television viewing depresses rates of participation most among precisely this same type of citizen. When these citizens watch only minimal amounts of television, their rates of participation are much higher than other citizens who watch the same amount; but when their viewing increases to three or more hours a day, they participate at only slightly greater rates than other segments of the population. In other words, rates of participation are much less differentiated among all types of citizens— educated or not, interested or not—when amounts of home viewing are large; and if new communications systems increase the amount of viewing among those most likely to be politically active, the decline in overall rates of participation may be particularly severe.

Impact of Increased Home Viewing on Different Types of Participation

What we have said in the previous section suggests that substantial increases in amounts of home viewing would be likely to reduce levels of all types of social and political participation, but this is not entirely true. Our data indicate that home viewing has a fundamentally different impact on voting as compared to all other types of social and political participation. Figure 4 displays the relationship between voting and number of viewing hours per day and the same relationship for three other types of political participation which are commonly performed by citizens.

The figure presents the proportion of the population who are active in each of the four types of participation according to the amounts of television watched.

Figure 4
The Effects of Television Viewing on Different Types of Participation.
Per Cent Who Are Regular Voters, Campaign Activists, Contactors, and
Group Activists Among Those Segments of the Population Who Watch
Different Amounts of Television.

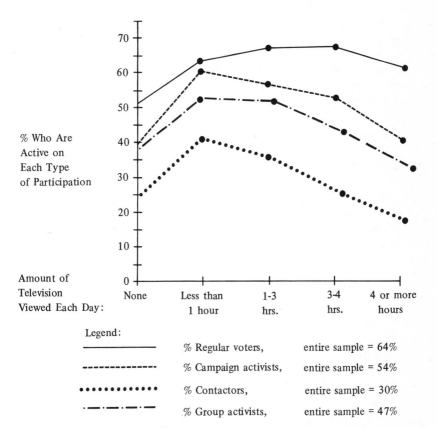

Legend:

	% Regular voters,	entire sample = 64%
	% Campaign activists,	entire sample = 54%
	% Contactors,	entire sample = 30%
	% Group activists,	entire sample = 47%

The almost expected curvilinear relationship, with moderately high levels of participation for those who watch limited amounts of television and a decline in activity with increased viewing, is evident for all of the types of participation but voting. Long hours of television viewing decreases the proportion of citizens who are active in election campaigns, reduces the probability that a citizen will initiate a contact with a governmental leader, and similarly reduces the likelihood of political participation through groups and organizations. Only the pattern for voting differs.

Those who watch no television at all are much less likely to be regular voters; and, in this sense, voting is like other forms of activity. From this point on, however, the relationship differs. Those who watch considerable amounts of television each day are *not* substantially less likely to be regular voters. In fact, the proportion who vote regularly increases slightly up to four hours of viewing each day, and the decline in voting is small even for those who watch in excess of four hours. Future increases in the amounts of home viewing are therefore much less likely to depress rates of voting than those of other forms of participation.

There may be several explanations for why voting is not affected in the same way or to the same degree as are other types of social and political activity. First, voting is not a very time-consuming activity—it requires only a few minutes out of a very infrequent election day. Thus the types of time-budgeting conflicts that viewing presents for campaign activity or contacting government officials may simply not be present in this case. Second, there is much to suggest that media exposure can stimulate and mobilize voting to a degree which cannot be duplicated for other more difficult and time-consuming activities. In this way, those who are exposed to large amounts of television may also be exposed to large amounts of vote-stimulating messages which act to counterbalance the time factors.

In either event, these patterns suggest an interesting profile of citizen participation in the future. While rates of most forms of participation may decline, voting turnout may remain unaffected. Unfortunately, voting is not much of a compensation for the losses of other forms of activity. This is true for at least three reasons. First, as one of millions of voters, the individual does not exercise much influence over the outcome of the election. Second, voting, unlike many other forms of participation, does not enable the citizen to gain any effective control over the substance or content of his participation—he simply chooses between a set of structured alternatives, and these alternatives are not necessarily ones that are salient to him. When a citizen contacts an official or organizes with other individuals, on the other hand, he controls the agenda of his participation; and the issues which are the subject of his activities are by definition relevant and salient to him. Third, and finally, voting is a very blunt and imprecise instrument that conveys very little in the way of specific information on the needs and problems of the citizen. In short, even if new communications systems were to increase rates of voting by creating a national voting registry or a home voting system, this would not compensate for the losses in effective citizen control produced by decreases in other more precise, relevant, and powerful modes of participation.

The Effects of Media Content

While substantial increases in home viewing are likely to decrease participation, the amounts of politically relevant material carried by this new media may also have some impact on rates of citizen participation. It seems, after all, reasonable to assume that if citizens are exposed to more politically relevant programming, they may increase their interest in, and appetite for, political activity; and the opposite would also seem to be true. Will the new Home Entertainment and Information System be likely to carry more or less politically relevant information? And perhaps even more important, will citizens be likely to watch more or less of this type of material when they have greater control over what they view?

There is some reason to believe that new communications systems will make available greater amounts of politically relevant programming. Cable transmissions will probably be quite inexpensive compared to the present costs of air time; and public officials, political parties, candidates for office, and even pressure groups might therefore have easier access to the living rooms of the nation. Such communications systems would seem to be particularly attractive and efficient for these purposes, because transmissions could be targeted to very small geographical areas and even to particular social groups. In short, new communications systems (such as the individualized home entertainment and information system) would present political elites with a more economical and focused media for transmitting information and propaganda to the citizenry.

However, individualized transmission is a blade that cuts with both edges—for when the viewer has virtual control over what he watches (as well as a wide selection to choose from), it may be increasingly difficult to get politically relevant information through to him no matter how much of this type of material is produced. In a situation where the individual may choose entertainment or information which closely fits his mood or needs, politics and public affairs may indeed find the competition stiff. Presently, politically relevant materials are limited, but they are also concentrated in certain hours of the day and in particular periods such as during national elections. Therefore, when a citizen wishes to view television during these periods, he may have no alternative but to watch this type of programming. But in the future this may very well not be the case.[18]

What then will the citizen of the future choose to watch—Sunday football all week long, Bogart movies by the dozen, westerns by the weekload, or a better mix of entertainment and public affairs? The answer, of course, depends to a large degree on the future quality of various types of programming; and, under conditions of user selection, citizens will undoubtedly spend their viewing hours in very different ways. We do, however, have some data on what current television viewers (and different types of viewers) choose to watch when they can select among a wide variety of very different kinds of programming, and this may provide us with some indications of what to expect in the future.

In a truly ingenious quasi-natural experiment into the process of program selection, Gary Steiner at the Bureau of Applied Social Research examined the detailed viewing habits (through viewing diaries) of seven hundred families in New York City for eight sample weeks over a six-month period.[19] These viewing diaries were then compared to what was actually broadcast by New York stations during the same period. All of the programs shown during this period were classified into three broad types: (1) light entertainment, (2) heavy entertainment, and (3) public information. There were 255 time periods during the eight sample weeks when all three types of programming were simultaneously being broadcast. In these periods, in other words, the viewers had an equal opportunity to select light entertainment, heavy entertainment, or public affairs programs.

Figure 5 shows what was actually selected for the entire sample, for various demographic groups, and for viewers who differed in their attitudes toward the present content of television programming. While programs containing information on public affairs had an equal chance of being selected in these time periods, they were actually selected only 5 percent of the time. Or, to put it somewhat differently, public information programs were available on each view-

Figure 5
Program Selection when Light Entertainment, Heavy Entertainment, and Public Affairs Are Available at the Same Time

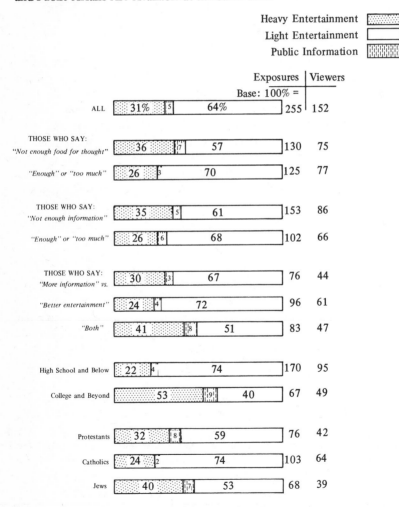

Source: Adapted directly from Steiner, *op. cit.*, p. 201.

ing occasion, but they were watched on the average in only one out of twenty possible instances. The data further indicate that the selection rate of public information varies only slightly from one social group to another, and almost not at all among those who have very different opinions concerning the amounts of informational programming which should be available.

The conclusions to be drawn from these data are, for our limited purposes, quite clear. *When citizens have the opportunity to choose between public information and entertainment, they choose entertainment.* Furthermore, this is true for all major social groups and for those whose attitudes would lead one to believe otherwise. There is little evidence to suggest that this would change in the future simply because the variety would be greater or the ability to choose more regularized. If future home information and entertainment systems are to alter rates of political participation, it is not likely—these data suggest—that this will come about through greater attentiveness to informational and political programming.

Alterations in the Composition of the Participant Stratum: Some Predictions and Their Implications

Up to this point in our discussion, we have been concerned primarily with rates of participation and the size of the activist strata. However, the most important consequences of new communications systems may have less to do with the size of the participating population than with its social and political composition. Changes in the composition of this activist group are important, for these are the citizens who have the greatest voice in determining what government *is* and *does*. Alterations in the social composition of this stratum may affect the influence of different social groupings within the society. Changes in the amount of participation of different social groups who differ in their political preferences and persuasions may also affect the types of decisions—electoral and otherwise—which emerge out of our participatory processes. The Republican party, for example, presently enjoys a considerable turnout advantage, because Republican party identifiers are found in their largest numbers among those social groups—namely middle-aged, upper-middle-class whites—who have the highest rates of turnout. Changes in their voting rates or those of other groups more prone to identify with the Democratic party may therefore alter the balance of power between the parties. Other types of changes in the composition of the participating citizenry may also affect, for example, the "quality" of participation (*e.g.*, the amount of information and interest maintained by those who participate) or the proportion of the participators who are committed to basic democratic values. It is to these possibly most important political implications of the new communications systems that we now turn.

Representativeness of the Participant Stratum

The motivational factors which impel citizens to participate are not equally distributed among all social groupings. Furthermore, these distortions in the social composition of the activist stratum—which are highly significant in their own right—contribute directly to distortions in its political composition. How might the new communications systems we have been discussing affect the social and political composition of the participant stratum? Will the individualized home entertainment and information system produce a different as well as a smaller participant stratum, and if it does, is it likely to be one which is more or less representative of the larger population?

A number of factors lead me to believe that new home entertainment systems, while producing a smaller activist stratum, will nevertheless produce one which is more representative. This appears to be true first because of the manner in which these devices are likely to spread through the population. If they disseminate in a pattern similar to previous and analogous technical devices, the more wealthy and better educated citizens are likely to be exposed to their influences long before they are acquired by those on the lower rungs of the socioeconomic ladder. Therefore, the rates of participation among the wealthy and better educated are likely to be reduced first; and since these are the citizens who are currently most overrepresented, there may be strong short-term forces for a more representative activist stratum.

Even more important than these short-term consequences resulting from the likely pattern of dissemination is the fact that home viewing, by all of our indicators, seems to act as a major leveler of rates of participation. Differences in rates of participation between all social groups are smallest among those who spend large portions of their day viewing. The data in Table 1 demonstrate this finding rather dramatically. Here are presented the mean differences in rates of participation among six pairs of social groups according to the amount of television viewed each day. In every instance, as the amount of viewing increases, the difference in rates of participation between the groups declines.

For example, white collar workers who watch no television engage, on the average, in 1.2 more political acts than nonviewing blue-collar workers. However, the difference in rates of participation among these two occupational groups declines with each additional hour of television viewing, and the difference all but disappears for those who watch four or more hours a day. In the very same manner, television viewing reduces the difference in rates of participation between men and women, whites and blacks, those of high and low income, the highly educated and the uneducated, and between Catholics and Protestants. The average difference for all of the six social dichotomies presented in the table is .78 for those who watch no television but .18 among those who watch four or more hours a day. In short, if new and more attractive home entertainment and information systems substantially increase amounts of viewing, then the leveling effects are likely to produce a participatory stratum composed of large numbers of those who are currently underrepresented and smaller numbers of those who are presently overrepresented.

Table 1
Television Viewing Reduces Differences in Rates of
Participation among Social Groups

Mean Difference in Number of Political Activities
Performed between Six Pairs of Social Groups
According to the Amount of Television Viewed Each Day.

Mean Difference Between	Amount of Television Viewed Daily				
	None	Less than 1 hour	1-3 hours	3-4 hours	4 or more hours
Low Income & High Income	.5	.4	.3	.2	.1
Low Education & High Education	1.4	1.5	1.5	1.4	.6
Blue-Collar Jobs & White-Collar Jobs	1.2	.9	.9	.7	.3
Whites & Blacks	.6	.8	.4	.1	.0
Men & Women	.5	.4	.3	.2	.1
Catholics & Protestants	.5	.0	.1	.1	.0
Average of the Difference for All Six Pairs	.78	.67	.58	.45	.18

Finally, new mass communications systems are likely to produce a more representative participatory stratum because, as we have argued, they are likely to have their greatest attractiveness to the more educated and generally upper-status citizens. One of the reasons these groups seem to participate more now is that they watch less, and a change in this pattern itself will be likely to produce a participatory stratum which has proportionally fewer upper-status individuals.

We should be wary, however, of confusing a more socially and politically *representative* stratum with more or better *representation*. For any significant reduction in the amount of participation or the size of the participant stratum—no matter how it takes place—will in effect turn over more control and influence to political elites. In some instances, a small but representative stratum may result in less one-sided and distorted political decisions; but, at other times, it may result in a less responsive and responsible political leadership. Furthermore, political leaders are not neutral brokers of competing interest groups; they too have backgrounds which color their political perspectives, and their social characteristics and attitudes are even more skewed and nonrepresentative than those of the current activist strata. In short, the implications of a smaller yet more representative political stratum are less than clear.

Effects on the Quality of Participation

The quality of a nation's political participation may be even more important for the maintenance of democracy than either the size or the representativeness of the participant stratum; some of our evidence suggests that new communications systems may result in a larger proportion of highly active citizens who have little interest in politics and public affairs as well as low levels of information about such matters. Figure 6 presents the relevant data. Here we report the mean levels of political participation by amount of television viewed for those in the lowest and highest thirds of our sample according to their levels of interest and informa-

Figure 6
Television Viewing Reduces the Differences in Rates of Participation
Between Those Who Vary Widely in Both Political Interest and Information

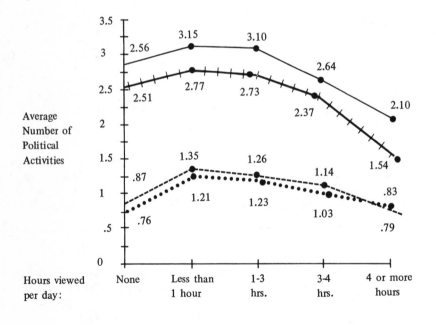

Legend:

----------	No interest,	$\bar{x}$ = 1.13, (N) 788
—————	A great deal of interest,	$\bar{x}$ = 2.94, (N) 969
• • • • • • • • •	Low information,	$\bar{x}$ = 1.19, (N) 952
+++++++	High Information,	$\bar{x}$ = 2.76, (N) 871

tion. Differences in rates of participation between those with more and less interest and more and less information are substantial among those who watch little or no television, but become increasingly smaller with additional hours of television viewing; and this pattern is clearly the result of the fact that long hours of television viewing have their greatest effect on rates of participation among those who are highly interested and informed.

If long hours of home viewing decrease rates of participation most among those with high interest and information, then it would suggest that a substantial increase in home viewing might produce a participant stratum with lower levels of these important characteristics. In short, the differential impact of home viewing on the more interested and informed citizen could in this way act to reduce the overall quality of participation by leveling the differences in rates of political activity among those who vary in interest and information. The mechanisms are virtually identical to the ones which we have argued might produce a more representative group of participators; but, in this instance, it is the bias towards high levels of interest and information which is likely to be reduced rather than biases which favor one or another social group.

How great an impact new communications systems might have on the quality of participation will again depend on how much they increase rates of home viewing and particularly on how they affect the viewing habits of those at different levels of interest and information. If the interested and informed citizen continues to watch less, then the effects may not be very large; however, one can here, as was done in the case of education, make a strong case for the fact that these systems are likely to have the most to offer these more interested and informed citizens.

Just what a reduction in the amount of interest and information among high participators would actually imply for our political processes is hard to say, but it clearly raises once again the specter of "mass irrationality" and "ignorant involvement" which has haunted democratic theorists since the Greeks. This may be counterbalanced by the fact that fewer citizens will be participating and that mass activity may therefore have less influence on what the government says or does.

Concluding Remarks

While offering great increases in the technical capacities for direct citizen participation, new communications systems, paradoxically, are not only unlikely to increase social and political participation greatly, but may even indirectly contribute to a substantial decrease. Much of the evidence seems to point in this direction. While instant referenda and nationwide electronic town meetings are interesting to contemplate, they seem to fade quickly into the realm of utopian myths when faced with the harsh realities of political decision-making in a large and complex modern society. On the other side, the indirect participatory consequences of these new systems through their impact on the interests and activity patterns of the citizenry seem all too real, and such factors may already be having some effects on rates of participation in our society. Paradoxically or not, improvements in mass communications in the future may quite likely contribute to a privatization of social life.

However, our data suggest that not all forms of participation will be equally affected, for there seems to be much less contention between home viewing and voting than is true for other forms of activity. Furthermore, new communications systems may even increase rates of voting by making possible a national voting registry and perhaps even an electronic home voting system. Increases in the proportion of the population voting and changes in the composition and quality of the active electorate will be all the more important if rates of other forms of participation decline. The selection of leadership clearly becomes more critical if other mechanisms for popular control wane.

New communications systems, and the individualized home entertainment system in particular, may affect not only the numbers of citizens who participate in various types of activity but also the kinds of citizens who are likely to be active. A number of types of evidence suggest that these systems may produce a participant stratum which is more representative of the social grouping of the larger population. Groups that are now rather severely underrepresented among the highly active may have more equitable influence in the future, and those that are presently overrepresented may have a less dominant voice. Such changes in the social composition of the participant stratum may lead to change in the balance of party strength as well as to altered distributions of policy preferences in this more visible and influential segment of the citizenry. However, the same mechanisms which act to create a more representative political stratum may also produce one which is of reduced quality. An activist stratum composed of larger proportions of uninterested and uninformed citizens is not an enticing prospect, though its concrete implications are difficult to foretell. Changes in the composition and the quality of the activist citizenry may prove to be less important than they would presently appear, for the stratum may be so constricted in size as to have little influence on the conduct or quality of government.

All of these predictions will, I firmly hope, be taken with a large grain of salt, for they are obviously little more than speculation. However, I am less concerned with the accuracy or inaccuracy of specific predictions than with what may be an inadvertant overemphasis of the importance of new communications systems to participation. We have based all of our predictions of future patterns of political participation on new communications systems while such systems are obviously only one of a large number of factors which will play a role in determining what these patterns will actually be. New trends toward local citizen control of government programs, continuing increases in educational attainment, changes in the amounts of leisure time, as well as a host of other factors may overshadow the effects of new communications media. It is impossible from this vantage point to tell which factors will play what type of role. I believe that we have isolated the directions in which new communications systems will push, but the shape of participation in the future may be determined by other factors which exert an even more powerful influence on the nature of citizen participation.

Notes

1. For some of the recent literature, see *Toward a Social Report* (Washington: U.S. Department of Health, Education, and Welfare, January, 1969).

2. As Eulau and MacRae make clear, however, changes in information are not equivalent to changes in representation. *See* Heinz Eulau, "Some Potential Effects of the Information Utility on Political Decision-Makers and the Role of the Representative," and Duncan MacRae, Jr., "Some Political Choices in the Development of Communications Technology", in this volume [*The Information Utility and Social Choice*].

3. This is not totally true. There is some polling on major national issues, but it is conducted almost exclusively by private organizations rather than by government, and does not constitute the type of regular mechanism we are discussing.

4. See Dwaine Marvick, "The Potential Effects of the Information Utility on Citizen Participation," in this volume [*The Information Utility and Social Choice*].

5. Television viewing by minority groups, however, may stimulate demands and *increase* political activity by creating a sense of relative deprivation.

6. These data are from a survey on political participation collected under the auspices of the "Cross National Research Program in Political and Social Change." I would like to thank Sidney Verba, the director of this research program and the other participants for allowing me to present this data. The index of political participation is a simple additive scale constructed by summing reports of activity on nine different individual political acts. Included among these activities were frequency of voting, contacting governmental officials, various types of campaign activities, such as attending meetings, canvassing, etc., and participation through groups and organizations.

7. This finding is *not* explained by coincidence of low socioeconomic status and non-ownership of a television, for there is only a small difference in rates of television viewing and ownership between the rich and the poor. See *Current Housing Reports, Housing Characteristics*, Series H-121 No. 15, U.S. Department of Commerce, Bureau of the Census, (June, 1969).

8. A later section will explore the implications of these findings for the social composition and representativeness of the participant stratum.

9. While we have argued that long hours of viewing acts to decrease social and political participation, it is possible that causality runs in the reverse direction—those who are not prone to be socially active simply have more time available for television viewing. In other words, rather than participating less because they watch more, people may simply watch more because they participate less. There are two types of data, however, which suggest that this is not the usual pattern. First, as Figure 3 shows, among those who have the motivations and attitudes characteristic of high participators, television viewing reduces participation even more than among those who report lesser amounts of interest in politics and public affairs; viewing would therefore appear not to be dependent on a more generally passive orientation. Second, the overwhelming majority of television viewers, when interviewed in depth, report a daily conflict in their lives between television viewing and all other forms of leisure-time activity. The theme is a recurring one, as viewers repeatedly report being captured by television when they feel they should be taking care of other matters. The evidence is summed up in the title of one of Steiner's chapters in his intensive study of the viewing audience—"Television and Leisure: A Basic Conflict," in Gary A. Steiner, *The People Look at Television: A Study of Audience Attitudes* (New York: Alfred A. Knopf, 1963).

10. The campaign participation data were compiled from the University of Michigan Survey Research Center's presidential election studies. The activities are membership in

political clubs and organizations, donations of money, attending political meetings and rallies, and other types of work for parties and candidates. The exact wording of the questions and the frequency distributions for the presidential elections of 1952 through 1964 can be found in the SRC codebooks.

11. These data were complied from the *Statistical Abstract of the U. S.*, 1969, Department of Commerce, Bureau of the Budget.

12. Nie, Powell, and Prewitt, for example, find that 19.5 percent of the variance in political participation in the United States is explained by a simple Social Status index composed of income, education, and occupation. See Nie, *et al.*, "Social Structure and Political Participation: Developmental Relationships," Part I, *American Political Science Review*, LXIII, 2 (June, 1969).

13. One of the major methodological difficulties with this type of analysis is that it is impossible to link simple frequency distributions directly to the behavior of individuals. To really test this proposition, we would need systematic data at the level of the individual on participation and television viewing across a large number of points in time. However, there are a number of natural experiments which suggest how modern conveniences affect behavior. The rather notorious peak in the birth rate in New York City nine months after the blackout and the rather dramatic reduction in a number of rural areas directly following electrification programs suggest how powerful such factors can be.

14. Television Household is defined as that population which has at least one television set. This 33 percent increase, therefore, cannot be explained simply by an increase in the number of households with televisions.

15. Nielsen data cited by John P. Robinson, "Television and Leisure Time," *Public Opinion Quarterly* (Summer, 1969), p. 215.

16. Both average number of hours per day spent watching and actual number of programs seen during the week decrease with higher education. This finding does not hold, however, during the prime view hours of 8:00 p.m. to midnight; in this period, both during the week and on weekends, highly educated people are equally or more likely than the less educated to watch television (*see* Steiner, *op. cit.*, p. 75).

17. The data from several studies indicate that lack of relevant programming for the better educated is a major reason such groups give for viewing less television. (*see* Steiner, *op. cit.*) Several Harris polls have also reported similar findings. (*see* Robinson, *op. cit.*)

18. Precisely because of this, the national government will probably maintain some legal and technical ability to saturate the media with major national events and emergencies parallel to its current practice of broadcasting important presidential messages on all three networks.

19. Steiner, *op. cit.*, pp. 198-204.

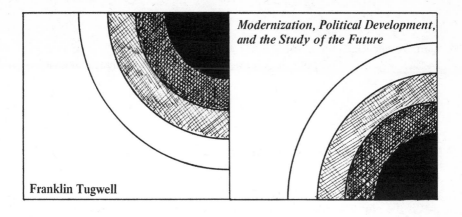

Modernization, Political Development, and the Study of the Future

Franklin Tugwell

For the past decade, the study of modernization and political development has been one of the most innovative and dynamic fields within political science. A response primarily to the rapid rise to independence of Afro-Asian peoples, it has served as a point of entry to the discipline for a number of important currents of thought. Many of these comprise part of what Gabriel Almond has called the "comparative politics movement," a movement that has been instrumental in leading the discipline beyond the rather parochial Western-democratic orientation typical of the forties and fifties; indeed, it has introduced a new concern for functional categorization and a heightened sensitivity to the ties between politics and other dimensions of social life.[1]

Quite recently, however, a new mood of questioning has come to the fore among students of modernization and political development. Increasingly, they have turned a critical eye upon the results of the decade's work and found it wanting. Several have complained about its continuing conceptual and terminological ambiguity. Rustow, for example, has warned that the concept of modernization is in danger of becoming a "brooding omnipresence," suggestive, but cloudy and vague, with few intermediary concepts to bring it down to earth.[2] Others have complained about the continuing tendency to treat modernization and political development as generally irreversible, unilinear processes suffused with an implied but unexamined set of teleological assumptions, or, in a nearly opposite vein, about the generally static quality of theory, a characteristic in most cases traced to systems-derived preoccupation with equilibrium and integration as opposed to evolution and conflict.[3] A number of critics have pointed to the persistent normative ambiguity—even cowardice—of past work as a source of problems. Finally, still others have expressed concern about the lack of policy applicability of knowledge being generated.[4] In sum, the study of modernization and political development is currently, as one writer has phrased it, "turgid and suffused with anxiety."[5]

There are many reasons for this state of affairs. It can be explained in part as a normal pattern of growth within a young field, in which periodic self-criticism is to be expected. However, much of this sense of confusion, even malaise, is surely due to the very depressing state of the underdeveloped world itself. For one of the most important and unfortunate "surprises" of the misnamed "Development Decade" has been the rather widespread failures in nation-building, state-building, and economic growth—failures that have left us deeply conscious of the optimistic bias of our early expectations, and of the immense tasks that lie ahead.

The Role of Future-oriented Analysis

It is in the light of the ongoing collapse of the "development paradigm" of the sixties that still another weakness in the decade's work comes to the fore—one that is the primary concern of this essay: the failure to pay sufficient attention to the future, *per se*, as an explicit object of study. Only a small number of individuals have ventured to touch upon the future, and their work has focused primarily on the high GNP countries.[6] This is not to say that the future has been absent from the thoughts of political development analysts; on the contrary, it has become a kind of "brooding omnipresence" of its own, especially in view of the gloomy forecasts that have been offered by those working on ecological prospectives for the planet.[7] Still, it has remained always implicit—in the background, but rarely touched.[8]

It is my contention here that explicit and extensive future-oriented analysis has an essential, though unrecognized, role in the production of a body of useful knowledge about modernization and political development. More specifically, I believe that it can (1) help assure a continuous consideration of the policy utility of new ideas; (2) force into the open the normative dimensions of analytical concepts and stimulate new and more sophisticated thinking about how to define human welfare and dignity for the future; and, finally, (3) help guide and invigorate the process of theory building itself by suggesting new relationships, contexts, and evaluative criteria that might otherwise be neglected. Taken together, these contributions may even help remedy some of the very serious problems in the field that have been diagnosed by recent critics.

In order to comprehend these contributions, it is necessary first to consider the problem of what may be called "past-directed" scholarship. This refers to the elaboration of theoretical generalizations with predictive intent for conditions that are never likely to exist again (at least not in the same form), but without explicit treatment of the effects of changing circumstances upon the future utility of the generalizations. An excellent example of this is provided by Barrington Moore's *Social Origins of Dictatorship and Democracy*.[9] Although much criticized, it is unquestionably a major contribution to the analysis of social and economic relations as they affected the political outcomes of the modernization process. The "routes" to the modern world Moore depicts in this study are well-constructed and very coherent, as are his more detailed propositions about the socioeconomic preconditions of democracy, fascism, and, above all, peasant-based revolution. But what of "new" routes for those who must try to map out an understanding of ongoing changes for the future? At the end of his book, Moore points out that peasant revolution, "one of the most distinctive features of the twentieth century, may . . . have already spent its force," yet he leaves to others the task of considering what might come after.[10]

Regarding the relative costs of violent change, Moore asserts: "the costs of moderation have been at least as atrocious as those of revolution, perhaps a great deal more."[11] Even though he qualifies this statement by noting that "the claims of existing socialist states to represent a higher form of freedom than Western democratic capitalism rest on promise, not performance," it is the original statement that rings out loudest and clearest.[12] And, as might be expected, it has been widely invoked as *predictive* evidence in support of revolution as an option for leaders of underdeveloped countries, and, even, on occasion, developed countries. It should be so used, but not without carefully considering new contexts and conditions, and not without asking cautiously whether the costs of old forms of revolution may not increase very significantly in a more modernized, differentiated, bureaucratized, and industrialized setting.

The argument here is that Moore's work would have been strengthened if he had tried to struggle with questions such as these as he came to his conclusions; that too often and too easily predictive utility is read into propositions of this kind without consideration for the future. After all, it is clear that a large part of the self-justification of Moore's work lies in its ability to contribute to the "map" of knowledge upon which important choices for the future are continually being made.

Past-directed analysis may do very well in helping produce "tested statements of probability of relations between variables which will gradually turn our heuristic macro-theories into proven propositions cumulated in an orderly way"—to use one writer's view of the field's purpose.[13] But of what value will they be if the author does not pause to ask, and do his best to answer, such questions as: will these statements continue to be true tomorrow? In ten years? How will they be shaped by ongoing patterns of change? By possible but unlikely events and trends? Unfortunately, questions such as these are normally left for others to explore—others who are necessarily less acquainted with the reasoning behind the original analysis. This is a criticism which may be directed, in varying degrees, at many of the most important studies of modernization and political development.[14]

Actually, I have identified two kinds of sins here. The first, and more serious, is the implication on the part of an analyst who offers a proposition that it will continue to hold true—equally true—in the future. The second is simply neglect of the future, usually on grounds of scientific rigor.[15] Such neglect is unfortunate for many reasons, not the least of which is that it reflects a mistaken conception of the uses of evidence from the past in the social sciences. Such evidence, and generalizations derived therefrom, are clearly of central importance, since they are the most secure building blocks we have for investigating tendencies and regularities in behavior, both individual and institutional. But there is a common tendency in this process to neglect one of the most important "lessons" that historical evidence offers: that change continues. Thus neglect of the future also reflects a common epistemological error in the application of the scientific method to the social sciences and other "inexact" sciences: the assumption that scientifically derived generalizations have predictive utility simply because they are scientifically derived.[16]

This, of course, is incorrect, if, as in most social settings today, the units or relationships being studied are in the process of continuous qualitative and quantitative transformation. Put more concretely, knowledge about, say, the oxidation of iron, is not the same as knowledge about the capitalist route to development, though both may have been derived as scientifically as possible. The former retains predictive utility; the latter does not, unless it is systematically related to changed future contexts. If the iron were becoming nickel, then lead, then some as yet undetermined substance, the relationship of explanation to prediction would be analogous in the two. Unfortunately, we simply do not work well with time and change insofar as our explanatory theory is concerned, and the weaknesses of past-directed theory reflect this. In particular, the distinction between static and dynamic, or equilibrium and developmental forms of understanding—a distinction recognized in the abstract in most social theory—is not emphasized sufficiently. It is ironic that many of those who are quietly neglecting the future in this way are those who at the same time are most deeply aware of the rate and extent of transformative change in the world today.

It is hardly surprising, therefore, that political development theorists are criticized for not being attentive to policy needs. Policies are made for and about the future and require careful and explicit elaboration of likely and possible alternatives and consequences. Although policy applicability requires more than a futurist orientation—indeed, one of the criticisms leveled against futurist work is that it, too, is phrased in such stratospheric conceptualizations that it is of little practical use—it can hardly be achieved without more systematic attention to the future in its relationships to past-derived propositions.

Closely related to policy utility is the problem of the place of values in ongoing work on modernization and political development. As indicated, the ambiguity of the normative component of theory has become a principal focus of criticism. One reason for this is the somewhat belated realization among political scientists that there are no theories of development that are "value-free," though there are many that are "value-ignorant." As Runciman has put it, values and science are "distinct but inseparable."[17] Fortunately, the normative component of political development theory has been rising closer to the surface, as the most recent writing of such analysts as Gabriel Almond and Samuel P. Huntington reveals.[18] And at least one writer, Dennis Goulet, has made the examination of normative assumptions in development concepts his primary concern.[19]

Future-oriented analysis is particularly well equipped to bring normative questions to the fore, and, to an extent, force a self-conscious normative engagement upon those who might otherwise prefer to avoid it. This is because futurist methodologies are usually structured so as to elucidate the value-laden consequences of possible choices. The alternative futures approach, for example—one of the most widespread methods of futurist analysis—serves this purpose if done well. And utopias and anti-utopias, of course, are first and foremost normative methodologies.

The time is clearly at hand for a thoroughgoing reconsideration of goals and objectives in the process of modernization. As Dennis Goulet has recently pointed out:[20]

In the strictest literal sense, we cannot be sure that development as a goal is a good thing for mankind. What we do know is that underdevelopment is a very bad state of affairs, and that the process of development is an imponderable mix of goods and evils.

The place of man in the biosphere is currently unstable and is likely soon to become untenable, due primarily to the spread of the "world culture" of modernization to all peoples and societies. Transitional man is desperate and insecure because he knows no stable, viable life system, yet prevailing images of such systems are either specious or unavailable. And the constantly enlarging role of man as an agent in the process of change suggests that good and viable modalities will never come into being unless they are imagined and constructed by men acting collectively.

Only if we attempt to clarify and help specify values and goals—even as we press ahead in macro-heuristic theorizing and enlarge our data-handling abilities—can we hope meaningfully to contribute to our principal task as social scientists: widening man's range of choice among available alternatives.[21] This is especially true for the political scientist, since political systems not only embody, depend upon, and tend to preserve values, but also serve as the chief vehicles by which value changes are confirmed and implemented. Thus political values take on transcendental importance—facilitating, distorting, or impeding our capacity to make collective choices of any kind. Unfortunately, our first task remains that of reconciling the philosopher and the scientist of politics, and convincing each that the other is indispensible if either is to serve mankind.

The proposition that more attention to the future by students of modernization and political development can also help guide and invigorate the process of scientific theory building is really the chanciest of the assertions made here, because it is dependent upon the willingness of those concerned to turn around and re-examine many of their assumptions—especially regarding time and change—in response to the needs of a future-oriented and policy-related perspective. Fortunately, however, the prospects here seem excellent since several of the best thinkers in the field have already begun to do this, just as they have begun to come to grips with normative problems.[22] Indeed, a listing of some of the areas of analysis that a futurist perspective is likely to promote, and contribute to, covers many of the subjects upon which new work is being concentrated. Such a listing includes:

1. "Big" syntheses and multidisciplinary interpretations of modernization as human transition, addressing directly the teleological questions that inevitably arise with such work. There is a broad agreement among specialists about what modernization is. Now we need to ask more persistent questions about why and

how this process of expanding choice and control got under way, how it relates to our biological nature or inheritance, where it is going, and how political systems fit into it. These are awesome and difficult questions, and the attempt to answer them can be expected to help students of political development, in particular, locate themselves more securely in the setting of transformation.

2. Forms of analytical conjecture: alternative futures, scenarios, developmental constructs, utopias and anti-utopias, plus the predictive techniques needed to work them out and relate them to the present. Key here also is the increased use of simulations in order to utilize clusters of hypotheses to depict alternatives.

3. Multidimensional ongoing change, not just change viewed as a disequilibrium of presumed systemic stability. Included here are "leaps" or revolutionary acts of will leading to refashioned social contexts.

4. The relationship of elites to change, not only passive responses but attempts to engineer change; the whole question of elite organizational and problem-solving behavior; leadership as a process; creativity, foresight, and intuition as applicable and tangible skills.

5. Generally, a continuing redefinition of the meaning of political development to stress the capacity to shape the future by managing transformation, thus treating the polity as an independent variable and the principal means of collective action to achieve this goal; also, closely related to this, a greatly increased concern for political *dis*velopment and political *over*development.

6. Political ecology; forms of polity appropriate to societies with differing technologies and ecological contexts, especially those identifiable with ecosystem stabilization and sanctification at low energy levels; a focus upon biosphere politics as an organizing concept, ties of human, organic, and inorganic systems to processes of choice and control; the search for man and computer-managed forms of planetary stabilization.

The Future of Political Development: An Exploration

Up to this point, I have agrued the importance of more future-oriented work in the study of modernization and political development. In the following pages, I offer a few thoughts—tentative and quite crude, but perhaps suggestive—about the future of political development itself. I do so in part because I feel the best argument for the study of the future *is* the future, and in part to help illustrate how several of the central concepts made available by recent studies do in fact lend themselves to thinking about the future, even if this dimension has been insufficiently explored to date.

To accomplish this, I have prepared a rough forecast of what I feel is one of the most likely future patterns of politics in the underdeveloped areas of the world. It is intended as a dynamic ideal-type, or developmental construct, rather than a detailed prediction of events in any particular country.[23] Elaboration of this construct, or "standard run" as I call it, is supplemented by a brief statement of the relationship between it and the material dimension of development;

a summary of alternative forms that seem likely or possible candidates to replace it; and, finally, a short discussion of some of the implications of the images presented.

The "standard run" forecast depicts a generalized failure of political development and the emergence among the late modernizing countries of a persistent and self-reinforcing form of institutionalized incompetence in the determination, validation, and implementation of guiding public policies. In addition, it maintains that this will be matched by a parallel and related malperformance in the work of material development. This forecast is based on two analytical components: first, an evaluation of recent trends; and second, a rough model, or cluster of propositions, explaining those trends and the reasons for expecting them to continue. Before I turn to these, however, some terminological clarification is in order.

Political development, as the term is used here, is both a condition and a process. As a condition, it refers to the will and competence of a polity in absorbing and handling changing and increasing demands while determining, validating, and implementing collective goals; to its ability to sustain the traditional "regulative" function of the state by maintaining order and providing authoritative resolutions to conflicts, and at the same time to lead society by providing strong and self-conscious choices among alternatives for the future.[24] As a process, political development is an increase in these capacities in relationship to the rapid changes in the society brought on by the impact of modernization. Therefore, it must be viewed as relational, to be judged in the context of differential rates of change in polity and society. Because of the explosive transformation in which mankind is currently involved, a higher degree of these capacities is becoming necessary for people to associate together effectively. If modernization can be viewed as a sudden expansion in the range of choice about the future, political development can be viewed as a statement about the capacity of society collectively to take advantage of this expansion to assure that the cumulative result will be coherent rather than incoherent, desirable rather than tragic. At the same time, however, the very conditions of rapid change are making this capacity more difficult to acquire. In summary form, this is the dilemma of political development; and it is a dilemma facing the developed as well as the underdeveloped, as we are all aware.

A polity with a high degree of the kind of competence described, plus substantial provision for widespread participation of groups and individuals in collective choices—a condition many writers feel is actually necessary if this competence is to endure—is both unusual in human affairs and a highly difficult accomplishment. There is no single formula for success, and success itself is no guarantee of continuity. Such a polity requires constant effort to sustain, since it is a complex and dynamic mixture of cultural attitudes and institutional arrangements. And recent trends indicate overwhelmingly that efforts to create such instruments among the late modernizing countries are rapidly faltering.

In this three-volume study of underdevelopment in Asia, and in the special policy-oriented essay stemming therefrom, Swedish economist Gunnar Myrdal places heavy emphasis upon what he calls the "soft state" as one of the most pressing problems to be overcome. By a "soft state" he means one characterized by widespread "social indiscipline." "There will in a soft state be a much wider spread, in all strata, of a general inclination of people to resist public controls and their implementation."[25] Similarly, Samuel P. Huntington has pointed out that:[26]

In politics as in economics the gap between developed political systems and underdeveloped political systems, between civic polities and corrupt polities, has broadened.

This is a generalization that is confirmed by nearly every measure of political development, statistical and impressionistic alike, including governmental continuity, revolts, uprisings, coups, civil and guerilla wars, the formation of coherent political organizations, and the ability of underdeveloped countries to provide a flow of public policies. Little aided by colonial masters, newly independent countries of Africa and Asia have clearly been faring badly in the struggle for political development. And Latin American countries, trend-setters in this respect, have been doing little better.

An evaluation of the conditions contributing to this rather universal failure provides material for an even more dismal forecast for the future: it seems that success in political development will continue to become increasingly more difficult. Generally speaking, in most underdeveloped countries, the processes of change have occurred, and will continue to occur, prior to the emergence of a sense of identity and unity, and prior to the establishment of strong and legitimate governmental institutions. The political arena has thus rapidly filled up with individuals, groups, and movements, all with strong policy needs and demands, before the polity has developed the ability to manage their participation or to satisfy their claims. As a result, violence, coercion, personalist and ideological appeals, and control of wealth have typically become key instruments of political participation, while elections have lost legitimizing force, and the state has remained weak and unable to acquire a managing role in society.

Samuel Huntington describes this situation as one in which "social forces" are more powerful than the government, and the cumulative result of social conflicts and competition is generalized chaos and incoherence.[27]

In all societies specialized social groups engage in politics. What makes such groups seem more "politicized" . . . is the absence of effective political institutions capable of mediating, refining, and moderating group political action . . . social forces confront each other nakedly; no political institutions, no corps of professional political leaders are recognized or accepted as the legitimate intermediaries to moderate group conflict.

Such a society is a "transient" society, to adopt Manfred Halpern's highly descriptive term, one that is undergoing change but is incapable of either handling the consequences of that change or making choices about its content or direction.[28] It is incapable of shaping the future by managing transformation to any degree; instead, it is caught adrift in the global process of modernization.

There are five basic reasons why the recent trend of poor performance in political development is likely to continue, and very probably, worsen:

1. *There is a tendency for the condition of transience to become institutionalized over time.* Historical experience in Latin America (as well as France, to a considerable degree), confirms this; and it is clearly occurring in other underdeveloped areas.[29] Although we as yet know very little about this as a process, it consists primarily in the emergence of generally accepted "rules of the game" for political conduct which take into account state incompetence and then tend to perpetuate it. Semi-corporatist patterns of access to public policy arenas are established, and private, particularistic functional groups carve out arenas of policy and tend to dominate them at the expense of the state. Military involvement in politics, weak parties, obstructionist legislatures, feeble executives, corruption, instability, and relatively high levels of violence become patterned. Individuals and groups, unable to transform such a situation, learn to accommodate the pursuit of their interests to the transient society. Once they have done so, they then create a supportive culture and set of behaviors around it. New participants learn appropriate behaviors and are incorporated into the system via powerful cooptational mechanisms.

2. *The creation of political development becomes more difficult as the political arena enlarges.* The forces contributing to this enlargement, subsumed under the term "social mobilization"—growth in literacy, media exposure, urbanization, and so on—have been growing, and very likely will continue to grow, despite political underdevelopment. Put another way, the condition of transience is no obstacle to the entry of new individuals, groups, and social classes into the political arena; on the contrary, there are reasons to believe that it solicits their entry. What it also does is assure that their entry will not contribute to political order but rather add to the complexity of the system and make the creation of political competence more difficult.

3. *Modernization activates ethnic and primordial identifications and conflicts, making the creation of a sense of unity and national (country-wide) identity more difficult.* We are learning the truth of this axiom with considerable pain in the United States, as the Europeans have and are. It is notable, in this regard, that the presently industrialized societies have almost entirely failed in their efforts to find formulae by which ethnically and culturally different people can live together within the same state. Yet such diversity is more prevalent, and rates of change are greater, in the underdeveloped areas. India alone has greater cultural and linguistic diversity than the entire European continent. Therefore, there is little reason to expect greater success than in Europe; rather there is every reason to anticipate a steady increase in conflict centered about ethnic and cultural matters—more civil wars such as the Nigerian and Pakistani; more fragmentation and breakup of existing political communities; and generally very

little success in creating political development in any ethnically diverse under-developed country.

4. *Revolution appears to be becoming more difficult.* Among other things, revolution is an act of will that seeks to create order, and a form of political development, out of chaos. It does not always succeed and is normally immensely costly in terms of immediate human suffering. Nevertheless, it represents a possible means of overcoming institutionalized transience and should be considered in thinking about the future of political underdevelopment. There is perhaps nothing more pathetic in social life than a society trapped in institutionalized chaos and corruption, yet unable to restructure itself even by revolution.[30]

Yet it seems that the option of revolution is becoming, for the near future at least, more difficult. Of all of the predictors in this list, this is the most tenuous and seems to be the most likely source of surprises. However, the conditions described above in the mobilized, institutionalized transient society indicate that revolution is almost sure to become more difficult to engineer internally. The reasons for this are many, and can only be indicated here in broad outline:

(a) the standard revolutionary coalition of urban middle-class leaders and radical peasants is becoming less likely, if only because the peasants are rapidly becoming less than a majority of the population; thus the effects of rural radicalism are likely to decrease in scope and impact. (Latin America is more than 50 percent urban.)

(b) Only a "new" form of revolution, an urban form, can compensate for this demographic shift—indeed, much of the attention of revolutionaries in Latin America has been placed upon this—yet urban poor seem to have been unresponsive to revolution as an option. It may be that this is because they have experienced an increase in welfare and will become revolutionary later; but this is difficult to predict, since urban shanty areas typically grow and develop into increasingly more permanent and affluent communities over time.[31]

(c) More nondomestic interests are involved in the questions of revolution, and these in general are becoming increasingly wary of any form of instability because of its effects on the probability of nuclear warfare. Certainly this has become the case with the United States and the Soviet Union, and will also increasingly be the case with China. Just as important, such wariness is likely to be a more prominent attitude among underdeveloped countries themselves over time. Consider the probable attitude of Argentina and Brazil to a revolution in either, or the attitude of the Dominican Republic (and the United States) should the coming turmoil in Haiti lead to revolution. Revolution has always been difficult—in fact, it has been a relatively rare phenomenon in history; and the more complex the political arena, domestic and international, the more difficult it is likely to become. Disruption will become easier; revolution harder.

5. *The trend toward political transience is related to a parallel failure in material growth performance; in fact, the two tend to reinforce each other, and will do so increasingly.* The following tables illustrate recent trends in GNP growth rates and give projections to the year 2000 based upon average annual

growth rates for the years 1950-1965. A series of "dichotomized images" highlight comparative performances of a selected group of high and low GNP countries, and estimate the "gap" dividing them. These are "persistence" forecasts, and therefore cannot take into account any changes in trends; but they do serve notice of the likely outcome if the surprisingly poor performance of the last decade continues to be the case.[32]

Table 1
Per Capita GNP and Average Annual Growth Rates
(U.S. dollars and percentages)

	1950	1965	Rate 1950-60	Rate 1960-67(8)
United States	2,300	3,557	1.1	3.6
Canada	1,750	2,464	1.2	3.7
Britain	1,200	1,804	2.3	2.3
France	750	1,924	3.4	4.3
West Germany	600	1,905	6.8	3.2
Argentina	500	492	1.4	1.3
Czechoslovakia	450	1,554	6.3	2.9
U.S.S.R.	400	1,288	8.6	5.8
Italy	350	1,101	4.9	4.2
Poland	320	962	6.1	5.3
Brazil	235	280	3.6	1.1
Mexico	225	455	3.0	3.1
Colombia	220	277	1.5	1.5
Japan	190	857	6.5	9.1
Egypt	135	166	—	2.2*
Indonesia	120	99	—	−0.2
Thailand	85	126	—	—
Nigeria	70	83	8.4	2.2**
Pakistan	70	91	0.4	3.4
India	70	99	1.6	0.3
China	50	—	—	—

* Only available figure, for 1962-66.
** Only available figure, for 1960-66.

Source: 1950 GNP per capita, Russett, *World Handbook, op. cit.*, p. 110; 1965 GNP per capita, Kahn and Wiener (Eds.), *op. cit.*, pp. 161, 165; average annual growth rates, U.N. *Statistical Yearbook*, 1969 (New York: United Nations, 1970), chart 179, giving Gross Domestic Product per capita at market prices, p. 550.

The growth failures indicated on these tables may be explained to a degree, probably a large degree, as the result of the increasing interpenetration and interdependence between polity and economy in the countries examined. Statistical evidence indicates that an expansion in the role of the government in practically every sector of social life has accompanied the onset of modernization. This is especially true of its role in the economy, as measured by government expenditues as a percentage of GNP. Correlations completed by Russet and others indicate that the sharpest rise of all has been measured in the movement from the category of countries with a mean per capita income of eighty-seven dollars to the category of countries with a mean per capita income of one hundred seventy-three dollars; and that it continues to rise, but at a much slower rate, in higher categories.[33] Nearly everywhere in the underdeveloped world, societies have been turning to their governments to accomplish tasks of development that were performed to a significant extent by private groups in the first countries to develop. The role of the state enlarged in response to economic growth in the United States and Western Europe; it has been enlarged to create such a growth among the underdeveloped countries today. And it has enlarged externally as well as internally in the sense that state management of national-international linkages (trade, aid, and so forth) is becoming increasingly vital.

Table 2
Forecasts of GNP Per Capita: 2000*
(U.S. dollars)

Country	2000
United States	8,157.947
Canada	5,847.553
Britain	3,998.350
France	7,340.864
West Germany	10,507.964
Argentina	789.306
Czechoslovakia	7,499.942
U.S.S.R.	14,680.159
Italy	5,313.654
Poland	6,334.633
Brazil	642.153
Mexico	1,324.513
Colombia	466.411
Japan	11,875.024
Egypt	355.517
Indonesia	92.501
Thailand	—
Nigeria	505.863
Pakistan	166.175
India	138.831
China	—

* Rate used: average for 1950-1967(8).

Baseline: 1965 per capita GNP.

As a result, the consequences of political underdevelopment, in terms of growth failure, have been increasing, and can be expected to continue to do so. And vice-versa: developmental performance is becoming increasingly necessary for the acquisition of legitimacy and popular consent by a government. This is the first hard lesson aspiring reformers learn. Successful economic policies are becoming a standard measure of a government's worth and a prerequisite for citizen loyalty and commitment, which are in turn necessary for building a strong public authority. Yet authority with citizen loyalty are prerequisite to setting out the hard and effective programs needed to achieve developmental performance. Thus ill-performance in one area can be expected to damage in turn the possibilities for success in the other, creating a downward spiral.

Table 3
High and Low Performers: 1950

(U.S. dollars and percentages)

Country	GNP per capita	% of forecasted GNP per capita, Total Table 1 countries
United States	2,300	22.8
U.S.S.R.	400	4.0
Japan	190	1.9
West Germany	600	5.9
France	750	7.4
Canada	1,750	17.3
Total	5,990	59.3
India	70	7
Indonesia	120	1.2
Brazil	235	2.3
Pakistan	70	.7
Colombia	220	2.2
Egypt	135	1.3
Argentina	500	5.0
Total	1,350	13.4
ratio: $\frac{\text{total rich}}{\text{total poor}}$	$\frac{4.44}{1}$	$\frac{4.4}{1}$

In addition, there is reason to believe that material development itself is likely to become more costly in the future, in part because of increasing resource scarcity, but primarily because of the heavy extra costs required to control pollution. In retrospect, we can now see that the development of the early modernizing countries was easier, because it was wasteful and used resources such as air, wood and water as free goods, paying only insignificant economic costs for them. It is becoming evident, however, that the developed world cannot allow such "wasteful" development to be repeated in the underdeveloped areas. A duplication of per capita pollution levels by the heavily populated underdeveloped areas would choke and poison the biosphere as a whole. Indeed, how much pollution will be allowed is sure to be one of the central questions of emerging biosphere politics.

Table 4
High and Low Performers: 1975
(U.S. dollars and percentages)

Country	GNP per capita	% of forecasted GNP per capita Total Table 1 countries
United States	5,066.184	17.7
U.S.S.R.	2,263.452	7.9
Japan	2,047.513	7.2
West Germany	2,601.304	9.1
France	2,931.212	10.3
Canada	3,543.463	12.4
Total	18,453.128	64.6
India	102.006	0.4
Indonesia	97.042	0.3
Brazil	312.365	1.1
Pakistan	127.124	0.4
Colombia	321.465	1.1
Egypt	206.352	0.7
Argentina	559.837	2.0
Total	1,726.191	6.0
ratio: $\frac{\text{total rich}}{\text{total poor}}$	$\frac{10.7}{1}$	$\frac{10.8}{1}$

When the forecast derived from the projection of recent trends plus these analytical propositions is assembled, there emerges one of the most dismal, nightmare visions this writer has been forced to face. It is a specter of degradation and indignity; of disorder and injustice; of "permanent" misery and helplessness. Although oversimplified and perhaps avoidable, it is so strongly suggested by the indicators available that it stands clearly in the fore as the most likely future for nearly a majority of the earth's people. If it proves even partly correct, then we are faced with a multidimensional "gap" emerging on the planet of proportions that few have been considering seriously.

Although the developed countries are finding the transition to high levels of political development very difficult, there is reason to hope that they will be able to bring to bear the skills and commitments necessary to begin to manage the transformation process in which they find themselves. Social invention, technology assessment, organizational development, planning systems—all are becoming important themes in these countries as they seek to harness human organizations and post-modern technology to build a society capable, increasingly, of making self-conscious choices among carefully envisioned alternative futures. Clearly, all developed societies are endangered by varieties of warfare as well as by the possibility that the pace of change will simply be too swift for them. But there seems a reasonable chance that political development will continue.

Table 5
High and Low Performers: 2000
(U.S. dollars and percentages)

Country	Per capita GNP	% of forecasted GNP per capita, Total Table 1 countries
United States	8,157.947	9.5
U.S.S.R.	14,680.159	17.1
Japan	11,875.024	13.8
West Germany	10,507.964	12.2
France	7,340.864	8.5
Canada	5,847.553	6.8
Total	58,409.511	67.9
India	138.831	0.2
Indonesia	92.501	0.1
Brazil	642.153	0.7
Pakistan	166.175	0.2
Colombia	466.411	0.5
Egypt	355.517	0.4
Argentina	789.306	0.9
Total	2,650.894	3.0
ratio: $\dfrac{\text{total rich}}{\text{total poor}}$	$\dfrac{22.4}{1}$	$\dfrac{22.6}{1}$

It is difficult to conceive of such a thing among the underdeveloped "transient" countries, especially the worst off—those combining low GNP per capita, low resource endowment per capita, and ethnic diversity. If the trends described continue, the "choice" gap will surely widen just as the material gap will. Furthermore, as indicated, a joining of material and political prospectives strongly suggests the emergence of an interlocked downward spiral, with each form of underdevelopment affecting the other in such a way as to make success even less available. In a very real sense, this points to not a breakdown, but a collapse of the modernization process itself for this portion of humanity. Such a vision is closely analagous to what animal psychologists have called a "behavioral sink," a condition in which unusual stresses and crowding brings on multiple forms of social pathology, including most behavior extremes and perversions, along with anarchy.[34]

Overall, it is a profoundly dismal specter; and it is difficult to see how the developed, the semideveloped, and the overdeveloped could realistically expect to avoid being greatly affected by such a "sink," especially since communications media will increasingly allow the inhabitants of each side to watch the other with increasing intimacy. It would, in addition, seem reasonable to expect a variety of forms of international disruption to result from this condition—especially at its edge, where perhaps one-third of the people of the world would find themselves caught between affluence and degradation.

Is there nothing that can be done? What about political alternatives? Clearly there are many kinds of political forms that offer greater possibilities than the "standard run" of transience. The most likely alternatives are authoritarian regimes created by some positive act of will that enables society to break out of the downward spiral. These include "mobilization" or "movement" regimes, which are rapidly becoming a kind of ideal among political scientists concerned with the creation of political competence.[35] They also include varieties of more pluralistic, usually corporatist, authoritarian systems, designed to demobilize the lower classes and control the representation of their interests while assuring political access to functional and associational interests. As yet these have been little analyzed. Totalitarianism also seems a relatively likely result of such "breakaway" movements, a prospect that raises fears about the rise of a generation of atomic age sociopolitical monstrosities of Nazi genre. Indeed, it would be very surprising if these do not appear, since developmental breakdown has been closely associated with the rise of total leaders in the past, and the forces supporting their appearance will likely be at work among the underdeveloped countries of the future.

Foreign or external control, perhaps called "integration" or "free association," and managed by individual or consociated governments, international organizations, or even multinational corporations, also seems a very likely possibility—especially when the costs of transience become particularly high, internally as well as internationally. Indeed, government by contract with a multinational corporation is an option that may soon become possible, especially if the power and complexity of these organizations continues to expand at current rates.[36]

Among the least likely political forms is democracy. One thing that historical studies demonstrate pretty clearly is that the old "route" by which existing democratic polities came into being is likely never again to be available.[37] However, it does seem possible that new routes will come into being—chiefly, it would seem, through the evolution of authoritarian forms.

Other, even less likely alternatives include theocracy, perhaps following the emergence of a new global Messianic religion, founded on eco-system sanctification; cybernocracy, involving cybernated and cyborganic systems in the direct and indirect governance of man—although governance by multinational corporations may well take this form; and varieties of transhuman systems—for example, rule by Neo-man, by drug infusion, and so forth.

To conclude, there really are no likely political forms that are either attractive in terms of our conceptions of welfare, freedom, and justice, or that hold much promise of acquiring the capacity to manage transformation. The enlightenment dream of rational, civil, peaceful politics is probably further from realization for the majority of mankind than it was at the time of Rome's collapse, and it may very well have actually passed beyond the realm of reasonable possibility in any future.

In this essay, I have touched upon two futures: the future of an area of study, and the political future of the living communities that are the objects of that study. The two are intimately connected. Science cannot tell us what is important to know; nor can it motivate us to invest our lives and energies in a search for understanding. Our future images of the future can and must do both.

Notes

1. Gabriel Almond, *Political Development: Essays in Heuristic Theory* (Boston: Little, Brown, 1970), ch. 9.

2. Dankwart Rustow, "Modernization and Comparative Politics: Prospects in Research and Theory," *Comparative Politics* 1, 1 (October, 1968), p. 40. For similar complaints, *see also* J. P. Nettle and Roland Robertson, "Industrialization, Development, and Modernization," *British Journal of Sociology*, 17, pp. 275-91.

3. *See*, for example, Almond, *op. cit.*, and Fred Riggs, "The Dialectic of Developmental Conflict," *Comparative Political Studies*, 1, 2 (July, 1968), pp. 197-226.

4. Dennis Goulet, "Development for What?" *Comparative Political Studies*, 1, 2 (July, 1968), pp. 295-312; and Robert A. Packenham, "Political Development Research," in Michael Haas and Henry S. Kariel (eds.), *Approaches to The Study of Political Science* (Scranton: Chandler, 1970), pp. 169-93.

5. Almond, *op. cit.*, p. 289.

6. There are a few exceptions to this. In *Futuribles*, I, edited by Bertrand de Jouvenel, there are essays on the political futures of Burma and Pakistan, by Edmund Leach and Leicester Webb, respectively (Geneva: Droz, 1963). More limited treatments can be found in Herman Kahn and Anthony Wiener (eds.), *The Year 2000: A Framework for Speculation* (New York: Macmillan, 1967); Zbigniew Brzezinski, *Between Two Ages: America in the Technetronic Era* (New York: Viking Press, 1970), especially ch. 3; Bruce M. Russett, "The Ecology of Future International Politics," in James N. Rosenau (ed.), *International Politics and Foreign Policy*, revised edition (New York: The Free Press, 1969); and Kalman Silvert, "Latin America and Its Alternative Futures," *International Journal*, 24, 3 (Summer, 1969), pp. 403-26.

7. *See*, for example: Harrison Brown, *The Challenge of Man's Future* (New York: Ballantine, 1954); Harrison Brown with James Bonner and John Weir, *The Next Hundred Years* (Pasadena: Cal-Tech, 1967); Kenneth Boulding, "The Economics of the Coming Spaceship Earth," in H. Jarrett (ed.), *Environmental Quality in a Growing Economy* (Washington: Johns Hopkins, 1966).

8. This is often true even where the principal conclusions are obviously suggestive of likely future outcomes, as in the recent work of Samuel P. Huntington, *Political Order in Changing Societies* (New Haven: Yale University Press, 1968), which is richly laden with such ideas.

9. Barrington Moore, Jr., *Social Origins of Dictatorship and Democracy* (Boston: Beacon Press, 1966).

10. *Ibid.*, p. 483.

11. *Ibid.*, p. 499.

12. *Ibid.*, p. 500.

13. Almond, *op. cit.*, p. 282.

14. Including, for example, Huntington, *op. cit.*; Robert Holt and John E. Turner, *The Political Basis of Economic Development* (Princeton: Van Nostrand, 1966); and much of the work published in the Princeton University series on political development.

15. A defense of neglect of the future on these grounds is provided in an epilogue to the Holt and Turner book, *op. cit.*

16. On the relationship of prediction to explanation in the "inexact" sciences, *see* Olaf Helmer and Nicholas Rescher, "On the Epistemology of the Inexact Sciences," *Management Science*, 6, 1 (October, 1959), pp. 25-52.

17. Cited from W. G. Runciman's *Social Science and Political Theory* (Cambridge, England: Cambridge University Press, 1963), p. 174, by Dankwart Rustow in " 'The Organization Triumphs over its Function': Huntington on Modernization," in *Journal of International Affairs* (New York), 23, 1 (January, 1969), p. 123.

18. Almond, *op. cit.*; Huntington, *op. cit.*

19. Goulet, *op. cit.*

20. Goulet, *op. cit.*, p. 307.

21. For an especially clear statement of this, *see* Robert S. Lynd, *Knowledge for What?* (Princeton: Princeton University Press, 1939), ch. 5.

22. *See*, for example, the most recent publications of Almond, Packenham, Riggs, Huntington, Rustow, *op. cit.*, plus Manfred Halpern and David Apter, to name a few of the most influential minds.

23. On the concept of "developmental construct," *see* H. D. Lasswell, *The Analysis of Political Behavior* (New York: Oxford University Press, 1948); and Heinz Eulau, "Harold Lasswell's Developmental Analysis," *Western Political Quarterly* 11 (June, 1958). For Lasswell's most recent version, *see* "The Garrison State Hypothesis Today," in Samuel P. Huntington (ed.), *Changing Patterns of Military Politics* (Glencoe: The Free Press, 1962).

24. This conception of political development is similar in many ways to those of Karl Deutsch, Manfred Halpern, and Amatai Etzioni. Deutsch stresses the role of the polity as "helmsman" involved in control and steering as well as charting the course. See *Politics and Government: How People Decide Their Fate* (New York: Houghton Mifflin, 1970) as well as his earlier *Nerves of Government*. Manfred Halpern stresses continuous capacity to manage change, making it coherent rather than incoherent. *See* "The Revolution of Modernization in National and International Society," in Carl Friedrich (ed.), *Revolution* (New York: Atherton Press, 1966). Etzioni's image of the "active society" is very similar to the ideal expressed here also: "A society that knows itself, is committed to moving toward a fuller realization of its values, that commands the levers such transformation requires, and is able to set limits on its capacity for self-alteration—lest it become self-mutilation. This would be an active society." See *The Active Society* (New York: The Free Press, 1968), p. 16.

25. Gunnar Myrdal, *The Challenge of World Poverty: A World Anti-Poverty Program in Outline* (New York: Random House, 1970), ch. 7, pp. 208-10.

26. Huntington, *Political Order in Changing Societies, op. cit.*, p. 2.

27. *Ibid.*, pp. 196-7.

28. Manfred Halpern, "A Redefinition of the Revolutionary Situation," *Journal of International Affairs*, 23, 1 (January, 1968).

29. Latin American experts have long suspected (feared) that their area might be a trend-setter for other underdeveloped areas, in spite of large cultural differences, and to a certain extent this appears to be happening. Edmund Leach, one of a few futurists who have completed analytical conjectures for individual countries, concluded his study of Burma in this way: "In general I predict a continuation of stagnation in Burma. . . . the dreary pattern

of South American politics will be reproduced in the Burma of the next half-century." *See* Leach, *op. cit.* Also noteworthy: In the last decade, there have been more military coups in Africa than in Latin America. In the next decade, the Middle East may outdo Africa in this respect.

30. Huntington, *Political Order in Changing Societies, op. cit.*, pp. 262-63.

31. William Mangin, "Squatter Settlements," in *Scientific American*, 217, 4 (October, 1967), pp. 21-25.

32. Note that these forecasts indicate a considerably greater failure in performance than the calculations of the other two principal persistence forecasts available, those by Bruce Russett and Herman Kahn and Anthony Wiener. This is primarily because of different years used as base line and to calculate growth rates. *See* Kahn and Wiener (Eds.), *op. cit.*; and Bruce M. Russett, et. al., *World Handbook of Political and Social Indicators* (New Haven: Yale University Press, 1964).

33. Russett, *World Handbook, op. cit.*, pp. 294, 299.

34. *See* John B. Calhoun, "Population Density and Social Pathology," *Scientific American*, 206, 3 (February, 1962), pp. 139-50.

35. For an excellent collection of studies of these regimes, *see* Clement Moore, Jr., and Samuel P. Huntington (eds.), *Authoritarian Politics in Modern Society: The Dynamics of Established One-Party Systems* (New York: Basic Books, 1970).

36. *See* Charles Kindleberger (ed.), *The International Corporation* (Cambridge: M.I.T. Press, 1970).

37. *See* Barrington Moore, Jr., *op. cit.;* plus Dankwart Rustow, "Transitions to Democracy: Toward a Dynamic Model," a paper presented at the APSA meeting, September, 1969.

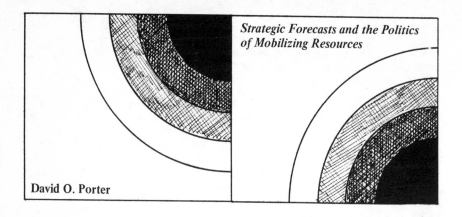

Strategic Forecasts and the Politics of Mobilizing Resources

David O. Porter

A forecast of the future can be both an exercise in objective techniques and an instrument of political strategy. Technical forecasts speculate on the future course of such things as the present (and foreseeable) trends in human values, technologies, and social structures. These forecasts are often prepared in the "long range" planning divisions of corporations or governments. The overriding concern is the accuracy of the forecasts; relatively little attention is given to interpreting the social or political implications of the trends they project.

The more politically oriented prophecies, which we shall call strategic forecasts, are made by actors more interested in controlling or shaping the future than in devising methodologies to predict it accurately. Their forecasts are not the value-free projections of a planner; rather, they are political instruments designed to assist them in the mobilization of the resources necessary to fulfill their prophecies. The practitioners of these strategic forecasts include a rather disparate collection of actors, ranging from humanists predicating the possibilities of utopia to the crassest of interest group partisans—each with a vision of the future they would like to bring to pass.

This paper will discuss some of the characteristics of strategic forecasts, when they can be realistically used, and by whom such forecasts can be effectively made.

Characteristics of Strategic Forecasts

A strategic forecast does more than coldly predict some future state. There is a motive behind such forecasts. But regardless of the character of the motive, the resources mobilized through the forecast make some things possible that otherwise would not occur. Herman Kahn makes this point well as he looks back to the military budgets of the 1950's:

The authorization to increase the defense budget enormously in June 1950 completely changed the technological picture. Without it people would have been saying throughout the 1950's that such weapons systems as the B-52 and Minuteman were "technologically infeasible." So they are if the budget is $15 *billion a year. But they are by no means technologically infeasible if the budget is increased by a factor of five. In the conditions of the year 2000 things may be no different. A budget increase by a factor of five makes a great many things techologically feasible.*[1]

The forecasts that military leaders made during this period had a substantial effect on the size of their budgets. Proponents of higher defense budgets still look back on the period from 1950-1965 with nostalgia. During that period, the American public generally accepted a view of the future (propounded by defense "planners") which portrayed the U.S.S.R. as an evil power, doing everything within its capacity to overtake the U.S. in military technology. Once this objective was achieved, it would then rain down death and destruction upon our population until we submitted to its despotic rule. The only way to prevent this feared scenario from being fulfilled, so the military asserted, was to spend billions on the development and deployment of weapons. This view of the future is no longer unchallenged, and the consequences of this change in belief about the future have drastically altered the size of the defense budget. In 1971, *The Wall Street Journal* reported that:

Many West Coast economists who have studied the industry say it would be folly for the aerospace companies to assume any return to the spending of the mid-1960s. Walter Hoadley, chief economist for Bank of America, says only events posing "a personal threat" to Americans, such as Russia's launching of Sputnik or the Cuban missile crisis, could create a defense-spending situation equal to the 60's.

Possible crises, however, are "a weak reed to base hopes on," says Wells Fargo Bank's Mr. [Harold] Buma.[2]

The editorial writers of *The Washington Post*, although conceding the possibility of the dread course of events outlined above, doubt its probability. This doubt about the military's forecasts leads the writers to look for other responses and alternatives which they think may move the world away from another round in the arms race. They offer the counter-prediction that a new round in the arms race may increase the likelihood of the dread scenario being fulfilled.[3]

This brings us to an important point in terms of understanding the nature of a strategic forecast. Since the future does not exist objectively, it can be manipulated to suit the purposes of a strategic forecaster. In his classic essay on self-fulfilling prophecies, Robert K. Merton makes it very clear that in thinking of a future event, "men respond not only to the objective features of a situation, but also, and at times primarily, to the meaning this situation has for them."[4] From a different perspective, Alberto Guerreiro-Ramos says essentially the same thing: "No course of events can be viewed as resulting from the interplay of absolutely necessary causes. The course of events results continuously from the interplay of objective factors and human choices."[5]

There is an interplay between what is objectively possible and what the human will decides in choosing among many feasible courses of action. The initial prophecy may rest on specious arguments, but the belief in these arguments evokes "a new behavior which makes the originally false conception come *true*. The specious validity of the self-fulfilling prophecy perpetuates a reign of error. For the prophet will cite the actual course of events as proof that he was right from the very beginning."[6] In the military example above, the belief in the intentions of the Soviets strongly encouraged a response on their part which verified the initial American forecasts. In such a situation, their "true" motives would be impossible to discover.

More generally, it should be emphasized that a strategic forecast need not be scientifically or methodologically valid. Its proponents are using the forecast to mobilize resources, and will attempt to orchestrate a course of events which will verify their assertions. This course of events is in no way inevitable, as may be implied (or stated) in the forecast; it is simply one of many possibilities. Thus, strategic forecasts are not made in a social vacuum. Such prophecies do not fulfill themselves. Their purpose is to help mobilize the resources needed to achieve the desired outcome.

Two other lines of analysis help clarify the character of strategic forecasts. The first relates to the more general debate over synoptic and incremental planning. Many planners, forecasters, and social theorists are accused of adopting a synoptic or comprehensive view of the future. In such a view, the "present's direction is inexorably determined, and we must make an effort to know it exhaustively. We fail to acquire a comprehensiveness of the present only because our intelligence is obscured by interest, prejudices, and distortions. . . . A powerful mind as a faithful mirror can have an exact picture of reality."[7] Some variations on this extreme characterization are more subtle. The synoptic analyst may realize that he cannot understand all of the significant variables without some aids to his calculations; but with the help of such devices as a computer, he can understand much more. Further, this view tries to treat the future as a relatively closed system. An effort is made to find a few significant determinants from which the analyst can predict the directions in which the society may be moving. If the right determinants can be found, then the analyst can create a clear map of the future by projecting the trends in these determinants.

On the other hand, the incrementalist approach assumes a more limited capacity on the part of the actors in understanding social futures, and puts less faith in projections based primarily on objective determinants. Incrementalists assume "that there are no absolutely necessary causes and that human choices are always in interplay with objective factors to produce events. . . ."[8] Thus, even in the short run, no one can predict the exact course of events. Instead, a course is arrived at through a process of trial and error, a partial satisfaction of a variety of interests, a partial fulfillment of several plans that were all objectively possible. This view is fairly widely accepted as an accurate description of social and political activity in the United States.[9]

The second set of ideas relates to the objective possibilities of *what* is being forecast. All forecasts are dependent on the level of technical knowledge (whether physical, natural, or social science technologies) available to fulfill the prediction. Regardless of the political power or determination of a strategic forecaster, he cannot bring about something that is impossible. "Predictions of Halley's comet do not influence its orbit."[10] True, as Herman Kahn noted, significant increases in resources and effort can speed up the development of technologies in selected areas and make things possible which formerly were not. But many problems are so complex, and research on them in such a primitive state, that more resources can only result in incremental gains. In large-scale societal predictions, such as ending crime in the streets or making our larger cities into lovely, humanistic communities, the likelihood of having (or soon developing) an adequate technical knowledge to accomplish such forecasts is relatively remote.[11]

Many people make strategic forecasts, but most of them are never fulfilled. The balance of the paper will suggest some lines of analysis which may assist in determining who is more likely to make effective strategic forecasts.

Forecasts and Power

Bringing a strategic forecast to pass is an exercise of power. The future does not exist objectively, unalterable or discoverable through careful techniques of prediction. The future is shaped from many alternatives. The alternative which becomes "the present" is a combination of objective possibilities, chance, and social power. Objective possibilities can be explored through research and conventional planning techniques; and some rather sophisticated techniques have been developed for coping with the contingencies of chance. But social power has been more resistant to systematic analysis.

Power has been an elusive concept for social scientists even to define. However, there seems to be some consensus on the elements that are important to the arguments presented in this paper. Power is rather generally conceived of as the ability to affect the outcome of social activities. Marvin E. Olsen lists two elements in his definition: (1) power is a rather broad and general phenomenon, and (2) there is always resistance to its exercise. "Reference to resistance does remind us that the exercise of power is usually a reciprocal process among all participants, and is rarely determined by a single actor no matter how unequal the situation may appear."[12] De Jouvenel adds an important point relative to power and strategic forecasts. Each actor has a differential ability to handle a situation or to control a certain course of events. "In human affairs the future is often dominating as far as I am concerned, but masterable by a more powerful agent, an agent from a different level."[13]

In exercising power and overcoming resistance to its exercise, writers have generally agreed that two factors—the mobilization of resources and social organization of some sort—are critical elements.[14] These are the two factors focused on in the balance of this paper. It is suggested that as a society becomes increasingly reliant on complicated technologies, these two factors may be even more important in the exercise of power as it relates to shaping the future.

Forecasts in Technological Societies

De Jouvenel argues that tradition and custom in societies governed by old and established social relationships are good methods to predict the future. Simply follow the tried and proven methods. Age and inherited position become credentials for making strategic forecasts and for enforcing these forecasts within the limits of objective possibilities. Max Weber wrote that in some societies authority based on tradition or charisma may have been sufficient to provide the power to accomplish the ends of the possessors.[15] Weber foresaw an increasingly "rational" society where formal, legal organizations would be needed to cope with its complex problems. This seemed particularly appropriate in the industrializing societies Weber was observing. Perhaps more fluid, and less formal organizations will be necessary as we move into a highly technological post-industrial society. More will be said on this topic later.

But even in such rapidly changing societies, there are regularities that keep appearing. Two of the salient characteristics of modern society are (1) an increasingly complicated and changing technological base and (2) an increasing number of complex and large organizations. A larger proportion of these organizations is moving away from the conventional bureaucratic pattern, and resembles what Toffler has labeled "ad-hocracy."[16] In such organizations, knowledge and professionalism are playing a greater role in decision-making, often at the expense of the holders of formal titles or positions in a hierarchy. However, even though bureaucratic organizations are not as widely used or as effective as in the past, careful organization is needed to coordinate the technologies and large populations of modern society. If a person or coalition hopes to influence or exercise power over the future in such a society, they must operate within a base that is capable of mobilizing and coordinating technological and human resources.

Competition Among Organizations

Some quick generalizations can be made, based on earlier discussion. If your forecast requires substantial human and material resources and involves a fairly complex technology, you must be located in a country or society which has substantial resources, social organizations capable of handling the coordination requirements of the technologies involved, and a reservoir of technical knowledge. Further, the forecaster is more effective if he belongs to an organization which commands a large share of these resources. The competition for resources among groups, organizations, and even networks of organizations will directly influence the objective possibilities open to a particular forecaster. He will, to use de Jouvenel's categories, have more opportunities to master a situation, rather than be dominated, if he is part of a highly developed organization within a highly developed society.

Many writers have observed that some organizations are able to mobilize more resources than others. C. Wright Mills argued that economic, political, and military organizations were able to mobilize most of the resources in the United States during the 1950's. In *The Power Elite*, he wrote:

Within American society, major national power now resides in the economic, the political and the military domains. Other institutions seem off to the side of modern history, and, on occasion, duly subordinated to these. . . .

Families and churches and schools adapt to modern life; governments and armies and corporations shape it. . . . And the symbols of all these lesser institutions are used to legitimate the power and the decisions of the big three. [17]

Along the same line, de Jouvenel observed that the organizations which control the allocation of research and development funds in an advanced country such as the United States will control the major allocations of resources in the future. He lamented that four-fifths (or more) of the Research and Development funds in the United States are used for military or related purposes. [18]

Mills identified the categories of organizations which did best in the 1950's. But later writers have suggested a different set of organizations, using different bases of power, which may do better in mobilizing resources in the 1960's and 1970's. Daniel Bell[19] and John Kenneth Galbraith,[20] for instance, have suggested that certain technocratic professionals and the institutions with which they are associated—*i.e.*, universities and consulting firms—are gaining control over ever greater shares of available resources. In a similar argument, James D. Carroll suggests that:

The central economic roles of land in a feudal society and of machinery and technological processes in an industrial society are filled by knowledge in a noetic society. This century the pursuit of knowledge has become the pursuit of wealth, and the pursuit of wealth has become the pursuit of knowledge. . . .

In a sense he who will control the schools and the universities will control the world. [21]

In summary, the success of a strategic forecaster may depend in large part on the nation and the organization to which he belongs. Some types of organizations are able to mobilize more effectively than others, and are thus in a better position to make effective strategic forecasts.

Competition Within Organizations

There are a number of factors from within an organization which influence whether a forecaster will be able to mobilize the resources that he needs to fulfill his prophecies. There is, for example, an obvious difference between John F. Kennedy predicting that the United States would reach the moon before 1970 and a scientist competent in space technology making the same prediction. They speak from different vantage points in the government. Persons higher in the formal hierarchy have, but with a growing number of exceptions, been able to influence more futures than those in lower positions. In some circumstances, the technical expert may be able to mobilize sufficient resources to fulfill some of his prophecies, or at least to frustrate the prophecies of others who may be his "superiors" in the formal sense. Albert Speer, for example, was able to undermine some of Hitler's orders to destroy German bridges, roads, and industry as the Allies advanced into Germany in 1945, even though he was unable to persuade the German leadership to end the war. [22]

The factors which affect the mobilization of resources within organizations are becoming more complex and more difficult to understand as organizational tasks become less routine and less subject to simple divisions of labor. Following James D. Thompson, this paper will deal with these factors under three broad headings: intraorganizational concerns, technology, and environment. [23]

Talcott Parsons took the concept of hierarchy as outlined in Weber's ideal type of bureaucracy beyond the simple notion of a single chain of command and simple divisions of labor. He identified three levels of suborganization—institutional, managerial, and technical—within any organization. [24] These refinements, and some further work by Thompson, [25] expand the concepts of social organizations so they can deal more effectively with the very complex and rapidly changing organizations characteristic of post-industrial societies.

The separations between suborganizational levels are qualitatively different from simple hierarchies. There is a two-way interaction between these levels, with each level having the power to interfere with the functioning of the other two. Each level has rather distinct patterns of relating to the organization's environment, distinct patterns of mobilizing resources, and distinct types of personnel.

The institutional level is the most open to influence from within and outside the organization. It legitimizes the goals and outputs of the organization within the context of the community or society. Examples are corporate boards of directors or school boards (but institutional functions are not restricted to such boards). Interactions with the environment, such as input acquisition or output disposal, are extensive and boundary-spanning considerations, and are dealt with in relatively broad terms. Emphasis is on a long-range perspective, flexibility, and the examination of the underlying assumptions behind specific proposals.

The managerial level serves a mediating role between the institutional and technical levels. Managers adjust and supplement the inputs provided by the institutional level to the more specific needs of the technical level. Discretion in the selection of alternative sources of input or alternative courses of action tends to be rather restricted. At the institutional level, discretion is much broader, as it can shift the basic goals and values sought. Both the managerial and institutional levels shield the technical level (or operating "core") from most of the contingencies and constraints of the environment, provide it with a stream of inputs, and dispose of outputs.

The technical level most nearly approximates a "closed" system. There is less uncertainty, and the interrelationships of fewer variables are (relatively) better understood than at the other two levels. There is a strong product or output orientation at this level; most mobilizing efforts are incremental and intraorganizational. Supplies and the choice of techniques are usually provided by the managerial level. Boundary-spanning activity is restricted to interdepartmental linkages. Time considerations are relatively short-run, and variables in the system are less numerous than at higher suborganizational levels. The primary concern at the technical level is in solving the problems of coordination posed by the basic types of technology used in the organization.

The broadest strategic forecasts, in terms of societal impact, are made by persons at the institutional levels of organizations. It is here that large organizations, or clusters of organizations, are persuaded to change their direction or maintain a basic status quo, or that decisions are made to commit large quantities of resources to research and development. These are sometimes changes in the basic values of the organization. It is only at the institutional level that there is a regular scanning of the horizons for future courses of action, or that a sufficiently long-range perspective can be consistently pursued. Some of this scanning is done by conventional planners, but its implementation usually requires a commitment of basic political capital to make effective strategic forecasts (and not simply "plans" that are duly accepted and filed). In a highly technological society such as the United States, these long-range perspectives are required to effect substantial shifts in present trends.

Some changes at institutional levels almost seem to fall outside the context of any organization. Ideas for change filter into organizations from many directions, particularly from the professionals working as staff to the institutional and managerial levels of the organization. Thompson argues that judgments at the institutional level are based on rather indefinite criteria—i.e., primarily by referring to "images" of the fitness of an organization for future action and effectiveness.[26] In this context, more than many others, it is not simply the organizational position of the forecaster, but the persuasiveness of his argument and the organizational position of the "ear" he can reach that are critical in determining the fate of his forecast. Even though staff professionals may not have formal power, they exercise considerable informal influence.

Successful strategic forecasts at the managerial and technical levels are distinguished from those made at the institutional level mainly by their scope and specificity. Fewer future alternatives are masterable and more are dominating, especially in organizations involved in routine, repetitive tasks. The time considerations are shorter, and any strategic forecasts are much more specific and detailed, matching the more specific and detailed knowledge of people working at these levels. Also, managers and technocrats often assist those at the institutional level in fulfilling their strategic forecasts.

However, (1) the character of the technology used in an organization, (2) the character of its environment, and (3) the development of professionalism are having a profound influence on the ability of actors at any level of organizations to make strategic forecasts. In routine technical processes, the inputs and outputs are highly standardized and the technology relatively well developed. Basic changes in the processes can be made only through shifts in the entire process. Persons at the managerial or technical level may be the only ones technically competent to suggest changes, but it is at the institutional level that decisions can be made to abandon large capital plants and undertake massive new investments. A classic example may be found in the transportation industry. The need for alternatives to the internal combustion engine is almost undisputed. But even if a substantial number of General Motors personnel at the technical level began to make strategic forecasts about a shift to some alternative power plant for automobiles (which they are not), their forecasts would be empty without the active backing of the institutional level. No manager or technician at GM controls enough resources to fulfill his prediction.

Power is more decentralized in custom or intensive technologies. Actors at all levels of organizations have a greater opportunity for independent action, and therefore a better chance for gathering the resources they need to make effective strategic forecasts. Even so, such predictions will be of relatively small scale, since the independent professional has very limited resources. If he is working within a large organization, he is constrained by the interests of other professionals, managers, and workmen. Further, organizations utilizing intensive technologies are usually much smaller than those using simpler technologies, because the complexity of their technology limits the number of units that can be effectively managed.

High rates of change in technologies create opportunities to make strategic forecasts. A classic example is in the field of mental health. As research improves the knowledge about therapeutic techniques, the custodial function of mental institutions is challenged. Although all institutions have not adopted therapeutic orientations, the possibility is open to them. In technologies associated with more routine processes, a changing technology may provide a framework for such organizations to change to different or more capital intensive processes. Changes in product, services provided, or technique can be made as an organization abandons an outdated technology.

Thompson deals with the environment of organizations along two dimensions.[27] Environments are homogeneous or heterogeneous, and stable or shifting. Thompson suggests that these dimensions will shape the structure of organizations. This paper suggests that they will also influence the ability of actors to make strategic forecasts. For example, in a homogeneous and stable environment, the organization will be able to deal with its environment in a routine manner. Such situations will be characterized by rather highly centralized firms and agencies. Persons at the managerial and technical levels of the organization will not be in a position to influence significantly the activities of the organization. Any large scale strategic forecasts within organizations of this type will come from the upper reaches of the organizational hierarchy.

But, as Bennis and Toffler have emphatically stated, the environments of organizations are becoming proportionately more heterogeneous and shifting. "Adaptive, problem-solving, temporary systems of diverse specialists, linked together by coordinating executives in an organic flux—this is the organizational form that will gradually replace bureaucracy."[28] These specialists tend to work in decentralized components of larger organizations, and exercise considerable discretion. Often, actors operating within boundary-spanning units of such organizations have substantial power relative to the rest of the organization, especially if the resources they control are scarce. They may be able to back up their strategic forecasts with resources that they are able to mobilize directly from the environment, without sanction of, or interference from, actors who may hold more formal authority.

Perhaps a more significant factor in modifying the influence formal hierarchies have on the course of events within organizations is the growth of professionalism and the specialization of knowledge. An increasing number of writers are predicting an end to bureaucracy. Weber, writing in the first third of the twentieth century, saw a trend toward rational, hierarchically dominated organizations. Collegial types of leadership and administration would take on a lesser role. Only through monocratic leadership and bureaucracy could "large-scale tasks which require quick and consistent solutions" be effectively carried out.[29] It was because of the need for such decisions that "the general tendency of monocracy, and hence, bureaucracy, in the organization has become definitely victorious."[30]

Bennis, looking at organizations in the last third of the twentieth century, sees a reversal of this trend toward monocratic bureaucracy. For him, bureaucracy is a form of social organization ill-suited and inappropriate to our age of change, growth, complexity, and changing values.[31] Professionals and specialists are increasingly influential in organizations. Tasks are less routine, less repetitive, more complex, and more customized to each situation. Loyalty to the organization "appears to be going up in smoke. In its place we are watching the rise of professional loyalty."[32] Professionals move frequently from project to project, organization to organization, working in *ad hoc* teams to solve novel problems. In such circumstances, "even professional loyalties turn into short term commitments."[33]

In these kinds of "nonroutine" organizations, workers are harder to control. They have independent bases of power rooted in their professions and in the esoteric bodies of knowledge they master. It is easier for them to pursue some professional goal which may or may not be in agreement with the goals of their host organization, or they may choose to satisfy their own needs rather than the narrower, technically rational objectives of their employer.[34]

Collegial forms of administration, instead of dying out as Weber thought, are becoming more prevalent. Bennis called these bodies executive constellations;[35] Bertram M. Gross labeled them control guidance clusters.[36] They allow the expression of many different values, and the pooling of several professional specialties in the accomplishment of highly complicated and novel tasks.[37] No one person or organization can claim credit for the completion of a program; it is too decentralized. A good example of such an activity was the moon-landing program. Hundreds of firms and government agencies participated, but none can claim to have played the dominant role in producing a system capable of putting a man on the moon.

In such processes, professionals are able to make major policy decisions, largely unrestricted by the formal power of superiors whose base of authority rests only in their hierarchical position. Professionals are able to seek their own fortunes much more openly and with greater ease. Further, this feeling of freedom, based on independent knowledge and buttressed by the development of unemployment and old-age insurance, is spreading throughout the entire society. The impact of these developments, as it relates to the question of who will be able to make effective strategic forecasts, is hard to evaluate with any precision; but certainly these are factors that will have to be considered as the trends become clearer.

Concluding Statements

We have attempted to define strategic forecasts and suggest how and by whom they may be used. Only a few of the obvious factors affecting strategic forecasts have been covered. Many have not even been mentioned.

We have found that there are almost an infinite number of social futures. Strategic forecasts are made in an effort to bring about one particular course of events among the many possible.

There are several implications for the study of politics and the future in this paper:

First, it provides some tentative guides for understanding and evaluating strategic forecasts.

Second, it reminds us that forecasts are usually loaded with the values of the forecaster. Often, the very act of making the forecast is an effort to begin mobilizing the resources needed to make the prophecy self-fulfilling.

Third, it gives us a few insights into the subtle influences of professionalism and technology on our futures. As the professions become more organized and their jargons more esoteric, and as technologies become more complex, the power to make effective strategic forecasts may be redistributed. To date, this shift in relative power is not fully accomplished, as there has not yet been a complete shift of power from one group to another. The top managers, who are not highly trained (or at least currently trained) in a profession or a technology, still govern many of the decisions regarding even research and development.[38]

Finally, the paper suggests that we may need to know more about how individuals, organizations, and societies interact and organize before we can make plausible predictions. Social structure, power, and strategic forecasts are all interrelated and jointly have an important impact on the shape of the future.

Notes

1. Herman Kahn, "The Military," in Harvey Perloff (ed.), *The Future of the United States Government: Toward the Year 2000* (New York: George Braziller, 1971), p. 204.

2. William McAllister, "Aerospace Crisis: Defense Firms Find It Isn't Easy To Switch to Peacetime Work," *The Wall Street Journal*, Pacific Coast Edition (February 25, 1971), p. 1.

3. "Strategic Arms: The Heart of the Issue," *The Washington Post* (August 14, 1972), p. A20.

4. Robert K. Merton, "The Self-Fulfilling Prophecy," in Alvar O. Elbing (ed.), *Be-*

havioral Decisions in Organizations (Glenview: Scott, Foresman, 1970), pp. 642-43. This essay originally appeared in Merton's *Social Theory and Social Structure* (New York: The Free Press, 1949).

5. Alberto Guerreiro-Ramos, "Modernization: Towards a Possibility Model," in Willard A. Beling and George O. Totten (eds.), *Developing Nations: A Quest for a Model* (New York: Van Nostrand Reinhold, 1971), p. 37.

6. Merton, *op. cit*, p. 644. (Italics in original.)

7. Guerreiro-Ramos, *op. cit*, p. 47.

8. *Ibid.*, pp. 47-48.

9. *See* David Braybrooke and Charles E. Lindblom, *A Strategy of Decision* (New York: The Free Press, 1963); Robert A. Dahl, *Who Governs?* (New Haven: Yale University Press, 1961); Amitai Etzioni, "Mixed Scanning: A 'Third' Approach to Decision-Making," *Public Administration Review*, XXVII (1967), pp. 385-92; Charles E. Lindblom, *The Intelligence of Democracy* (New York: Macmillan, 1965).

10. Merton, *op. cit*, p. 644.

11. Bertrand de Jouvenel, *The Art of Conjecture*, translated by Nikita Lary (New York: Basic Books, 1967), p. 55; James D. Thompson, *Organizations in Action* (New York: McGraw-Hill, 1967), pp. 83-98.

12. Marvin E. Olsen, "Power as a Social Process," in Marvin E. Olsen (ed.), *Power in Societies* (New York: Macmillan, 1970), p. 3.

13. de Jouvenel, *op. cit.*, p. 52.

14. Olsen, *op. cit*, pp. 4-6; Amos H. Hawley, "Power as an Attribute of Social Systems," in Olsen (ed.), *op. cit.,* p. 11; and Robert Bierstedt, "An Analysis of Social Power," *ibid.*, p. 17.

15. Max Weber, *The Theory of Social and Economic Organizations*, translated by A. M. Henderson and Talcott Parsons (New York: The Free Press, 1964), pp. 324-63.

16. Alvin Toffler, *Future Shock* (New York: Bantam Books, 1971), pp. 124-51.

17. C. Wright Mills, *The Power Elite* (New York: Oxford University Press, 1959), p. 6.

18. Bertrand de Jouvenel, "Technology as a Means," in Kurt Baier and Nicholas Rescher (eds.), *Values and the Future* (New York: The Free Press, 1969), pp. 225, 230.

19. Daniel Bell, "The Post-Industrial Society," in Eli Ginzberg (ed.), *Technology and Social Change* (New York: Columbia University Press, 1964), pp. 44-59.

20. John Kenneth Galbraith, "Technology, Planning and Organizations," in Baier and Rescher (eds.), *op. cit.*, pp. 353-67.

21. James D. Carroll, "Noetic Authority," *Public Administration Review*, XXIX (1969), p. 495.

22. Albert Speer, *Inside the Third Reich: Memoirs by Albert Speer*, translated by Richard and Clara Winston (New York: Macmillan, 1970), pp. 433-43.

23. *See* Thompson, *op. cit.*

24. Talcott Parsons, *Structure and Process in Modern Society* (Glencoe: The Free Press, 1960), pp. 66-67.

25. Thompson, *op. cit.*, pp. 3-13.

26. *Ibid.*, pp. 88-93.

27. *Ibid.*, pp. 70-73.

28. Warren G. Bennis, "Post-Bureaucratic Leadership," *Trans-action*, 6 (1969), p. 45.

29. Weber, *op. cit.*, p. 399.

30. *Ibid.*, p. 403.

31. Bennis, *op. cit.*, pp. 44-45.

32. Toffler, *op. cit.*, p. 146.

33. *Ibid.*, p. 148.

34. Guerreiro-Ramos, *op. cit.*, p. 245.

35. Bennis, *op. cit.*, p. 47.

36. Bertram M. Gross, "The State of the Nation: Social Systems Accounting," in Raymond A. Bauer (ed.), *Social Indicators* (Cambridge: M.I.T. Press, 1966), pp. 208-11.

37. Carroll, *op. cit.*, p. 497.

38. Bela Gold. "The Framework of Decision for Major Technological Innovations," in Baier and Rescher (eds.), *op. cit.*, p. 408.

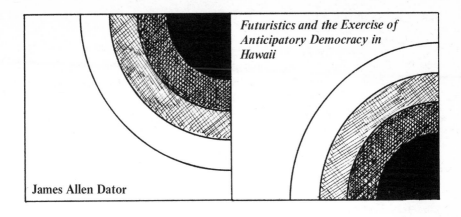

Futuristics and the Exercise of Anticipatory Democracy in Hawaii

James Allen Dator

The State of Hawaii, through activities first authorized by the State Legislature in 1969, is attempting to do what no other political entity has done in quite the same way: to get a running start on its future; to determine and discuss the likely consequences of unanticipated movement into the future, and then to develop and design a "better" future for the state. The current target date for these "futuristic" activites is the popular "Year 2000." But what may set Hawaii apart from other political or private groups attempting to study and invent their future is the somewhat more "grass roots" approach which Hawaii has taken.

In 1969, the State Legislature authorized the convening of a Governor's Conference on Hawaii 2000, and appropriated a modest sum of money for the planning and execution of that Conference. In the fall of the same year, a broadly representative group of twenty Hawaiian citizens was appointed to an advisory committee by Governor John A. Burns, with George Chaplin, editor of the Honolulu *Advertiser*, as chairman of the committee. Subsequent organization within the group resulted in Floyd Matson, of the Department of American Studies at the University of Hawaii, being placed in charge of interim activities (held between January 1970 and the Conference in August of the same year); Glenn Paige, Professor in the Department of Political Science of the University of Hawaii, being made program chairman for the Conference itself; and Anne King, prominent in Hawaiian social and cultural life, and wife of former State judge and Republican candidate for governor, Sam King, being appointed Conference arrangements chairman.

In spite of the literary/academic orientation of this leadership, many of the other members of the advisory committee were people who were representative of the major economic, ethnic, and regional groupings of the State. Care was also taken to see that women and young people of both college and high school age were full participants in planning for and carrying out the Conference.

From the very first meeting, the advisory committee was deeply committed to the idea of participatory futuristics, or "anticipatory democracy," in Alvin Toffler's words.[1] Keiji Kawakami, President of Iolani Sportswear in Honolulu, made an eloquent plea at the first general meeting of the advisory committee for keeping in close and constant touch with the dreams and fears about the future which the ordinary citizens of Hawaii possessed. He expressed special concern that the Conference might become a sterile intellectual and elitist exercise, divorced from the real interests and perceptions of the people. Although everyone on the committee shared Mr. Kawakami's concern, he was constant in his reiteration of this point in all that followed.

The details of the organization of the interim period and the Conference itself have been described partially and in detail elsewhere.[2] I do not wish to summarize them here again. However, I did have the privilege of serving as general consultant to the advisory committee; and, in this role, I had the opportunity of discussing my notions of futuristics with most of the varied participants in the Conference activities. The remainder of this paper, then, is a summary of the general notions of futuristics which I expressed during the planning period, and an elaboration of the basic idea of socio-political value formation and change which underlay the orientation and actions I suggested.

The Scope of Futuristics

The statement of the scope of futuristics which I proposed and subsequently will elaborate on here is as follows: "Futuristics is the study, forecasting, design, and realization of alternative social values, institutions, and organizations for immediate, intermediate, and distant futures."[3] Let me comment on the components of this statement.

A. Futures, in the first instance, are appropriate areas for study. If the past merits study as "history," then futures deserve study as "futuristics." If it be objected that futures cannot be studied because they cannot be analyzed scientifically—that statements about specific futures cannot be tested empirically—then the same must certainly be said of the past. Indeed, given the limitation of our current inability to reverse time, it might be argued that the study of futures is more justified than the study of the past, because claims about futures can be tested when a specific future becomes the present, while many claims about the past can never be validated.

Of course, I am not arguing against history. To the contrary, the study of the past, whether through the academic discipline called "history," or through anthropology, archeology, biology (evolution), or any other such area, is a very necessary component for futuristics itself for two broad reasons: (1) One of the plainest lessons of these studies of the past is that, in order to survive, organisms and societies must in some way adapt to their environment. "Adapt or die" seems to be a clear message of history, in this sense. The organisms or societies which fail to adapt to a changed environment are the very ones which become extinct. Those which adapt survive, though perhaps in modified form or behavior. (2) It is also clear that there is an enormous variety of appropriate adaptive responses. "Nature" has not responded in just one way to the possibility of life. On the contrary, the response is varied in the extreme. Thus, a claim that any particular adaptive social mechanism or social value is required because it is "natural" or "in accord with human nature" can be put to rest.[4]

However, the study both of the past and of the futures is justified for yet another very important reason—*i.e.*, because our *images* of what we have been and what we are likely to become are vital determinants of what we *do* in the present. If we shrink in fear of the future, we are likely to act—or fail to act— in such a way in the present that the feared future will actually materialize. If, however, we look forward to the future positively, optimistically, we may act now in such a way that the anticipated "bright" future will actually appear.

Unfortunately, while everyone probably has some image of his, and society's, future, few people have examined their images systematically. Until recently, there have been no classes in school where students' images of futures were analyzed and discussed.[5] Orientations toward futures typically are not examined in schools and universities, though orientations toward the past have long been a vital ingredient of most curricula.

Futuristics, at this first level, then, tries to correct this lack by incorporating the study of futures into formal academic situations, as well as into other broad socialization experiences in our society.

Secondly, futuristics is concerned with *forecasting* or predicting futures. To some extent, futures are seen as being "out there," to be predicted by appropriate statistical techniques. Thus, futuristics is concerned with developing methods for predicting complex personal and social situations with at least the accuracy with which physical scientists can predict physical phenomena. No claim is being made, however, that futuristics is capable at the present time of such predictive sophistication, nor am I maintaining that the techniques of the physical sciences are necessarily the ones most—or least—appropriate for futuristics.[6] But clearly the assumption of the type of futuristics being described here is that some relevant future social events are in principle susceptible of scientific prediction, and that futurists should be concerned with generating the desired techniques.

But futuristics is emphatically concerned with more than passively predicting the future. In this formulation, futuristics is also involved with actually designing or, in Dennis Gabor's fine phrase, "inventing" futures.

Futuristics recognizes that, as Robert Kennedy said, "Our future may lie beyond our vision, but it is not completely beyond our control." The assumption is clearly made that man can determine his own future in more or less specific detail, and that, rather than simply forecasting what will probably happen, he should design and, if possible, *realize* "desired" futures.

Thus, in its final stage, futuristics is action-oriented. It is deeply concerned about the present and wants to "improve" it. But in order to determine what to change and how to change it, the futurist insists that it is necessary to be as clear as possible about the future consequences of current activities. Perceiving that a considerable portion of the "mess" of the present is due to unwary modification of a more or less balanced past social *system*, the futurist cautions against further modifications until a desired future system has been determined and priorities for present action specified.

This does not mean that the futurist counsels maintenance of the status quo.

To the contrary, as will become clear shortly, the particular futuristics I am describing works for massive changes in the current social structure and behavior. It is simply that we wish to avoid further unnecessary disruption and unintended agonies caused by uncoordinated, unsystemic, and undemocratic action.[7]

In addition, it seems that another substantial element in the "mess" of the present is the continuation of obsolete adaptive functions that are now relatively inadequate. As John McHale says, "The constraining myths that bind us to obsolete forms, old fears, and insecurities may be our most dangerous deterrents. Our traditional attitudes and ideologies are inadequate guides to the future, serving mainly to perpetuate old inequities and insecurities. . . . We have few guides to follow and almost no usable precedents. 'Many of the old moralities have suddenly become immoralities of the most devastating character.' "[8]

An important implication of this contention is that, as a strategy for obtaining rapid and effective social change, it is advisable to avoid looking for people to "blame" for the inadequacies of the present. It is not the "capitalists," or the "hippies," or the "communists," or "outside agitators," or any other evil group which is to blame for our unsettled and unsettling society. Rather, it is in large measure the lingering inadequacies of our dominant but obsolete social attitudes and institutions. These attitudes and institutions linger not primarily because evil people perpetuate and profit from them—though some may—but because, while rapid social change is a relatively new phenomena, most social institutions and values were intended for what was considered to be a stable and essentially unchanging environment. At the present time—and for the foreseeable future—however, our environment will almost certainly continue to alter rapidly. Thus, the tension between our social institutions and attitudes posited on the normalcy of social stability, on the one hand, and the fact of continuing and accelerating environmental change, on the other, indicates that it is to the advantage of almost everyone for this tension to be reduced. If it cannot be reduced by ending the factors behind social change and returning to a stable condition (and I believe it cannot), then new social attitudes and institutions should be devised which will enable mankind to cope with flux as the new normalcy.

Hence, developing ways to cope with rapid social change is to almost everybody's advantage; and, in contrast with earlier reforms where one group's gain might result in another's loss, virtually everyone can be enhanced now by adequately planned and democratically determined changed attitudes and institutions. Scapegoating is then out of the question. The motherfuckers can be unchained from the walls.

B. The futuristic perspective being presented here suggests the desirability of dividing futures into three time zones: immediate, intermediate, and distant futures. The specific time intervals depend upon the particular aspect of the social system being considered, and presumably will not themselves be constant over time (that is, for example, the location in time of the "distant future" that I am about to specify here may itself alter). For many significant events, however, I would suggest that the *immediate future* is essentially one, five, or ten years from the present; the *intermediate future* is twenty-five to thirty years off; and the *distant future* is fifty to one hundred or more years hence.

This periodization has important consequences for the distinction made above between predicting and designing futures. Immediate futures are relatively easy to predict but difficult to design and alter, while distant futures are very difficult to predict but much easier to design. It is partly for this reason that a target date of the "Year 2000" makes so much sense for current futuristic activities: twenty-five to thirty years in the future is close enough to the present to enable us to have some notion of its general contours and to feel that we or our loved ones will be around to live in that future. Yet twenty-five to thirty years is far enough away for us to imagine that we will find solutions to the pressing problems of the present.

In a paper prepared for a panel on "cultural futurology" at the American Anthropological Association meeting in San Diego, California, November 20, 1970, Albert and Donna Wilson made a distinction between the elements of social change that is quite relevant to our discussion here:

> *Our experience with technical and social change suggests that a comprehensive model of change should allow for determinative, normative, and random processes.* Determinative *processes are those that provide the recognizable patterns of social change. They are the processes . . . that provide the continuity of society.* Normative *processes are those that have their origin in the needs, goals, and preferences of social groups and sub-groups and whose implementation bends the course of the determinative toward the chosen goals and increases their probability of occurrence.* Random *processes introduce unforeseen discontinuities or new directions into the patterns of change, launching new sequences of events that may overrule established determinative and normative courses.* [9]

In our formulation, it is the determinative aspects of the future that are most susceptible to our understanding through predictive and forecasting techniques; they are also the predominant forces in the immediate future. The random elements are the things that make prediction of distant futures especially hazardous, while the normative processes are those that we seek to elicit in support of rapid but guided social change towards intermediate future goals—and which therefore further interfere with our ability to foresee the distant future clearly.

C. Futuristics of the sort under description here focuses on three kinds of entities—social values (and hence attitudes and behavior), social institutions, and social organisms. I believe mankind is entering an unprecedented social situation—one in which he comes to realize for the first time that there are no givens, no fixed parameters, no unquestionable certainties upon which he can base either his private or his social life. Rather all is actually or potentially variable, changeable, subject to man's own alteration and control. Thus the futurist must consider the implication of the adoption of alternative social values; attempt to delineate the consequences of establishing a variety of new social institutions; and explore the probable impact of new organisms, new beings—*e.g.*, chimeras, cyborgs, machine-augmented beings, and genetically engineered creatures, including socially designed and biologically engineered human beings.[10]

D. Finally, throughout this elaboration of the scope of futuristics which was introduced to the Hawaii 2000 activities, it will be noted that I have frequently used the term "futures" in the plural in order to emphasize the desirability of acting as though the future is not totally determined independent of man's actions, and thus simply lying "out there" waiting to be realized. Rather, I stress man's ability to determine his future (the "normative processes") and thus, from the perspective of the present, that there are futures and not simply a future. There are alternatives, choices to be made, paths to be identified and explored. The actualization of some of these futures might be relatively simple. Others might be very difficult to bring about, given the force of determinative processes and the possible intrusion of random events. But none is inevitable, and thus all must be expressed in terms of probabilities of occurrence with or without conscious social effort being made to achieve or avoid them.

This has been a brief outline of the scope of futuristics as I see it, and as I presented it to the nearly one thousand persons who worked in a variety of capacities on the governor's conference on Hawaii 2000. What remains to be done in this article is to spell out the particular events that, in my opinion, made futuristics of this sort a desirable and necessary area of concern for so many citizens of the State of Hawaii.

Political Values and Structure Change as a Response to Technological Change

The major reason for the desirability of trying to encourage a whole community to engage in futuristic activities is that Hawaii, Western civilization, and essentially the entire world are well past the beginning stages of a continuing and accelerating period of rapid socio-environmental change. It very well may be that in some more distant future, mankind may enter a "new" period of social stability. Mankind may so gain control over his own evolution that continuity, stability, predictability, and order will become dominant (and worrisome) characteristics, and spontaneity, change, randomness, and chaos will be rare or essentially unknown.

But this is certainly not the situation for man now or in the foreseeable future. Instead, we seem to be in a unique situation where the dominant characteristics of our society and environment can best be depicted by exponential curves of growth in world population and the population of most countries; in the production of many goods (automobiles, television sets, houses, academic journals, scientific information) and of many "bads" as well (violent crimes, garbage, traffic deaths, etc.); in the utilization of exhaustible raw materials; and the like.[11]

Moreover, this environment of rapid change is new, unprecedented, and, indeed, contrary to man's whole previous experience. It is not that social change is for the first time occurring in history. Rather, it is that because of extraordinarily rapid change, of literacy, and scientific knowledge, man is for the first time becoming vividly aware of his changing environment in its negative as well as its positive consequences.

Marshall McLuhan has a very felicitous example, which should help us see the difference between mankind's current situation and his past. Social change, says McLuhan, is like a movie film which until recently has been off the projector, lying on the ground. Man in the past has seemed to be standing in the middle of but one frame of that film. As far as he could see in back of him, the frames preceding the present were exactly like the present. Before him also, there stretched seemingly undifferentiated frames.

"Thus," man concluded, "there is no change. At least, there is no predictable change, though floods, fires, earthquakes, and wars have brought discontinuities in the past. Since, barring these unforseeable events, the past and the present and the future are all essentially alike, it is my reasonable duty to learn the ways of the past; to perpetuate the values and institutions of the past; indeed, to venerate the past; to live in the present in accordance with the past—and to see that the ways of the past/present are transferred on unaltered into the future."

But, very suddenly and very recently, the film has been threaded on a projector, the switch thrown on, and at first gradually and subsequently with increasing speed, the film has begun moving past the illuminated lens. Man, for the first time, is being made acutely aware of accelerating change and the need to cope with it.

Now, social values and social institutions are the mechanisms by which men adapt to and mold their environment. Though the tendency is for men to make similar kinds of adaptive responses to similar environments, different men may develop different values and institutions as adaptive responses to essentially very similar environments. Whether the variations or similarities are due to chance, genes, experience, leadership, divine guidance, or something else is of less concern to us here than is our understanding of the contention that values and institutions are human adaptive mechanisms. That values and institutions differ even though their environments are similar should help us avoid ethnocentric adoration of our own particular values and structures. Apparently many adaptive responses are appropriate and perhaps we should not become overly attached to our own.

On the other hand, some anthropological evidence rather clearly indicates to me that social values and institutions can be typified, and that the typology appears to be related to levels of technological development. That is to say, while there will be variations around a mode, and while an occasional example can be found decidedly outside the "normal" range, the level of technology sets "limits" to the types of values and institutions one might expect to find in any given society, and renders more likely certain types of social structures. In short, given the level of technology of a specific human group, and the mode and range of social structures normally associated with this level, one should be able to predict with considerable accuracy the social values and institutions of the group in question.

If the society possesses pre-agricultural stone age technology, then its social structure should be expected to differ from that of most industrial age societies —indeed, it should also differ from that of agricultural technology societies— while it should possess a social structure similar to that of other stone age societies.

To repeat, this hypothesis is phrased as a statistical statement—an expectation of a positive correlation which might not be found in respect to any single society, but which should result in an accurate aggregate prediction of social structure from level of technology.

Moreover, it is plainly a causal statement as well. There is no use in denying that, even though it may not have been fully validated empirically. I am hypothesizing that a society's social values and institutions are caused by its level of technology, rather than the other way around, even though I will freely admit that there may be some significant counter-examples where non-technological features (for example, leadership) predominated.

Neither am I denying that social structure influences what specific technology is developed and how it is utilized by a society. The social setting is manifestly an important influencing condition. Kenneth Boulding says: "Changes in technology produce change in social institutions, and changes in institutions produce change in technology. In the enormously complex world of social interrelations we cannot say in any simple way that one change produces the other, only that they are enormously interrelated and both aspects of human life change together."[12]

To the contrary, I believe that we can specify the relation more clearly than that without denying the interaction. Chance, leadership, natural disasters, social needs, and the rest might influence what technologies will be invented, developed, and diffused. But once a technology has been diffused throughout a society, its impact is such that—unless conscious and effective effort is made to prevent it—the society is modified in significant and largely unintended ways by the technology. The overwhelming tendency, I believe, is too clear to avoid; as Marshall McLuhan puts it, "We shape our tools, and thereafter our tools shape us."

Now, in the past, as we have seen above, technological development was very slow, and hence technologically induced environmental modification was virtually imperceptible to the members of a given society. It is reasonable to assume, however, that such major technological developments as agriculture, for example, did have powerful effects on the attitudes and behaviors of the persons who lived through them. In a sense, these people, too, suffered from "future shock."[13] But the domestication of man which agricultural technology brought about took 10,000 to 20,000 years, while technological innovations today are being introduced into modern society at a fantastic rate, with little or no anticipation, concern, or preparation for their social impact. Indeed, it is for this reason that I refer to modern agricultural experts, engineers, biologists, and research and development scientists operating on federal and private funds as the real "revolutionaries" in our society. The SDS, the Progressive Labor Party, the Weathermen, the Black Panthers—these groups are ineffective indeed in changing society in comparison with those men of science and learning whose very job it is, in effect, to destroy the structure of the society they live in without bearing the responsiblity for, or perhaps even the awareness of, their part in the destruction.

Thus, in this environment of rapid change, we need to examine all our values and institutions—virtually all of which were produced in response to what was expected to be a stable or only slowly changing environment—and ask whether or not they are appropriate for this new, permanently dynamic social situation.

Some Implications for the Structure of Current American Government

There have been other periods in man's recent past where it has been necessary for him consciously to modify values and institutions in order to account for technologically induced changes in the environment, even if the calls for the changes were not always expressed in these terms.

One of the most recent and most important for current American government is that period during the seventeenth and eighteenth centuries when the social values and institutions appropriate for an incipient industrial society were hammered out. The medieval order was crumbling, being destroyed by the cumulative effects of new technologies, such as the water wheel, the stirrup, the horse collar, the single-horse-drawn plow, the compass and sextant, metal-refining techniques, and, most obviously, the printing press, which was perhaps the most politically potent technology of all because it served not only as a mass disseminator of political information, but also as the model of organization for industrial—i.e., mass-producing—society. In addition, and as an apparent consequence of many of these and other technological developments, population began to grow rapidly; and many of the social values and institutions of the past became inoperable among so large, and so increasingly mobile, a people.

Thus the broad outlines of parliamentary, representative government—as discussed by the British and French philosophers of the seventeenth, eighteenth, and early nineteenth centuries (Hume, Locke, Hobbes, Montesquieu, Rousseau, Mill) and as enacted into British, French, and American political structures (most notably the American Constitution of 1789, as justified by the *Federalist Papers*) must be viewed as relatively appropriate responses to the demands of new political values and institutions which were largely the consequence of technological developments and population growth.

Let me simply outline some of these political inventions:

1. An elected, "representative" government as a special technology designed to enable a large number of people who lack a common interest to participate in some way in determining those public rules that will guide their individual actions. Plainly, if every person could be present when social decisions are being made, as had been possible within a small population, or if some other technology were extant—such as electronic circuitry (computers, television, telephone, etc.) or cloned teletransport (the possibility of "beaming" yourself

instantly from place to place a la *Star Trek*, combined with the capability of making duplicates of yourself, via Xeroxed cloning)—then representative government would have less inevitability or desirability as a solution to the problem of enabling a large number of people to "participate" in public policy-making.

2. Majority rule within the elected assembly as a way of determining policy when a "natural" consensus is not apparent (as it is in most continuing face-to-face groups characteristic of tribal or village communities, or of small elite groups). Majority rule in political decisions and mass production in economics are similar solutions to problems of large scale and are especially characteristic of industrial-level technology (though of course not restricted to it). When everyone speaks for himself politically and has status, privilege, and reponsibility assigned to himself personally, then there is no need for an "averaging" (*i.e.*, de-individualizing) device like "majority rule." Similarly, when all goods are custom-made by individual artisans for individual consumers, "average sizes" are also unnecessary. But when it becomes necèssary to provide goods for a very great number of people, individualized sizing must give way to some sort of averaging technique. Here, also, cybernetic technology permits that which industrial technology does not—increased individual choice and power in a large population.[14]

3. Multicameral assemblies to reflect the interests of irreconcilably different constituencies which are equal in political power or importance.

4. The division of power, or federalism, as a way of making minimal political cooperation possible among separate "sovereign" states where actually they had little experience with cooperation, virtually no avenues of communication and transportation, a pre-industrial technology, and a small, scattered rural population—conditions which exist almost nowhere in the world now; certainly not in the United States.

5. The separation of powers and the balance of powers as techniques for handling the alleged evil nature of man. As the *Federalist Papers* said:

> But the great security against a gradual concentration of the several powers in the same department, consists in giving to those who administer each department the necessary constitutional means and personal motives to resist encroachments of the others. The provision for defence must, in this, as in all other cases, be made commensurate to the danger of attack. Ambition must be made to counteract ambition. The interest of the man must be connected with the constitutional rights of the place. It may be a reflection on human nature, that such devices should be necessary to control the abuses of government. But what is government itself, but the greatest of all reflections on human nature? If men were angels, no government would be necessary. If angels were to govern men, neither external nor internal controls on government would be necessary. In framing a government which is to be administered by men over men, the great difficulty lies in this: you must first enable the government to control the

governed; and in the next place oblige it to control itself. A dependence on the people is, no doubt, the primary control on the government; but experience has taught mankind the necessity of auxiliary precautions.[15]

A brilliant analysis—for the times. Truly, this arrangement of checks and balances was a masterly feat of social engineering in the face of an intractable quality of human nature. But our situation is quite different now. The behavioral and biological sciences seem about to make "human nature" within the control of man, as we have shown above. What, then, is our justification for continuing the rococo structure of American government? Men may not be angels, but how do cyborgs govern themselves?

6. Constitutional law (in the United States) and codified, written, and objective civil law in Europe to replace the oral, personal, and situational common law. What clearer evidence for the incredible power of the printing press than industrial man's belief that by enshrining custom in the printed word, he had made it "higher" and permanent. Marshall McLuhan asks us to imagine what the world would have been like if television and the computer had been invented before the printing press (he suggests that the tendency towards mass urbanization might have been reversed). We might wonder what effect this counterposition of inventions might have had on how our government was structured. If that is too hypothetical, at least we might ask how our government might be structured *now* that we can rely on (for example) a voice-sensitive computer, instead of the printed page.

7. An elevated, bewigged, enrobed, august, solemn, precedent- and procedure-bound, and impersonal (*i.e.*, inhuman and mechanical) judiciary to decide disputes between men; and an aloof, expert, rule-ridden bureaucracy to administer representatively determined policy—in short, in both instances, "a government of laws and not of men," which must determine blindly and equally when the pressures of a large number of people prevent them from acting individually and specifically. What might these structures be like if their functions were turned over to a computer which could be *both* objective and individualizing?

8. A "strong" president, elected indirectly by "competent people" in each of the states who had a national perspective as to who the "best" and "second best" men in the nation were. The ordinary citizens—illiterate, isolated, provincial—knew nothing of the world beyond their own small communities, or so the Founding Fathers believed; and on that belief they erected the Electoral College. Then came the railroad, the telegraph, the telephone, automobile, airplane, television, satellite . . . but the Electoral College, only slightly modified from 1789, remains.

The socio-environmental situation that evoked the American Constitution has changed very drastically since 1789. Whereas the American states were then on the verge of the industrial revolution, we are now moving swiftly into some type of a post-industrial society.[16]

Thus, it seems to me imperative that we seek rapid and radical modifications of our current political values and institutions, so that we can bring our social structure into congruence without environmental imperatives; and also that we attempt not to diffuse new technologies until we have forecast and discussed the implications of their probable impact upon existing societal arrangements.

This search for alternative futures in the light of alternative technological developments and varied human values was the main concern of the Hawaii 2000 interim and conference activities. The results of these activities, which only indicate our initial awareness of our obligations, our opportunities, and our obstacles, are contained in a book being edited by George Chaplin, chairman of the Conference, and myself.

Though the Conference itself is over, futuristic activities in Hawaii have by no means come to an end. On the contrary, the anticipation and invention of alternative social futures may become a major characteristic of political and educational activities in this state.

But if there is any validity in the attempt and any reason for the insistence on the urgency of the undertaking (whatever reservations one might have on the specific orientation suggested, or the actions taken in Hawaii), then we hope that other political communities, in the United States and throughout the world, will be encouraged to undertake activities in anticipatory democracy.

Hawaii's Response to the Challenge from the Future

As states of the American Union go, Hawaii is a relatively progressive political community. Whether as a result of the "Aloha spirit," the fact that no single ethnic group is in a majority,[17] the absence of a dominant historical tradition,[18] the relative youth and prosperity of the population,[19] or some other factor, Hawaii's current delegation to Congress is, with one exception, very "liberal;"[20] its State Legislature quite enlightened; its police—though not unconcerned with "law and order"—well appreciated locally for their comparative reasonableness; its legalization of abortion one of the first and most liberal (and most easily enacted); and its constitution only recently revised.[21]

But the new constitution remains only an updated eighteenth/nineteenth century document; and legislation, administration, and adjudication is still conducted on a piecemeal, "analytic" (i.e., non-systemic, unintegrated) basis like that which has characterized Western governments since the first English parliaments. That is to say, the unstated assumption underlying governmental activities in Hawaii seems to be that the social system in Hawaii usually is somehow "naturally" balanced, and that all the government needs to do from time to time is to act to "restore" that balance when it is temporarily disturbed beyond natural redress—e.g., the Legislature passes laws when specific problems are brought before it which seem to merit general approval—or which have the support of significant groups; the courts decide, on a piece-by-piece basis, specific disputes brought before them.[22]

In a stable environment and an essentially equilibrated social system, this piecemeal correction might be appropriate; but Hawaii, like other American political communities, does not appear to me to be in natural social equilibrium; and thus current analytic governmental actions tend to exacerbate the problems they seek to solve—they throw the system further out of equilibrium.[23]

Perhaps as a result of the discussions before, during, and after the Governor's Conference on Hawaii 2000, there is some indication that the government may have come to the conclusion that it should try to organize itself in such a way as to increase its potential for systemic decision-making rather than either to rush legislatively into the ecological/population/future shock breach, or to ignore the urgency of the problems and do nothing. I believe that theirs is the preferred response.

Among the actions by the Legislature which strike me as appropriate steps towards its own reorganized future are the creation of:

Office on Environmental Quality Control
Commission on Population Stabilization
Transportation Control Commission
Commission on Socio-Economic Indicators
Commission on the Year 2000 (supported by the Hawaii Research Center for Futures Study)

and by such specific actions as:

Legalization of abortion.
Thorough revision of the criminal code in the direction of eliminating "crimes without victims;" permitting previously outlawed sexual acts and expressions; considering "drug taking" to be a personal decision unless it has clearly negative social effects, at which point it is then treated more as a psycho-medical problem than a criminal one.
Consideration of "no-fault" divorce laws; strengthening the rights of children against their parents and other adults.
Government-initiated action to encourage public land to be used by experimental communities.

At the University of Hawaii, a teaching program on futures studies is being put into operation. The goals of the program are:

1. To provide a well-rounded interdisciplinary undergraduate and graduate major in futures studies to meet the student demand for such a course.

2. To encourage existing university departments, teachers, and administrators to develop to a futuristic orientation in their own academic discipline.

3. To respond to the considerable popular demand for more public discussion and action on futuristics by expanding activities into the Hawaiian community so that a broad futuristic orientation can be encouraged throughout the com-

munity, and so that the futures studies program will remain in close contact with the citizens' dreams and fears for the future.

4. To serve as a point of contact with other futures studies programs throughout the United States, Europe, and the world—especially in Asia, Latin America, and Africa.

Professor Fred Riggs, Director of the Social Science Research Institute of the University of Hawaii, also is developing a program in futures research to encourage both basic futures research itself and the incorporation of a futuristic orientation into all social science research at the University.

The University's College of Continuing Education (Ralph Miwa, Dean) and the State Department of Education have undertaken, and are continuing to sponsor, a variety of seminars and institutes intended to introduce futuristics to schoolteachers and to middle-level public decision-makers. The Hawaii Curriculum Center has already developed some futuristic material, and is making more under the direction of Theodore Rogers.

A variety of private and professional groups—especially the TB Association of the State (John Leifhelm, Sam Yoshida, and Deborah Coombs)—have also taken a leading role in encouraging community involvement in anticipating and designing the future of Hawaii.

It would, of course, be a great error to over-emphasize what Hawaii has done. What it has *not* done, what it has done somewhat "unfortunately," or what it *may* do certainly outnumbers its few significant steps forward. For example, as good as were the ten interim panel discussions (held between February and July, 1970), the thirteen task force reports presented to and discussed at the August Conference, and the proceedings of the Governor's Conference generally, it is only in a comparative sense (compared to the relative inaction of other communities, and compared to no previous concern in Hawaii) that these futuristic activities of the State can be considered in any way significant; they leave much to be desired otherwise.

"Ecology"—the backward-looking desire to recapture some environmentally preferable past—certainly predominates over futuristics in Hawaii; and, if the leaders of the ecology movement in Hawaii—especially Tony Hodges and Jan Newhouse—are correct, unrestrained "growth, development, and tourism" remain the predominating goals for the future in the minds of the decision-makers of Hawaii. This may indeed be the case, though I personally do not believe so.

Certainly, significant action lies ahead. The newly appointed (March, 1971) Commission on the Year 2000 has begun its meetings, and intends to solicit from the public, and generate for popular discussion, a number of clearly developed alternative futures for Hawaii.

This is plainly very hard work, demanding a rare blend of good social science, genuine humanism, a healthy appreciation of natural science and technology, and an enormous imagination. Whether such a blend can be found in Hawaii—or anywhere in the world—remains to be seen. Whatever the outcome, we hope that other communities, in the United States and throughout the world, will be encouraged to undertake their own activities in anticipatory democracy.

Notes

1. Indeed, in a special film which he prepared for the opening ceremonies of the Governor's Conference on Hawaii 2000, Toffler (whose book, *Future Shock* (New York: Random House, 1970 coincidentally was published the week the Conference was held) remarked that developments in futuristics moved so swiftly that the idea of anticipatory democracy which he first described in his book (pp. 416-30) was already in operation in Hawaii, and independent of his specific direction. Toffler's comment about specific independence is correct, but I should point out that Toffler's intellectual contribution to the style and focus of futuristic activities in Hawaii was considerable: his original *Horizon* article, "The Future As a Way of Life," *Horizon* (Summer, 1965), pp. 109-15; his two *Playboy* articles, "Future Shock," and "Coping with Future Shock," *Playboy* (March and April, 1970); and his introduction to Kurt Baier and Nicholas Rescher (eds.), *Values and the Future* (New York:) The Free Press, 1969), titled "Value Impact Forecaster–A Profession of the Future," were all part of the literature read by the persons most active in the work surrounding the Governor's Conference.

2. George Chaplin and myself are to edit the proceedings of the Conference for a yet-untitled volume. *See also*, Magoroh Maruyama and James Dator (eds.), *Human Futuristics* (Honolulu: Social Science Research Institute, 1971), and a report by myself in the volumes on the International Futures Research Conference, held in Kyoto, Japan, April, 1970.

3. There are a number of terms in use to describe this new orientation towards the future. I prefer the term "futuristics," though "futurology," "future(s) research," and "future(s) studies" are also popular. *See* the discussion of terminology in *The Futurist* (February, 1967), p. 5; (April 1967), p. 23; and (August 1967), p. 64.

4. This position is well-stated by the biologist, Theodosius Dobzhansky: "One stands in bewilderment before a mentality that claims to know exactly what is natural and what is unnatural. Man has changed nature in innumerable ways and will doubtless continue doing so. It is, indeed, 'natural' for man to recast nature." "Human Values in an Evolving World," in Cameron Hall (ed.), *Human Values and Advancing Technology* (New York: Friendship Press, 1967), p. 64. Or, in the words of Ortega y Gasset: "Man has no nature; what he has is a history."

5. For an indication of what is beginning to be done, *see* the recent edition of *The Futurist* (December, 1970) devoted to "Education and Futurism."

6. Probably the most sophisticated nongovernmental attempts at predicting and extrapolating (rather than inventing or designing) social futures is being done by the Hudson Institute and the Institute for the Future.

7. This would be the basis of my own criticism of many current ameliorative political activities or programs–whether of the "left" or the "right," of "ecologists" or "technocrats:" the programs are *uncoordinated*, in that the interaction of the parts is not anticipated adequately or at all; they are *unsystemic* in that the uncoordinated parts are then not articulated with other components of the system or with the significant elements of the environment; they are *undemocratic* not only because the policies are often generated independently of the wishes of the people, but also, and more importantly, because frequently little effort is made to stretch the visions of the people–to get them to want "better" things than they are likely to express in their naive, oversocialized situations. Democratic futuristics, in my opinion, involves not simply doing what the people say they want done, but encouraging them to consider more than the most obvious, or currently visible, alternatives before choosing. Thus, designing and implementing futuristic programs

in accordance with the peoples' wishes must be kept in a continuous feedback loop, as new popular awarenesses of the openness of the future create new definitions of desirable and realistic goals for the future.

8. John McHale, *The Future of the Future* (New York: George Braziller, 1969), pp. 11, 15. The interior quotation is from R. C. Cook, "Truth and Consequences in a New Era," *Population Bulletin* (November, 1966).

9. The Wilsons' paper is a working paper of the Institute for the Future, and is also found in slightly revised form in Maruyama and Dator, (eds.), *op. cit.*

10. In addition to the articles by Dobzhansky and Jose Delgado in Hall, (ed.), *op. cit.*, see D. S. Halacy, Jr., *Cyborg: The Evolution of the Superman* (New York: Harper and Row, 1965) and Gordon Rattray Taylor, *The Biological Time Bomb* (New York: World, 1968).

11. By now, the list of sources emphasizing these aspects of the present and the future has itself expanded exponentially. Paul Ehrlich, *The Population Bomb* (New York: Ballantine, 1968) remains the most influential. Garrett De Bell (ed.), *The Environmental Handbook* (New York: Ballantine, 1970) is a very convenient collection of analyses and proposed corrective actions.

12. Kenneth Boulding, *The Meaning of the 20th Century* (New York: Harper, 1964), p. 9.

13. It has been brought to my attention by Terry Rogers of the School of Medicine of the University of Hawaii that trolls "who lived in caves and under bridges" were actually stone age men who, unable to accept the changes brought about by the agricultural revolution, refused to move into cities. One can imagine the grumbling around the cave-fire: "It's unnatural for man to live in houses. If God had intended man to live in houses, he would have. . ."

14. For arguments that cybernetic technology (of the present and foreseeable future) is quite unlike industrial technology (of the present and the recent past) in its implications for social structures and individual decision making, *see* Richard Kostelanetz (ed.), *Beyond Left and Right*, (New York: William Morrow, 1968) especially Kostelanetz's excellent introduction, and the section on "Technology and Society."

15. In *The Federalist* Number 51, attributed to either Alexander Hamilton or James Madison, on page 337 in the Modern Library (Random House) edition.

16. Daniel Bell is probably the person responsible for popularizing this particular designation of a most probable immediate future. Kostelanetz, *op. cit.*, contains a handy summary of some of the major arguments for it.

17. The ethnic composition of the State of Hawaii (listed according to locally significant ethnic groups) is as follows: Japanese–30 percent, Caucasian–15 percent, Hawaiian (almost entirely part-Hawaiian)–19 percent, Filipino–8 percent, Chinese–6 percent, Other (mainly Korean, Portuguese, Puerto Rican, Samoan, or Micronesian–12 percent. Source: State of Hawaii, Department of Planning and Economic Development, *The Population of Hawaii, 1970,* Statistical Report #77 (November 19, 1970), p. 12.

18. Probably the best single history of Hawaii is Gavan Daws, *Shoal of Time* (New York: Macmillan, 1968).

19. Thirty-nine percent of the population in Hawaii is under eighteen years of age; another thirty-nine percent is between eighteen and 44 years of age. The median family income in Oahu (which has 80 percent of the population in Hawaii) was $8,046 between 1964 and 1967. Source: State of Hawaii, Department of Planning and Economic Development, *State of Hawaii, Data Book 1970,* Tables 5 and 74 respectively.

20. Senator Daniel Inouye, and Representatives Patsy Mink and Spark Matsunaga always rank very high on the various measures of "liberalism" as determined by voting records in Congress. They are Democrats. Senator Hiram Fong, a Republican, is somewhat more "conservative" by the same indicators.

21. For the constitution itself and the discussions of the constitutional convention, see *1968 Con-Con* in seven volumes (Honolulu: State of Hawaii, 1968). Benjamin Sigal and

Joyce Najita (eds.), *Convention Issues: The Changing Constitution* (Honolulu: University of Hawaii, 1968), contains some interesting commentary.

22. *See* Theodore Becker, "A Survey Study of Hawaiian Judges: The Effect on Decisions of Individual Role Variations," *American Political Science Review* (September, 1966), pp. 677-80.

23. Legislative, administrative and judicial action in Hawaii can be termed "unsystemic" for at least two fundamental reasons: (1) There is no clearly articulated model (or even description) of the presumed equilibrated social system of Hawaii—what its components are, how they are interrelated, how the system operates, etc. (2) Legislative, administrative, judicial—and private—actions are taken with only vague reference being made to their effect on the total system and its components.

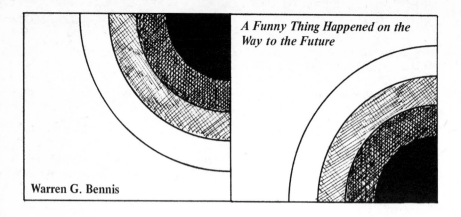

A Funny Thing Happened on the Way to the Future

Warren G. Bennis

In recent years, analysis of the "future" or, more precisely, inventing relevant futures has become as respectable for the scientist as the shaman. Writing in a recent issue of the *Antioch Review*, I groped for a definition of the future:

> For me, the "future" is a portmanteau word. It embraces several notions. It is an exercise of the imagination which allows us to compete with and try to outwit future events. Controlling the anticipated future is, in addition, a social invention that legitimizes the process of forward planning. There is no other way I know of to resist the 'tyranny of blind forces' than by looking facts in the face (as we experience them in the present) and extrapolating to the future—nor is there any other sure way to detect compromise. Most importantly, the future is a conscious dream, a set of imaginative hypotheses groping toward whatever vivid utopias lie at the heart of our consciousness. "In dreams begin responsibilities," said Yeats, and it is to our future responsibilities as educators, researchers, and practitioners that these dreams are dedicated.[1]

Most students of the future would argue with that definition, claiming that it is "poetic" or possibly even "pre-scientific." The argument has validity, I believe, though it is difficult to define "futurology," let alone distinguish between and among such terms as "inventing relevant futures," scenarios, forecasts, self-fulfilling prophecies, predictions, goals, normative theories, evolutionary hypotheses, prescriptions, and so on. Philosophers and sociologists, for example, are still arguing over whether Weber's theory of bureaucracy was in fact a theory, a poignant and scholarly admonition, an evolutionary hypothesis, or a descriptive statement.

However difficult it may be to identify a truly scientific study of the future, most scholars would agree that it should include a number of objectives:

1. It should provide a survey of possible futures in terms of a spectrum of major potential alternatives.
2. It should ascribe to the occurrence of these alternatives some estimates of relative a priori probabilities.
3. It should, for given basic policies, identify preferred alternatives.
4. It should identify those decisions which are subject to control as well as

those developments which are not, whose occurrence would be likely to have a major effect on the probabilities of these alternatives.[2]

With these objectives only dimly in mind, I wrote a paper on the future of organizations which was called, "Organizational Developments and the Fate of Bureaucracy."[3] Essentially, it was based on an evolutionary hypothesis which asserted that every age develops the form of organization most appropriate to its genius. I then went on to forecast certain changes in a "post-bureaucratic world" and to predict how these changes would affect the structure and environment of human organizations, their leadership and motivational patterns, and their cultural and ecological values. A number of things have occurred since that first excursion into the future in September, 1964, which are worth mentioning at this point for they have served to reorient and revise substantially some of the earlier forecasts.

Perhaps only a Homer, a Herodotus, or a first-rate folk-rock composer could capture the tumult and tragedy of the events which have occurred since that paper was written and measure their impact on our lives. The bitter agony of Vietnam, the convulsive stirrings of Black America, the assassinations, and the bloody streets of Chicago have each left their mark. What appears is a panorama that goes in and out of focus as it is transmitted through the mass media and as it is expressed through the new, less familiar media—strikes, injunctions, disruptions, bombings, and campus occupations and riots.

Political Futurism

The 1964 paper I mentioned was written within the liberal-democratic framework, and it contained many of the inherent problems and advantages of that perspective. The main strategy of this paper and its focus of convenience will be to review briefly the main points of that paper, to indicate its shortcomings and lacunae in light of several years experience (not the least of which has been serving as an administrator in a large, complex public bureaucracy), and then to proceed to develop some new perspectives relevant to the future of public bureaucracies.

I might add, parenthetically, that I feel far less certainty and closure at this time than I did then. The importance of inventing relevant futures and directions is never more crucial than in a revolutionary period, exactly and paradoxically at the point in time when the radical transition blurs the shape and direction of the present. This is the dilemma of our time and most certainly the dilemma of this paper.

The Future: 1964 Version

Bureaucracy, I argued, was an elegant social invention ingeniously capable of organizing and coordinating the productive processes of the Industrial Revolution, but hopelessly out of joint with contemporary realities. There would be new shapes, patterns, and models emerging which promised drastic changes in the conduct of the organization and of managerial practices in general. In the next twenty-five to fifty years, I argued, we should witness, and participate in, the end of bureaucracy as we know it and the rise of new social systems better suited to twentieth-century demands of industrialization.

This argument was based on a number of factors:

1. The exponential growth of science, the growth of intellectual technology, and the growth of research and development activities.
2. The growing confluence between men of knowledge and men of power, or, as I put it then, "a growing affinity between those who make history and those who write it."
3. A fundamental change in the basic philosophy which underlies managerial behavior, reflected most of all in the following three areas:
   a. A new concept of man, based on increased knowledge of his complex and shifting needs, which replaces the oversimplified, innocent push-button concept of man.
   b. A new concept of power, based on collaboration and reason, which replaces a model of power based on coercion and fear.
   c. A new concept of organizational values, based on humanistic-democratic ideals, which replaces the depersonalized mechanistic value system of bureaucracy.
4. A turbulent environment which would hold relative uncertainty due to the increase of research and development activities. The environment would become increasingly differentiated, interdependent, and more salient to the organization. There would be greater interpenetration of the legal policy and economic features of an oligopolistic and government-business controlled economy. Three main features of the environment would be: interdependence rather than competition, a turbulent rather than a steady, predictable state, and large rather than small enterprises.
5. A population characterized by a younger, more mobile, and better educated work force.

These conditions, I believed, would lead to some significant changes:

A. The increased level of education and rate of mobility would bring about certain changes in values held toward work. People would tend to: (1) be more rational, be intellectually committed, and rely more heavily on forms of social influence which correspond to their value system; (2) be more "other-directed," and rely on their temporary neighbors and workmates for companionship; in other words, have relationships, not relatives; and (3) require more involvement, participation, and autonomy in their work.

B. As far as organizational structure goes, given the population characteristics and features of environmental turbulence, the social structure in organizations of the future would take on some unique characteristics. I will quote from the original paper:

First of all, the key word will be temporary: Organizations will become adaptive, rapidly changing temporary systems. Second, they will be organized around problems-to-be-solved. Third, these problems will be solved by relative groups of strangers who represent a diverse set of professional skills. Fourth, given the requirements of coordinating the various projects, articulating points or "linking pin" personnel will be necessary who can speak the diverse languages of research and who can relay and mediate between various project groups. Fifth, the groups will be conducted on organic rather than on mechanical lines; they will emerge and adapt to the problems, and leadership and influence will fall to those who seem most able to solve the problems rather than to pro- grammed role expectations. People will be differentiated, not according to rank or roles, but according to skills and training.

Adaptive, temporary systems of diverse specialists solving problems, coordinated organically via articulating points will gradually replace the theory and practice of bureaucracy. Though no catchy phrase comes to mind, it might be called an organic-adaptive structure.

(As an aside: what will happen to the rest of society, to the manual laborers, to the poorly educated, to those who desire to work in conditions of dependency, and so forth? Many such jobs will disappear; automatic jobs will be automated. However, there will be a corresponding growth in the service-type of occupation, such as organizations like the Peace Corps and AID. There will also be jobs, now being seeded, to aid in the enormous challenge of coordinating activities between groups and organizations. For certainly, consortia of various kinds are growing in number and scope and they will require careful attention. In times of change, where there is a wide discrepancy between cultures and generations, and increase in industrialization, and especially urbanization, society becomes the client for skills in human resources. Let us hypothesize that approximately 40% of the population would be involved in jobs of this nature, 40% in technological jobs, making an organic-adaptive majority with, say, a 20% bureaucratic minority.[4]

Toward the end of the paper, I wrote that "The need for instinctual renuncia- tion decreases as man achieves rational mastery over nature. In short, organiza- tions of the future will require fewer restrictions and repressive techniques because of the legitimization of play and fantasy, accelerated through the rise of science and intellectual achievements."[4]

To summarize the changes in emphasis of social patterns in the "post- bureaucratic world" I was then describing (borrowing from Eric Trist),[5] the following paradigm may be useful:

	From	*Toward*
Cultural Values	Achievement	Self-Actualization
	Self-Control	Self-Expression
	Independence	Interdependence
	Endurance of Stress	Capacity for Joy
	Full Employment	Full Lives

	From	*Toward*
Organizational	Mechanistic Forms	Organic Forms
Philosophies	Competitive Relations	Collaborative Relations
	Separate Objectives	Linked Objectives
	Own Resources	Own Resources
	Regarded as Owned	Regarded also as
	Absolutely	Society's Resources

I hope I've summarized the paper without boring you in the process. One thing is clear: looking back and re-examining one's own work several years later is a useful exercise. Aside from the protracted de-cathexis from the original ideas, new experiences and other emergent factors all help to provide a new perspective which casts some doubt on a number of assumptions only half implied in the earlier statement. For example:

1. The organizations I had in mind then were of a single class: instrumental, large-scale, science-based, international bureaucracies, operating under rapid growth conditions. Service industries and public bureaucracies, as well as non-salaried employees, were excluded from analysis.
2. Practically no attention was paid to the boundary transactions of the firm or to inter-institutional linkages.
3. The management of conflict was emphasized, while the strategy of conflict was ignored.
4. Power of all types was underplayed, while the role of the leader as facilitator—"linking pin"—using an "agricultural model" of nurturance and climate building, was stressed. Put in Gamson's terms,[6] I utilized a domesticated version of power, emphasizing the process by which the authorities attempt to achieve collective goals and to maintain legitimacy and compliance with their decisions, rather than the perspective of "potential partisans," which involves a diversity of interest groups attempting to influence the choices of authorities.
5. A theory of change was implied, based on gentle nudges from the environment coupled with a truth-love strategy—*i.e.*, with sufficient trust and collaboration along with valid data, organizations would progress monotonically along a democratic continuum.

In short, the organizations of the future I envisaged would most certainly be, along with a Bach Chorale and Chartres Cathedral, the epiphany of an ideal Western civilization.

The striking thing about truth and love is that, whereas I once held them up as the answer to our institution's predicaments, they have now become the problem. And, to make matters worse, the world I envisaged as emergent in 1964 has become not necessarily inaccurate, but overwhelmingly problematical. It might be useful to review some of the main organizational dilemmas before going any further, both as a check on the previous forecast as well as a preface to some new and tentative ideas about contemporary human organizations.

A Funny Thing Happened . . . Some New Dilemmas

The Problem of Legitimacy

The key difference between the Berkeley riots of 1964 and the later Columbia crisis is that at Berkeley the major impetus for unrest stemmed from the perceived abuse or misuse of authority ("Do not bend, fold, or mutilate"), whereas the Columbia protest denied the legitimacy of authority. The breakdown of legitimacy in our country has many reasons and explanations, not the least of which is the increasing difficulty of converting political questions into technical-managerial ones. Or, put differently, questions of legitimacy arise whenever "expert power" becomes ineffective. Thus, black militants, drug users, draft resisters, student protestors, and liberated women all deny the legitimacy of those authorities who are not black, drug-experienced, pacifists, students, women.

The university is in an excruciating predicament with respect to the breakdown of legitimacy. Questions about admissions, grades, curriculum, police involvement—even questions concerning rejection of journal articles—stand the chance of being converted into political-legal issues. This jeopardizes the use of universalistic-achievement criteria, upon which the very moral imperatives of our institutions are based. The problem is related, of course, to the inclusion of those minority groups in our society who have been excluded from participation in American life and tend to define their goals in particularistic and political terms.

Herbert Kelman[7] cites three major reasons for the crisis in legitimacy: (1) serious failings of the system in living up to its basic values and in maintaining a proper relationship between means and ends; (2) decreasing trust in leadership; and (3) dispositions of our current youth. On this last point, Richard Flacks suggests

the existence of an increasingly distinct "humanist" sub-culture in the middle class, consisting primarily of highly educated and urbanized families, based in professional occupations, who encourage humanist orientations in their offspring as well as questioning attitudes to traditional middle class values and to arbitrary authority and conventional politics . . . Although this humanist sub-culture represents a small minority of the population, many of its attributes are more widely distributed, and the great increase in the number of college graduates suggests that the ranks of this sub-culture will rapidly grow.[8]

In short: as the gap widens between new shared moralities and authoritative norms (*i.e.* the law), questions of legitimacy inevitably arise.

Populist Versus Elite Functions?

Can American institutions continue to fulfill the possibly incompatible goals of their elitist and populist functions? Again, the American university is an example of this dilemma, for the same institution tries to balance its autonomous-elite function of disinterested inquiry and criticism with an increasingly service-populist oriented function. This has been accomplished by insulating the elite (autonomous) functions of liberal education, basic research, and scholarship from the direct impact of the larger society, whose demands for vocational training, certification, service, and the like are reflected and met in the popular functions of the university. As Martin Trow puts it:

These insulations take various forms of a division of labor within the university. There is a division of labor between departments, as for example, between a department of English or Classics, and a department of Education. There is a division of labor in the relatively unselective universities between the undergraduate and graduate schools, the former given over largely to mass higher education in the service of social mobility and occupational placement, entertainment, and custodial care, while the graduate departments in the same institutions are often able to maintain a climate in which scholarship and scientific research can be done to the highest standards. There is a familiar division of labor, though far from clear-cut, between graduate departments and professional schools. Among the faculty there is a division of labor, within many departments, between scientists and consultants, scholars and journalists, teachers and entertainers. More dangerously, there is a division of labor between regular faculty and a variety of fringe or marginal teachers—teaching assistants, visitors and lecturers—who in some schools carry a disproportionate load of the mass teaching. Within the administration there is a division of labor between the Dean of Faculty and Graduate Dean, and the Dean of Students. And among students there is a marked separation between the "collegiate" and "vocational" subcultures, on the one hand, and academically or intellectually oriented subcultures on the other.[9]

To a certain extent, the genius of American higher education is that it *has* fulfilled both of these functions, to the wonder of all, and especially to observers from European universities, where proportional strains are being placed on their insulating mechanisms.

Interdependence or Complicity in the Environment

The environment I talked about in 1964, with its interdependence and turbulence, is flourishing today. But my optimism must now be tempered, for what appeared then to be a "correlation of fates" turns out to have blocked the view of some serious problems. The university is a good example of this tension.

The relationship between the university and its environment has never been defined in more than an overly abstract way. For some, the university is a citadel, aloof, occasionally lobbing in on society the shells of social criticism.

Both the radical left and the conservative right seem to agree on this model, maintaining that to yield to the claims of society will fragment and ultimately destroy the university. Others, for different reasons, prefer a somewhat similar model—that of the "speculatorium," where scholars, protected by garden walls, meditate away from society's pollutants. Still others envisage the university as an "agent of change," a catalytic institution capable of revolutionizing the nation's organizations and professions. In fact, a recent sociological study listed almost fifty viable goals for the university[10] (a reflection of our ambivalence and confusion as much as anything), and university catalogues usually list them all.

The role of the university in society might be easier to define if it were not for one unpalatable fact. Though it is not usually recognized, the truth is that the university is not self-supporting. The amount available for its educational expenditures (including funds necessary to support autonomous functions) relates directly to the valuation of the university by the general community. The extent to which the university's personnel, ideas, and research are valued is commensurate with the amount of economic support it receives.[11] This has always been true. During the Great Awakening, universities educated ministers; during the agricultural and industrial revolutions, the land-grant colleges and engineering schools flourished; during the rise of the service professions, the universities set up schools of social welfare, nursing, public health, and so on. And, during the past thirty years or so, the universities have been increasingly geared to educate individuals to man the Galbraithean "techno-structure."

Thus, the charge of "complicity" of the universities with the power structure is both valid and absurd; without this alleged "complicity," there would be no university, or only terribly poor ones. In the late 1960's, the same attack came from the New Left. The paradox can be blinding, and often leads to one of two pseudo-solutions—total involvement or total withdrawal; these pseudo-solutions are familiar on other fronts, too—*e.g.*, in foreign policy.

If I am right that the university must be valued by society in order to be supported, the question is not should the university be involved with society, but what should be the *quality* of this involvement and *with whom*? For years, there has been tacit acceptance of the idea that the university must supply industry, the professions, defense, and the techno-structure with the brains necessary to carry on their work. Now there are emerging constituencies, new dependent populations, new problems, many without technical solutions, that are demanding the attention of the university. We are being called upon to direct our limited and already scattered resources to newly defined areas of concern— the quality of life, the shape and nature of our human institutions, the staggering problems of the city, legislative processes, and the management of human resources.

Will it be possible for the modern university to involve itself with these problems and at the same time to avoid the politicization that will threaten its autonomous functions? One thing is clear. We will never find answers to these problems if we allow rational thought to be replaced by a search for villains. To blame the Establishment, Wall Street, or the New Left for our problem is lazy, thoughtless, and frivolous. It would be comforting if we *could* isolate and personalize the problems facing the university, but we cannot.

The last two dilemmas that I've just mentioned—elitist *versus* populist strains vying within our single institution, and the shifting, uncertain symbiosis between university and society—contain many of the unclear problems we face today; and I suspect that they account for much of the existential groaning we hear in practically all of our institutions, not just the university.

The Search for the Correct Metaphor

Metaphors have tremendous power to establish new social realities, to give life and meaning to what was formerly perceived only dimly and imprecisely. What *did* students experience before Erikson's "identity crisis?" Scott Greer wrote recently:

[But] much of our individual experience is symbolized in vague and unstandardized ways. There is, as we say, no word for it. One of the great contributions of creative scientists and artists is to make communicable what was previously moot, to sense new meanings possible in the emerging nature of human experience, giving them a form which makes communication possible. The phrase-maker is not to be despised, he may be creating the grounds for new social reality. (On the other hand, he may merely be repackaging an old product).[12]

Most of us have internalized a metaphor about organizational life—however crude or utopian, conscious or unconscious it may be—which governs our perceptions of our social systems. How these metaphors evolve isn't clear, though I don't think Freud was far off the mark with his focus on the family, the military, and the church as the germinating institutions.

Macro Versus Micro Systems

One of the crude discoveries I painfully made during the course of recent administrative experience in a large public bureaucracy turns on the discontinuities between micro and macro systems. For quite a while, I have had more than passing *theoretical* interest in this problem, which undoubtedly many of you share; but my interest now, due to a sometimes eroding despair, has gone well beyond the purely theoretical problems involved.

My own intellectual "upbringing," to use an old-fashioned term, was steeped in the Lewinian tradition of small-group behavior, processes of social influence, and "action-research." This isn't terribly exceptional, I suppose, for a social psychologist. In fact, I suppose that the major methodological and theoretical influences in the social sciences for the last two decades have concentrated on more microscopic, "manageable" topics. Also, it is not easy to define precisely where a micro social science begins or where a macro social science ends. Formally, I suppose, micro systems consist of roles and actors, while macro systems have as their constituent parts other sub-systems, sub-cultures, and parts of society. In any case, my intellectual heritage has resulted in an erratic batting average in transferring concepts from macro systems into the macro system of a university.

An example of this dilemma can be seen in a letter Leonard Duhl wrote in response to an article by Carl Rogers which stressed an increased concern with human relationships as a necessary prerequisite for managing society's institutions. Duhl wrote:

> *Though I agree with [Rogers] heartily, I have some very strong questions about whether, indeed, this kind of future is in the cards for us. I raise this primarily because out of my experiences working in the U.S. Department of Housing and Urban Development and out of experiences working in and with cities, it is clear that in the basic decision making that takes place, the values Dr. Rogers and I hold so dear have an extremely low priority. Indeed, the old-fashioned concerns with power, prestige, money and profit so far outdistance the concerns for human warmth and love and concern that many people consider the latter extremely irrelevant in the basic decision making. Sadly, it is my feeling that they will continue to do so.* [13]

The following examples from my own recent experience tend to confirm Duhl's gloomy outlook:

1. The theory of consensus falters under those conditions where competing groups bring to the conference table vested interests based on group membership, what Mannhein referred to as "perspectivistic orientation." Where goals are competitive and group—or sub-system-oriented, despite the fact that a consensus might rationally create a new situation where all parties may benefit—*i.e.*, move closer to the Paretian optimal frontier—a negotiated position may be the only practical solution. There was a time when I believed that consensus was a valid operating procedure. I no longer think this is realistic given the scale and diversity of organizations. In fact, I've come to think that the quest for consensus, except for some micro systems where it may be feasible, is a misplaced nostalgia for a folk society as chimerical, incidentally, as the American "identity" for which we search.

2. The collaborative relationship between superiors and subordinates falters as well under those conditions where "subordinates"—if that word is appropriate—are *delegates* of certain sub-systems. Under this condition, collaboration may be perceived by constituents as a threat because of perceived co-option or encroachment on their formal, legal rights.

3. To take another example: in the area of leadership, my former colleagues at SUNY-Buffalo, Ed Hollander and Jim Julian,[14] have written for *Psychological Bulletin* one of the most thoughtful and penetrating articles on the leadership process. In one of their own studies,[15] reported in the article, they found that aside from the significance of task competence, the "leader's interest in group members and interest in group activity" was significantly related to the group acceptance of the leader. Yet, in macro-power situations, the leader is almost

always involved in boundary exchanges with salient interorganizational activities which inescapably reduce not necessarily interest in group members or activities, but the amount of interaction he can maintain with group members. This may have more the overtones of a rationalization than an explanation, but I know of few organizations where the top leadership's commitment to internal programs and needs fully meets constituent expectations.

In short, the interorganizational role set of the leader, plus the scale, diversity, and formal relations that ensue in a pluralistic system place heavy burdens on those managers and leaders who expect an easy transferability between the cozy *gemütlichkeit* of a Theory Y orientation and the realities of macro power.

Current Sources for the Adoption or Rejection of Democratic Ideals

I. A. Richards once said that "language has succeeded until recently in hiding from us almost all things we talk about." This is singularly true when men start to talk of complex and wondrous things like democracy and the like.[16] For these are issues anchored in an existential core of personality. And today I am confused about the presence or absence of conditions which could lead to more democratic functioning. Some days I wake up feeling "nasty, brutish, and short;" other days, I rise feeling "benign, generous, and short." This may be true of the general population, for the national mood is erratic, labile, depending on repression or anarchy for the "short" solution to long problems.

Let us consider Robert Lane's "democraticness scale,"[17] consisting of five items:

a. willingness or reluctance to deny the franchise to the "ignorant or careless."
b. patience or impatience with the delays and confusions of democratic processes.
c. willingness or reluctance to give absolute authority to a single leader in times of threat.
d. where democratic forms are followed, degree of emphasis (and often disguised approval) of underlying oligarchical methods.
e. belief that the future of democracy in the United States is reasonably secure.

Unfortunately, there has been relatively little research on the "democratic personality," which makes it risky to forecast whether conditions today will facilitate or detract from its effective functioning. On the one hand, there is interesting evidence that would lead one to forecast an increased commitment to democratic ideals. Earlier I mentioned Richard Flacks' work on the "transformation of the American middle class family," which would involve increased equality between husband and wife, declining distinctiveness of sex roles in the family, increased opportunity for self-expression on the part of the children, fewer parental demands for self-discipline, and more parental support for autonomous behavior on the part of the children. In addition, the increase in educated persons, whose status is less dependent on property, will likely increase the investment of individuals in having autonomy and a voice in decision-making.

On the other hand, it is not difficult to detect some formidable threats to the democratic process which make me extremely apprehensive about an optimistic prediction. Two are basically psychological, one derived from some previous assumptions about the environment, the other derived from some recent personal experience. The third is a venerable structural weakness which at this time takes on a new urgency.

A. Given the turbulent and dynamic texture of the environment, we can observe a growing uncertainty about the deepest human concerns: jobs, neighborhoods, regulation of social norms, life styles, child-rearing, law and order; in short, the only basic questions, according to Tolstoi, that interest human beings: how to live? what to live for? The ambiguities and changes in American life that occupy discussion in university seminars, annual meetings, and policy debates in Washington, and that form the backbone of contemporary popular psychology and sociology, become increasingly the conditions of trauma and frustration in the lower-middle class. Suddenly the rules are changing—all the rules.

Already clearly foreshadowed is a clashy dissensus of values that will tax to the utmost two of the previously mentioned democraticness scales: "patience or impatience with the delays and confusions of democratic processes" and "belief that the future of democracy in the United States is reasonably secure."

The inability to tolerate ambiguity and the consequent frustration, plus the mood of dissensus, may lead to a proliferation of "mini-societies" and relatively impermeable subcultures, from George Wallace's blue-collar strongholds to rigidly circumscribed communal ventures. Because of their rejection of incremental reform and the Establishment, and their impatience with bureaucratic-pragmatic leadership, their movements and leadership will be likely to resemble a "revolutionary-charismatic" style.[18]

B. The personal observation has to do with my experience over the past few years as an academic administrator—an experience obtained during a particularly spastic period for all of us in the academy. At Buffalo, we had been trying for governance through a thorough and complete democratic process, with as much participation as anyone can bear. There are many difficulties in building this process: The tensions between collegiality and the bureaucratic-pragmatic style of administrators, the difficulty in arousing faculty and students to participate, etc. I might add, parenthetically, that Buffalo, as is true of many state universities, had long cherished a tradition of strong faculty autonomy and academic control. Our intention was to facilitate this direction as well as to encourage more student participation.

When trouble erupted on the campus, I was disturbed to discover—to the surprise of many of my colleagues, particularly historians and political scientists —that the democratic process we were building seemed so fragile and certainly weakened in comparison to the aphrodisia of direct action, mass meetings, and frankly autocratic maneuverings. The quiet workings of the bureaucratic-democratic style seemed bland, too complex and prismatic for easy comprehension, and even banal in contrast to the headiness of the disruptions. Even those of us who were attempting to infuse and reinforce democratic functioning found ourselves caught up in the excitement and chilling risks involved.

Erich Fromm said it all, I reflected later on, in his *Escape from Freedom*; but what was missing for me in his formulation was the psychic equivalent for democratic participants.

During this same period, I came across a paper by Chris Argyris[19] which reinforced my doubts about the psychological attractiveness of democracy. He used a thirty-six-category group observational system on nearly thirty groups. These groups represented a wide cross-section of bureaucratic organizations, research & development labs, universities, service and business industries. In four hundred separate meetings, amounting to almost forty-six thousand behavioral units, he found that only six of the thirty-six categories were used over 75 percent of the time, and these six were "task" items such as "gives information, asks for information," etc. Almost 60 percent of the groups showed no affect or interpersonal feelings at all, and 24 percent expressed only 1 percent affect or feelings.

Argyris' data, along with my own personal experience, have made me wonder if democratic functioning can ever develop the deep emotional commitments and satisfactions that other forms of governance evoke—as for example, revolutionary-charismatic or ideological movements. The question which I will leave with you at this time is not "is democracy inevitable?" (Taken from the original paper), but rather "is democracy sexy?"

C. The structural weakness in present-day democracy, using that term in the broadest possible political sense, is the two hundred-year-old idea first popularized by Adam Smith in *The Wealth of the Nations*. This was "the idea that an individual who intends only his own gain is led by an invisible hand to promote the public interest." The American Revolution brought about a deep concern for the constitutional guarantees of personal rights and a passionate interest in individuals' emotions and growth, but it did so without a concomitant concern for the community.

In a recent issue of *Science*, biologist Garrett Hardin discusses this in an important article, "The Tragedy of the Commons."[20] Herdsmen who keep their cattle on the commons ask themselves: "What is the utility to me of adding one more animal to my herd?" Being rational, each herdsman seeks to maximize his gain. It becomes clear that if he adds even one animal, the positive utility is nearly +1, as he receives all the proceeds from the sale of the additional increment; whereas the negative utility is only a fraction of −1, because the effects of overgrazing are shared by all herdsmen. Thus, the rational herdsman concludes that the only sensible course for him to pursue is to add another animal to his herd. And another, and another, until each man is locked into a system that compels him to increase his herd without limit. Ruin is the destination toward which all the men rush. Freedom in a commons brings ruin to all.

The democratic process, as expressed through majority vote, contains many built-in guarantees for individual freedom without any equivalent mechanisms for the "public interest" as argued in a recent article by Herbert Gans.[21]

A character in Nigel Balchin's *A Sort of Traitors*[22] expresses this structural problem with some force:

You think that people want democracy and justice and peace. You're right. They do. But what you forget is that they want them on their own terms. And their own terms don't add up. They want decency and justice without interference with their liberty to do as they like.

These are the dilemmas as I see them now: the threat to legitimacy of authority, the tensions between populist and elitist functions and between interdependence and complicity in the environment, the need for fresh metaphors, the discontinuities between micro and macro systems, and the baffling competition between forces which support and those which suppress the adoption of democratic ideology. All together, they curb one's optimism and blur the vision; at the same time, they most certainly force a new perspective upon us.

The reader has by now guessed that the generalizations already behind us and those yet to come are based on recent experiences at American universities, and, more precisely, recent *personal* experiences at my own university where I have engaged in first-hand administrative work. Whether or not the aforementioned reversals and confusions are due to a change in roles, a change in times, or a change in site is hard to say. What should be made clear is that the generalizations are based on a single unit, however "representative" or microcosmic, and a unique one, at that. "Practice" has an awesome capacity to restrict and possibly distort theory. In my own case, it has generated experiences which elude conceptualization and has made previous conceptualization somewhat confining. The above may be overly obvious to the reader, and I mention it here only as an admission of probable bias.

A New Perspective

These profound changes lead me to suggest that any forecast one makes about trends in human institutions must take into account the following:

1. The need for fundamental reform in the purpose and organization of our institutions to enable them to adapt responsively in an exponentially changing social, cultural, political, and economic environment.

2. The need to develop such institutions on a human scale which permits the individual to retain his identity and integrity in a society increasingly characterized by massive, urban, highly centralized governmental, business, educational, mass media, and other organizations.

3. The significant movement of young persons who are posing basic challenges to existing values and institutions and who are beginning to create radical new life styles in an attempt to preserve individual identity or to opt out of society.

4. The increasing demands placed upon all American institutions to partici-

pate more actively in social, cultural, and political programs designed to improve the quality of American life.

5. The accelerating technical changes which require the development of a scientific humanism: a world view of the social and humanistic implications of such changes.

6. The necessity of a world movement to bring man in better harmony with his physical environment.

7. The need for change towards a sensitive and flexible planning capability on the part of the management of major institutions.

8. The rising demand for social and political justice and freedom, particularly from the American black community and other deprived sectors of society.

9. The compelling need for a world order which gives greater attention to the maintenance of peace without violence between nations, groups, and individuals.

A New Forecast for Public Bureaucracy

The imponderables are youth and tradition and change. Where these predicaments, dilemmas, and second thoughts take us, I'm not exactly sure. However, by way of a summary and conclusion, there are a number of trends and emphases worth considering.

1. *The organization's response to the environment will continue to be the crucial determinant for its effectiveness.* Economists and political scientists have been telling us this for years; but only recently have sociologists and social psychologists, like Terreberry,[23] Emery and Trist,[24] Levine and White,[25] Litwak and Hylton,[26] and Evan[27] done so.

Three derivatives of this protean environment can be anticipated: First, we will witness new ecological strategies that are capable of anticipating crisis instead of responding to crisis, that require participation instead of consent, that confront conflict instead of dampening conflict, that include comprehensive measures instead of specific measures, and that include a long planning horizon instead of a short planning horizon.

Second, we will identify new roles for linking and correlating interorganizational transactions—"interstitial men."

Third, and most problematical, I anticipate an erratic environment where various organizations coexist at different stages of evolution. Rather than neat, linear, and uniform evolutionary developments, I expect that we will see both more centralization (in large-scale instrumental bureaucracies) and more decentralization (in delivery of health, education, and welfare services); both the increase of bureaucratic-pragmatic leadership and the growth of revolutionary-charismatic leadership; both the increase in size and centralization of many municipal and governmental units and the proliferation of self-contained mini-societies, from the "status-spheres" that Tom Wolfe writes about—like Ken Kesey's "electric, cool-aid, acid-heads" and the pump-house gang of La Jolla surfers—to various citizen groups. Ethnic groups organize to "get theirs," and so do the police, firemen, small property owners, "mothers fighting sex education and bussing," and so on.

2. *Large-scale public and private bureaucracies will become more vulnerable than ever before to the infusion of legislative and juridical organs.* I have always been fascinated by Harold Lasswell's famous analogy between the Freudian trinity of personality and the tripartite division of the federal government. Most bureaucracies today contain only one formal mechanism—*i.e.*, the executive or ego function. The legislative (id) and the judicial (superego) have been under-represented. In the future, however, these underrepresented organs probably will become formalized, much like the Inspector General's office in the army. In one day's issue of a recent *New York Times*, three front-page stories featured: (a) the "young Turks" within the State Department who are planning to ask the department to recognize the Foreign Service Association as the exclusive agent with which the department would bargain on a wide scale of personnel matters: (b) the anti-poverty lawyers within the Office of Equal Opportunity who have organized for greater voice in setting policy; and (c) the civil rights lawyers in the Justice Department who have formed an informal caucus to draft a protest against what they consider a recent softening of enforcement of the civil rights laws.

But why, one might ask, have these legislative and judicial functions been so grossly underrepresented? Well, for one thing, the labor unions have been relatively unsuccessful in organizing either top levels of management or professionals. They have failed to do so, in my view, because they have operated at the lowest level of the Maslow Hierarchy of Needs—economic, physiological, safety —and have failed to understand the inducements of most professionals: achievement, recognition, intrinsic quality of work, and professional development. Ironically, this has provided more "due process"—and, in some cases, more legitimate participation—to non-salaried employees than to higher level personnel. It is no coincidence that, in addition to the students, the cutting edge of last year's French revolution consisted of middle-class professional employees and technicians.

3. *There will be more legitimization for "leave-taking" and shorter tenure at the highest levels of leadership.* One aspect of "temporary systems" that was underplayed in the 1964 paper was the human cost of task efficiency. Recently, James Reston observed that the reason it is difficult to find good men for the most responsible jobs in government is that the good men have burnt out—or, as my old infantry company commander once said, "In this company, the good guys get killed." Perhaps this creates the appearance of the Peter Principle—*i.e.*, that people advance to the level of their greatest incompetence. What's more likely is that people get burnt out, psychologically killed. Many industries are now experimenting with variations on sabbaticals for their executives; and I think it's about time that universities woke up to the fact that a seven-year period, for a legalized moratorium, is simply out of joint with the recurring need for self and professional renewal.

It may also be that leaders with shorter time horizons will be more effective in the same way that interregnum popes have proven to be the most competent.

4. *New organizational roles will develop—roles emphasizing different loci and commitments of colleague-iality.* Aside from consultants and external advisory groups, organizations tend to arrogate the full working time and commitments of their membership. One works for Ford, or HEW, or Macy's, or Yale. Moonlighting is permitted, sometimes reluctantly; but there is usually no doubt about the primary organization, or where there might be a possible "conflict of interest." This idea of the mono-organizational commitment will likely erode in the future, as more and more people create pluralistic commitments to a number of organizations.

To use Buffalo as an example once again, we set up one new experimental department which includes three different kinds of professors—different in terms of their loci and relatedness to the department. There is a core group of faculty who have full-time membership in the department. There is an associated faculty, who have part-time commitments to the department, but whose appointments are in another department. And finally, there is a "network faculty" who spend varying periods of time in the departments, but whose principal affiliation is with another university or organization. Similar plans are now being drawn up for students.

Along the same lines, a number of people have talked about "invisible colleges" of true colleagues, located throughout the world; they would be convened on special occasions, but would communicate mainly by telephone, the mail, and during hasty meetings at airports. I would wager that these "floating crapgames" will increase, and that we will see at least three distinct sets of roles emerge within organizations: those that are *pivotal* and more or less permanent; those that are *relevant* but not necessarily permanent; and those that are *peripheral*. A person who is pivotal and permanent to one organization may have a variety of relevant and peripheral roles in others.

There are many reasons for this development. First and most obvious is the fact that we live in a jet age where air travel is cheap and very accessible. (A good friend of mine living in Boston commutes daily to New York City for his analytic hour and manages to get back to his office by about 10:30 A.M.) Second, the scarcity of talent and the number of institutions "on the make" will very likely lead more of the top talent to start dividing their time among a number of institutions. Third, the genuine motivational satisfactions gained from working within a variety of comparable institutions seems to be important not for all, but for an increasingly growing fraction of the general population.

5. *We will learn the necessity of educating our leaders in at least two competencies*: (1) To cope efficiently, imaginatively, and perceptively with information overload. Marxist power was property. Today much power is based on control of relevant information. (2) As Donald Michael[28] says in *The Unprepared Society*, "we must educate for empathy, compassion, trust, nonexploitiveness, nonmanipulativeness, for self-growth and self-esteem, for tolerance of ambiguity, for acknowledgement of error, for patience, for suffering."

Without affective competence, and the strength that comes with it, it is difficult to see how the leader can confront the important ethical and political decisions without succumbing to compromise or to "petite Eichmannism."

6. *We will observe in America a society which has experienced the consequences of unpreparedness and which has become more sanguine about the effects of planning.* There will be planning—not to restrict choice or to prohibit serendipity, but to structure possibilities and practical visions.

Whether or not these forecasts are desirable, assuming their validity for the moment, really depends on one's status, values, and normative biases. One man's agony is another's ecstasy. It does appear that we will have to reckon with a number of contradictory and confusing tendencies, however, which can quickly be summarized:

1. More self and social consciousness with respect to the governance of public bureaucracies.
2. More participation in this governance by the clients who are served as well as those doing the service, including the lower levels of the hierarchy.
3. More formal, quasi-legal processes of conflict resolution.
4. More direct confrontations when the negotiation and bargaining process fails.
5. More attention to moral-ethical issues relative to technical-efficiency imperatives.
6. More rapid turnover and varying relationships with institutions.

I think it would be appropriate if I concluded this paper with a quotation from the earlier 1964 paper—a quotation which still seems valid and especially pertinent in light of the new perspectives gained over the past several years. I was writing about the educational requirements necessary for coping with a turbulent environment:

Our educational system should (1) help us to identify with the adaptive process without fear of losing our identity, (2) increase tolerance of ambiguity without fear of losing intellectual mastery, (3) increase our ability to collaborate without fear of losing our individuality, and (4) develop a willingness to participate in social evolution while recognizing implacable forces. In short, we need an educational system that can help make a virtue out of contingency rather than one which induces hesitancy or its reckless companion, expedience.[29]

Notes

1. W. G. Bennis, "Future of the Social Sciences," *Antioch Review*, 28, (Summer, 1968), p. 227.

2. O. Helmer, "Political Analysis of the Future," a paper presented at the 1969 annual meeting of the American Political Science Association, New York, September 4, 1969, p. 3.

3. W. G. Bennis, "Organizational Developments and the Fate of Bureaucracy," invited address, American Psychological Association, Los Angeles, California, September 4, 1964.

4. W. G. Bennis, "Organizational Developments and the Fate of Bureaucracy," *Industrial Management Review* (Spring, 1966), pp. 41-55.

5. E. Trist, *The Relation of Welfare and Development in the Transition to Post-industrialism* (U.C.L.A.: Western Management Science Institute, February, 1968).

6. W. A. Gamson, *Power and Discontent* (Homewood: Dorsey Press, 1968).

7. H. C. Kelman, "In Search of New Bases for Legitimacy: Some Social Psychological Dimensions of the Black Power and Student Power Movements," the Richard M. Elliott Lecture, delivered at the University of Michigan, April 21, 1969.

8. R. Flacks, "Protest or Conform: Some Social Psychological Perspectives on Legitimacy," *The Journal of Applied Behavioral Science* (April-June, 1969).

9. M. Trow, "Urban Problems and University Problems," a paper presented at the Twenty-fourth All-University Conference, University of California, Riverside, March 23-25, 1969, p. 2.

10. E. Gross, "Universities As Organizations: A Research Approach," *American Sociological Review* (August, 1968), pp. 518-44.

11. T. Parsons, "The Academic System: A Sociologist's View," *The Public Interest* 13, (Fall, 1968) pp. 179-197.

12. S. Greer, *The Logic of Social Inquiry* (Chicago-Aldine, 1969), p. 46.

13. L. Duhl, Letter to the Editor, *The Journal of Applied Behavioral Science*, 5, 2 (1969), pp. 279-80.

14. E. P. Hollander and J. W. Julian, "Contemporary Trends in the Analysis of Leadership Processes," *Psychological Bulletin*, 71 (1969), pp. 387-97.

15. J. W. Julian and E. P. Hollander, "A Study of Some Role Dimensions of Leader-Follower Relations," Technical Report No. 3, State University of New York at Buffalo, Department of Psychology, Contract 4679, Office of Naval Research (April, 1966).

16. G. Sartori, "Democracy," *Encyclopedia of Social Sciences*, (New York: Macmillan), pp. 112-22.

17. R. E. Lane, *Political Ideology* (New York: The Free Press, 1962), pp. 94-97.

18. H. A. Kissinger, "Domestic Structures and Foreign Policy," *Daedalus* (Spring, 1966), pp. 503-29.

19. C. Argyris, "Small Group Field Research and Implications for Cognitive Consistency and Social Comparison Theories," *The American Psychologist* (October, 1969).

20. G. Hardin, "The Tragedy of the Commons," *Science* (December 13, 1968), pp. 1243-48.

21. H. J. Gans, "We Won't End the Urban Crisis Until We End Majority Rule," *New York Times Magazine* (August 3, 1969).

22. N. Balchin, *A Sort of Traitors* (Collins, 1949).

23. S. Terreberry, "The Evolution of Organizational Environments," *Administrative Science Quarterly* (March, 1968), pp. 590-613.

24. F. E. Emery, and E. L. Trist, "The Causal Texture of Organizational Environments," *Human Relations* (1965), pp. 1-10.

25. S. Levine and P. E. White, "Exchange As a Conceptual Framework for the Study of Interorganizational Relationships," *Administrative Science Quarterly* (1961), pp. 583-601.

26. E. Litwak, and L. Hylton, "Interorganizational Analysis: A Hypothesis on Coordinating Agencies," *Administrative Science Quarterly* (1962), pp. 395-420.

27. W. M. Evan, "The Organization-Set: Toward A Theory of Interorganizational Relationships," in James D. Thompson (ed.), *Approaches to Organizational Design* (Pittsburgh: University of Pittsburgh Press, 1966), pp. 177-80.

28. D. Michael, *The Unprepared Society* (New York: Basic Books, 1968) pp. 108-10.

29. Bennis, "Organizational Developments and the Fate of Bureaucracy," 1964, *op. cit.*

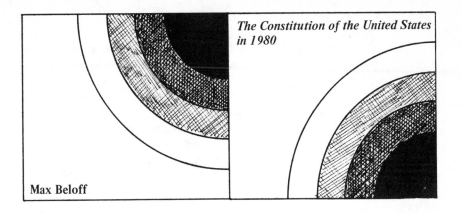

The Constitution of the United States in 1980

Max Beloff

To predict in politics is always dangerous; to do it twice, foolhardy. In 1963, I wrote an article endeavoring to foresee what constitutional changes might come about or be considered in the United States by the year 1970.[1] Well, 1970 is· here; what do my efforts then indicate about the way in which the position in 1980 might be predicted?

Changes in constitutional arrangements in a country like the United States where hitherto the presumption has been against change will normally arise from some immediate problem that appears to indicate a defect in the system. Until it crops up, it is unlikely that the political-scientist will guess at it. Had the world situation in 1940 and 1944 not provided President Roosevelt with reasons (and justifications) for breaking Washington's precedent and seeking a third and fourth term, it is doubtful whether there would have been the impetus behind the movement to prevent such action in the future, as was done in the Twenty-Second Amendment. I should perhaps have foreseen, but did not, that President Eisenhower's illnesses would make people feel that the ambiguity over the status of the vice-presidency, the possibility of a vacancy in that office, and the lack of a provision for declaring the President unfit to perform his duties had become intolerable and that what is now the Twenty-Fifth Amendment would come into effect. The problem posed to the major parties by the Wallace candidacy in 1968 has helped to precipitate the movement to abolish the electoral college and to replace its functioning by the direct popular election of the President, a movement which seems likely to succeed before very long.

More far-reaching changes or attempts at change will obviously arise from deeper causes, so that in order to predict the constitutional future one has to be able to peer into the social and political future. Here one may be wrong through no particular weakness in the method of analysis, but simply because history is contingent, and accident plays its part.

Writing in 1963, I said that, barring accident or national catastrophe, President Kennedy would remain in office until 1968; it would then be a question of whether the Democrats would still hold office, and, if so, what kind of man they would select for the succession. The question would then have been open as to whether the distinct accent of the Kennedy administration on external problems would continue under Democrats or Republicans, or whether there would be a renewed and more consistent effort at dealing with domestic issues.

The assassination of Kennedy and the involvement in the Vietnam war, which was his legacy to his successor, destroyed this seemingly probable timetable. President Johnson brought forward the date at which a real effort was made to deal with domestic issues, but this program was distorted and finally brought to a halt through financial and other pressures arising from the war. It was not possible in 1963 to foresee the extent of radical protest on either the war or the racial issue; and, in consequence, the Republican victory on a "law and order" platform in 1968 could not be foreseen either. Nor could one have foretold the growing assertiveness of Congress in the external field and the re-emergence under President Nixon of tensions between the executive and legislative branches of government to the extent that these became apparent in the first half of 1970.

What is hard to estimate is the extent to which President Johnson's attempt, sanctioned by a benevolent Supreme Court, to hurry the progress of the southern Negro in the direction of full political equality and greater educational opportunity may actually have contributed to the subsequent radicalization of positions on both sides. It is a common historical experience that it is when hope begins to flower that a revolutionary upsurge is to be expected. Where there is no hope, acquiescence is somehow easier.

The two aspects of the direct attack on the racial issue—programs for dealing with poverty as such are indirect parts of the same strategy and raise different constitutional issues. The first, the political, is the easier to grasp. Unless one admits, as few Americans white or black have so far admitted, that some territorial solution to the problem is possible, the American Negro will have to ameliorate his position through the ordinary political process; therefore, the full exercise of the right to vote and to stand for office is all important.

The progress that was foreseeable for the 1960s is likely to continue in the 1970s, so that one might suppose that by 1980 it would be almost complete.

The Twenty-Fourth Amendment outlawing the poll tax, which was passed by Congress during the Kennedy presidency and ratified in the Johnson era, may have been of more symbolical than real significance, since other measures of discrimination are possible and have of course been used. But the general pressure in this field does seem to have proved irresistible. The redistricting decisions of the Supreme Court may not be as important in this respect as in altering the balance of the electorate in other ways, and it is possible that a Supreme Court of a more conservative temper will have the effect of slightly slowing down the process; though the rejection of President Nixon's two southern nominees for the bench does not indicate the change in its substantive attitudes on the race issue will be a radical one. By 1980 then, the United States will have adult suffrage with the voting strengths of different portions of the electorate fairly evenly represented for the first time. In this way, as some municipal successes show, black Americans will be able in larger numbers to participate at all levels in the political process; the question remains as to whether by then a substantial proportion will want to contract out of it or not.

The use of political power effectively obviously depends in part upon the educational opportunities open to different groups. Educational desegregation—in the South by design, in the North by the operation of the neighborhood principle—has been harder to uproot than political discrimination. It is one of those areas in which the constitutional separation of powers makes advance most difficult where there is no local consensus in its favor. It does depend upon the executive branch being willing to enforce through financial and even coercive powers the interpretation by the courts of Congress's intentions. The advent of the Nixon administration with its "southern strategy" and states-rights inclinations has obviously slowed down the movement and made the relative optimism of the 1950s seem a little euphoric. But it is difficult to see what more can be done within the constitutional and legal sphere, even supposing that President Nixon's successor in 1972 or more probably 1976 reverts to the Johnson view. The whole issue is one where the action of so many individuals and different public authorities is involved that opinion rather than law must always in some measure be decisive. Nor is it easy to be certain whether black radicalism is likely to hasten or retard the process. Insofar as it has induced institutions of higher education to make room for "black studies" programs or to lower the demands made upon black students in order to keep up their numbers, it could be argued that in the long run it will have produced a retarding effect upon the Negro community and hence made it more difficult for it to profit by the greater measure of political opportunity it now enjoys.

I certainly regarded it as likely that sooner or later a more active interventionist policy by the federal government in the educational field was probable and that this would extend to other aspects of social action. But I did say in 1963 that any such program would come up against certain obstacles of an institutional kind which could ultimately be regarded as deriving from some aspects of the constitutional system. The fate of President Johnson's programs has justified my view.

I held and still hold that the units of American government—the states, counties, and cities—are too numerous and too unrelated to the present population map, particularly in the great conurbations. The right to act and the power to tax are too rarely united. With problems of urban decay and environmental pollution even more alive than a decade ago, this claim seems more than ever justified. The friction between New York City and New York State is only one example among many. It is impossible to say whether by 1980 the need to tidy up the map of subordinate authorities will be so manifest that action will have been taken—and if states are to be involved, as they must be, this might need a constitutional amendment—but one can say that if some action has not been taken, the problems will be even worse than today.

Less obviously crucial is the other deficiency which I pointed out: the lack of fully professionalized government service at all levels which would make it possible for agreed programs—for instance, in respect to poverty—to be implemented with maximum efficiency and at minimum cost. Nothing has done more to discredit the notion of the "welfare state" in Congress and in opinion at large than the conviction that money voted will largely be swallowed up in graft or near-graft. On the other hand, the powerful prejudice in Congress against giving the Federal executive branch clear lines of authority and adequate staffing made any other outcome very difficult to expect. Whether a change in congressional attitudes is possible in this or many other fields so long as the Senate is as monstrously unrepresentative a body as the Constitution now makes it, one may doubt. The most far-reaching amendment to the Constitution one could envisage in terms of its probable consequences would be to end the equal representation of the states in the Senate. I do not think this is likely to happen by 1980.

One area in which I did not foresee any great problems in the 1960s and therefore no great likelihood of constitutional change, was that of the basic rights of the individual. It looked as though, after some undoubted encroachments upon human rights under the stress of war, the Court had pretty well re-established the necessary equilibrium between the just claims of the state and the human rights enshrined in the Constitution.

That balance has now been adversely affected in two ways. Technological developments have permitted an invasion of privacy by both the public authorities and private corporations or persons to a hitherto undreamed of extent, while modern methods of storing data have made this information all too easy to preserve and utilize. How to add a right to privacy to the Bill of Rights is a question that may well occupy lawyers for quite some time; the first requirement is that public opinion should be alive to the need of it. Do Americans value privacy as much as most Europeans? One does not know.

The other and more obvious change has been the challenge to the law itself and the development of new techniques of protest both in the black ghettos and on the campuses. It is too early to say whether this phenomenon—not adequately summed up in catch phrases about law and order—will outlive the Vietnam war which has done the most to spark it off.

It is of course not the first time that the unpopularity of a war has in itself added to the normal human reluctance to be conscripted—one is reminded of the Civil War draft riots—but the extent to which defiance has been encouraged by sections of the country's intellectual leadership is perhaps unique in American history. And it is certainly the case that the new techniques of resistance—the "sit-in" for instance—are very easily exploited for any cause or even for no cause.

The ordinary constitutional principles about the rights of free speech, assembly, petition, and the like, which have served the United States and the rest of the liberal West for a couple of centuries, cannot easily cope with the activities of those who deny the validity of the whole legal-constitutional system and insist on operating outside it; this is particularly true where the passive techniques of protest spill over into the destruction of property and the inflicting of personal violence, as they inevitably must. Can the law be amended to draw the line at some acceptable point without infringing upon the liberties that are demanded by the nature of an open society itself? This question is now at issue in many countries, but it is particularly poignant in the United States where the Bill of Rights is so central to the nation's creed.

Quite apart from the changes in legal norms that may be necessary, the new forms of protest have raised a rather muted problem in American institutional arrangements—*i.e.*, the disposition and control of the forces of coercion: police, national guard, and regular military. One of the difficulties in trying to control these new movements has obviously been the deep distrust which so many Americans—particularly young Americans—feel toward their police. (It is an interesting mark of difference between the British and the American scene in this respect that the attempt to direct hostility against the police on the part of some youthful leaders in Britain—particularly those with an American or other foreign background—was an almost complete failure. The British citizen regards the policeman as a friend not an enemy, and the police have put up with a great deal rather than destroy that image. Like so many things, however, this is not the same in Northern Ireland.)

It is quite obvious that the national guard is not an appropriate body to call to the aid of the civil power, and that the regular armed forces ought only to be used as a last resort. It may be that the states will have to be provided with some new and trained force for the preservation of public order if the present threat of disorder continues; but it will take a good deal of thinking and perhaps of experiment before the right formula can be found. Both society and the individual need protection; violent disorder is itself a crime and a cover for crimes, but the measures taken must not be such as further to exacerbate group or generational tensions.

The Kennedy accent on the United States world role made me believe in 1963 that civil-military relations would be as they had been under Truman, an important area of constitutional debate, which has been the case; but it also led to my seeing the question solely in the light of operations outside the United States. Here, in fact, the problems of the 1960s have not been acute. Whatever errors the military may have made in giving their advice about entering the war in Southeast Asia and about the method of trying to terminate it, there has been no question of their not channeling their advice through the civilian authorities. It may be that the advice given to Johnson and Nixon was not altogether explicit as to the probable consequences of following it—or it may be that the military were really self-deceived—but there has been no question of a MacArthur-type defiance of presidential directives, or of an attempt to appeal over the head of the President to the people or to Congress; perhaps because there has so far been little need to do so.

There is however a susceptibility in the people and in Congress about the degree to which the military claim, and probably must claim, a free hand in the tactics they pursue in the course of their allotted missions. Nor can an army even when fighting as far away as Southeast Asia be readily insulated from domestic opinion, particularly when it is so largely a conscript army. Hence the indignation expressed at the suggestion of undue violence toward civilians and the counter-feeling that soldiers are being improperly victimized for behaving as soldiers in tight spots have always done.

It is difficult to say whether this kind of issue could raise general problems of civil-military relations once more. If the apparent intention of the administration to move toward the abolition of selective service in favor of an all-professional army of the old American and present British type can be carried into effect, one will have a rather different situation from the one in which army and civilian life is closely interwoven. But Americans are always likely to react sharply to any suggestions of a praetorian guard situation; if American constitutional democracy comes to an end, it will not be at the hands of "colonels"–not by 1980 anyhow.

But there are within the civilian apparatus of government itself certain tensions about actual policy–defense and foreign–which do provide a wedge for the activities of the civilian-military complex and which were already talked about when I wrote in 1963. The delicate calculations about the balance of terror which have influenced Presidential decisions in defense policy and in arms control negotiations have not always commended themselves to Congress. For example, congressmen find it hard to see, as do their constituents, that "defensive weapons" like ABM systems can actually have a destabilizing effect. So the President has to walk warily in these fields, knowing that some branches of the military and of the defense industries may be advocating policies which do not fit in with his overall objectives.

If Congress (like the public) may well be more bellicose in the matter of preparing for war than the executive branch, in the actual decision to use force it has usually been warier, or thought to be so. One aspect of the Constitution which time has rendered it hard to apply literally has been the placing of the war-making power in the hands of the legislature. It has long been realized that as far as getting the country into war is concerned, the President's powers as commander-in-chief are more important. But it does not necessarily follow that this is a responsibility that every President relishes; though Kennedy used it unflinchingly in the 1962 Cuba crisis. Both President Eisenhower and, to some extent, President Johnson tried by the use of congressional resolutions to get guidelines for presidential action which would in a sense force Congress to underwrite any actions they might undertake in certain specific situations. How far this responsibility can be shared under the Constitution, or whether the war-making and troop-moving power ought to be redefined in a new Constitutional amendment and the separation of powers abandoned in this sphere, are open questions unlikely to be resolved before 1980.

Under President Nixon, the problem has also been attacked the other way round; can Congress by the use of the power of appropriation deny certain freedoms that the President would otherwise enjoy as commander-in-chief, and, if so, how far could this go? Could the power be used to dictate how a war is to be fought as well as where? So long as a separation of powers does exist, it is difficult to see that Congress can ultimately replace the President's policies by its own or that any legislature is well-fitted to do so. And if the war in S.E. Asia is brought to an end, it may be that the present bout of Congressional self-assertiveness in this sphere will come to an end. If the executive branch cannot be trusted with the main issues of national security, then it is necessary to find some way of making changes in it; and that course leads away from the essence of the American system toward the "responsible government" of the British parliamentary type, where you know you have to change the men in order to change the policies. It won't happen by 1980.

In my article in 1963, I pointed out that both the separation of powers and the strong element of genuine federalism in the American system militated against the possibility of the United States entering any international organization involving some surrender of sovereignty. The events of the last few years have, if anything, strengthened my convictions in this respect. It seems almost certain both that the mood in the United States will be inward-looking over most of the next decade and that the demand will be for greater governmental powers to deal with internal problems rather than for any allocation of such powers to international or supra-national organizations. I would not therefore expect the Constitution to be altered by 1980 in such a way as to facilitate the incorporation of the United States in some wider entity; advocates of "world government" and of "Atlantic unity" seem destined to be disappointed.

It will be seen that in 1963 looking forward to 1970, I forecast no major changes in the American constitution; similarly in 1970, looking forward to 1980, my inclination is to think that all the strains will be met somehow within the system and that changes will be marginal. Whether this is desirable or not depends upon social predictions and social values which fall outside the purview of the purely political inquirer.

Inherent in the whole approach of political studies is the fact that it is difficult to escape from the confines of what is; the tendency is, and rightly so, to think that there are good reasons for existing institutions and practices, and that equally good reasons are necessary before they ought to be altered. We are beginning to realize that if it exceeds a certain rate, change itself has deleterious consequences for the life of a community; and therefore, if technological changes and the changes in social mores which are in part their consequence are exceptionally rapid, people may seek solace in the immutability of other institutions and practices. Even the routine of elections, with all the well-known meretricious elements that it involves, may be a certain solace. One must not press the argument too far; abuses which violate the fundamental beliefs of a system can only undermine the confidence that people should have in it. But that is not an argument for perpetual tinkering.

A foreign observer is likely to expect that the Constitution of the United States will be in 1980 what it is in 1970, and to assume that the people of the United States will solve their most pressing problems within its confines.

Note

1. "La Constitution des Etats-Unis en 1970," *Futuribles*, I (Geneva: Droz, 1963).

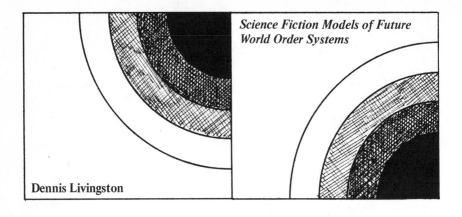

Science Fiction Models of Future World Order Systems

Dennis Livingston

In recent years, the necessity of attempting to anticipate the shape of things to come has achieved widespread recognition by individuals in government, business, and academia. The result has been a large body of literature concerned with the projection of ascertainable trends and the presentation of alternative societal models. Although it is more difficult to forecast future social and political developments than to engage in economic and technological forecasting, this has not deterred speculation about the development of future social systems. The series of books on *The Future of the International Legal Order* and the World Order Models Project of the World Law Fund are examples of programs in the field of international relations explicitly involved in the projection of models of an international political system capable of effectively dealing with the global issues of arms control, tension management, economic development, and social justice.[1] The study of alternative futures has become a legitimate area of scholarship.

In the absence of data directly connected with the subject at hand, investigators of possible futures have developed a methodology that includes the extrapolation of current trends, the systematic survey of expert opinion, and the comparative analysis of the present with the analogous past. The literature of science fiction can be an additional source of relevant material, in two respects: first, the content of its stories comprises an archive of speculative insights into the future; this content has often been generated by the implicit use of the same techniques as nonfiction futurology, leavened by the unquantifiable ingredient of creative imagination. Second, the nature of the themes selected for science fiction works may both reveal the contemporary concerns of society and directly influence the stock of futuristic images available to society. The purpose of this essay, then, is to inquire into the availability of alternative models of the future international political system that may be found in science fiction, and to evaluate the utility of these models in the context of international political forecasting.

I

Science fiction has not received great attention to date as a possible research tool in political futurology. Several factors may account for this.

First, the literature is still a captive of its past reputation as escapist adventure, or "space opera," in which an often atrocious writing style (*e.g.*, unexplained or undeveloped character motivation) was combined with technocratic megalomania to stimulate adolescent fantasies in future Dr. Strangeloves. But this objection to taking science fiction seriously, while the most common, is the least relevant to the kind of analysis of interest here. The fact that there are works of science fiction that are excellent by any criteria of literary esthetics is not the point either. What is important to a sociological perspective of science fiction are the basic hopes and fears of a society as revealed in this literature and the impact of its visions upon the popular culture, even though given works within the genre may vary widely in their literary quality.

Second, it may be held that science fiction is not very useful because, taking the literature as a whole, its predictions have not been overly accurate. While I know of no empirical investigation of this point, it seems reasonable to suppose that the quantity of output has been such over the years as to render it not surprising that some stories have been close in their anticipations of the future, but not for any systematic reasons inherent in writing science fiction. However, the accuracy of science fiction predictions is not a primary consideration here, nor is it such to science fiction authors, who write simply to provide entertainment. What *is* significant in science fiction is not its predictions or prophecies of what will be, but its speculations about what might be.

The third, and most serious, problem with science fiction as a source of models of future societal patterns lies in the basic characteristics of many of its plots. With the exception of utopian and dystopian works, science fiction as a whole has not detailed the nature and operation of domestic or international political systems. Much of the literature, especially that prior to World War II, consisted of straight-line extrapolations of dramatic technologies invented by heroes when in difficulty, or tales dealing with the rise and fall of galactic empires.[2] Thus, in any given story, there was not likely to be much material on the society in which the characters operated: nor was this a matter of great concern.

Even after science fiction started to devote more attention to the social consequences of science and technology and to projections of social trends themselves, an implicit conservative bias was observable in many stories. Science fiction authors have let their imaginations roam freely in regard to developments in future science and technology, but they have generally been less bold in considering the social systems whose operations would be heavily affected by those developments. Whatever its track record in technical predictions, many social forces—birth control, women's liberation, the anti-colonial and black revolutions, the youth culture, the ecological crusade—received relatively little attention in science fiction prior to their impingement on the public consciousness. The majority of authors have found it hard to extrapolate social mores different from those operating within their own time and culture.[3]

When some attention is paid to social systems or governmental affairs in science fiction, many authors model their societies on abstractions of historical political systems reshuffled whole-cloth into the future. Science fiction's favorite models include the Roman Empire (often copied for galactic civilizations), feudal Western Europe (the model for primitive or postnuclear worlds), the federal United States, and Stalin's Soviet Union. It has often been noted that science fiction authors seem to have a predilection for creating stories set in totalitarian dictatorships.[4] Typical to these tales is the protagonist, the hero-dissenter, who, for reasons never quite clear, has managed to escape the usual brainwashing and enters the tight little world of the authoritarian state. The hero contacts the local underground and in due course overthrows the government, with a little help from his friends. The reasons behind this attention to elitist dictatorships may be nothing more complex than the difficulty of writing dramatically of a situation where all is going well and the relief of readers at being presented with societies where it is easy to separate the bad guys from the heroes. A more subtle factor may be that many authors of commercial science fiction writing prior to World War II received their professional training in science and engineering and, one might speculate, were therefore not equipped or inclined to devise future societal settings any more ambiguous than the current status quo or its totally evil variant.

This situation still leaves one with a negative kind of benefit. To charge that much of science fiction takes for granted the political myths of its time, that it relies heavily on historical analogy, that it does not pay enough attention to positive alternatives to present societies, or that it is not imaginative in its social extrapolations is only to repeat criticism that could equally well be leveled at nonfiction futurology or systems analysis.[5] Forecasters could gain something from reading science fiction by learning to avoid its errors, for they are prone to the same pitfalls. Similarly, science fiction authors could be enriched by gaining some familiarity with those works of political analysis that attempt to devise a sophisticated array of alternative international systems.[6]

Yet, that is not the end of the game. While it is possible that a great part of the literature of science fiction may be useful only in providing warning signs to the toilers in the think tanks, it is worthwhile sifting through what is available in order to locate the many works that can be perused with some profit by social scientists. Specifically, there does exist a significant substratum of science fiction stories which is distinguished from the rest of science fiction by the fact that it devotes some thought to how varying models of world order allocate authoritative decision-making processes on both national and global levels.

A survey of this portion of the literature has resulted in the formulation of five catagories representative of the kinds of societies found in these models and the nature and status of the international actors that emerge from them. The first two categories are relevant to the socio-economic setting in which plots take place, while the remaining three are relevant to the international setting.

The first category in which these science fiction social systems fall involves a traditional, three-class, hierarchically stratified society, consisting of a mass of workers and peasants at the bottom, salaried personnel and lower echelon managers at the middle level, and a small group with ultimate decision-making authority at the top level. Technology is used to repress the masses and keep the elite comfortable. In the second category, technology is used to liberate man from routine drudgery, resulting in a two-class structure of affluent masses and, again, a small group of leaders at the top.

The institutions through which these societies express themselves and by which they are regulated on the international scene fall into three patterns. Generally, the stories selected for survey here avoid models reminiscent of the pre-World War I international system in which a multitude of states shared relatively similar notions of the rules of the game and were the only significant actors on the global stage. In the variety of international futures presented in science fiction, the more or less sovereign nation-state continues to be a major element of future political systems, but it no longer enjoys either a monopoly of legitimate decision-making authority or the supreme institutional loyalty of its citizens. Three transformations are possible for the state system as we know it. First, power to allocate human and material resources may be concentrated in one or a few superstates evolved from today's Soviet, American, and Communist Chinese blocs. Second, power may be diffused from the state to a variety of transnational actors, such as business corporations, international organizations, and organized crime. Third, the bureaucratic structure typified by the modern state and corporation may be entirely superseded by alternate forms of governance.

Finally, in order to describe and compare the societies thus categorized, I have chosen seven stories for review which contain thematic components representative of the socio-political settings of interest here.[7]

II

The three-class society, stratified by status and wealth, comprises a pattern which has appeared with remarkable consistency throughout the history of science fiction. The highest and lowest class members may receive different names—in *1984* they are the Party and the proles, in *Gather, Darkness!* they are the Hierarchy and the commoners, and in *The Space Merchants* they are the heads of the largest advertising agencies and the consumers—but their respective roles are generally similar.[8]

These societies are distinguished from historical examples by the efficiency and ruthlessness with which the elite managers use modern techniques of psychosocial manipulation to induce mass conformity to the prevailing belief system and by the fact that membership in the elite is usually not hereditary. Thus, in *Gather, Darkness!* it is the scientists themselves who have seized power after a time of war and revolution and have perpetuated their rule by cynically establishing a priesthood comprised of seven ascending circles. The skills of an advanced technology are used to perform "miracles" and hoodwink citizens into believing the veracity of the official religion, as if Elmer Gantry had teamed up with Thomas Edison. The Party in *1984* goes one step further by dispensing entirely with the rationalization that it is in control to restore stability for the citizens' own good. The party leaders desire power for its own sake, for the control it gives over the minds of party members.

Of course, technology may be used not only as a repressive mechanism, but also as a form of liberation by which man is freed from menial labor. It is interesting that the rulers of Oceania, one of the three superstates in *1984*, are quite aware that technology could enable all men in their society to achieve a decent standard of living. This, however, is perceived as a condition that would destabilize their rigid society, since a literate and prosperous population is less susceptible to control. The solution to this problem is to utilize industrial output in the nonproductive game of continual war. Inner Party members, however, retain some economic luxuries for themselves and use this advantage to demonstrate their superiority over the other classes.

On the other hand, the beneficial fruits of technology need not be restricted to a favored minority. Yet even if affluence is widely shared, the societies that result are seldom presented as utopian. Many science fiction authors long anticipated the New Left critique that materialistic perfection may also be a kind of tyranny; for man, if his physical needs are too well cared for, is liable to grow weak, flabby, intellectually lazy, and degenerate, and his society will be prone to stagnation.[9] While both *Teg's 1994* and "The Five Way Secret Agent" are examples of the automated society complete with universal credit card, the threat of mass mental decay is presumably avoided by encouraging citizens to fulfill their psychic needs for self-development through continual education and, in *Teg's 1994*, by joining together in mutually compatible environments supportive of personal growth.

Societies in which affluence is artificially restricted to a privileged class or allowed to diffuse throughout the system are two possible futures. More probable than either a completely repressive or utopian society, however, would be a world in which automation has proceeded apace, but without eliminating all jobs below the managerial level; in which techniques for personality manipulation have improved, but without turning the masses into mindless robots; and in which the widespread availability of consumer products has continued, but without alleviating conditions of poverty everywhere in the world.

Stand on Zanzibar is an attempt to envision a realistically complex society and is perhaps the most sophisticated social and political description of a future world yet to appear in science fiction. Manhattan of the year 2010 is depicted along Wellsian lines, modernized and extrapolated. The government policy of eugenic breeding maintains the small family social norm; but the citizens packed under the city's Fuller dome lead lives of public apathy and private drug trips, enlivened by periodic riots, murderous rampages, and incidents of sabotage engaged in by some as a hobby. Walled off from the natural world by a screen of consumer goods and advertising, stripped of most of his privacy, and unable to feel a sense of territoriality or permanency in an environment of disposable possessions and rapid social change, Western man is on the road to mass insanity. Employment is still possible, though by and large the jobs are makework. In spite of an improvement in public services, one important new economic phenomenon has served to make the ostensibly more affluent average man less well-off than his predecessor of the mid-twentieth century: inclusion of the expense of reclamation or purification of resources in the price of products has made the cost of living much higher than could be explained by normal inflation alone.

This state of affairs stands in interesting contrast to both *Teg's 1994* and *1984*. Citizens of the more developed countries in *Stand on Zanzibar*, unlike those in *Teg's 1994*, have not used their release from drudgery to improve their educational skills and interpersonal relationships, and, unlike *1984*, seem perfectly able to turn themselves into a conformist, apathetic herd without help from Big Brother or the threat of physical brutality. This picture is all the more depressing because the quality of life deteriorates in spite of the efforts of governments in *Stand on Zanzibar* to carry out population and pollution control, evidently no panaceas in themselves.

III

Internationally, the present state system could evolve, first, in the direction of a greater concentration of institutional power. As one would expect from the nature of their societies, the worlds of *Gather, Darkness!* and *1984* are highly structured dictatorships. In the former story, a golden age of mankind is followed by war, apparently involving colonies of Earth on Mars and Venus, and general social disorder. The scientists assume power in a struggle to restore law and order and then become entrenched in their own administrative establishment. This is the priesthood of the Hierarchy which holds ultimate authority in what amounts to a centralized world government headed by an apex Council of archpriests who sit in the capital city of Megatheopolis.[10]

In *1984*, a similar period of chaos, including atomic war, revolution, and ideological purges, serves as the prelude to the restructuring of the planet into three superstates: Oceania (the Americas, the United Kingdom, and the British Empire), Eurasia (the USSR and Europe), and, ten years after the formation of these two, Eastasia (China, Japan, and southern Asia). While the three empires are in a state of perpetual war, the fighting is restricted to a zone which extends from North Africa to India, lands which serve as sources of raw materials and slave labor. Having seen how close the world came to the point of destruction in the previous atomic war, the leaders of the three states maintain a condition of nuclear deterrence and hold their nuclear weapons in reserve for the all-out attack to end the war—an attack which never comes. This situation, plus the desire of the rulers of each state to retain their lands as self-enclosed socioeconomic spheres, prevents a direct invasion by any one of the states against its enemies.

In both scenarios, the very basis of an international system and the art of statecraft which it requires have disappeared. For the scientist-priests of the Hierarchy, governmental relations consist of communicating with the major cities in the provinces and receiving delegations of local officials when necessary.

In *1984*, any normalization of relations by a state with one of the others with which it is temporarily allied would be unthinkable. It is a fundamental prerequisite for the functioning of each closed society that there be no contact with the others aside from unavoidable battles which take place in peripheral border regions. The ruling elite in each land mass can maintain control over its followers only if the latter are carefully shielded from the fact that the societies of their alleged enemies are ideologically and structurally identical to their own. Of course, this total lack of contact between individuals from the three states perfectly mirrors the internal nature of their societies.

Authority need not become concentrated within states of continental size. In the second pattern, authority may shift to institutions other than those of formal, national government, although the latter may still be used to effectuate or legitimize decisions reached elsewhere. Several transnational or supranational supplementary institutions to the state are available in science fiction.

In *The Space Merchants*, government continues to exist as the ostensible source of rule-making, but the actual nexus of power is maintained by private individuals who effectively rule the world in their capacity as the heads of the top advertising companies. The motivating philosophy of the executive class here is nothing more complicated than corporate greed, buttressed by firm belief in the value of ever higher standards of consumption and rising population levels. The individual citizen is continually subjected to a barrage of both subliminal and overt advertising messages and, if he should fall into debt, enters perforce into the lowest ranks of the consumer class, the contract laborers, from which he is unlikely to emerge. Industrialization has resulted in smog so bad that one must wear a nose-filter on the city streets, although pedicabs have replaced fuel-powered vehicles. Formal organs of government are used as convenient meeting grounds for corporate leaders to hammer out bargaining positions. For example, United States Senators directly represent commercial interests and vote in proportion to the economic power of their clients.

As in many science fiction stories of this kind, there is a small band of conspirators, organized here into the World Conservationist Association, who do not see continually increasing consumption as the only way to maintain a viable economy and who are prepared to sabotage the system to propagate their beliefs—a fascinating speculation for a book originally published before the current ecology movement. However, there is little the "Consies" can do except escape to Venus and try to build a sane society there. This rather cynical and satirical view of the moral bankruptcy of society's leaders is a classic example of the use of science fiction as a medium for criticizing major contemporary trends and for warning us about the condition we may be in if these trends are allowed to continue unchecked.

Rather than the co-optation of power by big business exercised through the sham of formal government, a more complex vision along this line would have authority to make decisions and command personal loyalty shared between states and multinational corporations, both global actors in their own right with both conflicting and overlapping interests. Serious efforts to envision possible world futures in which the state must share the prerogatives of sovereignty with business, but without being entirely supplanted by it, are made in "The Five Way Secret Agent" and *Stand on Zanzibar*.

In the world of "The Five Way Secret Agent," global corporations called "cosmocorps" have evolved to the point where their directors perceive the state as a threat to world stability and to their companies' continuing development. The managers of the cosmocorps, which are run as meritocracies, desire to locate resources, manufacture products, and employ skilled personnel solely on the basis of the dictates of geography and technology. A majority of those individuals who are still employed work for and owe their primary loyalty to one or the other of these businesses. Reflecting the functionalist concept of how the world may be brought together, the cosmocorps executives believe that if allowed to grow, their organizations will evolve into an effective world government capable of coping with the problems of a technologically interdependent globe. This naturally conflicts with the needs of states, which are still prone to rely on the balance of terror and the national interest as their guiding principles in world affairs.

The head of the largest cosmocorps, International Communications Incorporated, decides to accelerate the process of evolution toward world order. He hires an American to make contact with meritocrats in the Soviet Complex who have grown disillusioned with the inefficiency of the Soviet government bureaucracy and desire to cooperate in the common goal of achieving a more rational global allocation of authority. Interesting to note in this plot is the account of those who would be opposed to such a development—nationalists, of course, operating through the United States intelligence bureau; descendants of the old entrepreneurial families, rapidly losing prestige to the meritocrats; and, in a thought-provoking extrapolation, the Mafia, organized into a cosmocorps of its own and hardly eager to be policed by any powerful world government.

In *Stand on Zanzibar*, a corporation is again emphasized as the major institutional addition to the international scene, although in this case it cooperates with the United States Department of State in a project of mutual benefit. The political system of 2010 projected here is basically similar to that of the present. Internationally, Communist China, the Soviet Union, and the United States remain major world powers, but none of them has predominant influence in the international political structure. Of course, there have been changes: A "Common Europe" exists; Puerto Rico is an American state; the Catholic church has undergone schism upon approval of the Vatican of the birth control pill; the black majority rules in the Republic of South Africa; and two new powerful federations, composed of English-speaking and French-speaking states, have arisen in western Africa.

One of the major scenarios of the book involves the impoverished African country of "Beninia," strategically important because of its position as a buffer zone between the large federations of "Dahomalia" and the "Republican Union of Nigeria with Ghana." The Department of State fears that a major regional war could erupt between the two states if Beninia is unable to resist their continual tug-of-war over its territory. At the same time, the multinational corporation is faced with the problem of how to develop a rich load of mineral resources it has located in the middle of the Atlantic Ocean. The interests of the state and the corporation converge when the latter agrees, with the covert backing of the United States, to finance and supply personnel for a project to upgrade the educational skills of the next generation of Beninians and to build the necessary port and industrial facilities for processing the offshore minerals.

In short, here is a model of a situation in which a potential threat to world stability, in the interest of neither the United States nor big business, is to be defused by a cooperative, though covert, pooling of the technological and advertising skills of the company and the diplomatic support of the government. The global corporation has assumed its role in the international system as an autonomous, though not completely independent, actor capable of choosing the grounds on which it will cooperate with larger states in the achievement of its own interests.

Of course, the multinational corporation or organized crime are not the only institutions which might gain significant influence in international affairs. A range of functional international organizations, particularly the United Nations system, is evolving important decision-making powers as they perform and co-ordinate essential worldwide services. For the most part, however, this layer of international organization is absent in science fiction, perhaps more from the authors' unfamiliarity with the nature and operation of such groups than from any conscious extrapolation of their insignificant status in the future.

One of the few stories, however, which does project the United Nations as a major system actor working for world order is "Un-Man," a play on the words "man who works for the UN." As in *Stand on Zanzibar*, the international arena comprises familiar patterns of interstate competition, in a world buffeted by the forces of sweeping technological and social change. Improved geriatric and birth control techniques, together with the automation of jobs in which individuals with only average intelligence could once find employment, are leading to an older population increasingly unable to cope with the new institutional framework that such a world requires.[11] The world is in desperate need of those who can formulate and implement imaginative plans that might build some kind of socio-economic stability in a time of social stress. In this case, it is not the multinational corporation but the UN which is the rallying point for such efforts.

The UN in this story is not exactly the organization known to us. Humanity has survived World War III and the ensuing period of hunger and economic depression, but it is still divided into nation-states. On the other hand, the UN is strengthened after a charter-revision conference. An Inspectorate, which reports on matters like violations of disarmament agreements, a small police force, and a Lunar Guard have been added to its structure. Attached to the Inspectorate is a secret service with authority for preventive intervention to forestall the development of tension between states and to wind down cases of serious civil disorder. On occasion, and sometimes without the knowledge of member governments, the secret service uses methods such as political assassination. As in "The Five Way Secret Agent," those with the ability to grasp synergistic patterns see the probability that the UN can evolve into a world government if it can survive attacks by those for whom a more just and secure world order is not desirable—the nationalists, militarists, and power-hungry personalities likely to be found in the ranks of the Party by 1984. The opposition is itself organizing into what amounts to an ad hoc world body to halt the evolution of the UN. Although portions of this scenario sound more like James Bond than the *Yearbook of International Organizations*, "Un-Man" remains one of the few science fiction stories to speculate about the role of the UN acting on its own cognizance as an agent for institutional reform in a world of accelerating change.

In the two basic patterns presented thus far, the locus of decision-making power is concentrated in one or a few superstates or is diffused among an additional variety of international actors. While the systems that result are in some ways qualitatively different from those that presently exist, there is nothing essentially unfamiliar about the actors in the international system or the motivations for their interaction in these stories. Whether in nonfiction or science fiction, it is exceedingly difficult to describe novel patterns of interpersonal or international relationships. Nonetheless, in recent years, there have been increased attempts in science fiction to develop stylistic experimentation in the literature as well as a greater variety of societal models consciously different from present and historical examples.[12] The pattern most relevant to this discussion, and the final category here, is the societal arrangement which combines highly automated technology, a just distribution of economic products, intentional communities, an emphasis on self-actualization as the primary social goal, and decentralization of political affairs. This format, perhaps what one could expect if the political and cultural philosophies behind the New Left and the counter-culture should become major social forces, is used as the background of *Teg's 1994*.

This story is stylistically similar to the classical utopian novels—the main character ("Teg" is the heroine's nickname) travels through her world and records her observations for the enlightenment of future readers. While this story is not explicitly clear about how a postulated change in the world view of citizens in the affluent societies has drastically altered the fate of states, the cold war, or the military-industrial complex, it does provide a more detailed account of the transition period from the present to the story's future than is usually found in science fiction. The phasing out of the Vietnam War during the early 1970s sets the stage for the fruition of several social movements that had previously emerged in American life—the struggles for community control over decisions which affect the community, for an educational system relevant to the individual's needs, for consumer goods designed to make efficient use of available natural resources, for limitation of population increase to a zero-growth rate, for rational planning to a full use of the potential of automation, and for the free and open flow of scientific information. The result of these converging forces, unhampered in this scenario by any waves of repression, is that by the mid-

1980s a movement back to smaller communities has reversed the trend toward the ever larger megalopolis and achieved the free distribution of goods.

In this world, bureaucratic organization and structural authority in general have given way to a society based on decentralized communities ("multihogan complexes") and sapiential authority. As each community is bound together by the implicit consent of its members to engage in related research and productive social activity, a rich variety of life styles is available to those who wish to travel among the communities as a means of supplementing their education. Educational training and the leisure time of citizens released from industrial labor by automation is focused on interdisciplinary research projects called "problem/possibility [p/p] areas." Communities and individuals may engage the aid of "synergistic facilitators" to further the development of both interpersonal and educational skills in any given p/p area.

The closest thing to a central government for this confederation of technologically sophisticated, yet individualistic, communities is the Terran Center in Hawaii. This center consists of facilities for studying overall global patterns of development, stimulating research in unexplored fields, and aiding the communications centers that form the headquarters for each p/p area. While those who staff the Terran Center, chosen for their expertise much like the meritocrats in "The Five Way Secret Agent," are in a position to exercise potentially great power because of their dominance over the information networks and the lack of any parliamentary check on their performance, there is no hint that these benevolent experts of the communications era are at all eager to assume dictatorial control. Rather, Teg discovers by the end of her travels that the problem facing the world is just the opposite—communities are diverging so much in basic social values, and even language, that entropy leading to system breakdown could develop.[13]

IV

The essential contribution of the kind of science fiction surveyed here consists in its offerings of heuristic, speculative models of social systems that speak to the major issues raised in nonfiction works. The seven stories that have been reviewed collectively address issues that are presently on the frontier of international relations research: the disappearance of distinctions between domestic and foreign policy; the effect of new system actors on the international political system; the possibilities for, and alternative outcomes of, nonviolent system change; the consequences for international relations of new forms of communications, alterations in life styles, and an environment of accelerating change; the viability of the nation-state and its possible replacements. Two of these issues in particular can be traced through the stories.

One deals with the significant linkages between the nature of domestic society postulated in the large states and the quality of international politics in which they are engaged. In both *1984* and *The Space Merchants*, although the techniques of repression differ, a relatively rigid social order is maintained by an elite group of individuals skilled in the technology of social manipulation. In both stories, this domestic order is correlated with the concentration of power in the international sphere in the hands of a few major system actors coequal with those who exert the most influence within states.

On the other hand, more benevolent inclinations on the part of a meritocratic elite are accompanied by an effort to achieve more flexible democratic forms of world order. Thus, the establishment of cybernetic societies in "The Five Way Secret Agent" and *Teg's 1994* leads to attempts to construct a planetary system capable of achieving a just distribution of goods and services. In both plots, the kind of synergistic cooperation that enabled the richer states to reach their affluence is sought after in the international sphere. However, in "The Five Way Secret Agent," the path leads to the functional coordination of large international corporations, while in *Teg's 1994* an enlightened anarchism of decentralized communications communities prevails.

In "Un-Man" and *Stand on Zanzibar*, conditions of domestic social stress, technological change, and urban disorder are intricate components of an international system subject to great tension and painful gropings toward a more stable world order.

The other issue is the possibility for system change at the international level. In *Gather, Darkness!*, *1984*, and "Un-Man," the world is restructured or reformed only after a breakdown of the previous system by war and revolution.[14] However, we also have an alternative to such catastrophic processes of change: when political evolution is allowed to proceed without interruption by widespread war or social chaos, the outcome is seen as an inexorable trend toward some kind of world government. This may result either from a straightforward transference of governmental power to functional international organizations ("The Five Way Secret Agent" and "Un-Man") or from a system combining a central coordinator of research services, redistribution of governmental authority to the local level, and complex communications links between skilled individuals (*Teg's 1994*). Indeed, all three plots end on hopeful notes as the major characters accomplish their goals of perceiving or removing major obstacles in the path of the ongoing evolution.[15]

Of course, when these questions are dealt with in scholarly literature, data will be gathered and studied in great detail, and trends will be derived from more explicit application of forecasting techniques than appear in science fiction. Nevertheless, the framework of narrative fiction has its own advantages. Science fiction allows authors to use their informed, creative imagination to speculate about alternative futures. The models that result may be closely reasoned extrapolations from present trends, as in *Stand on Zanzibar*, or they may be formulated out of any combination of social elements of which the author can conceive. Unlike academic forecasting, which must be restricted to the realm of the feasible or the probable, science fiction has no compulsion to be respectable. As long as stories maintain an aura of credibility, a matter of the internal consistency of the plot, the author is bound only by the limits of the conceivable, not by the limits of the possible: world government, postnuclear societies, and technological breakdowns are all possibilities for the future.[16] Indeed, if it is true that forecasters implicitly take for granted their own cultural standards as the base lines for projections, then the more outlandish concepts in science fiction may come closer to the actual shape of future events.

Thematic elements used in the description of future societies may be of as much interest to scholars as the descriptive content. The science fiction of any particular historical era picks up and magnifies the fundamental aspirations and anxieties characteristic of the given popular culture and transmutes these themes into its plots. Space travel to other planets, alien invasion of Earth, creation of artificial or mechanical life, establishment of world dictatorships or democratic governments, the operations of great corporations and the megalopolis—all these are the present's mythology of the future, man's hopes and fears metaphorically stylized in science fiction; and the fact that these themes are prominent in the literature may be as significant as their content. If it is true that what we desire to achieve or avoid plays an important role in shaping the future, then science fiction, along with other popular art forms, becomes an important source in which to identify basic cultural assumptions and motivations.[17]

What one may find in the kind of science fiction reviewed here are insightful speculations on the social orders man is capable of creating. The value of this literature lies in the ability of skillful authors to take the myriad strands of data about man's potential available from experience and research and to weave them intuitively into coherent wholes.[18] It may be obvious that corporations and international organizations will be increasingly important system actors in future global affairs, but it need not be at all obvious how the system is affected by the introduction of such new actors. One may be able to graph and project various economic trends without gaining any appreciation, thereby, of the quality of existence that could result from the interaction of the disparate trends. To appreciate the many ways in which the elements of personal and organizational life may combine and mutate in the future, the political forecaster should turn, on occasion, to the works of science fiction.[19]

Notes

1. Two volumes in the five-volume series have appeared: Richard A. Falk and Cyril E. Black (eds.), Volume I, *Trends and Patterns*, and Volume 2, *Wealth and Resources* (Princeton: Princeton University Press, 1969 and 1970, respectively). The World Order Models Project is described in the *World Law Fund Progress Report*, 2, 1 (Winter, 1970), pp. 1-8.

2. On this period in science fiction history in the pulp magazines, *see* Sam Moskowitz (ed.), *Science Fiction by Gaslight: A History and Anthology of Science Fiction in the Popular Magazines, 1891-1911* (Cleveland: World, 1968), and *Under the Moons of Mars: A History and Anthology of the "Scientific Romance" in the Munsey Magazines, 1912-1920* (New York: Holt, Rinehart, and Winston, 1970).

3. L. Sprague de Camp, "Imaginative Fiction and Creative Imagination," in Reginald Bretnor (ed.), *Modern Science Fiction: Its Meaning and Its Future* (New York: Coward-McCann, 1953), pp. 141-52; Robert Block, "Imagination and Modern Social Criticism," in Basil Davenport (ed.), *The Science Fiction Novel: Imagination and Social Criticism*

(Chicago: Advent, 1964), pp. 126-55; R. Gordon Kelley, "Ideology in Some Modern Science Fiction Novels," *Journal of Popular Culture*, 2, 2 (Fall, 1968), pp. 211-27. Perhaps because so much of modern science fiction originates in the English-speaking world in general, and the United States in particular, a certain parochialism emerges. The cultural assumptions, dramatic problems, and even last names of characters commonly reflect an Anglo-Saxon background.

4. Sam Moskowitz, in *Seekers of Tomorrow: Masters of Modern Science Fiction* (New York: Ballantine, 1967), has noted: "Since the heyday of, first, Heinlein and then van Vogt, the bulk of modern science fiction has visualized governments of the future as outright dictatorships, religious dictatorships, military dictatorships, or unvarnished monarchies. There has been precious little utopianism, let alone liberalism." (p. 222.) *See also* Kingsley Amis, *New Maps of Hell: A Survey of Science Fiction* (New York: Harcourt, Brace, 1960), pp. 90, 95-110; and Block, *op. cit.*, pp. 139-41.

5. For example, Henry David, in "Assumptions about Man and Society and Historical Constructs in Futures Research," *Futures*, 2, 3 (September, 1970), pp. 222-30, charges forecasters with being more explicit about the assumptions they make regarding human nature and the historical analogies they use to extrapolate trends; Marion J. Levy, Jr., "Our Ever and Future Jungle," *World Politics*, 22, 2 (January, 1970), pp. 301-27, criticizes Herman Kahn and Anthony Wiener's *The Year 2000* for lacking imagination and restating the obvious; and George Modelski, "The Promise of Geocentric Politics," *World Politics*, 22, 4 (July, 1970) pp. 617-35, complains of the status quo bias inherent in theories of international relations that assume the continuing reality of the nation-state system.

6. Given its limitations, I believe that a stimulating collection of scenarios suitable for transformation into good science fiction plots is available in Herman Kahn and Anthony J. Wiener, *The Year 2000: A Framework for Speculation on the Next Thirty-three Years* (New York: Macmillan, 1967), pp. 248-385 (especially the "canonical variations" on the "standard world"). Other valuable works on possibilities for change in the present international system include Richard A. Falk, *This Endangered Planet* (New York: Random House, 1971); John Galtung, "On the Future of the International System," *Journal of Peace Research* 4, 4 (1967) pp. 305-33; and Bruce M. Russett, "The Ecology of Future International Politics," *International Studies Quarterly*, 11, 1 (March, 1967), pp. 12-31.

7. These stories are as follows (the date following the bibliographic reference is the approximate time setting for the story):

Anderson, Poul. "Un-Man." In Martin Greenberg (ed.), *All About the Future*, pp. 81-160. New York: Gnome Press, 1955. (2050)

Brunner, John. *Stand on Zanzibar*. New York: Ballantine, 1969. 650 pages. (2010)

Leiber, Fritz. *Gather, Darkness!* New York: Pellegrini and Cudahy, 1950. 240 pages. (2305)

Orwell, George. *1984*. New York: Harcourt, Brace and World, 1949. 314 pages. (1984)

Pohl, Frederick, and Kornbluth, C. M. *The Space Merchants*. New York: Walker, 1969. 158 pages. (circa 2000)

Reynolds, Mack. "The Five Way Secret Agent." In *Analog*, 83, 2 (April, 1969), pp. 6-54; and 83, 3 (May, 1969), pp. 96-142. (circa 2000)

Theobald, Robert, and Scott, J. M. *Teg's 1994: An Anticipation of the Near Future*. Chicago: Swallow Press, 1971. 211 pages. (1994)

8. The prototype of this genre was "When the Sleeper Wakes," by H. G. Wells, now conveniently available with its sequel, "A Story of the Days to Come," and "The Time Machine," in *Three Prophetic Novels of H. G. Wells* (New York: Dover, 1960). Modern authors owe to Wells not only this vision of the socio-economic structure of future society but the physical setting in which social life takes place—the great city in which the masses carry out their daily tasks, tall, gleaming, and efficient in its commercial and governmental quarters, but gaunt, dirty, and noisy in the homes and work places of the lower classes. The stresses of population density and lack of personalized associations that lead to urban pathologies of alienation and destruction also appear continuously in science fiction since

Wells. *See* in general, Mark R. Hillegas, *The Future as Nightmare: H. G. Wells and the Anti-Utopians* (New York: Oxford University Press, 1967).

9. In a sense, this is the fate of the Eloi people in "The Time Machine" by Wells. Over millions of years, they have de-evolved into a childlike species used as cattle by a race of underground beings in turn descended from the laboring class. For other examples of affluent stagnation, *see* Arthur C. Clarke, *The City and the Stars* (New York: Harcourt, Brace, 1956); Kurt Vonnegut, Jr., *Player Piano* (New York: Harcourt, Brace, 1952); and Mack Reynolds' ironically titled "Utopian," in Harry Harrison (ed.), *The Year 2000: An Anthology* (Garden City: Doubleday, 1970), pp. 91-110.

10. An operational world government is seldom described in science fiction. One favorable portrait is in Robert Heinlein, *Double Star* (New York: Signet, 1964), whose world government is federal, parliamentary, constitutional, and monarchial! The monarch is descended from the Dutch House of Orange; states within the empire are allowed to retain their local constitutional regimes, so that the emperor is not king of the United States (analogous to the British Commonwealth system).

11. This resembles the kind of situation described by Alvin Toffler in *Future Shock* (New York: Random House, 1970).

12. One reason for the change might be the greater number of writers with a humanistic or social science background who have taken up science fiction as a convenient format in which to express their feelings about present society and its trends. *See,* for example, Ursula K. LeGuin, *The Left Hand of Darkness* (New York: Walker, 1969) (a unisexual human society); Joanna Russ, *And Chaos Died* (New York: Ace, 1970) (a society based on psychic powers); Norman Spinrad, *Bug Jack Barron* (New York: Walker, 1969); and Fritz Leiber, *A Specter Is Haunting Texas* (New York: Walker, 1969).

13. Interestingly, a claim is made in *1984* that Oceania has neither capital nor central government. Cohesion for the empire is provided by the ideology of Ingsoc (English Socialism). Another example of a decentralized, quasi-anarchical world order guided by a benevolent, technocratic elite may be found in two related stories by Rudyard Kipling: "As Easy as A.B.C.," in Groff Conklin (ed.), *17 X Infinity* (New York: Dell, 1963), pp. 172-201, and "With the Night Mail: A Story of 2000 A.D.," in Damon Knight (ed.), *100 Years of Science Fiction* (New York: Simon and Schuster, 1968), pp. 13-51. (A.B.D. is the Aerial Board of Control, a group of people who do whatever is necessary to keep the all-important lines of air traffic open, including a very loose administration of any areas that wish to come under their control.) Also notable in this vein are H. G. Wells, "Men Like Gods," in *28 Science Fiction Stories of H. G. Wells* (New York: Dover, 1952), pp. 1-268; James Cooke Brown, *The Troika Incident: A Tetralogue in Two Parts* (Garden City: Doubleday, 1970); and Eric Frank Russell, "And Then There Were None," in William Sloane (ed.), *Stories for Tomorrow: An Anthology of Modern Science Fiction* (New York: Funk and Wagnalls, 1954), pp. 425-90.

14. One possibility that has occurred to several authors is Earth's nations uniting under the threat, real or imagined, of alien invasion. In André Maurois, "The War Against the Moon," a group of men who control the mass media decide to present the Earth with a convenient common enemy by fooling people into believing the planet is under attack from the moon; an Earth scientist then sends a heat-ray to the moon to answer the alleged lunar aggression, whereupon the all-too-real lunar inhabitants promptly retaliate by wiping out Darmstadt, and the first interplanetary war is on. In Groff Conklin (ed.), *Omnibus of Science Fiction* (New York: Crown, 1952), pp. 450-63.

15. It is fascinating to note that both *1984* and *Teg's 1994*, whose political systems are otherwise polar opposites, have in common a stress on the importance of basing system change to some degree on an alteration of the linguistic forms by which people interpret reality. Thus, in *1984*, the substitution of "Newspeak" for English in Oceania will presumably make it literally unthinkable for the citizen to comprehend such concepts as freedom or democracy in any way other than that which the Party establishes. In *Teg's 1994*, the evolution of three variants of English more precise and appropriate to differing

interpersonal contexts than is common English has helped make the response of aggression inappropriate to most social situations.

16. The utility of positing nonexistent world models in the study of comparative international systems and their processes of macrochange is noted by Richard A. Falk in "The Interplay of Westphalia and Charter Conceptions of International Legal Order," *The Future of the International Legal Order*, I, p. 36, though the editors also state in their introduction to the series that the project is based on the assumption "that there would be no major change in the structure of international society during the period that concerns us." (p. vii.)

17. On this historical role of science fiction, *see* Marjorie Hope Nicolson, *Voyages to the Moon* (New York: Macmillan, 1960); Fred L. Polak, *The Image of the Future: Enlightening the Past, Orientating the Present, Forecasting the Future*, two volumes (Dobbs Ferry: Oceana, 1961); H. Bruce Franklin, *Future Perfect: American Science Fiction of the Nineteenth Century* (New York: Oxford University Press, 1966); I. F. Clarke, *Voices Prophesying War, 1763-1984* (New York: Oxford University Press, 1967); W. H. G. Armytage, *Yesterday's Tomorrows: A Historical Survey of Future Societies* (Toronto: University of Toronto Press, 1968); Robert M. Philmus, *Into the Unknown: The Evolution of Science Fiction from Francis Godwin to H. G. Wells* (Berkeley: University of California Press, 1970). Recent overviews of science fiction include Donald A. Wollheim, *The Universe Makers: Science Fiction Today* (New York: Harper and Row, 1971); Sam J. Lundwall, *Science Fiction: What It's All About* (New York: Ace, 1971); Dick Allen (ed.), *Science Fiction: The Future* (New York: Harcourt, Brace, Jovanovitch, 1971); William Atheling, Jr., *More Issues at Hand* (Chicago: Advent, 1970); and Thomas D. Clareson (ed.), *The Other Side of Realism* (Bowling Green: Bowling Green State University Press, 1971).

18. John Brunner, author of *Stand on Zanzibar*, in "The Genesis of *Stand on Zanzibar* and Digressions into the Remainder of Its Pentateuch," *Extrapolation*, 11, 2 (May, 1970), has described his procedure in this manner: "Two years of casual research seemed to have given me a kind of sense of pattern about the world I wanted to describe, such that I didn't need details, only an awareness of the point which certain discernible trends might have reached by my—entirely arbitrary—future date of 2010." (p. 35.)

In futurology, development of the technique of the cross-impact matrix is also an attempt to assess the possible outcomes of sets of trends. *See* T. J. Gordon and H. Hayward, "Initial Experiments with the Cross-Impact Matrix of Forecasting," *Futures*, Vol. 1, No. 2, (December, 1968), pp. 100-16.

19. The reader who has decided to take the plunge into science fiction need not despair at where to start. Several anthologies of the "best" science fiction of the year are issued annually, particularly Donald A. Wollheim and Terry Carr (eds.), *World's Best Science Fiction* (New York: Ace), and Judith Merril, (ed.), *The Year's Best S-F* (New York: Dell). Each year since 1966, the Science Fiction Writers of America have awarded the Nebula for best novel and shorter stories; the latter are collected as *Nebula Award Stories* (Garden City: Doubleday). This group is also compiling a multivolume series on the best science fiction, of which volume one has appeared: Robert Silverberg (ed.), *The Science Fiction Hall of Fame: The Greatest Science Fiction Stories of All Time Chosen by the Science Fiction Writers of America* (Garden City: Doubleday, 1970). Science fiction fans themselves have similarly awarded the Hugo at their world conventions each year since 1953 (this prize is named after Hugo Gernsback, publisher of the first all-science fiction magazine). A useful bibliographic tool is Edwin S. Strauss (comp.), *Index to the Science Fiction Magazines: 1951-1965* (Cambridge: New England Science Fiction Association, 1966, with annual supplements). An annotated bibliography of critical literature about science fiction will be published by the Kent State University Press in its Serif bibliographical series. The recent formation of a Science Fiction Research Association should also lead to an increased body of scholarly studies about science fiction.

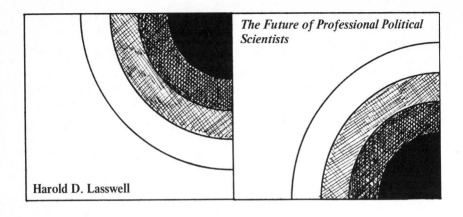

The Future of Professional Political Scientists

Harold D. Lasswell

The following pages outline a modified preference model of the future evolution of professional political scientists. The model is a "modified" construct of the future in the sense that, although the main outlines of the probable conform to my preferred goals, some developments do not. Attention is called to any major discrepancies between prediction and preference.

The term "political scientist" is employed in a conventional sense to designate persons who have received advanced training in government, public law, and politics, or whose preparation is equivalent to an academic exposure. The main thrust of the definition is to emphasize the importance of approaching the practice, study, and teaching of political science with an explicit map of the place of government, law, and politics in the life of society and reference to our historical period. To use the term "professional" implies a tradition of concern for the problems involved in adapting the institutions of public order to the valued goals of the body politic. Whatever their limitations may be—and they are not difficult to recognize—the schools and departments of higher education keep both the challenge and the effort alive. The stress on training acknowledges that the most explicit indicator of a "political scientist" is exposure, attended by some degree of success, in struggling with academic standards of performance.

The limits of "equivalent" training or experience will no doubt continue to be debated. We know the arguments for "broad construction" of "equivalence:" Isn't the sophistication of a political journalist equal to that of the holder of an academic degree? Doesn't a conscientious civil servant or legislator have a realistic map of politics that at least rivals that possessed by an advanced student or teacher?

The significant point about these questions is that they unwittingly use academic criteria to define the means of distinguishing one journalist, civil servant, or legislator from his colleagues. In the past, academic institutions have given professional recognition to "untrained" individuals who have demonstrated their capacity to apply and extend our knowledge of the political process. Substantial recognition has been given in the form of invitations to teach or to join in the research program of universities.

One of the principal obligations of a profession such as political science is generally accepted. The obligation is to contribute to the advancement of knowledge, hence to the preparation of individuals and institutions adequate to the task. It is worth dwelling on the point long enough to comment on a continuing confusion. "Knowledge" has at least two empirical orientations, one toward "enlightenment," the other toward "skill." To contribute to enlightenment is to improve the map of knowledge that depicts the role of political institutions in the social process. To contribute to skill, on the other hand, is to mobilize the knowledge required to achieve excellence in the performance of specific tasks defined within the context of the inclusive map. The key questions about political institution refer to enlightenment. They ask about the interplay between politics and the rest of society. Key questions about skill refer to such operations as the management of money and persons, or the manipulation of communication for diplomatic and ideological purposes.

It is usual to find various degrees of incompatibility between members of a profession who are principally concerned with enlightenment and colleagues who focus on specific skills. For instance, "theorists" have often been on noncomplimentary terms with "administrators," "lawyers," or other "technicians." Another line of separation is between those who are chiefly engaged in improving the fundamental map of politics and those whose primary concern is with transmitting the best available current map to young people. The skills of special relevance to the former objective are not always well adapted to the latter.

To an uncommitted outside observer, the internal stresses and strains of any profession seem to be much ado about little. For instance, outsiders look with some distaste, not unmixed with apprehension, at the struggles among physicians, surgeons, nurses, interns, and hospital superintendents and workers—to say nothing of the encounters that divide the organ specialists (heart, lungs, etc.) from the procedure specialists (anesthesiologists, radiologists, etc.), or separate the case-to-case specialists from environmentalists who deal with sanitation, housing, and the like.

Many of the factors that have contributed to past fragmentation are being weakened by factors that strengthen the discovery of new common interests generated by perceived interdependencies. The communications revolution, for instance, provides a means of introducing a map of an entire community or of a particular enterprise to everyone who participates in it. Motives to utilize these new instruments are increasing. In coming years, the consequences of these innovations will be increasingly evident throughout political science, as well as in the institutional sectors with which political scientists are involved.

The distinction between primary orientation toward enlightenment or skill has another dimension. The image of the political scientist is only partially distinct from the image of active politicians or practicing lawyers. To be a professionally trained person implies competence in analyzing and indicating how to cope with an *aggregate* process. Many businessmen are competent operators of specific business enterprises, but they are not necessarily possessed of a realistic map of how the whole economy works. For a cognitive map of the production, distribution, investment, and consumption of wealth, we turn increasingly to economists for advice. Economists have the image of a true profession to the extent that they are seen as the ones who have the best available model of the aggregate flow of economic activities. The prospects are improving that the image of political scientists will become more obviously professional as we establish the validity of our inclusive map of the political process at every level of community life—national, transnational, subnational.

Professionals are expected to assist in clarifying and serving a common interest. A common interest in health, it is assumed, is served if the trained health specialist deliberately kills no one (or allows him to die). Community interest in health is also served by a profession that outlines practicable goals for health policy, and assists in their implementation. Political scientists are fully professional when they accept responsiblity for formulating inclusive goals, structures, and operating strategies of public order.

It seems to me that professional political scientists will discover that the approach best suited to their role in society corresponds to what I have called the policy science orientation.[1] The point, of course, is to emphasize concepts, not terminology. The concepts are appropriately contextual and problem-oriented. Since I foresee a very considerable diffusion of this way of looking at the man of knowledge, it will be included in the following projection.

Preference Model: Today + 20 (1990)

The preference model outlined here is roughly scaled to political science as it will be observed by those in a position to describe the situation in twenty years. There is no magic about a twenty-year interval that uniquely qualifies it to be taken seriously as a slice through time. It does, however, have some obvious advantages for people brought up in our society. We often characterize the flow of generations in twenty-year periods. By the age of twenty, we expect young people to be fully adult and to have assumed, or to be near assuming, the obligations of a full member of society. The age of forty is a rough and ready estimate of the time when one generation is "taking over" the elite posts. Its maturity is precipitated by the impact of the rising wave of twenty-year-olds who expect to take advantage of a more complex educational experience and a new wave of value orientations partially crystallized in pre-adult years. The age of sixty often marks the high point of respected achievement in public service, and is a watershed after which performance is expected to be attenuated by advancing years. In the triangulation of the generations, the "grandparents" may form a temporary alliance with grandchildren to offset the assertiveness of the middle-aged who may resent the double burden of looking after both young and old. It is not inconvenient to throw the focus of attention back to 1950 or forward to 1990, and to recheck the construct as the years unfold.

We adopt the convention of treating 1990 in the present tense. The projection assumes no drastic disintegration of the world picture, such as would be the case in the aftermath of a major nuclear war.

1. Political science is widely recognized in the world of science and policy as a

leading example of a policy-oriented discipline. It is perceived as among "the most improved" among closely related professions specialized to various sectors of the social process (such as economics and public law).

2. Political scientists are expected to take a leading role—and do in fact play such a role—in all official and unofficial policy processes of large organizations.

3a. This is particularly evident in the *intelligence* component of the policy process of the organizations involved. The intelligence function includes planning. More generally, the task of intelligence gatherers, processors, and disseminators is to adopt postulates in terms of which the goals of policy can be clarified, time sequences described up to the present, scientific explanations compared, future projections presented, and policy options invented or evaluated. If an activity of such complexity and delicacy is to be performed with most effect, intelligence personnel must keep in close association with all the other policy functions (here classified as promotion, prescription, invocation, application, termination, and appraisal).

Political scientists are more influential in the intelligence functions of government than they were in 1970 because their well-established commitment to public administration has been amplified by better training in contextual theory, which has counteracted the tendency to be satisfied with traditional administrative routine. To an increasing degree, bureaucratizing tendencies are counteracted by the practice of migrating from public to academic and other private institutions.

Political scientists are active in making available to the community as a whole, and to all significant component elements, comprehensive maps of knowledge. Three innovations have been fully exploited in the last twenty years: (1) information storage, processing, and retrieval systems based on computer technology; (2) satellite communication systems for the simultaneous broadcasting of audio-visual images; (3) exhibit technology that allows permanent installations to be more effective.

It is recognized that communications technology is at a point that makes it practicable for an *image of the context* as a whole to be interpolated at any point in a sequence of interaction that relies on secondary media. The image may depict the past, present, and future of a territorial community at every level (global, regional, local). The pertinent context may present a pluralistic process, such as the policy forming and executing phases of a large-scale organization. Political scientists are relatively important in the public communication networks because they are able to make practical their long standing theoretical concern for "an intelligent public opinion." Their research on the political component of the social process emphasizes the impact of the frame of attention on beliefs, faiths, and loyalties.

Political scientists are leaders in improving the technique of such intelligence aids to decision (*e.g.,* continuing seminars and the social planetarium).

3b. Professional political scientists are prominent in the *promotional* phases of official and unofficial policy processes. This includes leaders and staff of political parties and pressure groups; and the promotional departments of organizations specialized in every area of social life (economic, health, education, etc.).

Many members of the profession perceive it as their responsibility and opportunity to give expression to every latent discontent with the structure of society, as well as with specific programs or persons. Similarly, they feel bound to clarify policy alternatives by speaking out for the criticized as well as for the critics. In a word, in the arenas of public agitation and propaganda, political scientists are performing the role traditionally taken by lawyers at later stages of the decision process. Despite the ambivalent attitudes entertained toward the legal profession in the body politic, it is generally accepted that every accused person should have at his disposal a qualified member of the bar who is able to assist justice by saying whatever can be said in his behalf. Political scientists are obtaining a parallel image by emphasizing the claim of all disaffected elements to have a spokesman who can formulate any latently rational justifications in their behalf.

It is recognized that political scientists are more vulnerable to public attack than lawyers, since a lawyer is formally obliged to be a servant of the legal process and is supervised by community decision makers (typically the court). The professional image of the political scientist is most seriously compromised when he moves beyond persuasion and acts to justify and engage in violence intended to change the established public order of any body politic.

Members of the profession are ideologically split on fundamental questions to a degree that renders it impossible for them to stay in the same professional associations. For example, those who commit themselves to violence are not tolerated by scholars who are committed to nonviolence, or who accept the use of violence only as a monopoly of popular government. Another cleavage separates political scientists who support or oppose the claims of a particular group to achieve or maintain the position of a superior caste that seeks to consolidate and perpetuate its power.

As a consequence of the cleavages referred to, there are sharp differences of opinion among political scientists in regard to the professional qualifications of persons who have been trained in schools committed to such ideologies as racism or the necessity and desirability of using violence against particular established orders.

I do not welcome this projection of the future, since I am opposed to ideologies that renounce the realization of human dignity as a goal (or adopt the words without providing definitions and encouraging behaviors that can be accepted in good faith). At the same time, I agree that a plausible case can be made for rival ideologies, and that the level of knowledge available to the champions of unwelcome ideological positions can be sufficiently high to meet workable standards of professional competence.

After all, deep normative differences are no novelty in political science. Many eminent thinkers have been identified with incompatible theological claims. Neither Plato nor Aristotle were champions of democracy. Efforts to excommunicate from the profession persons who identify themselves with particular normative postulates have not been successful; nor are they necessary to establish the public image of the professional student of government as a man whose level of knowledge and skill is high, whatever his beliefs; nor is the separation necessary to demonstrate differences of emphasis within the profession on the several problem-solving tasks. Problem-solving calls for goal clarification, the description of trends, the analysis of conditions, the projection of alternatives, and the invention (evaluation, selection) of alternative policies. Although in principle it is unnecessary to develop schismatic associations among those who are mainly concerned with philosophy, history, science, projection, or policy, schisms are likely to continue. Ultimately, it is not beyond the wit of man to understand that a division of labor among learned men who can agree to communicate with one another is mutually helpful.

The fact that qualified political scientists are to be distinguished from laymen can be more evident to the public during this literate and visually oriented epoch than it was during the period of limited literacy and print. The audio-visual media exposed everyone to displays of data and to methods of interpretation that are the fruit of research and analytic training. Individuals unacquainted with available data or at a loss to cope with advanced interpretations are not likely to hold their own in competition with rivals.

3c. Political scientists are more prominent than before in the organs of government that specialize in the *prescribing* function. Political scientists continue to be less prominent in old parliamentary regimes where lawyers have long had an accepted ascendancy. In single party systems, the political scientists are closely integrated with specialists on violence (military and police), with secretaries of the party, and with civil servants.

Political scientists are relatively conspicuous in countries which consider themselves industrially underdeveloped, or whose development is recent. Ex-colonial powers, in particular, have laid so much emphasis on relating goals to strategies that they are more hospitable to economists, political scientists, political sociologists, and political anthropologists than to lawyers, who are more dependent on an accepted frame of formal authority.

After a period of eclipse, religious and other traditional leaders have staged a partial comeback in countries where secularizing tendencies could be stigmatized as "imperialist" efforts to suppress traditional culture. The revival of symbols of identity marks the rise of more parochial elites than revolutionary innovators who obtained much of their original orientation abroad.

After years of relative indifference to written constitutions, many powers have sought to crystallize authoritative expectations by the preparation of acceptable documents. In some countries, the reluctance to emphasize such instruments depended on the unresolved allocation of effective power among older tribal formations and the institutions of detribalization. Many modernizing elites believed that tribal and local identities would rather rapidly wither away as industrial development changed the social structure of the nation. They also believed that any early effort to "finalize" the constitutional system would prove to be an obstacle to innovation. In recent years, however, the national situation has been sufficiently stabilized to suggest that skillfully written instruments would expedite the modernizing process. Sometimes the growth of legal and political science professions has strengthened the independent role of courts and other top policy structures. In any case, political scientists have been heavily involved as proposers of constitutive structure. They have prepared materials for the conventions and committees charged with producing satisfactory frames of government at national and subnational levels.

In some instances, political scientists (and lawyers) have been sufficiently innovative to go beyond the tradition of purely verbal drafting to utilize television and other audio-visual means of communicating the essential points to be made. It is entirely feasible to supervise the preparation of films that show what is meant by proper voting and deliberating procedures. (Such is the standard practice in legislative "draftsmanship" where, for example, the task is to delimit boundaries or to indicate the meaning of national and subnational plans.)

3d. Political scientists are much more active at the level of *invocation* than in the past. The growing interdependence of contemporary life carries with it much greater concern for discovering the permissible limits of behavioral deviation. An act of invocation occurs when conduct is *provisionally* characterized in terms of a prescription. It is the first step in the chain of events that involves the whole machinery of administrative action and law enforcement. Invocation includes the first initiatives of a civil servant who begins to execute a statute providing for an official enterprise, or the first acts of an inspector or a police officer who evaluates a situation as "lawful" or "unlawful."

Political scientists have become increasingly involved as a result of belated recognition of the theoretical and practical importance of the early stages of "law enforcement" and execution. The field of "criminal justice," for example, has attracted members of the profession who perceive that the decision to ignore the breach of a norm or to proceed against the perpetrator of the breach is a governmental act of critical importance for the entire system of public order. If, in a verbally "democratic" commonwealth, the weak are left unprotected against the depredations of the strong, the stability of the commonwealth is ultimately in question. Hence the involvement of political scientists in the formulation of public policies of law enforcement (or nonenforcement). Because of their policy orientation, political scientists have been able to supplement earlier approaches to the field that were made in the name of criminology, police science, forensic jurisprudence, penology and correction, probation, and the like.

Although criminal and civil justice are much spoken of, political scientists have been particularly active in providing guidelines for timing the execution of public programs. In the past, many students and practitioners of public administration were timid about facing the policy questions involved in allocating scarce administrative resources. They did not want to seem to say that their job was to decide what laws would be neglected or what legislative programs would be nullified. The growth of more comprehensive ways of presenting the whole political process has made it more evident to all that explicit criteria, not evasive tactics, are required if public policy is to be made more effective where popular government exists.

3e. It is less than surprising to find that political scientists continue to play a major part in civil service at all levels. The *application* function includes the final characterization of circumstances in prescriptive terms, and the completion of operations in harmony with prescriptive requirements. The most important change of the last few years is more "qualitative" than "quantitative" in the sense that somewhat different self-images are current among administrators. The change is in the direction of becoming less tied to government and more tied to the *administrative function*, whether it is exemplified in a large-scale organization that serves the political arena, the market, or another context. The administrative function includes responsibility for research, teaching, and consultation on problems of application, as well as involvement in executory duties.

The increased variety and mobility of the appliers in our society has had an important consequence for political scientists. They have perceived more clearly that a genuinely professional conception of themselves makes it possible to operate outside government posts without betraying the public interest. This has confronted them with intellectual problems comparable with the professional questions that lawyers have faced. Lawyers are supposed to act within the frame of public policy goals when they are retained by a private client. The intellectual problem is indicated by the distinction between tax "evasion" and tax "avoidance." The lawyer is never justified in the former; he is permitted to engage in the latter—especially if he is sufficiently responsible to call attention to "loopholes" and to recommend changes in public policy. Administrators are only gradually rising from the status of "employees" to the status of "professionals"; and this is happening as the political scientists, among others, are able to move from one post to another without losing much economic security. This change is a matter of collective bargaining on behalf of professional standards (exemplified in the case of teachers by demands for research time, salary, and facilities; and by parallel demands on private and public corporations).

3f. The presence of political scientists among those engaged in *termination* is a novelty, and testifies among other things to the new importance of the function itself. To put an end to a prescription that is in force is not necessarily a simple matter. It may initiate a long series of adjustments whose role is to compensate all who have established justifiable expectations during the period when the prescription was in effect. Specialized agencies may be needed to negotiate claims for compensation or for equivalent services (such as houses in a congenial community neighborhood).

In a world of changing science-based technology, the terminating function is a permanent feature of public life. In transnational terms, the problems appear in the form of claims for just compensation for expropriated property. In international areas, the demand for security means that people who are able and willing to work, but who have no job commensurate with legitimate past expectations, are at least provided with an income enabling them to maintain an accustomed standard of living. Demands for equivalent services are especially difficult to satisfy since they depend on less simple criteria than the market.

Lawyers continue to play their traditional role in compensation matters. But political scientists come into the picture as a result of their increasing involvement in planning, and their concern for methods of conflict resolution to supplement the formal arrangements of litigation. Termination may involve programs of "re-education" amd "redirection" of human skills and aspirations.

3g. The prominence of political scientists in the *appraisal* function is closely bound up with the enlarged part that they are taking in promotion and intelligence. One task of appraisal is to report the degree to which policy objectives have been realized. A more complex problem is to identify the factors responsible for success or failure. The expansion of scientific knowledge has contributed to the viability of such a program; so, too, has computer technology.

Political scientists have taken the lead in supplementing official agencies of appraisal with a network of "counterpart seminars" whose primary role is to strengthen civic order, and hence to strengthen public order. The conception of a counterpart seminar can be applied to particular structures, selected problems, or territorial communities. For instance, a continuing seminar may parallel a court, a legislative committee, a regulatory commission, or some other organ of government at the national, transnational, or subnational level. The structures may be selected from other value-institution sectors than government; for example, economic, ecclesiastical, or educational organizations. If a problem like resource pollution is taken, all the structures affecting pollution are considered. Also, an effort may be made to view the body politic as a whole at each level.

A counterpart seminar may specialize in studying the trend of decision, attempting to locate the factors that account for what has gone on. But the seminar can be utilized in a more inclusive fashion to perform all the problem-solving tasks pertinent to a given area (goal clarification, trend description, analysis of conditions, projection, alternatives).

Concluding Comment

The brief developmental construct outlined above does not consider in needed detail the prospects of a garrison-police state in the United States and other bodies politic. It is evident that if the expectation of violence (external, internal) dominates the world arenas of power, the professional evolution of political scientists will be severely curtailed. Competitive arenas will fold up in the world as a whole, in every component territory, and at every phase of decision processing. It is not within the scope of the present discussion to deal directly with these possibilities, which have been fruitfully reconsidered by Bertram M. Gross, for instance, in recent publications. On the whole, the prospect for the next two decades is positive for the profession.

Note

1. *See* Harold D. Lasswell, "The Emerging Conception of the Policy Sciences," *Policy Sciences*, 1 (1970), pp. 3-14.

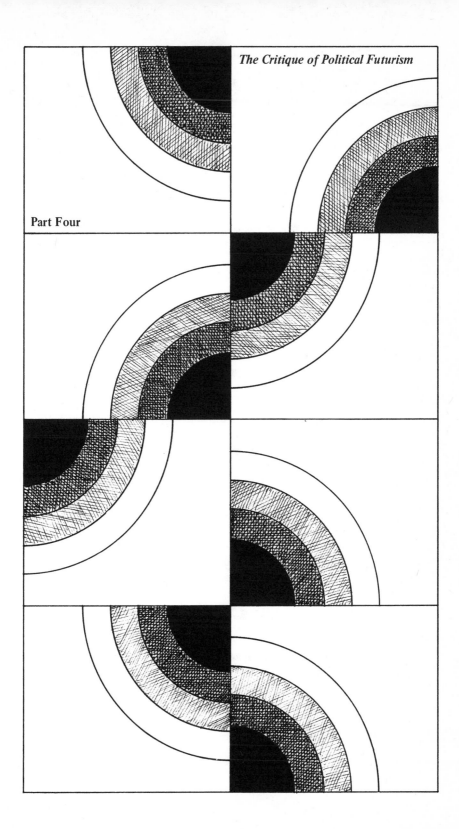

Part Four

Very few intellectual movements—or industries—lack critics, and futurism is no exception. The three commentators represented in this section base their criticism on quite different grounds. One writes from a philosophical perspective, another from a pragmatic viewpoint, and the third, to use a somewhat strained term, from a pedagogical orientation.

Among the most incisive analyses of the philosophical assumptions on which futurism rests was Robert A. Nisbet's 1968 article entitled "The Year 2000 and All That." The futurists, Nisbet argued, take for granted the validity of Leibniz's law of continuity, a law which holds that "the present is big with the future, the future might be read in the past, the distant is expressed in the near." Nisbet rejected this assumption, contending that "(1) events do not marry and have little events that grow into big events which in turn marry and have little events, etc.; (2) small changes do not accumulate directionally and continuously to become big changes." In asking Nisbet for permission to reprint the original brief essay, it was only natural also to ask if he would be willing to develop his case at greater length. To my delight, he answered in the affirmative. "Postscript: June, 1971" represents both an amplification and a sharpened restatement of his earlier views.[1]

Quite another type of critique is provided by Paul Seabury. Although by no means unconcerned with the philosophical or metaphysical aspects of the issue, Seabury focuses his attention on the practical utility of futurism, particularly as applied to international affairs and international relations. The track record of the futurists in this respect, he holds, leaves a great deal to be desired. His criticisms, I think it safe to say, are more directed at the manner in which futurism has been practiced than at the basic concept itself.

The third, and gentlest, critique looks neither at the assumptions nor the practice of futurism, but rather, at the manner in which it has been taught. H. Wentworth Eldredge reports on his analysis of futurist offerings at some ninety institutions of higher education. He concludes his discussion of the contents and objectives of these courses with "seventeen summary propositions." Taken collectively, these suggest that while education for futurism is doing some things moderately well, there is vast room for improvement in other areas.

Note

1. For a somewhat different line of attack, *see* the paper by Fred C. Iklé, "Can Social Predictions Be Evaluated?," *Daedalus op. cit.*, pp. 733-58.

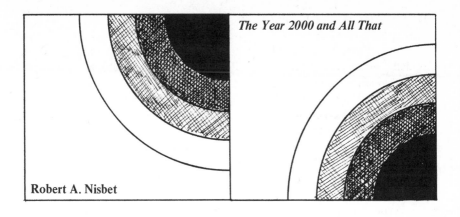

Robert A. Nisbet

The approach of the year 2000 is certain to be attended by a greater fanfare of predictions, prophecies, surmises, and forewarnings than any millennial year in history. In the past twelve months, at least four books on this subject have appeared, all of them concerned with the probable shape of American and world society in the year 2000.[1] How many articles have appeared I cannot even guess. But books and articles are in any event only the exposed part of the iceberg. There are today centers, institutes, and bureaus, not to mention specific commissions, whose principal business it is to forecast or predict the future. There is with us, in short, as part of the already huge knowledge industry, the historical-prediction business; and this business is certain to become ever larger, ever more ramified. Through every conceivable means—game theory, linear programming, systems analysis, cybernetics, even old-fashioned intuition or hunch—individuals and organizations are working systematically on what lies ahead during the next thirty-two years, and indeed during the century or two after that. Nor is this an American enterprise only. In France there is the *Futuribles* project under the distinguished direction of Bertrand de Jouvenel. In England, the Social Science Research Council has established the Committee on the Next Thirty Years. There will be other forays into the future, in this country and abroad, for the lure of the game is spreading fast. An official of the State Department's Bureau of Educational and Cultural Affairs, Frank Snowden Hopkins, has already proposed the organization of an institute in which "rising young government administrators would each year spend some nine or ten months . . . studying the American future in all its aspects," to which one can only say, nice work if you can find it—the future, that is.

Why the fascination with the future at a time when so many of us are preoccupied with the roots of our not always clear cultural identity? Daniel Bell, whose knowledge of what is going on in this matter is vast, suggests two rather different forces operating in human consciousness today. There is, first, the magic of the millennial number. Men have always been attracted, Bell reminds us, to the mystical allure of the *chiloi*, the Greek word for a thousand, from which we acquire our religious word *chiliasm*, the belief in a coming life free of imperfections.

258 / The Critique of Political Futurism

There is, certainly, no question of the power of the *chiloi* on the human, especially Western, consciousness. As Professor Bell notes, Plato, in the Myth of Er with which he concludes *The Republic*, foretold that departed souls would return on earth after spending a thousand years in the netherworld. And there were widespread expectations in the early Christian era of a Second Coming at the end of a thousand-year period. To which we might add that St. Augustine, although he was much too shrewd to assign a precise date for the ending of the world, seems to have been convinced that the inevitable holocaust would take place approximately a half a millennium after his time, which would have put it at about 1000 A.D.

(It is worth observing parenthetically that the fire which Augustine foresaw as eventually consuming the world has, in addition to Stoic intellectual roots, a certain flavor of Caltech modernity. We are told in *The Next Ninety Years* by Norman Brooks, Professor of Engineering at Caltech, that one of the prime dangers faced by contemporary society is "thermal pollution," the discharge of heat generated by technology. Professor Brooks estimates that the total amount of heat generated in Los Angeles alone is now 3 per cent of the incident solar radiation. And, independently, we are informed by two Rutgers scientists that at present rates of discharge of heat into American rivers "some of the rivers could reach their boiling point by 1980 and even evaporate by 2010." Here, surely, amid all the plights of modern man, is the most exasperating. The hotter our technology makes the atmosphere, the more we will use air-conditioning machinery to cool it, which means—under the unrepealable second law of thermodynamics—the more heat.)

By the late 17th century, Western philosophers, noting that the earth's frame had still not been consumed by Augustinian holocaust, took a kind of politician's courage in the fact, and declared bravely that the world was *never* going to end (Descartes, it seems, had proved this) and that mankind was going to become ever more knowledgeable and, who knows, progressively happy. Now, of a sudden, the year 2000 became the object of philosophical speculation. One of the more charming manifestations of this in the 18th century was a play, *L'An 2000*, written by the bohemian man of letters Restif de la Bretonne, which has been described as a heroic comedy representing how marriages would be arranged in the year 2000, at which time some twenty nations would be allied to France under the wise supremacy of "our well-beloved monarch Louis François XXII." (I almost wrote Charles de Gaulle.) A few years earlier Sébastien Mercier had written a small volume, much read and discussed, titled *L'An 2440*, in which a more or less ideal future is limned, one that we have no difficulty seeing as an extension into the future of economic, political, and intellectual "trends" that no doubt seemed as real to Mercier as current "trends" do to us at the present time.

It would not do, while still on the millennial magic of the year 2000, to forget the redoubtable Edward Bellamy in this country. His *Looking Backwards*, which deals with life as it might be expected to be in the year 2000, has just reappeared in a new edition by Harvard University Press, and has a splendid introduction by its editor, John L. Thomas. Considering the immense appeal that this book exerted for years on the minds of American citizens, politicians, and business men, it can be regarded as one more example of the occasional superiority of the "soft data" of ideas and fancies over the "hard data" of demography in shaping the future.

II

The second reason Daniel Bell gives for the recent upsurge of interest in the forecasting of the future is technology. As he writes, there is in our society a kind of "bewitchment of technology." So many other matters have been settled by technology, so much of space—including planetary—has been conquered by technology, why should not the marvelous skills of the computer conquer time by providing us with increasingly accurate glimpses of the future? As Bell puts it, "the possibility of prediction, the promise of technological wizardry, and the idea of a millennial turning point make an irresistible combination." There is no question of this.

What is in question, however, is whether the marvels of electronic technology, cybernetics, linear programming, systems analysis, game theory, and the like, do add anything, *can* add anything to our success in an enterprise that is at least two hundred years old in the West: the serious, conscious business of predicting the future by observation of real or imagined continuities of event, change, and circumstance in time.

The wizardry of contemporary technology notwithstanding, the essential and lasting methodology of future-predicting was set forth in the early 18th century by the great Leibniz. One sentence, taken from his "Principles of Nature and of Grace," will suffice to express the crucial elements of Leibniz's law of continuity: *The present is big with the future, the future might be read in the past, the distant is expressed in the near.*

I will come back in a moment to some of the premises and assumptions of Leibniz's law, for they are vital to our belief that predicting and forecasting are possible. For the moment, however, I want only to stress the fact that not all the marvels of computer technology and related devices have in any way supplanted our reliance upon this profound, if questionable, Leibnizian view of the relation among past, present, and future. Either the future *does* lie in the present, and hence is subject to observation through dissection, or it does not. And if it does not, all the computers and systems analysis and linear programming in the world will not help us. For it is sheer delusion to suppose that anything short of H. G. Wells's Time Machine can in fact get us into the future, as technology gets us across space to the moon.

For at least a couple of centuries, the essential meaning of Leibniz's law of historical continuity has been axiomatic in Western thought. It has been the basis of all that we call philosophy of history and social developmentalism. From it has come the widely accepted notion that there *is* an entity called civilization or culture, that this entity obeys certain immanent principles of growth in time, that the continuity of time is roughly the same as the continuity of this growth, that past, present, and future have not merely a chronological relation but a *genetic* relation, and that through sufficient study of the past and the present it is possible to foresee the future simply by extending or extrapolating ongoing process.

This is precisely the mode of investigation, the framework of analysis, that we find in such titans of the 19th century as Comte, Hegel, Marx, and Spencer. One and all they were operating in terms of Leibnizian assumptions about the genetic relation of past, present, and future. We call them philosophers of history. But they could as properly be called future-predicters. For, it was not antiquarianism or preoccupation with the present that generated the works of these individuals. Obviously, they were interested in the past and present—and provided their readers with a great deal of enlightenment about past and present, just as do our Herman Kahns and Stuart Chases today—but the motivating interest was the shape of the future. The vision of future society, organized around the trinity of scientist, statesman, and industrialist, that Comte gave us in his *The Positive Polity* was far from being simple, speculative utopianism. It was a vision, in its root essentials, formed of projections of trends and tendencies that Comte supposed (and not without much reason) to be sovereign in his present and the recent past. Marx spent decades in the British Museum studying economic history—of England chiefly—not because he was enamored of English economic life but because, under Leibnizian assumptions that he no more questioned than had Comte, he discerned something called "capitalism," something that was universal in type, actual or potential, and that would, he thought, obey laws of development which if correctly identified and clearly understood would make prediction of the future as scientifically unassailable as prediction of the movements of the earth around the sun. Marx and Engels, as we know, attacked the problem in two ways: *genetically*, by assessment of "iron" trends extending from past to present and, therefore, into the future; *analytically*, by study of the forces at hand, such as capitalism's supposed internal contradictions. The first gave overview; the second insight into mechanisms of change. Both, for Marx, were essential to the business of future-predicting.

There is no need of elaborating this. It is enough to stress that what Comte and Marx were engaged in exemplifies perfectly what other philosophers of history down to Spengler, Toynbee, and Sorokin (whose recent death took from us a mind matchless in this century for breadth of historical learning and insight) have been engaged in: prediction of the future in terms of extrapolation of discerned tendencies or trends in the present and recent past.

Nor are matters very different today. As one reads such a book as Herman Kahn's and Anthony Wiener's, *The Year 2000*, or their account in the *Daedalus* issue of the nature of their enterprise at the Hudson Institute, one has—if he has read the 19th-century philosophers of history mentioned above—almost the feeling of *déjà vu*. I would be the last to disparage anything simply because it has been done before, or because it exists in a line of like enterprises over a period of several centuries. The trouble is there are so many references of a "hard data" sort, so many allusions throughout the contemporary literature on the future to all the puncture-proof, self-sealing devices of models, programming, and systems, that the unwary reader may be deceived into thinking that projections and forecasts of the future have the same secure relation to these devices that our accounting systems, traffic controls, and market analyses do. It would really be a shabby trick if we somehow left the inference around, to be picked up by the public, that computers and systems-analysts *do* look into the future in ways that were denied to a Tocqueville or a Marx.

"At the Hudson Institute," Herman Kahn writes, "we have used three inter-related devices to facilitate making systematic conjectures about the future." I will paraphrase the description of the "devices." *First*, the Institute identifies "those long-term trends that seem likely to continue," such trends as secular humanism, institutionalization of scientific and technological innovation, and steady economic growth. *Second*, the Institute personnel "cluster significant events by thirty-three year intervals, starting with 1900." The purpose of this, we are informed with a straight face—though come to think of it, it may be deadpan—is to see which combinations give rise to new clusters, and to identify "emergent properties." *Third*, the Institute constructs "significant baselines, statistical where possible, to project key variables in society—population, literacy, GNP, energy sources, military strength, and the like."

I will not go into all the details that fill a four hundred-page book about what the future may be expected to look like. Suffice it to say that, cast in the terminology much favored by our "hard data" brethren in the social sciences today—"surprise-free projections," minimum versus maximum assumptions, "canonical variations," and the like—we have what turns out to be the by now familiar forecast of impending proliferation of bourgeois, bureaucratic, and democratic elites; continued accumulation of scientific and technological knowledge; worldwide industrialization; increasing affluence, urbanization, literacy, and education; increased capability for mass destruction; increasing tempo of change; and, capping this edifying assemblage, "the increasing universality of these trends."

Or take the indefatigable Stuart Chase. Obviously, he assures us solemnly, "this present book is not in the Utopian tradition . . . It takes a hardheaded look at ten current trends, all deriving from science since Galileo, and then attempts to project them into the next few decades, say to the year 2000." Mr. Chase admits that he is compelled to use his imagination like any writer of Utopias, "but there is very little that is imaginative about the description of the trends." No, indeed. Perish the thought. Let no contemporary apostle of the hardheaded look be thought guilty of imagination when there are computers and linear programmers to transpose old-fashioned imagination and guesswork into hard science. After all, look at the remarkable predictions regarding the course of events in Vietnam that the hardheaded Secretary McNamara furnished us with through the wizardry of technology.

Let me now state two equally important points: (1) contemporary forays into the future are no better, and generally worse, *ceteris paribus*, than the forays into the future that our great grandfathers—Tocqueville, Comte, Marx, *et al*—made; (2) the only real utility of these fast accumulating reports and books on the future is the often enlightening, generally informative, sometimes brilliant perceptions they contain about the *present*. No doubt this point alone makes "future-predicting" worthwhile, for there is nothing like an assignment to gaze into the future for sharpening one's awareness of what lies around him in the present.

It is in these terms that the *Daedalus* volume and the Caltech symposium are especially fascinating and worthwhile. Why shouldn't they be, given some of the participants: in the first-named, Daniel Bell, Karl Deutsch, Theodosius Dobzhansky, Erik Erikson, Fred Iklé, Ernst Mayr, Wassily Leontief, Wilbert Moore, Roger Revelle, David Riesman, Herman Kahn—these are but a few; and in the Caltech symposium, Harrison Brown, James Bonner, J. George Harrar, Norman Brooks, John Weir, Thayer Scudder, Athelstan Spilhaus.

What we have in these two volumes is a great deal that is important to know about *present* conditions, *present* structures, and *present* rates and their apparent relation to the recent past. We have much speculation about what the future might be, we have a good deal about historical "trends," and of course vast amounts of material on rates: birth rates, death rates, production rates, rates of air miles flown, entries into the national parks, investment rates, rates of just about everything in any way amenable to quantity-statement.

Reading all of these volumes, we can thrill with repressed horror at the thought of the mantle of too too solid flesh that will one day cover the earth (a mantle that the physicist-population expert, Sir Charles Darwin, once told an audience, much in the manner of the old fashioned temperance lecture, would reach, present rates continuing, one mile in height by the year 3500, or was it 2500?) One can feel his toes trampled on as he reads that by the year 2000 there will be two people for every foot of waterline in the U.S. One can hypnotize himself into a state of driver-fury by merely reading about the 250 million automobiles (we now have about 59 million) on American streets and highways. The thought of 225 billion passenger miles to be flown by the airlines in the year 2000, in contrast to a 1960 figure of 35 billion, is enough to keep everyone home, which would indeed be a change. But change is not, alas, what these books are predicting; they are only extrapolating present rates, many of which remind one of a mad physiologist predicting giants at age twenty on the basis of growth rates at age ten.

Only the unwary will be deluded into thinking that any of this is in fact the future. There have been statistician-soothsayers, I am certain, in all ages. In ancient Egypt there must have been such individuals to compute the number of pyramids there would be on the earth two thousand years later; before that someone to compute the number of pterodactyls; after that to compute the number of knights on horseback, wayfarer chapels, not to mention witches. It is a great game for the statistically-minded (like predictions year by year in the Pentagon of that infinitesimally small chunk of time represented by our engagement in Vietnam), and, as I say, I do not for a moment disparage it. It tells us about the present.

But to pretend, as many will pretend, that we are being treated to a look into the future—a look that is "hardheaded," that is technologically beyond what lay in the capacity of a Marx or Spencer—is to pretend nonsense. We do not even, apparently, have it in our technological power to make "predictions" that will themselves remain steady within the computer-priesthood for more than the shortest periods of time. Thus, when Daniel Bell opened one of his sessions by referring to the quite recent Rand projections of what the year 2000 would be like, he was promptly counter-punched by Fred Iklé with the horrendous disclosure that Rand predictions "already look a little foolish"; that among other inaccuracies, the population of the world will be "seven or eight billion" by that year instead of the "five billion" projected by Rand. Well, one could, of course, write quite an essay, if he were sufficiently bad-tempered, about the predictions made, the *hard data* predictions, during my short lifetime by the demographers.

III

Let me be very clear. I am not finding fault with, much less depreciating or scoffing at what demographers and other statistical analysts do by way of explicating the world we live in, its structures, processes, and rates. It is indeed important to know sometimes *how* big "big" is, *how* fast "fast" is. These activities are valuable, as are the technological devices that today accompany and reinforce them. They will not, however, (and Daniel Bell makes this point in one of the frequent observations—aloof but committed, skeptical but engaged—with which he interlards the proceedings in *Daedalus*) supplant speculation, raw speculation, when it comes to predictions that go more than a very very short time from the immediate present.

And the reason for this—I now go back to the Leibnizian law of continuity which remains as powerful today in its impact upon future-predicters as it did in the 18th and 19th centuries—the ineffaceable, unconquerable reason for this is that the present is *not* big with the future. Nor, let it be well understood, was the past ever big with what is now the present. We are confusing continuity of chronology with continuity of circumstance and event. We are mistaking our metaphoric reconstructions of the past, by which we assuage the pain of need for temporal order, for causal connection.

In the 18th century a distinguished physical philosopher (Laplace, I believe it was), declared that if he could but know *everything* in the present—every thought, motive, reflex, need, etc.—he could with ease and accuracy predict *everything* in the future. The surface plausibility of this is matched only by its lurking naivete. Since it is precisely the kind of naivete that reigns today, however, I do not apologize for introducing it. Nothing, I assume, could seem more certain to the individual for whom reality consists of the hard data of atoms, molecules, reflexes, social-security numbers, and the like than that absolute knowledge of the hard data of the present should yield—properly processed in the machines—knowledge of the future. But it won't and it never will. And the reason, I repeat, is that the present does not contain the future, the far is not to be found in the near, nor was our present ever contained in the past. Not if what we are concerned with is *change*.

True, institutions, structures, established ways of behavior, will extend themselves into the future just as geographic terrain will. There will be, barring catastrophe or the appearance of the Genius, or the Prophet, or the Maniac, or the Random Event, technology, schools, kinship systems, magazines like *Commentary*, and so on. This is safe predicting, for all we are predicting is persistence. And I do not depreciate this, for we would be a lot farther along in our understanding of the actual dynamics of change if there were real understanding, real *acceptance*, in the theoretical terms of social science, of the phenomena of stability and persistence of ways of social behavior. Wilbert Moore, in a wise utterance in the *Daedalus* issue, calls attention to our typical exaggeration of change in society and to our common confusion of change—actual, significant change—with mere motion, activity, and movement.

For some reason it is difficult to discuss stability and fixity with most social scientists. They do not believe in it. I am invariably told, gently, condescendingly, that what I mistake for hard, unchanging persistence in time is my inability to discern the actual changes—subterranean, microscopic—that go on incessantly, in the form of minute adaptations, conflicts, stresses, and strains which in the long view might be seen to be as directional and cumulative as the infinitesimal variations studied by the geneticist. But conflicts, stresses, and strains do not by any means bespeak change; all they can confidently be said to be are—conflicts, stresses, and strains! It is remarkable, as Lewis Coser has shown us in his classic study of the functions of social conflict, how much conflict actually turns out to be not merely containable within social structures but actually supportive of such structures. How many billions of role tensions and conflicts there have been in the long history of Western kinship it would be impossible to guess; but changes, basic, fundamental changes, in kinship structure in the West have been few and far between, and these changes have clearly had far more to do with the external and adventitious impacts of the Random Event, the Prophet, the Genius, and the Maniac in history than with any accumulation of minute role—or status—changes within the *kinship* system or with what are generally called trends of change in society.

"Trends" are particularly suspect. A trend, the dictionary tells us, is the general direction taken by a stream, a shoreline, etc.; it is an underlying or prevailing tendency or inclination. These are all tempting words for the historian or predicter of societal development. How easy it is, as we look back over the past—that is, of course, the "past" that has been selected for us by historians and social scientists—to see in it trends and tendencies that appear to possess the iron necessity and clear directionality of growth in a plant or organism. We think of these "trends" as cumulative movements, as genetic sequences, as actually *causal.* We forget that they are, one and all, *a posteriori* constructs, frequently metaphoric in character, always *post hoc, propter hoc.*

But the relation among past, present, and future is chronological, not causal. As one looks at the various sequences of events—"clusters," as Herman Kahn calls them—there is not a sequence or linkage that would not make just as much sense in causal terms were it in fact the obverse, were it any one of the literally hundreds of "patterns" that events and changes might as easily—and, in causal or genetic terms as "rationally," "logically"—have taken.

What Emile Durkheim wrote on all this is profound and, obviously, still relevant: It is said, writes Durkheim, "that history has for its object precisely the linking of events in their order of succession. But it is impossible to conceive how the stage which a civilization has reached at a given moment could be the determining cause of the subsequent state. *The stages that humanity successively traverses do not engender one another.*

"All that we can observe experimentally . . . is a series of changes among which a causal bond does not exist. *The antecedent stage does not produce the subsequent one, but the relation between them is exclusively chronological.* Under these circumstances all scientific prevision is impossible." (Italics added.) *Pace* Marx, Comte, Spengler, Toynbee, and, with them, any of those currently concerned with the year 2000 who might believe that sufficiently intensive analysis of the present will yield knowledge of future change.

That one can, through religious or philosophical metaphor, summarize, encapsulate, on the basis of skillful selection of a few events and changes from the past, is not to be doubted; that one can form in his mind, through this type of selection and through one or another metaphor, "trends" that have vivid meaning to his mind is not to be doubted either. We may with Tocqueville see Western history in the terms of a leveling that sweeps away all class differences; with Marx we may see the same Western history in terms of class conflict that sweeps away all equalities. Or we may see history in terms of magnification of power, rationalization of power, emancipation from power. All of these are philosophical constructions with which we seek to impose meaning upon the essentially meaningless. To confuse "trends," whether Marx's, Tocqueville's, Stuart Chase's, or Herman Kahn's, with processes that have in fact genetic continuity and causal connection in time is, however, to take the metaphor of growth much too seriously in its application to human behavior in time. The hypothesis of growth is useful only in the understanding of entities that do actually grow and develop—such as plants and organisms—and for all else it is either naive or dangerous.

As one who enjoys an occasional roll of the dice at Las Vegas, I have a model of change in time that seems to me much better than models drawn from organic growth. My model is based on what happens with the throw of the dice. I may, in a given evening, fancy all manner of trends and tendencies present in my dice-throwing. Hypnotized occasionally by either surpassing good luck or bad luck, I may imagine the existence of continuities too extraordinary to be explained by chance. Such continuities can even seem genetic. But my good sense usually comes quickly to the rescue. I know that such continuities are random and chronological, not causal. Even if I were to throw twenty naturals in succession I would know that no genetic trend existed; only that the laws of probability had been stretched. I would know that twenty or a hundred naturals would not, either in the experience or in retrospect, have, in their unbroken succession, the slightest influence upon what the next throw would yield. To predict anything on the basis of my five or twenty naturals in succession would be, plainly, impossible.

Could we therefore predict nothing? Not at all. We could confidently predict that the dice game would go on and on (we could make this prediction on the basis of surprise-free assumptions with, I should think, quite a high coefficient of probability), that the gambling casino would also go on and on, that Las Vegas would continue to sprawl ever farther out into the desert (just as the pyramids once went sprawling over the Egyptian desert), and that the number of Americans visiting Las Vegas, at present annual rates of increase, would by A.D. 2100 reach the point where there would be twenty-eight little old ladies in front of each slot machine in contrast to the two invariably there now.

Somehow this kind of predicting isn't very exciting once your hopes have been raised by apparent continuities of the dice, but it is still prediction, isn't it?, and it is the kind of prediction, like it or not, that you will get in books on the year 2000.

The crucial point, though, is this: What is significantly different and novel about American society in 1968 did not "grow out of" American society of 1868, fond though we may be of the lovely, thought-narcotizing metaphor of growth with all its comfortable words regarding genetic continuity, trends, causality, and the like. (One of the *Daedalus* participants observes that what is new and vital in science today—that is, what has *changed* in time—could not possibly have been predicted a generation ago. Of course not. What is manifest today was not then latent, was not "in" the science of that time. Why should matters be different elsewhere in culture?) True, a really surprising amount of what existed in 1868 is with us still, and it is this similarity that leads us to think of it all in terms of growth and continuity of change. But it is not continuity of change that has operated; only continuity in the sense of continuity of the river's *bed*, that is, persistence of the unchanging or the only slightly and infrequently changed. This is continuity too, but not the kind that is summarized in visions of trends and tendencies.

Let us be clear on two points (1) Events do not marry and have little events that grow into big events which in turn marry and have little events, etc.; (2) small social changes do not accumulate directionally and continuously to become big changes. We pretend in our histories and sociologies that such is the case, but it is all *a posteriori*, suffers badly from an affliction known as the pathetic fallacy, and does more to assuage the pain of intellectual disorder than it does to throw light on the actual processes of social change. Yes, the theory of natural selection might also be called *a posteriori* and poor in predictive power, but somehow the evolutionary biologist has been more successful at linking micro-changes in their additive and cumulative succession to macro-changes of speciation than we in the social sciences have (or ever will!).

And, of course, the biologist doesn't have to deal as we have to with the Random Event, the Maniac, the Prophet, and the Genius. Maybe there are equivalents in the timeless, structureless, typeless world of the biologist's "population thinking," but I doubt it.

It is very different with studies of change in human society. Here the Random Event, the Maniac, the Prophet, and the Genius have to be reckoned with. We have absolutely no way of escaping them. The future-predicters don't suggest that we can avoid or escape them—or ever be able to predict or forecast them. What the future-predicters, the change-analysts, and trend-tenders say in effect is that with the aid of institute resources, computers, linear programming, etc. they will deal with the kinds of change that are *not* the consequence of the Random Event, the Genius, the Maniac, and the Prophet.

To which I can only say: there really aren't any; not any worth looking at anyhow.

Note

1. *Toward the year 2000: Work in Progress.* This is a special issue of *Daedalus*, reporting the first study papers and proceedings of the American Academy of Arts and Sciences' Commission on the year 2000, of which Daniel Bell is chairman. Herman Kahn and Anthony J. Wiener (eds.), *The Year 2000* (Macmillan, 1967); *The Next Ninety Years* (California Institute of Technology, 1967); Stuart Chase, *The Most Probable World* (Harper and Row, 1968).

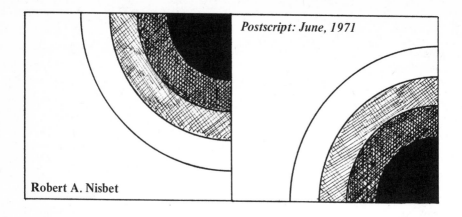

Robert A. Nisbet

The editor of this volume, with rare kindness, has asked me if I wished to say anything on my behalf at this late date, to qualify, alter, or repudiate any of the statements contained in my earlier article, first published exactly three years ago. Try as I might, however, I cannot. Futurology seems to me now as it did then: an unstable combination of statistical extrapolation, ordinary forecasting, occasionally shrewd insights into the present, and, now and then, some worthwhile, old-fashioned prophecy, based upon the kind of fertile imagination we are likely to see at its best in first-rate science fiction.

I like to think I have all possible admiration for what technology, computer science, and advanced mathematics have done for modern knowledge. I am no stranger to the excitement induced by the view that inasmuch as these have catapulted us through space to the moon and other planets, they should be able to catapult us across time, enabling us to pay visits, as it were, to the future. Those who were ever as enchanted as I was many years ago by H. G. Wells's story of the time machine can guess at the buoyancy of my fantasy, if not hope. But neither technology nor science as a whole will ever be able to get us any farther into the future, any more accurately into the future, than the imaginations and insights of men of common sense, of seers and forecasters and prophets, and of science fiction writers have in the past—and continue to do in the present.

The reason for this is simple in statement, massive in theoretical implication. *The future does not lie in the present.* Nor did the present, as we know it, ever lie in the past. What is at issue here is a whole, wide-ranging, encompassing habit of mind, one that has been deep in Western thought ever since the pre-Socratic Greeks made the momentous analogy between the biological organism and social structure, declaring that as growth is an inalienable attribute of organismic structure, so change—that is, a "natural" pattern of change needing only to be described by the sociologist as the life-cycle of growth is described by the biologist —is an inalienable part of the structure of whatever social system we may have in view at any given moment. What we have all around us, today, as in the days of the organism-intoxicated Greeks, is the spell of the metaphor of growth.

Closely associated is another metaphor: the metaphor of genealogy. This is of more interest to historians, and has been since the time of Thucydides, than it usually is to the growth-fascinated sociologists, economists, and political scientists. Here we are dealing with the imagined genealogical linkage of events, acts, and personages in history. The image of the genealogical series in the organic world—of genetic causality plainly to be seen in the act of generation—is made by the historian to serve the world of events, acts, and motives with which he deals. Who has not been beguiled by the persuasive historian into believing that the same genetically causal relation exists from event to event, act to act, and motive to motive, as so plainly exists from one generation to another in a family line.

But whereas growth and genealogy are actual enough in the world of plants and animals, a mighty act of metaphoric transference is required to give them acceptability in our theories of institutions, changes, and events through time. In the biological world, each is to be seen clearly and indisputably whether the canvas be small or large. In the social world, however, it is evident enough that these two metaphors gain greatly in verisimilitude the more abstract, distant in time, or vast in size the subject matter is. If the subject is Civilization, or a Parsonian social system, or some ancient empire, ideas of inexorable growth and of genealogical causality are easy enough to sustain. If the subject is, say, the United States in the twentieth century, or the caste system in India, or the Chinese family, the same ideas have a somewhat grotesque relation to subject matter. Whatever else we see in the concrete, circumstantial, and detailed record of each of these, we assuredly do not see processes which readily lend themselves to the metaphor of growth, with its commitment to immanence, genetic continuity, cumulation, and directionality; or to the metaphor of genealogy, with event begetting event, act begetting act, the whole forming an iron chain of causality in time.

Fundamental to futurology, it seems to me, is the deceptive, even fallacious, assumption *that the continuity of time is matched by the continuity of change or the continuity of events*. Time—at least as we arbitrarily and conventionally record it; who knows what time is in any substantive sense?—can easily be thought of as continuous and cumulative, and also directional. Seconds become minutes; minutes become hours, days, months, years, etc. The *temporal* present has indeed grown out of, emerged from, the *temporal* past. How could it be otherwise, with January invariably preceding February, with 1971 preceded by 1970, with the twentieth century emerging lineally in a time series out of the nineteenth century, and so on.

Change, however, is in no sense identical with time, in no sense a necessary aspect of time. Time, as we record it, can coexist with absolute fixity of position or condition. When we refer to change, we are referring to a *succession of differences in time in some persisting identity*. The last may be anything: a tree, dog, rock, language, structure of kinship, religion, state, or a human being. Change may be said to exist if, over a period of time, we can perceive differences in that persisting entity. Under the spell of the organic metaphors, we like to assume, so far as is possible, that these differences emerge, one from the other, genetically, subject, ideally, to uniform causation, and having the kind of continuity and directionality that genuine growth in nature invariably does. Above all, the continuity of time is held to be matched, if only we can supply enough data, by continuity of change. Just as seconds become minutes and then hours in cumulative, lineal sequence, so—it is assumed, and has been since the Greeks—do infinitesimal variations of human interaction become small changes and then larger changes, with the lineal sequence thus given the same attributes of continuity (*genetic* continuity) that are indisputable when it is time alone that is being considered.

In the organism, there is warrant for making time and change synchronous, if not identical. So long as an organism is alive at all, whether undergoing genesis or decay, each passing moment is simultaneous with some change, however microscopic, or even invisible, that is a genetic element of the overall process we call growth. No such warrant exists, or could conceivably exist, when the "persisting identity" is not the biological organism, but the social and cultural behavior of human beings.

The relevance of all this to futurology is, I think, evident. If futurology is, or is to become, what it so often now pretends to be—a *science* of the future, in contrast to old-fashioned, largely intuitive prophecies of the future—then it will have to be able to demonstrate, first, the undifferentiated character of time and change and, second, the applicability of concepts of growth to the small, finite, and circumstantial in society; this last in contrast to the great vistas of time and the immense, largely abstract units we call "civilization," "mankind," "the human race," and so on. In the study of biological evolution, the mechanisms of change studied by the geneticist, the micro-mechanisms, have patent relevance to the larger manifestations of evolutionary change involved in speciation. No such relevance exists in the study of society.

Futurology and old-fashioned social evolutionism of the Marxian, Comtean, and Spencerian kind have much in common. It is not strange that we should be getting at the present time, when futurological fancies are parading across the landscape toward the Year 2000, a distinct revival of old-fashioned social evolutionism in the recent works of Talcott Parsons, Gerhard Lenski, and Robert Bellah, among others. As I have stressed, futurology and social evolutionism are clearly founded on the same premises concerning the nature of change. Social evolutionary constructions differ from those of futurology chiefly in that the former are oriented toward the past, the latter toward the future. But just as futurology seeks to root its projections in trends supposedly reaching back to the past, so most theories of social evolution have at least passing reference to the future.[1]

Both types of construction are bound to come easily to a world of social science that is as suffused as ours by the genetic fallacy: the fallacy that change is derivable from social structure and that, like organic growth, it is largely immanent, cumulative, and directional. And this has to be said: if the premises of social evolutionism are correct regarding the relation between past and present, then the premises of futurology are equally correct. If by diligent study we can come up—objectively, as does the biologist—with embryonic beginnings of the present back in, say, the medieval period, then there is, on the face of it, no reason why sufficiently diligent study of the present should not yield social and cultural embryos of the future. Further, if the premises that we find throughout the literature of "developmentalism" in those areas of political science and economics concerned with the new or "emerging" nations, and that we find too in the sociological literature of "social systems," are correct, then futurology could no doubt be said to rest on sound conceptual foundations.

Alas, these premises do not hold up; not when we dismiss the metaphor of growth with its vocabulary of immanent, cumulative, and directional change or development; not when we dismiss the metaphor of genealogy with its vocabulary of linkages of events in time; not when we turn from abstractions such as social systems; not when we go from metaphor and abstraction to the actual, verifiable, concrete history of a given area or period. In referring as I did in the earlier article to the Genius, the Maniac, the Prophet, and the Random Event, I was only concerned, albeit somewhat dramatically, with making the point that try as we might we cannot detach the study of social change—past, present, or future—from these powerful, and entirely unpredictable, forces in history.

It would be very nice if each institution and social structure, ranging from the tiny family to the massive civilization, did indeed have a discoverable and verifiable pattern of change built into its structure, as any organism does. And it would be nice, given this pattern, if historical actuality were such as to permit it to unfold itself cumulatively, genetically, and directionally. But no matter what may be our dreams or secret hopes regarding patterns of "natural" change of development in institutions and civilizations, they do not exist. There is not an atom of evidence to suggest that a pattern of change *emerges* from a social structure—that is, that change or development is an attribute of a social structure, as, most obviously, growth is an attribute of any organism—or that any kind of cycle or trajectory for a civilization can be deduced from either intensive study of the present or as a consequence of those eminently subjective, arbitrary, and highly selective strings of events that historians assemble in the form of narrative history.

But let us assume for a moment the opposite of what I have just observed here. Let us assume that, as is true of any organism, there is indeed a built-in, normal, or natural pattern of change in institutions and cultures. We would still be confronted by the all-to-intrusive phenemona of the historical record: random events such as wars, invasions, migrations, catastrophes, etc., which by no stretch of anyone's imagination could ever be deduced or projected from analysis of structure; and, however much sociologists may despise them, the powerful impacts of the geniuses, prophets, and maniacs in history.

Tolstoi, in the epilogue to his great *War and Peace*, which is like nothing so much as an ode to the masses, thought that all the particularities and individualities of history could be dismissed from consideration. History, he thought, is no more, at bottom, than a record of those tidal movements in time which bespeak the risings and fallings of the masses. No one to my knowledge gives much shrift to Tolstoi's view of history. For everyone, it is a rather embarrassing addendum to what is probably the greatest novel ever written. But, as one reflects, Tolstoi's view of history is not different in essentials from that of social evolutionists and futurologists.

Futurologists, social evolutionists, and social systems theorists say, in effect: "We are not concerned with unique or random events, with the highly individual impact of the great (or maniacal) statesman, general, prophet, inventor, creator, or entrepreneur. No one could be expected to predict these. *Our* concern is with those patterns of change and development which exist independently of such forces." I can only repeat with emphasis what I said in the earlier article: the kinds of change which exist independently of the impacts registered by random events, geniuses, prophets, and maniacs are—despite the lulling testimony to the contrary of the metaphors of growth and genealogy—insignificant at best, and more likely to be the simple manifestations of motion, movement, flux, and interaction which are always present in social life.

I don't dispute the fact that one can work up quite an imposing picture of the future simply by projecting present modes of behavior. Inertia and persistence bulk large in human behavior. Undoubtedly, future mating patterns will be much like those around us, with usual defections from monogamy in the forms of adultery, premarital sex, serial marriage, communes—celibate and noncelibate— and so on. Beyond doubt, organizations analogous to our great economic corporations will still be around, and will have a major influence in economic and political matters. Labor unions, spectator sports, schools, universities (?), churches (!), public libraries, automobiles, national parks, etc., etc., will no doubt be around in one form or other. Whatever government may be in fact, assessed by present standards of democracy, almost certainly we shall live under a government that will call itself, and surely be regarded by most persons as, democratic.

If this kind of generalized projection of the present—present structures and also present rates of activity and motion—is what is meant by futurology, it is bound to have a good future. All one needs is to be sufficiently amorphous, general, and chameleonic in his "predictions," as are the practitioners of the so-called Delphi method in the Rand Corporation, and one cannot fail to be a futurologist. Looking at the matter from the point of view of the gambler's odds involved, one does best to predict—that is, for any date thirty or forty years removed—continuation of what one sees around him. He will lose here and there—sometimes, as in those rare periods of convulsive political and social change, heavily—but, given the well known tendency of human behavior to persist in generally recognizable ways from one age to the next, he will surely have the odds with him. The amount of certifiable change in history is extraordinarily small in comparison with the amount of sheer persistence and inertia, which of course includes much random motion, action, and interaction that often gives the illusion of change.

Forecasting, an old and indispensable part of social life in all its spheres, seems to me, basically, no more than a placing of bets on the likeliest of a finite number of alternatives. Information and knowledge are clearly important, just as these are important to the professional gambler; and I doubt that contemporary forecasting would reject out of hand the successful professional gambler's invariable qualities of acumen, insight, discipline, boldness—and luck! There are, obviously, some areas of forecasting—weather, crops, steel production—characterized by more success than others. There are none, however, in which forecasts of more than the shortest periods of time are worth much.

So is prophecy—long-range prophecy—a valuable part of social life. Prophecy integrates and gives meaning to the present in the very act of locating the distant future. Who today can do other than marvel at the prescience Tocqueville displayed in *Democracy in America* (though one could do a small book filled with nothing but his *bad* prophecies) or, say, at Jacob Burckhardt and his melancholy prophecy of the coming of the "terrible simplifiers" in Western governments—that is, the totalitarian rulers of the twentieth century. Or think of Dostoevski and his visions of a world under the torment of permanent revolutionaries and godless true believers.

At this point, I dare say, someone will think of Marx. Did he not, working from his "science of history" and his "social systems analysis" of capitalism accurately predict the coming of socialism? But where is socialism? If one refers to those nations such as Soviet Russia, Albania, and China which call themselves socialist, it can be assumed easily enough, I should think, that Marx, were he alive, would be among the first to say they are not what he had in mind. And even if they were, even if by objective judgment they are socialist, no one could say that their manner of coming into being, their processes of revolutionary inception, had the slightest resemblance to the processes Marx's study of capitalism led him to foresee. Marx was, however, in the Old Testament sense of the word, a mighty prophet—one of the prophets indeed, if not geniuses, whose impact, along with the impacts of random events and maniacs, has done much to shape the world we live in. (Question: could Marx the "scientist" have predicted the impact of Marx the religio-moral prophet?)

Much that occasionally looks like prophecy or forecasting—or, if we like, futurology—actually isn't. It is no more than assessment of a present condition before anyone else has so assessed it, with both the assessment *and the condition* persisting in public consciousness. Two years ago at this time, I wrote an article titled "The Death of the Student Revolution." This was the summer following the agonizing spring of turmoil at Columbia, Harvard, and Cornell—as well as at the scenes of earlier turmoil, such as Wisconsin, Berkeley, and San Francisco State. I said that the student revolution was over, that its back was broken, and, that apart from a few more lashings of the long tail it had acquired during the four preceding years, there would be nothing left of slightest significance.

The article was published September 13, 1969, in the *Montreal Star*. It was submitted at the same time, or just after, to *Encounter*, which, because of a crowded publication schedule, couldn't publish it until the following February, though the editor in friendly interest to me may well have wanted to see the dreaded fall academic term come and pass before subjecting me to public exposure. True, as the result of President Nixon's extraordinary and, for him, unwonted manner of announcing our military entry into Cambodia, there was one more brief period of conspicuous unrest on college campuses, including Kent State the following spring. But that was all. And I had clearly stated, at the very beginning of the article, that there would be a few more death-lashings of the revolution's tail, its back having already been broken.

"Embarrasing," "presumptuous," "fatuous," "blind" were among the politer responses my article drew. Several student revolutionaries—or would-be revolutionaries—managed to get space in the *Montreal Star* for a detailed rebuttal of my piece a month after it had first appeared there. They "proved" how false and unseeing I had been in declaring dead a movement they—and so many non-revolutionary others!—believed would go on and on.

I take some pleasure in that article. It has moreover been referred to now and then as a successful piece of "futurology," or prediction—written by someone who doesn't believe in futurology! But it was in no sense futurology—whether defined as prediction, prophecy, or forecast. It was simply an analysis of a *present condition* (the condition present in the summer of 1969) that proved, I am happy to say, eminently accurate. I was not declaring that the revolution *would* end in the near future. I was stating, with all evidence necessary, that the revolution was *already* over. Much so-called forecasting and prophecy is, at bottom, of this kind.

Recently, while engaged in some nostalgic rereading of issues of *The New Republic* published forty years ago, I came across the following, directed at an address that had just been made by President Herbert Hoover:

> *Of particular interest [wrote the editors] was his "twenty year plan" for America. . . . He says that in the next twenty years we shall add 20,000,000 to our population, build 4,000,000 new homes for them, increase our farm productivity 20 percent and improve our standard of living, which, he says, is already the highest in the world. . . ."*

Now hear this, from the editors of *The New Republic*. Their indignation is mighty; their confidence in the social sciences sublime:

> *It is so easy to answer Mr. Hoover on specific details that it is hardly worth doing. He is evidently ignorant of the studies made by population experts, which show that we are rapidly approaching a stationary or declining population, so that it is highly improbable that we shall add 20,000,000 persons in the next twenty years; even our present birth and death rates would add but 15,000,000 while our birth rate is rapidly falling and the death rate is almost certain to rise as the average age of the population increases. The statement that we shall build 4,000,000 houses in the next twenty years is of course a wild guess. . . ."*[2]

Well, as anyone with a handy reference volume can discover in a twinkling, it was Mr. Hoover who was right; and even he was scarcely right enough, for the population increased just under 30 million persons in the twenty years referred to. Nostalgia and a decent respect for the dead among editors of *The New*

Republic restrain me from citing other, relevant, and even more damning statistics. One does not have to look at the actual history of the period 1931-1951 to know that on any index the editors or President Hoover had cared to use, the editors—and their social science experts—were so wide of the mark that 1951 set, in fact, as to be somewhat hilarious.

Now, I can hear as I write the chorus of objections to my example, all telling me that on any sound, *scientific* (meaning here statistical-extrapolative) ground, the editors and social scientists were right and President Hoover didn't know what he was talking about. The birth rate trend was there, wasn't it, along with trends of the same kind in jobs, housing, profits, payrolls, etc.? And—usually said in high dudgeon—we are not expected to predict maniacs like Hitler and random events such as World War II, are we?

Indeed not. But my point is that the historical record is inseparable through all time from maniacs and random events, as well as prophets and geniuses, and that to seek to predict the future, or to account for past and present, without reference to these leaves us with something that may be defensible on grounds of games-playing but nothing more. The blunt fact remains that President Hoover, working from who knows what materials—political self-justification, sheer optimism, poker player's acumen, ignorance of social science, luck—made a prediction for a twenty-year period that was on the right track, whereas the editors turned with sublime confidence to the best of social science, and fell on their faces.

Everybody knows that the grounds on which President Hoover rested his twenty-year prophecy are notoriously unreliable (and as a depression child, I have a vivid recollection of how wrong Hoover was on some of his short-range prophecies—who will ever forget "prosperity is just around the corner"?). What fewer persons realize, however, is that the grounds on which social scientists and futurologists today rest their predictions of the future are—despite the panoply of computers and mathematical techniques—no better than were President Hoover's. And the reason, to repeat once again, is that the future does not lie in the present. And the present is all we have, or ever will have, to work with.

I find it interesting to look around at the America of 1971 and to contrast it with the America of 1931, which is about the time I was really becoming aware of the world, having just graduated from high school. Top-flight scientists of the present tell me that what is, and has been, distinctive for a decade or two in physical science simply was not present in the physical science of the 1920s or 1930s: not present in any form, shape, or fashion, not even as a tiny fertilized germ cell.

Neither was much if anything else of what most of us would regard as truly distinctive in our culture today—or distinctive, for that matter, in the 1950s and the 1960s present in the 1920s or 1930s. What was there, for example, in substance or embryo, however slight, to be picked up by even the most sensitive of futurological minds and instruments—had they existed—that would have made it possible to predict in even the most general terms those aspects of the cultural-intellectual present which we all today know as distinctive and important? I refer to such varied aspects as the utter collapse of an authentic, autonomous political left in the West; the collapse, too, of an intellectual buoyancy that remained strong throughout the Depression but that has whimpered out (that is, by the standards of the 1930s) in the familiar forms of identity-preoccupation, anomie, and other forms of obsessive alienation;[3] the astonishing reassertion of religion, orthodox and bizzarre alike, which even the religionaries of the 1930s assumed was being vanquished by secularism and technology; the spreading anti-intellectualism—not, be it noted, among the noneducated, but among the most educated, especially in the universities; the radicalization (by the criteria of 1931) of the whole, sprawling American middle class for which to be affluent means to be, if not actually guilty, at very least service-oriented and super-permissive in all respects; the radicalization (again by 1931 criteria) of the media—from the *New York Times* to the *Los Angeles Times*, and not overlooking the great radio and television centers in New York and Los Angeles; the virtual collapse among intellectuals of the once luminous vision not merely of socialism but of the larger, more encompassing political community; the collapse of humor in all its manifestations (the only remaining public comedians are those such as Jack Benny and Bob Hope who flourished among literally dozens of successful comedians in the 1930s.);[4] and, finally, the utter bankruptcy, in all senses of the word, of what was in the 1930s America's one great contribution to the history of the arts: the movies.

Clearly, the few items I've mentioned in the preceding paragraph vary substantially in importance; none of them, however, can be doubted to be real. Many other aspects of the present will suggest themselves to readers as being of equal or greater importance to our culture—or, rather, to the ever-required *springs* of culture, those we call motivation, context, and incentive. I doubt that any of these will suggest themselves as having been present in any kind of embryonic or otherwise discernible form in the 1930s either. Note that I am magnanimously omitting any mention of such events as World War II and its consequent militarization of the world we live in *or* the astonishing turns in population rates *or* the unprecedented economic boom of the postwar period *or* the ethnic explosion in all areas of the culture and society of the blacks, etc. For, as futurologists invariably say, crossing themselves in the utterance: "We don't pretend to be able to predict unique events!" My only question is, what *do* they claim to predict that can be lifted out of the realms of conjecture, surmise, and old-fashioned prophecy and that is of much significance—or, for that matter, reality?

There is a kind of hoax involved in futurological claims. When we are told that there are ways of foreseeing the future, we cannot help thinking that the reference is to the *differentness* of things—to those aspects of life thirty years hence that will be different from those now present. All the futurologist can, in fact, do, however, is extrapolate and project, rates included, *present* phenomena. Operating on the false premise that continuity of time is matched by continuity of change and event, he worships at the shrine of continuity to a degree hardly found among the most pious of nineteenth century evolutionists. Continuity is the futurologist's god. Alas, history is made up of *dis*continuities when we have the phenomena of difference, novelty, innovation, change in mind. However, as I have said, one can safely enough predict that human beings will still be mating—and this is continuity, too.

None of the above should be taken to mean that I lack confidence in the social sciences. Far from it. I think the worst effect of futurology may well prove to be the destruction, or at least serious reduction, of public confidence in the social sciences. There are too many social scientists who make the scientific character of their disciplines depend upon utterly mistaken conceptions of what genuine scientific prediction is. I shall come to this in a moment. I want only to emphasize here that I think the record of the social sciences, taking them at their best, is extremely good. They have contributed a great deal in the recent past. They should be able to contribute much more in the future. It would behoove all governing agencies to accept and make a good deal more use of the conclusions and judgments of the best of our social scientists than is now the case. Such conclusions and judgments, those at least that are genuinely scientific, have nothing to do, however, with the pretensions of futurology as they are being foisted upon an all too gullible public.

What are these pretensions? They are compounded precisely of a confusion—witting or unwitting—of *prediction*, as this is known in science, and of *prophecy*. Prediction in science has nothing intrinsically to do with the time-category of the future. When the astronomer "predicts" the eclipse, he is merely vouchsafing that part of a well known astronomical regularity that happens to be capable of statement in the public-pleasing terms of a certain day, hour, and even minute. The astronomer is not, however—or, at best, only incidentally—looking into the future of the cosmic system; he is only dealing with the "future" that is contained in our conventional chronology. The astronomer's "prediction" of an eclipse is not one bit different from the "prediction" that the sun will rise tomorrow at 5:39 A.M. Neither is, in substance, one bit different from the epidemiologist's "prediction" that malaria, or pellagra, will be found to be present in a given community if it is visited—the epidemiologist's "prediction" being no more than a statement of causal effect on the basis of his prior and certain intelligence that certain types of conditions prevail in that community.

Can social scientists predict? We can and do—with really rather remarkable success, it seems to me. We know enough about the conditions and functional relationships of certain social phenomena to make possible explanatory propositions much like those I have just borrowed from the physical sciences. To use a very important example, we have found—despite old wives' tales found in so many quarters, including editorial offices of the media—that hard-core poverty as such never, by itself, leads to revolutionary behavior. We are thus in a sound position to "predict," with the usual coefficent of error, of course, when we come upon, or hear about, some new enclave of poverty, that no revolutionary behavior will emerge apart from the addition of certain, easily specifiable elements—elements such as a sudden expectation-increasing rise in standard of living, or the addition to the enclave of change-minded, or revolutionary political intellectuals. There are, as one reflects on the matter, scores of "predictions" of that kind available to us.

Futurology, alas, and also much ostensibly nonfuturological writing by social scientists suggests that prediction in the social sciences, or in historiography, if it is to exist at all, must take the form of preview of the future. And, given the fallacies of the whole functional-structural, or social systems, view of the relation of change to structure or system, there is nothing really surprising about this. The quest for universal generalization, for so-called unified theory, is as powerful a quest today in human thought as the quest for community is in human behavior. Genetic causality, continuity, cumulation, directionality: all of these are, it would sometimes seem, as much icons in the intellectual spheres of history and the social sciences as belonging, identity, and membership are icons in the more popular spheres of contemporary society.

Notes

1. And have had ever since St. Augustine gave the West its first unilinear, developmental, cumulative, and directional picture of civilization—*one* civilization—in time. Contemporary social-evolutionary constructions, Parsonian and other, make the pretense of affiliating themselves with modern genetics and comparative biology. They are, in fact, Augustinian—with only God left out!

2. *The New Republic* (June 24, 1931), p. 135.

3. Who, with whatever instrument or genius, in the depression-ridden, collapse-haunted, jobless, hungry, social insurance-bereft, breadlined 1930s could ever have guessed that the decade would be the subject of America's favorite nostalgia by the time of the affluent 1960s?

4. The 1950s yielded some fine new comedians—Nichols and May, Berman, Sahl, and others—and some humor that was, for Gentiles at least, marvellously fresh. Some distinguished black comedians also came on the scene with humor rooted in black historical past. They are all gone as I write, leaving only those who have managed, like Benny, Hope, and Skelton, to continue with a 1930s-type of humor.

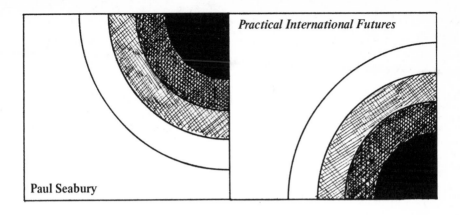

I tried years ago [Paul Valery once wrote] to form a positive idea of what is called progress. *Eliminating all considerations of a moral, political, or aesthetic character, I found that progress came down to the rapid and obvious growth of the mechanical* power *at man's disposal, and of the* accuracy *he can attain in his predictions. ("Remarks on Progress," in his* History and Politics, *p. 164.)*

*New powers, new constraints; and the world has never been less sure of where it was going. (*Ibid., *p. 161.)*

These thoughts are contradictory. A great enlargement of power enables things to happen (to be done) which heretofore were thought impossible or were not thought about at all. If this is so, then the capacity to predict, being but one of many human powers and talents, cannot keep pace. *In extremis*, prediction degenerates into the mere ability to speculate about a profusion of possibilities and/or unlikelihoods. Then is it not the case that power-in-general and predictive ability (a subcategory of power) must be at loggerheads with each other? Ecclesiastes ("nothing new under the sun"), in his time of relative human impotence, was then probably as good a forecaster as Bertrand de Jouvenel is today, although not because he had much special equipment or skills. It seems clear today that accurate predictive techniques do not develop as rapidly as do techniques for change.

To proceed: is it then not all the more necessary, precisely because power leaps far ahead of predictive accuracy, that there should be a constant sharpening and improving of predictive skills, especially those useful for speculation about some of the most important possibilities? Much of our current difficulty in prediction arises from the need now to think not about the "unthinkable," as Herman Kahn has called it, but the previously "nonthinkable"—matters which heretofore were not really questions or problems.

I make these points after spending several weeks reading a great deal of the recent "Year 2000" literature—especially that part of it which treats with futurist scenarios of international politics and with "end-state" depictions. A hazardous occupation, futurism: are such people any better than all those others who with much less data and equipment played this game in the past? Are all such scenarios simply inflated or extrapolated caricatures of present and past actuality? Or, at least, of actualities which most of us see about us *right now*—simply projected into the future?

Wandering through the literature of tomorrowland I came across a quaint early nineteenth century tale recently rescued from oblivion by an English writer, M. Maddison.[1] Written in 1827 by another Englishman, J. Webb, it was called *The Mummy! A Tale of the Twenty-Second Century.* It described Egypt as it would appear three hundred years hence:

No longer did the moving sands of the Desert rise in mighty waves, threatening to overwhelm the wayward traveler; macadamized turnpike roads supplied their place, over which postchaises with anti-attritioned wheels bowled at the rate of fifteen miles an hour. Steamboats glided down the canals and furnaces raised their smoky heads amidst groves of palm trees. . . .

just the way the smoky heads of furnaces were raising themselves over the stately elms of England at the very moment Webb was writing. A recent American book, *The Unprepared Society* by Donald Michael, does much the same thing. What does the future now hold for Americans? Why, hippies, drugs, giant airplanes that crash, pollution, agitated and incompetent bureaucrats, etc.! The point in both these instances simply is that the future *can* be seen simply as an exaggeration, a caricature, or a "linear extrapolation" of select, highly visible tendencies. In demographic forecasts of the 1930s, the Myrdals[2] sought to describe the future Europe that would actually have a declining population—much the same thing. It was declining, and their purpose was to examine the socio-economic conditions of such a future way of life.

II

Seeking to account for the recent fad of futurism, Daniel Bell has noted somewhere the *fin de siecle (fin de millenium!)* fad which started coming over Christian Europeans just before 1000 A.D.: chiliasm, derived from the Greek word, *chiloi,* meaning "thousand." This fad may now be being repeated as we get toward 2000 A.D.; but, in addition, Bell cites the current "bewitchment with technology." "The possibility of prediction, the promise of technological wizardry, and the idea of a millenial turning point make an irresistable combination," he says. The more impressive products of this kind of speculation (*e.g.,* Herman Kahn and associates' *The Year 2000*) seem to confirm this view. Doubtless (here I go, "doubtless," indeed!) in a few years there will be any number of chiliastic sects either making arks or writing manifestos rather than doing simply what most current futurists do—which is scrupulously to avoid determinism, fatalism, and what could be called proclamationism ("that's the way it's going to be").

In futurism, is accuracy or inaccuracy, truth or falseness only to be determined *after* the fact—*i.e.,* after what has been forecast has, or has not, occurred? This old philosophical issue—namely, whether the future is "real," or only partly so, or does not exist at all—has inspired quarrels among scholars ever since Aristotle started it.[3]

Among practical people, however, this metaphysical question is a luxury of philosophers—one must make calculations about the future; and people who do it better than other people can get rewarded for it. If you stay around long enough, of course, error and miscalculation will out—and thus the advantage to the long-term predictors is that the risks of their being found to be wrong are considerably less than for the short-runners. People may have forgotten, for instance, that you predicted anything: or by then they may not care. The short-term projectionists are much more likely to get into trouble.

Consider, for example, a piece written in 1965 by Professor Ithiel Pool of M.I.T. and published in *Daedalus* in 1967. Pool makes the usual acknowledgments of his human fallibility: ("The only thing of which one can be confident is that reality will depart radically from these predictions," but "the predictions chosen are those on which the author would prefer to bet.") He then enumerates a set of *futuribles* for the now-elapsed period of 1965-1970:

1. Mao Tse-tung will die.
2. De Gaulle will die.
3. Two years after (2), French presidential power will have atrophied; without a coalition government, France will be more pro-European but still as bad to NATO as was her dead leader—although she shall be considerably paralyzed.
4. Major fighting in Vietnam will have "petered out" by 1967. A "substantial American victory" will have occurred.
5. Lyndon Johnson will have been re-elected in 1968.
6. Chaos, famines, and military dictatorships will dominate Africa.
7. There will be greater economic discontent in the USSR than "now."

Fortune cookies, anyone? A reading of these predictions in conjunction with Pool's *principal* long-range one ("no nuclear war in the next fifty years") is enough to cause one to get out the old shovel and cement and start digging again in the back yard.

I cite the particular instance of Mr. Pool's bad guesses simply to get one aspect of this new discipline fixed in our minds: with respect to important matters, intelligent futurists can make big mistakes; while, with respect to unimportant ones, prediction can be quite accurate. For example, it is unlikely (very unlikely) that by 1975 Pakistan and Peru will be at war with each other, or that either of them will have a GNP of $100 billion, etc., etc. But then these are not matters of serious speculation anyhow. The sun quite likely will rise at about 6:53 P.S.T. on February 20, 1975, but that natural phenomenon also is not of much interest to us. North Vietnam will not have applied for admission to the United States as a state by 1975—the list could continue indefinitely.

Futurism has a way of centering on matters that are now regarded as important and whose outcomes are open to conjecture. Secondly, and this is where Professor Bell could have been more forceful in explaining why this craft exists, futurism is not inspired solely by technology and chiliasm but also by necessity. Much of its literature does not deal centrally with technological matters, important as these are; much of it does *not* focus on the Year 2000, but more modestly addresses itself to shorter time spans. Much as one might poke fun at its foibles, one might well ask what our human situation might be if no one practiced it. Even an existentialist, that wretched wayfarer floating on a slice of time, cannot afford to ignore such practical questions as whether (for instance) Simone de Beauvoir will or will not come for lunch tomorrow.

In matters of greater moment than this, conjecturing is indispensable to rational action of states. One needs estimates of future contingencies in order to decide what must be done, now. Whether the future is real, unreal, or partly unreal/real is a matter best left to semanticists and philosophers. As long as one rules out determinism (and even Marxists today are dumping this in favor of other modes of thought), conjecturing affirms the need for rational choice based upon intelligent guesses. Pool turned out remarkably wrong in this instance, but he was not playing dirty pool—the problems he chose to conjure with were undeniably important, within which choices had to be made. (Whether de Gaulle died before 1970 or in it is a moot point if one considers the consequence of assuming, to the contrary, that he would have lived and stayed in office indefinitely. The American policy of absorbing his various abuses with unaccustomed Christian charity was based upon conjectures not wholly different from Pool's.)

The difficulties intrinsic to forecasting in international politics can be best seen when we take note of the special kinds of questions uppermost in our minds in the relationships among nations, and then link these with the *kinds* of criteria which generally enter into any rational speculation about the "future." Let us take up the latter set of considerations first.

In general futurist speculation takes into account at least five kinds of evidence:

1. *Extrapolations*: linear curves of measurable phenomena, straight-line projections, and what for our purpose could be called "floating barges"—*i.e.*, major social institutions and aggregates which float down the "time river," giving some promise of durability.

2. *Surprises and catalytic disasters*: events which may or may not have been foreseen or assumed possible or probable, but which mess up extrapolations.

3. *Clouds-on-the-horizon*: this or that unfamiliar phenomenon which appears on the horizon. One, of course, inquires into its size, direction, benignity or malevolence, and its dirigibility.

4. *Noise*: static which deflects attention from significant signals or objects.

5. *Self-starters*: plans for the future based upon attempts to influence the direction of things. In international politics, of course, we have a bounteous supply of these. Some are constructive, others are preventive or deterrent.

It should be clear that the central questions in international macropolitics pertain to the twin matters of peace-war and the nature of relationships between the great blocs of states. Other matters—including now salient ones of ecology, demography, and the condition of the so-called Third World—must be considered subordinate to these; they contribute to the quality of the relationships mentioned above, but are less important. Likewise, the question of the evolution of political communities "beyond the nation-state" must also be contingent upon the character of bloc relations and the special relationship of the superpowers to each other and to their perceived external environments. The "American problem," the "Soviet problem," and the joint problem of Soviet-American relations constitute the core issues of the future, just as they have done since 1945. These configurations can change; qualitative alterations will occur as other states, or groups of states, change their affiliations or alliances; but it still remains true that due to their magnitude, their amplitude of technological power, and the extent of their current span of influence, the United States and the Soviet Union continue to be the arch keystones of the international system.

III

Since American foreign policy during the intense phases of the Cold War tended to be pragmatic and responsive rather than strategic and purposeful in a long-range sense, it is surprising that it maintained the degree of constancy that it did from the early 1950s through the late 1960s; so too, the general configurations or relationships that were being shaped in the first postwar decade (1945-1955) still correspond today to their initial forms. The only "surprise" of any magnitude in the basic international system might be said to be the Sino-Soviet split and the rivalries that this exacerbated in Communist movements in the Third World. Other major changes, especially in the character of the strategic distribution of power between the Soviet Union and the United States, important as these are, were predictable in the late 1950s and have been consummated in a "surprise-free" fashion.[4] Likewise, the recent tendency of the Soviet Union to behave like a "conventional" Great Power, cultivating new allies, "good neighbors," without at the same time demanding of these ideological and political subordination, is really no surprise. Since the mid-1960s, for the Soviet Union the continued spread of "Communism" was less to be welcomed than the spread of Soviet influence and power—quite a different matter.

Today the Soviet Union resembles Richelieu's France in the seventeenth century—not that it is an ideological power in a world of religious wars, but that it is a Great Power pursuing its purposes vigorously and with quite conventional means while compromising its ideological convictions; this at a moment in time when the United States, increasingly disillusioned and doubtful about its own role as a Great Power and the costs entailed by this, is turning "inward" to lick its domestic wounds. From an American perspective, the "surprise" of the late 1960s and early 1970s has come not from the outside environment but from signs of a lapse of will and international purpose among its leaders. That this has contributed to passivity and has intensified an American tendency simply to "react" in the international arena goes without saying. A new source of inter-national instability thus arises *within* the United States—a novelty, whose dur-ability remains to be seen, but one which clearly differs from the kind of isolationism that American leaders like Roosevelt feared in the 1940s.[5]

IV

Yet even the current twist of American moods to an inward-looking social hypochondria tells very little about the "future." Much is now made of the notion of "mood cycles" in American public opinion, the point being that it really is possible to discern twenty-five-year phases of "inward" vs "outward" directed American moods and preoccupations. Yet it is more probable that the current American malaise is contingent on specific events—including the para-doxical combination of a Soviet-American détente with the active American involvement in Vietnam. The former diminished American fears of a major confrontation with Russia just as a minor confrontation of wills was being transformed into a major test of arms.

I make this digression because I regard it as an unfortunate mistake in futurist speculations to fall victim either to cyclic theories or to "straight-line projec-tions" in anticipating future conditions. Most scenarios of either sort may serve as heuristic horror stories—*i.e.*, the scenario may be so unattractive that one recoils from it, like Scrooge from the ghost of Christmas future, and seeks to fend the unwanted future off by mending one's ways. In this fashion, the "fu-ture" may be corrected, modified, deterred, or even prevented.

In a general sense, it is extremely difficult to have any clear ideas about what the future actually holds; and this is most especially true with respect to future diagrams of the international system. It has been my impression that the most useful futurist "scenarios," such as those used in "diplomatic gaming," take off from some specific set of current concerns and move ahead through clear se-quences of action and decision to unfold new kinds of situations. Such forward-moving scenarios differ from those which simply hop ahead several decades to posit some set of future conditions that might then exist. Such speculation about definite conditions at some future base-point may, like Edward Bellamy's *Looking Backward*, have exhortatory and illustrative uses and can provide a sense of sure purpose to current endeavors. They cannot, of course, tell us where we *will* be; but they can show us where we do not or should not want to be—or where we should be, given some will and determination and strength.

To speak, for example, of the probabilities that an America of the year 2000 A.D. will exist or not, that it will or will not be as it now is—a rather messy, free, open society with great reservoirs of technical energy and know-how continuing to comprise the essential heart of a complex nontotalitarian world culture—accomplishes little. Such a statement, or even a quite contradictory one, really is quite bootless as a *prediction*. So, too, are the abstract statements about the condition of international and transnational integration at some determined future point in time. Here again, there is absolutely nothing to be gained other than a picture of some end-state, the general character of which might be desired or not. It might be deemed normatively desirable that the world be more, or less, politically integrated than it now is. Year 2000 pictorializations of such situations may, if done intelligently, anticipate some of the problems that this or that condition may pose or even ways in which the "new world" could be made a "better" one.

V

It is probably safe to say that an important factor that recently entered into future-oriented thinking about world politics has been a willingness to accept the possibility of abrupt *discontinuity* in social and organizational change—*i.e.*, the possibility of seismic upheavals that are occasions of violent reconfigurations of relationships. It is not that such seismic reconfigurations are a normal part of our lives—there has been a remarkable amount of organizational continuity in world politics since 1945, much more perhaps than might then have been assumed. The pacing of some changes—*e.g.*, emancipation from colonial rule—may have been underestimated; the rate of diffusion or nondiffusion of nuclear weapons may have been variously miscalculated; the pace of Europe's economic and cultural recovery after World War II may have been misestimated. Yet, by and large, the world of 1970 *is* a plausible extrapolation from the general situation of 1945.

In retrospect, it may seem surprising that all this is so, given the various apocalyptic possibilities inherent in every stage of our removal from that base point. What is quite interesting, for instance, is that in 1971 we are as far removed chronologically from 1945 as 1945, in turn, was removed from 1914. Yet between 1914 and 1945, the world underwent two major traumas of discontinuity, in which the entire structure of the international system was torn apart, only to be reassembled in vastly different fashion. The wars and revolutions of the first part of the twentieth century were, indeed, "unthinkably" discontinuous. They shattered every pleasant Victorian assumption held about the steady progress and improvement of the human race. The very agencies of human progress were brought to their knees. The powerhouse of Europe, which was the epicenter of human energy and progress everywhere in the world, was finally reduced to Athenian proportions. The authority of that European world to direct the advancement of a Europe-centered world was irretrievably smashed. Between 1914 and 1918, great empires fell, and others were nearly bankrupted. This process was consummated in World War II; at its onset, no one could have possibly known the nature of the systemic outcome which actually occurred.

The acceptance of very great systemic discontinuity as a *possibility* is now a hallmark of our situation: it has the authentic stamp of nuclear power on it. Nothing except some massive cataclysm[6] can now conceivably alter the situation. This fact deeply affects our perception of the future of international politics. For the Great Powers, it conduces to severe limits on their willingness to push things to a head; it has entailed a suspension of pressure to "solve" major irritating international problems quickly by force. Thus it has been more or less true in the past decade that the forces and movements which have been most eager to employ violence have not been the nuclear powers, the Great Powers, but forces and movements led by desperadoes that are either far removed from theaters of nuclear politics or able to exploit the nuclear stalemate of the Great Powers to their own advantage.

Europe, heavily impacted by nuclear weapons and conditioned to know full well the fatal consequences of any major recurrence of conflict there, now knows and enjoys a kind of "civic peace" whose price has entailed the suspension of wars of liberation. That there *might* be serious civil disorders in Europe (subnational uprisings, etc.) is far more probable than a war generated by the "ambitions" of states themselves. The price tag on such conflict in Europe is infinitely higher than ever before, and everyone knows this. Not so in the so-called Third World, which has been the principal scene of major international holocausts since 1950.

The very foreknowledge of possible systemic discontinuity thus far conduces to prudence the application of power by the Great Powers; and paradoxically, we may just possibly say that it is this very awareness and foreknowledge that has produced the conditions of relative stability in their relations with each other. A Hitler before 1939 *could* make what now would seem fantastic claims against other Great Powers and employ violence to carry them out. That was actually possible then, and even plausible; after all, had he succeeded in actually defeating Russia in 1941, he would have conquered all of Europe at a remarkably low price. A European Hitler now simply would not be believed by anyone unless, of course, both he and many others in positions of power were prepared to accept incineration as the inevitable price of such adventures.

VI

At the same time, it is also true that there has developed a kind of armistice concerning *contrived* end-states in world politics—*i.e.*, blueprint designs for future systemic states. Futurist literature for the most part is not innovative in a structural sense; the scenarios and depictions in this literature, interesting as they may be, skirt around the kinds of futurist assumptions that were quite common even as late as a decade ago. One may anticipate or predict certain kinds of transformations of functions of international organizations, for instance, yet not take seriously the prospect for significant *new* political institutions, say in the Year 2000. Structural speculations tend to focuse upon *de facto*, informal relationships: polycentrism, multipolarity, tripolarity, etc.; yet these most often are seen as tendencies and conditions rather than as purposeful contrivances. Thus a utopian concern for "world order" as a planned qualitative transformation designed to meet new needs seems to have been washed out, for the moment at least. The fragmentation of Communism into a congeries of mobilization societies and militant sects can now be seen in conjunction with the new phenomenon of the 1960s—the inward-turning of a once utopian America to its urban and cultural troubles.

A recent "futurist" best seller, Alvin Toffler's *Future Shock*, published in 1970, contains scarcely a word about future changes in international politics and contents itself almost exclusively with the personal, societal, and internal institutional aspects of change. The kinds of "inspired" architectural projections into the international future that were so common in America in the 1940s and 1950s are nowhere visible. They existed in America in the late 1960s in the writings of W. W. Rostow and in the exhortatory speeches of President Lyndon Johnson. But these now seem antique or demeaned by many manifestations of a currently unpopular "American imperialism."

With respect to aspects of international politics that are clearly dysfunctional, a wide body of revisionist *mea culpa* literature in America now regards them as products of American foolishness, stupidity, or wickedness. The new wisdom purveyed by pundits like John Kenneth Galbraith and other moderate critics of the American foreign policy process prescribes simply a reduced American posture in world politics. This, in turn, would seem to rule out any adventurous, constructive blueprinting of the international system requiring extensive U.S. contributions. Prescriptive futurism now seems passé. A dislike of greatness does not conduce to either the imagining of new ordered structures or the attempted consummation of them. The "future," then, is to be anticipated as the compounding of "tendencies." Rational, consensual willfulness in creating new structures of world politics seems "out" for the time being.

VII

In futurist literature, it is also interesting to note a general absence of what I would call here "future prevention" or "future deterrence," even though, in ordinary practice, a great deal of this goes on. One discerns tendencies, notes those which appear obviously undesirable, and undertakes to prevent them from going further. Dean Acheson once remarked (paraphrasing Oliver Wendell Holmes):

The judgment of nature upon error is death. We must make ourselves so strong that we will not be caught defenseless or dangerously exposed in any possible eventuality. The future is unpredictable [emphasis mine]. Only one thing—the unexpected—can be reasonably anticipated. . . . The part of wisdom is to be prepared for what may happen, rather than to base our course on what should happen. . . . Here you can be wrong only once. [7]

What Acheson seems to have been saying is not that nothing can be predicted but that *what may happen* includes a variety of unwelcome contingencies and that these contingencies must be identified in order to be deflected or deterred. In a certain sense, what this special attitude toward forecasting signifies is "conservative estimating"—presupposing "bad" eventualities in order to improve the prospects either that they will not eventuate or that, if they do, one will be prepared to cope with them adequately.

Planning for the worst can lead to absurdities. Since the worst can be very bad indeed, measures to anticipate or deter it could conceivably make life mean, grubby, and certainly perpetually anxious. One "knows," for instance, that the worst which can happen is a terrible earthquake,[8] one prepares for it, and other considerations are subordinated in some degree to the doleful eventuality.

Most reasonable people would not rule out such an earthquake, yet few in practice permit this *one* contingency to govern their affairs in the meantime. Why should they? For there are many, many contingencies, including a contingent earthquake. (There are, for instance, a lot of catastrophic nonearthquakes.)

When we turn to security policy and planning, however, we see two quite essentially different ways of thinking about future contingencies, if one adopts the habit of conservative estimating. Conservative estimating does not necessarily call into being the unpleasant reality it "imagines." *Si vis pacem, para bellum* is its meanest justification. It stresses the deterrence of the unwanted. One imagines the prospect and *takes measures*, the purpose of which is paradoxically twofold: to lessen the likelihood of the occurrence itself and to cope purposefully with it if and when it does occur. Indeed, conservative estimating necessarily must contain this basic paradox: one accepts the possibility of the deterrence's failure in order to strengthen the prospects for the deterrence's success. One holds out the prospect of salvaging something as the principal justification of possessing the means that come into play *if failure occurs*.

This lugubrious perspective differs from many other forms of futurist thinking in that its attention must focus upon "bad" futures that hopefully will not happen and that are to be avoided by what one does now. We can call this future deterrence. *One must be willing to accept* in advance the bad future.

It is here, of course, that the old question of self-fulfilling or self-negating prophecies raises its Janus head. One anticipates (conservative estimating) a series of likely hazardous alterations in the architecture of the security environment, and then takes new measures to cope with them. In the early 1960s, for instance, such projections and anticipations led to a shift of U.S. defense policy and strategic thinking to the problem of internal war, counterinsurgency, and guerilla strategy. New capabilities were developed. New orientations occurred. While the "old" and conventional problems of U.S. deterrence strategy, especially in Europe, remained substantially as they were, a new priority of attention was given to the problems of internal subversion in parts of the Third World—notably the Caribbean, Southeast Asia, and the Congo.

It has been argued somewhere by Kissinger that one peculiar feature of deterrence is, paradoxically, that one never knows when and where it has succeeded; one only knows for sure when and where it has failed. The successful deterrence of past unwelcome futures goes unnoticed because they "didn't happen." One can, for example, never know *for sure* whether the posture of strategic deterrence, applied in Europe from the early 1950s to date, has deflected Soviet expansion; so that today some retrospective Pollyannas now argue (on looking at *what actually happened* after NATO was put together) that Soviet intentions at the time were inherently conservative, reactive, and defensive, concerned only with preserving Russian hegemony in East Europe, and that the western strategic buildup was therefore unnecessary and provocative. In point of fact, the retrospective interpretation has on its side the known subsequent historical performance of the Soviet Union—*i.e.*, it did *not* expand further in Europe (although the dangerous pressures on Berlin in 1947-48, 1958, and 1962-63 raised severe questions of such expansionist intentions).

However, this interpretation does not have anything else on its side. Since so little is known, and can be known, of Soviet intentions, its own behavior and capabilities constitute the only evidence on which retrospective and futurist guesses may be made. Deterrence, and quite credible deterrence, existed. Did it work? Nobody will ever know for sure; yet there are probably few strategic theorists who would, if they could, rerun the reel of history from 1950 onward *without* U.S. deterrence just "to see how it might have turned out." As Acheson said, the part of wisdom is to be prepared for "what may happen" rather than base our course on "what should happen. . . ."

Live and learn: one's fascination or obsession with one set of futurist possibilities (which one is determined to avoid) may blind one to other sets of possible futurist scenarios that could easily be by-products of successful avoidance. Short-range military solutions which seem at the time to be essentially desirable may set in motion wholly unwished for new tendencies.

VIII

How in fact ought the policy sciences and policy makers to benefit from futurist thinking? On one level, there is the compulsion or sometimes the necessity of taking actions in quite uncertain circumstances: events usually control the theater program, not the dramatist or the production manager, and certainly not a research institute. As Robert Osgood has written:

The fundamental question of American interests and power is never posed or answered directly or in the abstract. It is posed implicitly in terms of a number of specific immediate issues and decisions; it is answered ambiguously, if at all, by a set of responses that emerge from the **unpredictable** *[emphasis mine] interaction of external events and domestic politics, of general policies and particular decisions, of underlying premises and pragmatic judgments.*[9]

Even with a briefcase of surpriseful and surprise-free scenarios to provide heuristic insights, the policy maker must keep his eye upon the uncertain context within which action should occur. (Even Bismarck, it is said, preferred to deal with the future on a *three*-year predictive basis.) Probably for this reason, it is true that the one kind of heuristic futurist device that has proven to be of most value to policy makers is the political-military scenario game, which takes off from some reasonably plausible description of present conditions and works its way through labyrinthine passages of choices and responses. In the playing of such games, it is said by one who has played many of them that people "accustomed to the realities of government service are reported to be much more reasonable players."[10] These people know from experience that no perfect scenario exists and that no perfect organization exists to deal with it.

Why are these special forms of futurism so valuable? Probably for two reasons. Such games, with built-in assumptions about surprises and innovations, are judged to correspond plausibly with some existing perceived situation; they are not intrinsically fantastic. Secondly, they permit participants to observe and act in an ongoing situation that *itself* opens up the inherent possibilities of the future, including some possibilities that might otherwise have been overlooked or regarded as unthinkable. They disprove the idea of the future as unilinear. They are dramatically instructive of the ambiguous relationship between intentions and outcomes.

Several years ago, I participated in a seven-team game of international politics that (by any reasonable standards) was won by a team whose chief "decision-maker" (a professor of Russian history) proved incapable of figuring out how to construct his national budget. Paralyzed by fiscal incompetence, his team took no action in the complex interplay of states, went virtually unnoticed during the strange holocausts, and escaped—unscathed, unhated, and respected for its sagacity—from any of the carnage.

IX

What is one to say then when we know from history that people have frequently been far more surprised by what actually happens than by the devised practical standard scenarios that are so useful? In one sense, it could be *suggested* that we discount the fantastic in futurism not only because this or that piece of fantasy, being plucked out of the air, is no better than several thousand others, but also because, on balance, we really cannot afford to risk choosing among so many implausibles.

What also is one to say about surprise-free scenarios when we know from history that people often have been greatly surprised by what occurs (not having anticipated anything like it)? Why are "sensible standard versions of the future" esteemed more useful than scenarios *with* surprises? In one sense, we may find surpriseful scenarios annoying and fantastic ones a waste of time simply because if this or that element of fantasy is selected out and placed in the center of the chain of events, we know that it is arbitrary and no better than the infinite numbers of others that were *not* picked. (Thus, for instance, a scenario about a huge South African armageddon, extrapolated from contemporary guerilla warfare in Angola and Rhodesia, may make interesting reading but be of little more significance than any number of other scenarios—including South African scenarios that are far less dramatic.)

Our distrust of surprises arises from the fact that our easy acceptance of one to the exclusion of others fixates upon one (or even several) sets of unexpecteds and rules out others. Harrison Salisbury may be correct about the high probability of Sino-Soviet nuclear war, yet an infatuation with this prospect could blind one to other related prospects and could certainly deflect attention from many other priority-attention problems.

Yet even more importantly, have we not good reason to rely upon the non-fantastic simply because to do otherwise would entail too heavy a burden of costs? Some sort of "standard world" must be assumed in order to act rationally.

Notes

1. "The Case Against Tomorrow," *Political Quarterly*, 36 (April-June, 1965), pp. 214-27.

2. Alva Myrdal, *Nation and Family* (New York: Harper, 1944).

3. *See* his *De Interpretatione*, IX, where he asks whether if one were *now* to say "there will be a sea battle tomorrow," such a statement could be said to be true or false. Logically, of course, to deny both truth and falsity to such a statement would be to deny reality to the future.

4. The most fundamental change here being that of the vulnerability of the continental United States to strategic attack, which became possible after 1957 but had been anticipated.

5. Roosevelt and other American interventionists feared that the United States would revert to a former condition of political nonentanglement ("isolationism"), impairing the discretionary powers of the American government to regulate the international system in concert with others. The current American malaise seems more fundamental; discouragement with the psychic and material costs of maintaining its international commitments now combines with pervasive doubts about the American ability to solve its internal cultural problems as well. This combination is historically unique for the United States.

6. *I.e.*, a catastrophe great enough to wipe out nuclear technological know-how—which, of course, would be a massive disordering of international politics anyway.

7. A speech he made in 1939, quoted in Senate Foreign Relations Committee hearings on the nomination of Dean Acheson as Secretary of State, 81st Congress, 1st Session, p. 20.

8. I use the earthquake metaphor rather than, say, an all-out nuclear war, since it avoids the question of self-fulfilling or self-negating prophecy—whatever we think about it, there will, or will not, be an earthquake tomorrow, or a year from next Saturday, etc. (Unless, of course, we learn more about how to trigger or forestall earthquakes. Then one will have to move further afield, say, to more unmanageable natural occurrences.)

9. Robert Osgood (ed.), *America and the World* (Baltimore: Johns Hopkins Press, 1970), p. 1.

10. H. A. DeWeerd, "Political-Military Scenarios," *Rand Paper P-3565*, February, 1967.

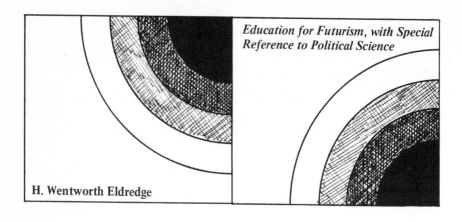

Education for Futurism, with Special
Reference to Political Science

H. Wentworth Eldredge

Political science is concerned with the *understanding* and the *operation* of political systems. Governments most assuredly attempt to enrich the life of the citizenry in the present and almost universally in the future. From Plato's *Republic* through St. Augustine's *City of God*, the Declaration of Independence and the Preamble of the Constitution, and on to Karl Marx's utopian "whithered away" state and Adolf Hitler's *Tausende Jahre Reich*, "good" and "evil" philosophers and practitioners of governance have had their eyes on the future. Presumably, a lively concern for this future separates the statesman from the politico. It thus behooves the social scientist devoted to government in both its internal and external functions to join wholeheartedly the emergent loose consortium of disciplines involved in futures research. Of the handful of political scientists at work in this direction, there are a small number identifiable as "teaching" futurism. Predictably, they represent a variety of points of view—ranging from a concern with methodology/theory to the contemporary preoccupation with *participatory democracy* (in the classroom as well) coupled with *experiential learning techniques*.

In a general survey of graduate and undergraduate futurism courses in the United States (actually North America, as Canada was included) made during 1969-70, some half dozen individuals were unearthed who did some instructing in the general area of political science futures. This number is patently too small and the data too incomplete (the sample undoubtedly missed significant operators) to form any particularly valid—much less quantifiable/qualitative—inductions for political science. But the overall experience in teaching futurism to date, from which certain tentative generalities can be drawn, may be instructive for the political scientist.

What actually is the extent of futurism teaching, which has developed here only in the past decade? Other than the unlikely beginnings in the *Recent Social Trends* study inaugurated by the conservative Republican President Herbert Hoover in 1929,[1] and, perhaps more importantly, by the brilliant pioneering works of the University of Chicago sociologist William F. Ogburn (who served in the 1930s as the research director for the *Recent Social Trends'* Presidential Committee on Technological Trends and Forecasting),[2] futurism courses in the

United States *per se* started in the 1960s. Pioneering work was done by Richard Meier[3] at Ann Arbor and Berkeley, and by Daniel Bell, teaching sociology at Columbia University. During the years 1966-67, futurism courses began to pop up all over the country; and the first attempt to summarize their extent appeared in *The Futurist* of April, 1969. This preliminary roundup, incidentally, served as the springboard for the collection of data for this survey and has been updated recently in the June, 1970, issue.

It should be stressed that currently there are at least two contributory streams of intellectual innovation (and resultant course work) that are feeding into the future study area. The first stream is *technological forecasting*[4] (foreshadowed by Ogburn and others in the thirties), which appeared to evolve initially within large corporations and military research establishments in the United States. It is probable that a like development has been occurring in Western Europe, and quite possibly in both Japan and the USSR. By 1961, exercises in tech forecasting were used in regular courses both by James R. Bright at Harvard Business School and by J. Brian Quinn at Dartmouth's Tuck School of Business Administration. The second contributory stream is the well-known tradition of *economic forecasting* with its hoary history of projecting business cycles and, more recent, productivity and economic growth (or GNP).

Clearly a tripartite symbiotic relationship should be established among these "three schools" of future watching. Actually, researchers, university faculty, and the latter's charges "are all students together" with the implicit or explicit intention of designing the future as long-range planners at the third level of science (level 1, understand; level 2, predict; and level 3, control). Such a relationship leading to a wholistic grasp of the future should be mutually rewarding in knowledge, intellectual technology, and operational skills. While all the evidence is not in, it appears likely that research institutes, government, and private corporate enterprises have produced more innovative thought and action—especially in tech forecasting—than has purely academic endeavor.

There is no doubt that the popular media have widely publicized futurism on both TV and in the "slick" magazine press as the latest fad. The notion of the *unprepared society*[5] has been hammered home by (a) the perceived urban and environmental mess and (b) the black revolt, both of which were more or less foreseen by the *Recent Social Trends* group almost forty years ago. Resources for the Future has played a basic educational role in the field as has the Center for the Study of Democratic Institutions. The three-year program on *Environment and Man* by the American Institute of Planners, at a cost of over $1 million should have alerted that profession. The appearance of new professional journals in the recent past—*The Futurist* (1967), the *World Future Society Bulletin* (1968), and *Technological Forecasting* (1969), as well as the action-oriented *Policy Sciences* (1970) in the United States, and *Futures* in the United Kingdom—signals this mood at a more sophisticated level.

Other intellectuals are slowly grasping the probability of a sea-change in the arrival all to soon of a post-industrial society (Bell) or a post-civilized society (Boulding)—with interesting and possibly dismal overtones in the meaning of the latter appellation. The possibility of basic discontinuities in human societal change is becoming more appreciated yearly. Further, the United States is acutely aware, in the face of the grinding Indochina war, coupled with harsh domestic inflation, that even the richest nation in the world cannot enjoy both *Kanonen und Butter*, but must assign priorities for scarce assets on a national scale in long-term capital budgeting schemes. It is difficult to be smug in the United States of 1970. Mention should be made further of the strident voices— young, black, poor—demanding participatory democracy for egalitarian goals and violently stoking the fires of societal change. Similar situations are not unknown in other nations. The American intellectual world and government is moving into the futures act; the atomic physicists, engineers, and life scientists are telling us how to run society and the social scientists how to manage technology. President Nixon announced the formation of the National Goals Research Staff on July 13, 1969, with five precise tasks:

1. Forecasting future developments and assessing the longer range consequences of present social trends.

2. Measuring the probable future impact of alternative courses of action, including measuring the degree to which change in one area would be likely to affect another.

3. Estimating the actual range of social choice—that is, what alternative sets of goals might be attainable in light of the availability of resources and possible rates of progress.

4. Developing and monitoring social (societal) indicators that can reflect the present and future quality of American life, and the direction and rate of its change.

5. Summarizing, integrating, and correlating the results of related research activities being carried on within the various federal agencies, and by state and local governments and private organizations.[6]

No one can fail to recognize that, if the more conservative of the two American parties advocates such an operation directly under the President, the United States is en route—if with all deliberate speed—toward national long-range planning, or futurism. As the Arabs say, "The camel's nose is under the tent." All of which does not suggest by any means a revolutionary attitude in the United States toward the conduct of human affairs; Marx and Engels at least verbalized futurism in the nineteenth century, the USSR did in the 1920s, and France and Sweden quite consciously began to allocate resources on a national scale with several decades of lead time in the 1960s. West Germany and Japan appear to be moving in that direction too. The so-called Jackson Committee Report on the use of systems planning in economic development for the UN lifts long-range planning to the international level.[7] From anarchic radicals, intent on busting up society's web, to staunch conservatives, eager to preserve it; from biotechnicians and nuclear physicists to social scientists, literary humanists, and philosophers; from design utopianists to religious sages; everyone is out to "invent the future." It is little wonder that alert individuals in the huge academic teaching community of the United States also joined up during the past decade.

This survey is an attempt to assess "lessons learned" to date in futurism education. Starting with *The Futurist*'s list of higher education courses of April, 1969, as a base, and the good offices of Edward Cornish of The World Future Society (Washington, D.C.) and Theodore Gordon of the Institute for the Future (Middletown, Connecticut), individually typed letters were mailed, commencing in July 1969, to all identified course-givers with a request for relevant written material, as well as some general evaluation of results. In most cases, respondents were further asked to identify other individuals making up the growing network of futurists. In November, 1969, a further input of tech forecasting names was added; up until now (July, 1970), economic forecasters have fallen into the survey only by pure chance. Further plans are to mine this latter group for information comparable to that set down below. Predictably, the academicians failed to respond to their mail adequately or at all, necessitating follow-up form letters and, more importantly, personal letters attempting to elicit more complete, more sensitive, and more precise data on their futurism teaching experience. Ideally, it now appears certain that a careful, personal, face-to-face interview based on the preliminary results of this survey with at least fifty identifiable persons could be extremely rewarding; patently, it would be costly and time-consuming.

As of July 1970, approximately ninety institutions of higher learning were located[8] offering futurism or tech forecasting courses—actually, seven of these were in Canadian universities. Several institutions had two or more courses in futurism—loosely defined. Of these ninety-plus identified courses, some forty-seven instructors replied in a useful fashion; of the remainder, perhaps fifteen are questionable. Thus a global guess-estimate of the extent of the art in North America at this point would be perhaps that at least one hundred academics are involved (group or team teaching in seminars or courses was quite usual—usually of an interdisciplinary nature). It is not clear how high this total would jump if economic forecasters (creeping toward a wholistic position) were to be identified and added; as a wild guess, it might be increased by 50 percent; this area needs further investigation. Since there are approximately twenty-five hundred "institutions of higher education"[9] in the United States and Canada, it does not appear that interest in futurism has overwhelmed the academic community and scene. But it is on the march; a surprising number of "dud" answers indicated the intention of offering a futurism course as soon as practicable—Bowdoin College, for example, is exploring an entire futures-oriented program.

The disciplines involved should surprise no one. Social scientists (Appendix C) are clearly in the lead, with sociologists (futurism has already crept into the official journals[10]), as traditionally interested in both meliorative behavior and social change theory, predominating. Political scientists followed closely. Economists (quite possibly due to poor coverage of "economic forecasting") were conspicuously absent. Business administration types (tech forecasting) appear very strongly as the potentially most numerous acolytes of the faith. It seemed odd that more urban planning courses—specializing in the long-term allocation of resources—could not be discovered.[11] Symptomatic of both popular and professional interest, futurist books of extremely varying merit are flooding the publishing market; no one should have much difficulty in identifying worthwhile teaching materials.[12]

What has been learned from this survey of course material and results to date? A tentative progress report is given below under four headings: intellectual roots, predictive techniques, teaching methods, and a synthesizing "lessons learned" as summary.

Intellectual Roots

Shallow, Generally Speaking

Our futurist and tech forecasting course-givers showed very little awareness in general of mankind's age-old Promethean strivings. It has been observed that modern futurism is merely rationalized utopian thought; if this be true, there was little evidence that futurism courses were even slightly aware of Christian (or Muslim) heaven (or the "reverse futuristics" Garden of Eden); nirvana in Buddhism; reincarnation in Hinduism; or even Karl Marx's dream world.[13] Utopian thinkers from Plato in *The Republic* to B. F. Skinner[14] were pretty generally ignored, as were the great modern distopias, *Brave New World*[15] and *1984*,[16] which extrapolate modern totalitaria into the future. The Goodmans' *Communitas*, an early alternative possible planning futures allegory,[17] was neglected too. The "design utopias" of Le Corbusier and Frank Lloyd Wright were unmentioned, as well as the entire tradition of Utopian socialism with its real communities scattered about the world, but especially in the new Eldorado of the Americas. Jeremy Bentham, the great utilitarian, opined that utopian thought was mind-stretching,[18] but that conclusion seemed not to be too widely understood.

Unquestionably, present future courses are too short to spread themselves intellectually into beginnings—especially in an a-historical age—but it might be very rewarding for students to realize that imaginative projection and planning into the "future" have been tried in various ways before, although it might have been aimed backward into the past or out to some odd place on the earth's surface (now space), with the goals of warning man, beating the present, or promoting certain values believed to be goods. It has all been done before, *but not* in the coldly rational, highly skilled fashion of the intellectual technology of our present mood. Perhaps, as a pragmatic society, we are more concerned with how to get there than with any theoretical ideal state, which may account for the rapid acceptance of tech forecasting.

Science fiction (perhaps a reflection of the times and of a gadget-minded society) is better treated, but only spasmodically and with a touch of condescension. However, see the imaginative work of political scientist Dennis Livingston;[19] it is waved at *en passant* by the tech forecasters. Leonardo da Vinci is not generally recognized as a "futurist," but Jules Verne, H. G. Wells, Buckminister Fuller, Arthur Clarke, and Asimov are paid slight obeisance and their on-target shots recorded.

The saints of futurism have been duly canonized; and Bertrand de Jouvenel, Robert Jungk, Daniel Bell, Buckminister Fuller, Olaf Helmer, John McHale, Theodore Gordon, Herman Kahn, and company are in the course bibliographies, as is the *Year 2000* study of the American Academy of Arts and Sciences (Bell ran this, of course). The latter group is generally regarded as Eastern Establishment in essence; it was amusing to watch California struggling to erect a similar West Coast futurist effort in 1967—after all, the Rand Corporation, in Santa Monica, California, did start things going with its weapons technology projections in the early days as an Air Force spin-off.

Social Change Theory

There was almost a complete lack of any implicit, much less explicit, social change theory (with the exception of the few involved sociologists); without such theory, there can be no wholistic prediction much less future planning. It should be evident that partial or micro-system extrapolation will almost inevitably fall on its face due to external variables *not* accounted for in such an undertaking (*i.e.*, tech forecasting without political, social, economic, or ecological factors being considered, or economic forecasting and physical planning for like reasons).

Under the present division of labor among social scientists, social change theory (better societal or socio-cultural change theory) falls to the somewhat grudging lot of the sociologists. Sociological beginnings go back both to naive Comtean, *Kulturgeschicte*, and social-Darwinian ideas of the nineteenth century and to the sweeping unilinear evolutionary thinking of the early classical anthropologists. American sociology, contaminated at its inception also with a simplistic theological-reformist zeal, backed away from both change theory and "doing good" in the 1930s and became bogged down (some say) in the function-structure analysis popularized by Talcott Parsons.[20] This social statics "moved" badly. Creating their identity as hard-data scientists, the American sociological profession (moved, too, by Emil Durkheim's statistical approach) developed a very precise and complex, quantitative questionnaire orientation—now computer-backed.

Curiously, once again the young sociologists are denying ethical neutralism (as are young political scientists) and demanding that the profession resume a strong meliorative (even revolutionary) role; futurism is obviously a stance with which to do this. In addition, an increasing number of senior sociologists are trying to get theory moving again with more adequate notions about social change. Kingsley Davis suggests that the function-structure is an interlocked moving equilibrium with change possible by new inputs at a variety of points.[21] Wilbert E. Moore, who has pioneered in societal indicators[22] so important to futurism, through studies financed by the Russell Sage Foundation, has recently published *Social Change*[23] and *Order and Change*,[24] symptomatic perhaps of a new orientation toward social change—basic to reasonable prediction and future planning.

There are a number of persons, the author included, who are searching for quasi-independent variables as central to socio-cultural change. Tech forecasting is symbolic of this, although it would appear that the truly basic golden thread in the evolution of human society and its culture is reliable knowledge (*i.e.*, science) from which technologies spring: (a) "gadget" or technical technology; (b) biotechnology; (c) behavioral technology; (d) organizational technology; and (e) the burgeoning intellectual technology (decision-making games theory, linear programming, mathematical models, systems analysis, etc., generally in symbiotic relationship with a computer).

Serious attention should be paid also to the anthropologists, who, too, have broken with the narrow American historical school and are now attempting to carry out the serious development of cross-cultural change theory.[25] The cultural anthropologists—and others—have never quite forgotten that it is a *whole society* that changes. They have, of course, been spurred by the incredible problems engendered by underdeveloped societies rushing pell-mell into the modern world—completely underprepared for such steps.[26]

William F. Ogburn[27] and *Recent Social Trends* (1933) have been rediscovered, as has the defunct National Resources Planning Board (slaughtered in the return to "normalcy" following World War II), by the increasing interest among professionals in social change and especially in its manipulation.[28] The brilliant work of the economic historian Robert L. Heilbroner in popularizing the notions of *The Future As History*—actually broad trend projection—should not be slighted for its influence in intellectual circles as well.[29] It would be manifestly unfair to leave out the key role of the demographers (marginal sociologists?) who, having badly underestimated gross population projection in the 1920s and 1930s, are the leading prophets of future troubles in surprise-free projections of population growth with such titles as: *The Population Dilemma; The Politics of Population; Population: The Vital Revolution; The Population Explosion*; etc.—all recently published. No demographer dare be other than wholistic in the 1970s.

This wholistic approach to societal change has been recently proposed in Herman Kahn and Anthony J. Wiener's "Basic Long Term Multifold Trend,"[30] which clearly grasps the interconnectedness of many-faceted societal change in the bold brush work of a series of thirteen interlocked, "surprise-free" projections of present trends—excluding (a) sharp discontinuities, such as thermonuclear war, of which both authors are quite aware,[31] and (b) heavy increments of planned change.

Beyond mere prediction of the multifold trend is the prediction of value trends, which along with pure science may be a key variable in societal change in the future. About this very little is presently known for certain. Is it just to be "more of the same"—straight-line extrapolation of present goal values—or may deep changes be expected? Nicholas Rescher, fittingly a philosopher with a specialty in the philosophy of science, has lately been concerned with this matter (as has Anthony J. Wiener of the Hudson Institute) and has gathered together projected value changes resulting from "the impact of current technological advances on American values" and vice versa. That values could change in and of themselves to influence technological change (and all change) is clear.[32]

Obviously, there is much sharpening needed in this standard multifold trend projection—recognized, of course, by Kahn and Wiener—such as possible value shifts, quantification, and a monitoring system under societal indicators. It is possible that the identification of the key variable (or variables) which tend to initiate change—such as reliable knowledge and/or values—could make this multi-fold trend analysis more manageable. The survey of courses so far has *not* revealed much understanding of, or attention to, social change theory, which appears to be a striking deficiency in the overall pattern of futurism education.

Predictive Techniques

Techniques Employed

The survey, without a meaningful quantification of results yet possible, indicates that all the well-known predictive techniques are in use in varying degrees in the courses reporting. A given course will emphasize one or more techniques for a variety of didactic reasons. Brief mention will be made of each technique with an impressionistic judgment of how and why each finds its way into course programs. It should be understood that the time limitation of a semester, or even worse an academic quarter, constricted the options open to each instructor to deal (a) with one predictive technique in reasonable depth or (b) with several superficially. A grouping of techniques under five major rubrics is employed here.[33]

1. *Intuitive methods and codified intuition of Delphi.* The physical designers in their old artistic tradition—especially the architects and planners—often enjoyed intuitive intellectual sprees (see *L'habitation, Brasilia,* and *Chandigarh*) and gave students very free creative reign. This approach appeared to develop great personal investment in the course. Social scientists and the business school group, on the other hand, used the Helmer/Rand-developed Delphi (time-consuming) method possibly for two reasons: (a) it might actually have considerable validity, and (b) it most certainly is a useful device for ego-involving students and developing a perfervid interaction—much admired by modern educators. All this at the cost of considerable man hours!

Whether students could be classified as "experts" under Delphi terms or not is an open question, but most certainly the current vogue of participatory planning entered into the classroom/workshop/studio picture, although participation seemingly is educational in and of itself. Take, for example, the work of two young political scientists: (1) James A. Dator (University of Hawaii), with the Governor's Commission on Hawaii 2000 in popular participation in future planning, and (2) Stuart Umpleby (University of Illinois), building psychologist Charles E. Osgood's work with Delphi techniques in a learning computer-based operation (PLATO), using citizens' and experts' participatory search for possible and desired futures.[34]

2. *Trend extrapolation.* Trend projection came into the majority of the syllabi with warnings that most curves seem to reach toward infinity. Thus S curves, substitution theory, step functions, and umbrella curves were stressed with determination always apparently at war with free will. Actually, there was an

amusing use of "shocker techniques" to get at the students, to alert them to possibilities of "good and evil." The most important projection of value change, one key to long-range planning, was approached gingerly with the respect it deserves. In a rapidly changing society, the extrapolation of trends—prior to their bending through planning—is clearly an overriding desideration. Here, too, is opportunity for quantification in a variety of indicators and no area for naive simplistic straight-line projection.

3. *Development of ideal state and/or alternate possible futures.* This is the planning technique for a micro- or macro-utopian situation with a follow-up "scenario" on "how to get there" by a valid planning, programming, budgeting system, operational research techniques, and the "policy sciences."[35] In present thinking about "planning as a process," utopian states turn out to be discardable plateaus in an ever-changing morphology of the wholistic future. Such scenario building may have a very valuable early warning effect in pointing a finger toward the lack of knowledge/technologies necessary to reach a desired state. Few, if any, courses appeared that sophisticated about either utopias or scenarios; nor did any appear specifically to note "prophecy" as a self-fulfilling device!

4. *Dynamic models.* Many of the courses leaned toward mathematical model building on computers where inputs could be introduced "to predict" results within certain parameters. John Taylor, an urban planner, has just published in England a study detailing some 125 city games and dynamic models which have been developed throughout the world to date. Some of these are "total" urban systems; some are "partial" systems, such as transport or transport/land use, or simply housing, etc.[36] As a reasonably valid induction, it would appear that practically all courses surveyed (with the exception of the "intuitive/artistic/ creative" few) were at least strongly hopeful that such a predictive technique could be included in a valid fashion—if it was not already a part of the course work. This is not to say that the various limitations of such dynamic models went unnoticed in application.

5. *Monitoring change.* There was some interest in an intellectual reconnaissance into emergent knowledge, technologies, and values, and into fresh social, political, and economic forms. The conception of pulse-taking is a barely organized activity, largely intuitive as yet, but perhaps capable of rationalization with growing sophistication in the societal indicator techniques briefly explored below.

Room for further expansion, reclassification, and refinement of the five techniques noted is readily visible and possible; one can expect both the operationally/oriented, applied government and corporate research people, as well as the university intellectuals, to provide further valuable grist for the academic mill— but how to get it all into one short "course" with firm temporal limits?

Planned Change

Explicitly in most courses, implicitly in others, the instructors involved were, in typical Western—not to mention American—style, out "to improve" the world in a planful way. No one, it seemed, was prepared to take the future lying down in a fatalistic fashion. Given modern students, it is moreover quite impossible to conceive of a "successful" teaching operation as merely a highly intellectualized statement of what is, what has been, and what might be. The "now" generation wants part of the action, and the academies understand what their clients desire/ demand. In short, *all courses* were in one fashion or another, in some degree or other, operationally oriented. How practical they were in sophisticated multi-thrust methods of total societal change in all its sensed present intricacies was *not* evident from the data at hand. It is probable that wholistic societal guidance techniques were hardly touched on—assuming they were available and, if available, understood.

Societal Indicators

Since futurists are "reformers," or better rationalist utopians, they are sorely in need of a reliable weighing system to evaluate, beyond monetary units, alternate possible future states and to monitor progress, or lack of progress, toward that state. Existing plans must be open to continuous modification in the planning process of reaching the lengthening series of desired states.[37] Benefit-cost analysis by econometrists has become an increasingly precise device, assuming a continuing societal pattern (actually impossible). "Hard-nosed" dollar evaluation on a relatively limited scale gives the illusion of precision.

For example, urban planners have a relatively easy decision to make on alternate possibilities for the location of a super-highway if simple monetary costs of alternate routes are weighed. The immediate dollar costs of land and construction are readily available; what is not evident is the costs/benefits of aesthetics, human community, housing, political processes, recreation, air pollution, crime, surface and ground water, noise levels, local business, national business, suburban development, etc. It may be possible eventually to place tags on various of these results in an orderly quantified fashion, but this appears for the moment very unlikely.

Thus we have the search for social (better societal)[38] indicators transeconomic in character. It has been noted that dollar benefit-cost analysis tends to skew governmental decisions toward a narrow definition of what is "good" and "bad"—"good" turns out to be "cheap" and "bad" "expensive." This is a rather dreadful way to run a society even if planning, programming, budgeting systems are of enormous merit for futurism and *not* to be brushed aside.

Present societal statistics are already gathered in a variety of governmental agencies (in most countries for a variety of reasons), but they were never designed to give aid to the executive branch in plotting benefit/costs for possible future plans, nor were they ever designed to make possible quick monitoring of ongoing plans. There is in the United States no complete social, political, economic, environmental barometer/compass of where we are and where we are going. It should be stated frankly that most nations—both developed and undeveloped—are obviously in the same boat; this includes those who fancy themselves as sophisticated future planners based on revered, if hypersimplistic, socialist theory/theology, long disproved.

The plans for the American National Goals Commission aim optimistically at making a sound start in building a set of societal indicators based on comprehensive societal statistics. It appears likely that sooner or later, decision makers will have "apples" to weigh against "lemons" against "public health" against "dollars" against "symphonies" in deciding on feasible priorities and in weighing the allocation of scarce resources for societal movement. A *common measuring unit* for all these variables seems far ahead. The courses surveyed generally showed little or no realization of the basic need for societal indicators in all futurism study as a required compass and barometer. The recent writings of Bertram Gross,[39] Wilbert Moore,[40] and Raymond A. Bauer[41] should play a major part in any sophisticated futurism course; as yet they do not.

A valid general conclusion to draw from all the courses on which data was available is that the epistemological underpinning is relatively slight. The corpus of knowledge of such a sophisticated depth *may not yet* be available for futurism. A pressing task in the field is to build theoretical foundations as well and as quickly as possible.

Teaching Methods

From "Participation" to Traditional Teaching

Teachers involved with futurism seem to be lively personalities—experimental, innovative individuals who certainly must be up-to-the-moment ("with it") in intellectual interests and, presumably, life-styles, since they are beyond the present and already future-oriented. That their teaching techniques are geared to their contemporary student clients ("groovy") who lack much contact with the traditional intellectual tradition (no "hang ups") should be hardly surprising.

Actually, two polar types of instructional styles appear to be visible, roughly correlated with age (indicated by academic rank) and undoubtedly correlated with the instructor's professional discipline. On one hand were the young radical social scientists and young "profs" in the humanities (broadly interpreted) who, in a number of cases, were out to "bust" the status quo. On the other were the more staid, senior faculty (establishment types) who engaged in the sturdy rational tradition of trying to build in an evolutionary fashion on the good of the present. To the latter group might be added the business school faculty people, engineers, and physical scientists, who tended to be allied with private corporations and government.

The best of the young futurist teachers identified with their student charges (as do most young American faculty anyway) and tried to be "relevant" in what they dealt with. They were great believers in experiential learning; the "now" generation seems to care little for what anyone else does, much less what they think. They, the students, wish "to learn by doing" and "make the future." Such phrases as "no one is an expert"; "no corpus of knowledge to impart"; "we are all learning together, faculty and students"; and "the course is always chang-ing" are symptomatic. "Do the future, not study with it," snapped one respon-dent when presented with a more traditionally oriented syllabus. To illustrate further this mood of classroom "participatory democracy": "the teacher is a resource person"; "break down student-teacher barriers"; "bull sessions"; "inter-disciplinary problem oriented"; "students do things"; and "all people should participate in designing the future."

At the other pole, but not mutually exclusive to the participatory characteris-tics listed above, are the few courses which explore the intellectual roots of futurism and adhere to established patterns of intellectual build up prior to "experiential learning." To this group should be added the hard-data, computer models people, whose rhetoric is tempered by precise quantitative scholarship—*i.e.*, "prepare defendable models!," etc.

These were dynamic learning operations: "team teaching"; "small group pro-cess"; "film discussions"; "open telephone line debates"; the World Game of Buckminister Fuller; "series of short- and long-run political scenarios of the future political system of the United States"; "the building of an Asiatic water city;" and "the rise of the library at the expense of the classroom." One innova-tive young faculty member gave a concise history of an unnamed Latin Ameri-can nation (actually Brazil) from its settlement to 1914, and asked his class to project it to the present; he reported that one bright youngster projected its "future" with remarkable precision, even plotting a Vargas-like figure.

It is not surprising that at least two "Free University Courses" were identified as "initiated by students and run by students for students," and that an "under-ground course" contrary to the wishes of a conservative institution's hierarchy also appeared. All this gave students "a feeling of exhilaration; they felt nothing was beyond their scope"; both student and teacher experienced through "gut-learning" "future shock."

Again, to polarize at the opposite quantitative and/or establishment end, "this was a methodology course"; "urban systems design"; "hard-data cybernetician and man;" "computer technology." A young woman instructor opined sourly that her colleagues on the faculty were "not interested in the future, they merely wished to bitch about it."

Subjects "studied"

A random catalogue of topics touched on in their kaleidoscopic variety is per-haps all that is needed to suggest the *embarrassment de richesse* and often random exploratory quality of the course contents:

the future of great cities	world development
the universe	ecological changes
biochemical futures	space programs
the urban scene	public policy for research and
war	development

peace	privacy
organized society	military technology
family	ocean programs
community	pollution and degradation of the
planet	environment
the future of information systems	Delphi methodology
energy	the future of the international system
scientific management	aesthetic education in the year 2000
communication	systems and decision theory

In this inchoate and exciting mish-mash, untrammeled minds soared freely; what could be produced—distilled—from all this is somewhat unclear. Certainly the field is in as much ferment as the future!

Creativity

Worthy of passing attention, at least, is the implication that futurism develops innovational minds. "The students were free to be creative for once," which may be a critique of our higher educational system. Certainly "thinking about the unthinkable" is an awesome operation and the invention of "alternate futures" a most exciting game; if possible is added, and the name of the game becomes "alternate *possible* futures," then hard measurement comes into decision-making about both societal and environmental inventions. Social scientists have seldom been trained as "societal inventors"; their forte[42] is analysis. It is quite difficult in fact to select the best "alternate possible future" if some searching and inventive mind has not produced a lively valid assortment. It was argued conversely by a respondent, who was a consultant to big business, that a thorough pedestrian exploration of all possibilities was more productive than creativity. Perhaps the well-worn Hegelian solution of inventive *possible futures* in an exhaustive array of *all* futures may be the answer.

Several of the respondents argued that there were evident personality changes in students who took their futurism course—changes which apparently spilled over into their stance in other courses and toward their peers. One instructor (a psychologist) has specifically tested his students for "creativity" both before and after exposure to futurism; unfortunately, to date the results are not yet at hand. Whether, as some of these courses seem to indicate, "group think" is conducive to the "lonely process" of creation is by no means clear; but such very innovative teaching on horizon-stretching subject matter should have behavioral spin-offs. Sooner or later a better grasp of what does happen to the intellectual set of students of futurism—on both sides of the lectern—ought to be explored thoroughly.[43]

Lessons Learned

There is enough evidence now at hand from this preliminary survey to make an evaluation of the education in futurism going on in American institutions of higher learning. Various disciplines are involved, including political science. Many promising experiments along these lines clearly have not been reported in and the data from others is patently incomplete and possibly too sanguine. It is hoped that this survey can continue to collect more data, and more valuable and incisive data, on futures courses all over the world for the benefit of futures teachers and the institutions and societies they now serve. The dual role of teacher-scholar is a key innovative source—joining with research institutes, government agencies, and corporate business enterprises—to further the stage of the art.

As a final synthesis of the admittedly tentative and imprecise findings, here are seventeen summary propositions.

The teaching of futurism:

1. Is part of the *general contemporary ferment in education* and incorporates such innovational aspects as new courses, revised traditional courses, interdisciplinary problem-oriented staffs, computer gaming and mathematical models, creativity development, systems analysis, long-range projections, wholistic or total environmental planning with macro-time scales, etc.

2. Serves as *intellectual horizon stretching* for both faculty and students; it is an exercise in "thinking about the unthinkable" as well as the very limits of the thinkable.

3. *Shakes up students' minds* as they are "awed by the enormity and complexity of the future." Called "future shock," this is a useful form of "gut-learning" for the generation whose arrogance has been said to exceed their ignorance. Speculation, powered by a growing intellectual technology, should be a potent weapon for the development of human civilization.

4. Underlines once more that modern (American?) *students appear to learn faster with more enthusiasm if they participate very actively in producing knowledge rather than reading about the process.* They prefer to "do futures" not study what others have done. Participatory learning requires energetic, devoted, flexible teachers; it is very time-consuming.

5. *Is generally based on shallow roots in intellectual history.* Seemingly unaware of religious heavens, utopian thought (and communities), the "design utopias" of Le Corbusier, Frank Lloyd Wright, and Kenzo Tange, futurism courses make only an occasional brief bow to modern science fiction (excluding the imaginative work of political scientist Dennis Livingston) and pay little attention to Leonardo da Vinci, Jules Verne, or, for that matter, H. G. Wells.

6. *Varies in worth* from the presentation of a certain modicum of drivel, plus whimsy, to extremely advanced symbiotic relationships between man and computer.

7. Indicates that *instructors in this field tend to be lively intellects*—experimental, resourceful, iconoclastic, and sometimes difficult. They range all the

way from marginal men ("kooks," "oddballs") to engineers and sturdy defenders (and would-be improvers) of the governmental/business corporate establishment who employ very sophisticated new intellectual techniques. Most futurism teachers appear to be highly innovational, and are stretching the horizons and parameters of their disciplines.

8. Makes it reasonably clear that, while there are a few deep pessimists in the field and some radical firebrands with anarchist leanings, *the general practitioners are optimistic* purveyors of an intellectual technology used primarily to think one's way into the future. This is counter to the current generally despondent American mood. "To design the future, one first has to believe in it."

9. *Requires more than one short term or semester course.* There is seemingly a futures dimension to almost all learning, and futurism conceivably should enter into the entire curriculum or perhaps serve as a minor within many major concentration areas leading to a degree.

10. Has created *a dedicated group of devotees* who, as intellectual missionaries, infectors, or gadflies, are establishing a network of contacts throughout the North American higher education scene.

11. By making many persons aware of probable/possible futures, may serve as a widespread *early warning system* alerting society.

12. *Shows little grasp of socio-cultural change theory* and further indicates the inadequacy of the theory presently available. Basic to all multifold projection is the development of a truly precise grasp of interdependent variables with some grasp of "more independent" factors, such as reliable knowledge (science) as the truly crescive factor in change. Values may well turn out to be a semi-independent variable.

13. Shows *creativity in producing alternate possible futures is a tender plant needing wise care.* While it can be argued that a methodical plotting and weighing of alternates is more realistic, truly innovational alternatives come from creative minds.

14. Requires before it proceeds much further a fairly rich and precise *system of societal indicators* (both qualitative and quantitative) for transeconomic cost/benefit analysis and monitoring of planning efforts.

15. Makes startlingly evident that the *projection of values* is a key element needed in any sensitive and sophisticated weighing of alternate possible futures.

16. Is *joining with technological forecasting (and perhaps economic forecasting) in a fruitful convergence.* Futurism can contribute with its wholistic point of view to forecasting and can gain some precise techniques for forecasting—especially if *technology* is recognized as divisible into its technical (gadget), biological, behavioral, organizational, and intellectual forms!

17. *Illuminates a growing clash between proponents of futurism/long-range*

planning with proponents of the incremental, segmental planning beloved of the pragmatic "practical man." The American conventional wisdom continually returns to this simplistic, traditional position despite the recent disasters of painting ourselves into corners, externally in Indochina and internally in urban renewal ("Negro removal"). Both of these performances rather obviously lacked any wholistic, clearly articulated, long-range goals, policy, and programming. A Hegelian synthesizing effort seems in order to unite these two approaches in a productive fashion, recognizing the merits of each ("strategy" and "tactics").

Finally, one firm—if not quantitative—prediction can be made that formal education in futurism and long-range planning, based on a growing reliable corpus of knowledge, will continue to expand in American colleges and universities. It will show itself in a "futures" point of view in many disciplines—in new courses and programs specifically oriented toward such a direction, and in altered subject matter within traditional courses in a variety of academic subjects. Whether intellectual futures research in government can be left to political scientists, and whether behavioral political science can join with systems anlysis and systems design along with the specifically behaviorally oriented social sciences to form a truly valid and operationally successful *policy science*, remains to be seen. It would appear that a challenge has been thrown down to political scientists by futures research to understand, predict, and control—be they philosophers, public administration adherents, behaviorally-oriented, computer modelists, or "with it" activists knee deep in the "real world creation of the future." If they can't, or won't, most certainly someone else will.

As noted above, the academicians—aided by research institutes, private corporations, and government laboratories/research teams—will play their dual role of developing new reliable information and transmitting it to the young in such areas as socio-cultural change theory, predictive techniques, value projection, and societal indicators. Their efforts will help to educate a rapidly growing network of people throughout the world who peer ever further and ever more clearly into the future. It is hoped that this ongoing survey and critical analysis will serve as a modest device for the continuing interchange of ideas among these teacher-researchers.

Notes

1. *Recent Social Trends*, one-volume edition (New York: McGraw-Hill, 1933).

2. William F. Ogburn, *Social Change* (New York: B. W. Huebsch, 1922). *See also* the publications of his student, S. C. Gilfillan, during the same period. Especially noteworthy was *Technological Trends and National Policy*, Report of the Subcommittee on Technology, headed by Ogburn, to the National Resources Committee, 1927.

3. Meier, a modern Leonardo, has produced an extraordinary series of publications (close to one hundred articles) meaningfully dealing with such matters as "The Polymerization of Olefines and Friedel-Crafts Catalysts," "Beyond Atomic Stalemate," and "Studies on the Future of Cities in Asia." He gave a seminar on new scientific development possibilities at the University of Chicago in 1949 which might better be subsumed under technological forecasting; *see* below.

4. Two useful publications on "tech forecasting" are: Robert V. Ayres, *Technological*

Forecasting and Long-Range Planning (New York: McGraw-Hill, 1969); James R. Bright (ed.), *Technological Forecasting for Industry and Government* (Englewood Cliffs: Prentice-Hall, 1968). For the international scene, *see* Erich Jantsch, *Technological Forecasting in Perspective* (Paris: OECD, April, 1967).

5. D. Michael, *The Unprepared Society: Planning for Precarious Futures* (New York: Basic Books, 1968).

6. The key designing consultant for this project was Anthony J. Wiener of the Hudson Institute, co-author with Herman Kahn of *The Year 2000* (New York: Macmillan, 1967).

7. Sir Robert G. Jackson, *A Study of the Capacity of the United Nations Development System*, UN, 1969. Alastair Buchon, who now heads the British Staff College, has used the "alternate possible futures" approach as editor. *Europe's Futures, Europe's Choices* (New York: Columbia University Press, 1969).

8. See Appendices A and B.

9. One wag crassly suggested that "at least 500 of these should be knocked on the head."

10. See Appendix C. Henry Winthrop, "The Sociologist and the Study of the Future," *The American Sociologist* (May, 1968), and Frank Hopkins, "The United States in the Year 2000; A Proposal for the Study of the American Future," *The American Sociologist* (August, 1967).

11. This author was initiated to *The Futurism of Urbanism and Cities* through City Planning 227, which he offered at the College of Environmental Design at the University of California (Berkeley) as a visiting professor of city planning.

12. Both the World Futurist Society and the Institute for the Future are at work on bibliographies. An international computerized bibliography is being constructed in Sweden, and several industrious individuals have lengthy compilations well in hand.

13. Actually all messianic religion can be considered "utopian."

14. B. F. Skinner, *Walden Two* (New York: Macmillan, 1948).

15. Aldous Huxley, *Brave New World* (1932).

16. George Orwell, *1984* (1949).

17. Paul and Percival Goodman, *Communities* second revised edition. (New York: Vintage Books, 1960). (The original edition was 1947.)

18. Lewis Mumford glimpsed this, too, almost fifty years ago in *The Story of Utopias* (New York: Boni and Liveright, 1922).

19. Dennis Livingston, "Science Fiction as a Source of Forecast Material," *Futures* (March, 1969), and "The Study of Science Fiction as a Forecasting Methodology," his paper prepared for the International Future Research Conference in Kyoto, Japan, April 1970.

20. Talcott Parsons, *The Social System* (Glencoe: The Free Press, 1953).

21. Kingsley Davis, *Human Society* (New York: Macmillan, 1949), p. 633.

22. *See* below the treatment of societal indicators. Eleanor B. Sheldon and Wilbert E. Moore (eds.), *Indicators of Social Change* (New York: Russell Sage Foundation), 1968.

23. Wilbert E. Moore, *Social Change*, Foundations of Modern Sociology Series (Englewood Cliffs: Prentice Hall, 1963).

24. Wilbert E. Moore, *Order and Change* (New York: Wiley). *See also* William J. Goode (ed.), *The Dynamics of Modern Society* (New York: Atherton Press, 1966), a rather elementary textbook level treatment.

25. For example: Leslie A. White, *The Evolution of Culture* (New York: McGraw-Hill, 1959), and Margaret Mead, *Continuities in Cultural Evolution* (New Haven: Yale University Press, 1964).

26. David C. McClelland, *The Achieving Society* (Princeton: Van Nostrand, 1961), and Everett E. Hagen, *On the Theory of Social Change* (Homewood: Dorsey Press, 1962).

27. Ogburn's *Social Change* was first published in 1922 and revised in 1950.

28. Amitai Etzioni, *The Active Society* (New York: The Free Press, 1968), and Sara Jane Heidt and Amitai Etzioni (eds.), *Societal Guidance* (New York: Thomas Y. Crowell, 1969).

29. Robert L. Heilbroner, *The Future As History* (New York: Harper, 1959, 1960).

30. Herman Kahn and Anthony J. Wiener (eds.), *The Year 2000* (New York: Macmillan, 1967), p. 7. Wiener remarked in personal conversation that the statement of these interlocking trends would now be altered.

31. *See* Herman Kahn, *On Thermonuclear War* (Princeton: Princeton University Press, 1960).

32. Kurt Baier and Nicholas Rescher (eds.), *Values and the Future* (New York: The Free Press, 1969). *See also* Gerald Feinberg, *The Prometheus Project: Mankind's Search for Long-Range Goals* (New York: Doubleday, 1969).

33. This synoptic scheme was derived from James W. Bright, "A Working Outline: Introduction to Technological Forecasting," Challenge IV: Environmental Forecasting Conference Graduate School of Business, University of Texas, January 1970.

34. *See* Dator's "Summary Report on Activities in Hawaii as an Example of an Approach to Popular Participation in Futures Awareness, Research and Planning" and Umpleby's "Citizen Sampling Simulations: A Method for Involving the Public in Social Planning," both prepared for the International Future Research Conference in Kyoto, Japan, April, 1970.

35. *See* Daniel Lerner and Harold D. Lasswell (eds.), *The Policy Sciences: Recent Developments in Scope and Methods* (Stanford: Stanford University Press, 1951), and Lasswell's "The Emerging Conceptions of the Policy Sciences," *International Encyclopedia of Social Sciences*, Volume Twelve, pp. 181-189, and his forthcoming book, *A Preview of Policy Sciences*. Yehezkel Dror has summarized the policy science field brilliantly and succinctly in *Prolegomena to Policy Sciences* (Santa Monica: Rand Corporation, January, 1970).

36. *See* R. H. R. Armstrong and John L. Taylor (eds.), "Instructional Simulation Systems in Higher Education," Monograph Series, Volume Two, Cambridge Institute of Education, Cambridge, England; and John L. Taylor (Ed.), "Social Science Instructional Simulation Systems: A Selected Bibliography," SURISS Project Paper No. 4, SURISS Project Department of Town and Regional Planning, Sheffield University, Sheffield, England.

37. Total modification or scrapping possible also.

38. In English-American usage, "social" tends to be a restrictive word which does not include (except in professional sociological language the entire structure/behavior of society in its political, economic, educational, religious, and technological aspects. "Societal" appears to be a more useful umbrella word subsuming all of these aspects of society and culture about which more *precise* quantified information is needed.

39. Bertram Gross, *Social Intelligence* (Boston: Allyn and Bacon, 1969). Note especially pp. 5-16 with a careful table of the sort of "societal intelligence" needed in the United States, both building on existing data already gathered, and suggesting additional information needed. Some fifteen categories are listed with an individual chapter or chapters devoted to upgrading the quantity and quality of each type of information.

40. Eleanor B. Sheldon and Wilbert E. Moore (eds.), *op. cit.*

41. Raymond A. Bauer (ed.), *Social Indicators* (Cambridge: M.I.T. Press, 1966).

42. "Bag" in youth argot.

43. The bibliography on creativity is a mixed collection. One good "educated-adult" level book is John Gardner, *Self-Renewal: The Individual and the Innovating Society* (New York: Harper & Row, 1964); *see also* his *Excellence: Can We Be Equal and Excellent Too?* (New York: Harper, 1961). Another seminal cross-cultural survey on innovation by an anthropologist is H. G. Barnett, *Innovation: The Basis of Cultural Change* (New York: McGraw-Hill Paperbacks, 1953).

Appendix A
Colleges and Universities From Whom Some Data was Obtained

State University of New York (Buffalo)
Florida State Univeristy (Tallahassee, Florida)
Massachusetts Institute of Technology
Harvard University
Stanford University
State University of New York (Albany)
Louisiana State University
LeMoyne University (Syracuse, N.Y.)
Syracuse University
Washington University (St. Louis, Mo.)
Purdue University
University of California (Berkeley)
San Jose State (San Jose, Calif.)
College of Marin (Kentfield, Calif.)
Columbia University
University of Denver
University of Tennessee
University of Oklahoma
St. Francis College (Brooklyn, N.Y.)
University of British Columbia (Vancouver)
Princeton University
Wright State University (Dayton, Ohio)
University of Southern California (L.A.)
Case Western Reserve University (Cleveland, Ohio)
Simon Fraser University (Burnaby, B.C.)
Loyola College (Montreal, P.Q.)
York University (Ontario)
Illinois Wesleyan University (Bloomington, Ill.)
Dartmouth College (Hanover, N.H.)
Drexel Institute of Technology (Philadelphia, Pa.)
University of Massachusetts (Amherst, Mass.)
University of Washington (Seattle)
University of Georgia
University of Illinois
Manhattan College (Bronxville, N.Y.)
Drew University (Madison, N.J.).
University of South Florida (Tampa)
George Washington University (Washington, D.C.)
St. Andrews Presbyterian College (Laurinburg, N.C.)
University of Texas (Austin)
University of Hawaii
Portland State University (Portland, Ore.)
University of Chicago (Chicago, Ill.)
Cornell University (Ithaca, N.Y.)

Appendix B
Material Collected

Data on:
46 college university level courses or seminars
(about 1/2 at the graduate level)

Identified:
17 almost certain additional courses   no data could
15 possible additional courses   be obtained

In addition: data on
2 high school courses
1 elementary school course
1 underground undergraduate course
(against the official college)
2 experimental courses
(run by students)
1 "Mountain Experience" School

Some material of general interest from 10 research institutes, seminars, and business or consulting firms.

Appendix C
Disciplines Involved

	Response	No Response
Interdisciplinary or Unidentifiable	7	3
Physical Science		
Biology	1	1
Zoology	1 (2)	1 (2)
Social Science		
General	1	1
Sociology	7	0
Political Science	5	1
History	0 (15)	1 (5)
Geography	1	1
Anthropology	1	0
Economics	0	1
General		
Business Administration	10	2
Communication	2	1
Philosophy	1	1
Engineering	4 (22)	0 (5)
Urban Planning	3	0
Education	1	1
Architecture	1	0
Totals	46	17
Grand Total		63

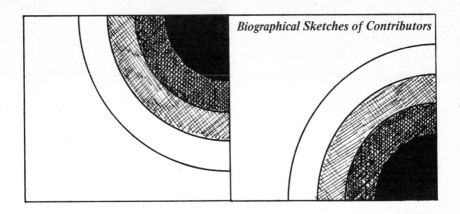

Bell, Daniel

Daniel Bell is professor of sociology at Harvard University. He is chairman of the Commission of the Year 2000 of the American Academy of Arts and Sciences, and editor of *Towards The Year 2000*, the interim report of the commission (Houghton Mifflin, 1968). The commission is ending its work in 1972, and a final report is due in 1973. Mr. Bell is the author, most recently, of *The Coming of Post-Industrial Society* (Basic Books), a venture in social forecasting.

Beloff, Max

Professor Beloff was born in London in 1913, and was educated at St. Paul's School and Oxford University. He has been the Gladstone Professor of Government and Public Administration at the University of Oxford, and a Fellow of All Souls College, since 1957. Professor Beloff has traveled and lectured widely in the United States and in other parts of the world, and has been a member of the Princeton Institute for Advanced Study and of the Brookings Institution in Washington, D.C. His books include a well-known short work on American federal government, and his writings have covered the Soviet and European as well as the American and British fields. He is at present engaged in a three-volume study of the world position of Britain in the present century. The first volume was published in New York in 1970 under the title of *Imperial Sunset, Volume I—Britain's Liberal Empire.*

Bennis, Warren G.

Dr. Warren Bennis is president of the University of Cincinnati. From 1967 to 1970, he served first as Provost of the Faculty of Social Science and Administration and, subsequently, as Vice-President for Academic Development at the State University of New York at Buffalo. Prior to that, Dr. Bennis was chairman of the Organization Studies Group at M.I.T.'s Sloan School of Management. He has written extensively in the field of organizational theory, and is the co-author, inter alia, of *The Temporary Society* (1968) and *Interpersonal Dynamics* (1968).

Dator, James Allen

James Dator is a professor in the Department of Political Science and is also head of the Program in Futures Research at the University of Hawaii. He was also an advisor to the Governor's Conference on the Year 2000 (August, 1970) and to the Hawaii State Commission on the Year 2000 (since 1971). Professor Dator is teaching courses in political futuristics, applied futuristics, and advanced futuristics at the graduate and undergraduate levels. He also conducted a television course for academic credit called "Tune to the Future" in 1971-72. Professor Dator is on the Continuing Committee of the World Future Research Conferences and is a member of the World Future Society. He was co-editor (with Magoroh Maruyama) of *Human Futuristics* (Social Science Research Institute of the University of Hawaii, 1971) and author of "Political Futuristics: Toward the Study of Alternative Political Futures," in David Plath (ed.), *Aware of Utopia* (University of Illinois Press, 1971); "A Framework for Futuristics in Hawaii," in *Challenges from the Future* (Proceedings of the International Future Research Conference, Kyoto, 1970): and "Futuristics and Modernization: An Asian Encounter," *Asian Forum* (October-December, 1970).

De Jouvenel, Bertrand

Bertrand de Jouvenel (1903-   ) is a distinguished French political philosopher. He has taught at Oxford, Yale, Cambridge, and Berkeley, and is presently a professor of law at the Sorbonne. He is the author of *On Power* (1948); *The Pure Theory of Politics* (1963); *Sovereignty* (1957); and *The Art of Conjecture* (1967). Professor de Jouvenel has also been editor of two important journals in the futures field —*Futuribles* and *Analyse et Prévision.*

Eldredge, H. Wentworth

Professor Eldredge is a professor of sociology at Dartmouth College, where he has served as chairman of the Sociology and Anthropology Department, director of the International Relations Major and of the Urban Studies Program. He has been a visiting lecturer in Urban Planning at Harvard, and a visiting professor of Urban Planning at the University of California (Berkeley), and a faculty member of the Salzburg Seminar in American Studies No. 97. He has lectured in urban and regional planning matters at some twenty American and foreign universities, government offices, and research institutes—twenty lectures at the NATO Defense College, Paris; the *Fuhrrungsakademie der Bundeswehr*, Hamburg; the *Ecole de Guerre*, Bruxelles; and *L'Institut des Hautes Etudes de Defense Nationale*, Paris, on strategic political, economic, and social planning. In addition, Professor Eldredge has served in the Department of State, the Department of

Justice, and the U.S. Joint Chiefs of Staff; and has been a consultant on the White House Staff to the Assistant for International Security Affairs and to the Department of Defense. He is the author of *The Second American Revolution* (1966); co-author of *Culture and Society* (1952); and editor of *Taming Megalopolis* (1967). His work in progress is *World Capitals, Toward Managed Urbanization and Urbanism.*

Gordon, T. J.

Formerly a vice-president and senior research fellow of the Institute for the Future, Mr. Gordon founded the Futures Group in April, 1971. He has also been a senior administrative officer at McDonnell-Douglas Astronautics Company, serving as chief engineer of the Saturn Program and as director of the advanced Space and Launch Systems. His association with universities has included service as a regents professor at the Graduate School of Business Administration, University of California at Los Angeles; and he has also lectured at Wesleyan University, Columbia, University of Texas, University of Indiana, and Harvard. His publications include a lengthy list of books and articles dealing with social technology, technological forecasting, and related subjects.

Helmer, Olaf

Olaf Helmer received Ph.D. degrees in mathematics and logic from the Universities of Berlin and London, respectively. He taught at the Universities of Chicago and Illinois, at New York City College, and at the New School for Social Research. In 1946, he joined Project Rand, which in 1948 became the Rand Corporation, of which he was a senior staff member of the Mathematics Department until 1968. He was one of the founders of the Institute for the Future, served as its president in 1970 and 1971, and is now its director of research. In 1946, he participated in the design of the historically first systems analysis. He also was a co-designer of the Delphi method. In recent years, his principal contributions have been in scientific methodology, in gaming and other simulation studies, and in long-range forecasting. Among his publications are *Social Technology*, a book which appeared in 1966 under the Basic Books imprint, and numerous articles, such as "On the Epistemology of the Inexact Sciences" (co-author: N. Rescher), *Management Science*, 6 (1959); "The Future of Science," *Science Journal* (October, 1967); *Political Analysis of the Future*, Paper P-1 (August, 1969); *On the Future State of the Union*, Report R-27, Institute for the Future (June, 1972).

Johnston, Denis F.

Dr. Johnston is Senior Demographic Statistician, Office of Manpower Structure and Trends, Bureau of Labor Statistics, U.S. Department of Labor, and Professorial Lecturer in Sociology, Georgetown University. His primary research interest at BLS is the development of long-range projections of labor force. He is the author or co-author of a number of articles on labor force characteristics and projections (published in the *Monthly Labor Review*), and recently completed illustrative projections of labor force for the Commission on Population Growth and the American Future. He has also served as consultant to the United Nations Secretariat and the International Labor Office on Demographic Aspects of Manpower Development.

Lasswell, Harold D.

Harold D. Lasswell is Ford Foundation Professor of Law and Social Sciences (Emeritus), Yale Law School, New Haven, Connecticut. He is currently a visiting professor of history and law at Temple University, Philadelphia, Pa. He is also Co-Chairman, Policy Sciences Center, 1, Lincoln Plaza (17B) New York, 10023. Lasswell has been concerned with interdisciplinary research and with the formulation of intellectual tools and procedures pertinent to the processing of knowledge,into action. He has been a visiting professor at several American universities and at universities in China, Japan, and elsewhere. He has been engaged in consultative activities relating to development activities in various federal departments and agencies. He is past president of the Policy Science Association and the American Society for International Law. His publications include: *A Pre-View of Policy Sciences; Psychopathology and Politics; World Politics and Personal Insecurity; Politics: Who Gets What, When, How?; Interpretation of Argreements and World Public Order* (with others); *Power and Society.*

Livingston, Dennis

Dennis Livingston obtained his Ph.D. degree in political science at Princeton University. He is generally interested in the influence of science and technology on international relations, on the interactions of the international political and environmental systems, and in the study of possible alternative world futures. He has taught courses at the University of California at Davis and Case Western Reserve University on such subjects as world futures, science fiction, and utopias. Most recently, he has done research on international efforts to cope with ocean pollution at Scripps Institution of Oceanography. Mr. Livingston presently is an independent consultant on curriculum development for high schools and colleges on education for alternative world futures. He resides in Cleveland Heights, Ohio.

Nie, Norman H.

Professor Nie is an assistant professor of political science at the University of Chicago and a senior study director of the National Opinion Research Center (NORC). His major research interests are in the areas of comparative political behavior and quantitative research methods. He is co-developer and co-author of the *Statistical Package for the Social Sciences* (McGraw-Hill, 1970), and co-author of *Information Utility and Social Choice* (AFIPS Press, 1970).

Nisbet, Robert A.

Robert Nisbet is a professor of sociology and history at the University of Arizona. He has taught at the University of California, Berkeley, and Riverside, where he was also a dean and vice chancellor, and has served as a visiting professor at the University of Bologna, Columbia University, Princeton University, and Smith College. A member of the American Academy of Arts and Sciences, he is a recipient of the Award of Merit from the Republic of Italy, the Berkeley Citation from the University of California, Berkeley, and was Phi Beta Kappa Visiting Scholar 1971-72. He is the author of *The Quest for Community; The Sociological Tradition; Social Change and History;* and *The Social Philosophers*, among other books.

Porter, David O.

Mr. Porter is an assistant professor of administration and political science at the University of California, Riverside. He is currently on leave for one year as an ASPA Public Administration Fellow in Washington, D.C. His primary research is in the areas of organization theory, urban fiscal administration, and urban studies. He has written a monograph, *Who Slices the Pie?* (Center for Urban Studies, Wayne State University), and several articles and papers in these areas. He received a Ph.D. degree in political science in 1970 from Syracuse University.

Sawhill, Isabel V.

Isabel V. Sawhill is an economist who has had frequent consulting assignments in Washington and is an assistant professor at Goucher College in Baltimore, Maryland. Dr. Sawhill served as a member of the Social Indicators Staff at the Department of Health, Education, and Welfare, and helped to produce *Toward a Social Report*, one of the first systematic, governmental attempts to monitor and analyze social conditions. Her other contributions in this area include an article written for the Joint Economic Committee in 1969 entitled, "The Role of Social Indicators and Social Reporting in Public Expenditure Decisions" in *The Analysis and Evaluation of Public Expenditures: The PPB System*. Portions of her contribution to this volume are based on this earlier work.

Seabury, Paul

Professor Seabury is a professor of political science at the University of California, Berkeley, and was educated at Columbia University and Swarthmore College. He is the author of various works in international politics and foreign policy, including: *The Rise and Decline of the Cold War; Power, Freedom and*

Diplomacy; and *The Wilhelmstrasse*. He is also an occasional commentator on problems in American culture and politics.

Somit, Albert

Albert Somit is presently Professor of Political Science and Executive Vice-President of the State University of New York at Buffalo, where he was previously chairman of the Department of Political Science. He has also taught at New York University and was Nimitz Professor of Social and Political Philosophy at the Naval War College. Dr. Somit is co-author of *The Development of American Political Science: From Burgess to Behavioralism (1967)* and *American Political Science: A Profile of a Discipline* (1964).

Tugwell, Franklin

Professor Tugwell was born March 29, 1942, in San Juan, Puerto Rico. He received a B.A., M.A., and Ph.D. from Columbia University, where he was Faculty Scholar and Latin American Institute Scholar. He was also the recipient of Foreign Area Fellowship (pre-doctoral) and Haynes Foundation and SSRC (post-doctoral) research grants. Since 1968, Professor Tugwell has served on the faculty of Pomona College in California, and is now on leave doing field research on development and interest-group politics in Venezuela. He is the editor of *Search for Alternatives: Public Policy and the Study of the Future* (Winthrop, forthcoming).

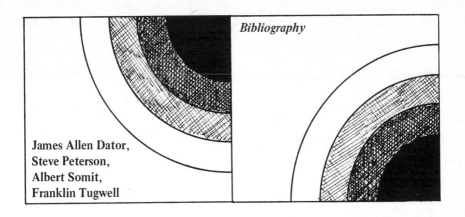

Bibliography

James Allen Dator,
Steve Peterson,
Albert Somit,
Franklin Tugwell

I. General Futuristics

Amis, Kingsley. *New Maps of Hell.* New York: Harcourt, 1960.

Anderson, Stanford. *Planning for Diversity and Choice.* Cambridge: M.I.T. Press, 1968.

Ayres, Robert U. *Technological Forecasting and Long-Range Planning.* New York: McGraw-Hill, 1969.

Baade, Fritz. *Race to the Year 2000.* Garden City: Doubleday, 1962.

Baier, Kurt, and Rescher, Nicholas (eds.). *Values and the Future.* New York: Collier-Macmillan, 1970.

Barach, Arnold B. *The U.S.A. and Its Economic Futures.* New York: Macmillan, 1964.

Bean, Louis H. *The Art of Forecasting.* New York: Random House, 1971.

Beckwith, Burnham P. *The Next 500 Years.* Jericho: Exposition Press, 1967.

Bell, Daniel "The Study of the Future." *The Public Interest*, 1 (Fall, 1965), pp. 119-30.

Bell, Wendell, and Mau, James (eds.). *The Sociology of the Future.* New York: Russell Sage Foundation, 1971.

Birkenhead, Earl of. *The World in 2030.* London: Hooper and Stoughton, 1930.

Boulding, Kenneth. "The Future of Individual Responsibility." *American Behavioral Scientist*, 15 (Janaury-February, 1972), pp. 329-60.

Boulding, Kenneth. *The Meaning of the Twentieth Century.* New York: Harper, 1963.

Bronwell, Arthur (ed.). *Science and Technology in the World of the Future.* New York: Wiley Interscience, 1970.

Brown, Harrison. *The Challenge of Man's Future.* New York: Viking Press, 1954.

Brown, Harrison. *The Next Hundred Years.* New York: Viking Press, 1957.

Brown, Harrison. *The Next Ninety Years.* Pasadena: California Institute of Technology, 1967.

Chase, Stuart. *Most Probable World.* New York: Harper, 1968.

Chung-Ho Choe (ed.). *An Inquiry into the Future.* Seoul: The Korean Society for Future Studies, 1970.

Clarke, Arthur C. *Profiles of the Future.* New York: Harper, 1962.

Clarke, I. F. *The Tale of the Future.* London: Library Association, 1961.

David, Paul T. "The Study of the Future." *Public Administration Review*, 28 (March-April, 1968), pp. 187-93.

de Jouvenel, Bertrand. *The Art of Conjecture.* New York: Basic Books, 1967.

Downs Anthony. "Alternative Forms of Future Urban Growth in the United States." *Urban Problems and Prospects.* Chicago: Markham, 1970.

Drucker, Peter. *The Age of Discontinuity.* New York: Harper, 1969.

Dunstan, Maryjane and Garlan, Patricia. *Worlds in the Making.* Englewood Cliffs: Prentice-Hall, 1970.

Evans, Wayne, O. and Kline, Nathan S. (eds.). *Psychotropic Drugs in the Year 2000*. Springfield: Charles C. Thomas, 1971.

Flechtheim, Ossip. "Futurology: The New Science of Probability." *Midwest Journal*, 2 (Winter, 1949), pp. 18-28.

Flechtheim, Ossip. *History and Futurology*. Meisenheim an Glan, Germany: Verlag Anton Hain, 1966.

Foreign Policy Association. *Toward the Year 2018*. Chicago: Cowles, 1968.

Forrester, Jay W. *Urban Dynamics*. Cambridge: M.I.T. Press, 1970.

Forrester, Jay W. *World Dynamics*. Cambridge: Wright-Allen Press, 1971.

Fuller, Buckminster. *Operating Manual for Spaceship Earth*. Carbondale: Southern Illinois University Press, 1969.

Furnas, Clifford. *The Next 100 Years*. New York: Reynal and Hitchcock, 1936.

Gibbs, Philip. *The Day After Tomorrow*. London: Hutchinson, 1928.

Ginzberg, Eli (ed.). *Technology and Social Change*. New York: Columbia, 1964.

Gleeson, Patrick. *America, Changing*. Columbus: Merrill, 1968.

Gordon, Theodore. *The Future*. New York: St. Martin's Press, 1965.

Graham, Robert K. *The Future of Man*. North Quincy: Christopher, 1971.

Gunn, James (ed.). *Man and the Future*. Lawrence: University of Kansas Press, 1968.

Halacy, Daniel S. *Beyond Tomorrow*. Philadelphia: Macrae Smith, 1965.

Halacy, Daniel S. *Century 21: Your Life in the Year 2000 and Beyond*. Philadelphia: Macrae Smith, 1968.

Heilbroner, Robert L. "The Future of Capitalism." *Commentary*, 41 (April, 1966), pp. 23-26.

Helmer, Olaf. *Social Technology*. New York: Basic Books, 1966.

Hopkins, Frank S. "The U.S. in the Year 2000, A Proposal for the Study of the American Future." *The American Sociologist*, 2 (1967), pp. 149ff.

Iklé, Fred Charles. "Social Forecasting and the Problem of Changing Values." *Futures*, 3 (June, 1971), pp. 142-50.

Israeli, Nathan. "Some Aspects of the Social Psychology of Futurism." *Journal of Abnormal and Social Psychology*, 25. (1930), pp. 121-32.

Jantsch, Erich. *Technological Forecasting in Perspective*. Paris: Organization for Economic Cooperation and Development, 1967.

Jungk, Robert. "The Future of Futures Research." *Science Journal*, 3 (October, 1967), pp. 3-40.

Kahn, Herman, and Bruce-Briggs, B. *Things to Come*. New York: Macmillan, 1972.

Kateb, George (ed.). *Utopia*. Chicago: Aldine, 1971.

Kopkind, Andrew. "The Future Planners." *American Psychologist*, 22 (November, 1967), pp. 1036-41.

Kostelanetz, Richard (ed.). *Human Alternatives: Visions for Us Now.* New York: William Morrow, 1971.

Kostelanetz, Richard (ed.). *Social Speculations: Visions for Our Time*. New York: William Morrow, 1971.

Langdon-Davies, John. *A Short History of the Future*. London: George Routledge and Sons, 1936.

Leach, Gerald. *Science Shapes Tomorrow*. New York: John Day, 1963.

McHale, John. *The Future of the Future*. New York: George Braziller, 1969.

McHale, John. *World Facts and Trends*. New York: Collier, 1972.

Manuel, Frank. *Utopias and Utopian Thought*. Boston: Houghton Mifflin, 1966.

Marty, M. E. *The Search for a Usable Future*. New York: Harper, 1969.

Massé Pierre. "Attitudes Toward the Future and Their Influence on the Present." *Futures*, 4 (March, 1972), pp. 24-29.

Mau, James. *Social Change and Images of the Future*. Cambridge: Schenkman, 1967.

Mesthene, Emmanuel. *Technological Change: Its Impact on Man and Society.* Cambridge: Harvard University Press, 1970.

Mesthene, Emmanuel (ed.). *Technology and Social Change.* Indianapolis: Bobbs-Merrill, 1967.

Meynaud, Jean. *Technocracy.* New York: The Free Press, 1969.

Michael, Donald (ed.). *The Future Society.* Chicago: Aldine, 1970.

Michael, Donald. *The Unprepared Society.* New York: Basic Books, 1968.

Miller, S. M., and Roby, Pamela. *The Future of Inquality.* New York: Basic Books, 1969.

Moore, Wilbert, "The Utility of Utopias." *American Sociological Review,* 31 (1966), pp. 765-72.

National Goals Research Staff. *Toward Balanced Growth: Quantity with Quality.* Washington: Government Printing Office, 1970.

Nostredame, Michel de. *Nostradamus: Life and Literature.* New York: Nosbooks, 1965 reprint edition.

Ozbekhan, Hasan. *Technology and Man's Future.* Santa Monica: Rand Corporation, 1966.

Platt, John. "How Men Can Shape Their Own Future." *World Future Society Bulletin, 3* (June, 1970).

Polak, Fred. *The Image of the Future.* Two volumes. Dobbs Ferry: Oceana Publications, 1961.

Prehoda, Robert. *Designing the Future.* Philadelphia: Chilton Books, 1967.

Rescher, Nicholas. *The Future As an Object of Research.* Santa Monica: Rand Corporation, 1967.

Sargent, Lyman, "Utopia and Dystopia in Contemporary Science Fiction." *The Futurist,* 6 (June, 1972), pp. 93-98.

Schon, Donald. *Beyond the Stable State.* New York: Random House, 1971.

Seidenberg, Roderick. *Anatomy of the Future.* Chapel Hill: University of North Carolina Press, 1961.

Seidenberg, Roderick. *Posthistoric Man.* Boston: Beacon Press, 1957.

Shipton, Ursula. *Prophesies of Mother Shipton, A.D. 1481.* Philadelphia: S.S. Thomas, 1881 edition.

Shubik, Martin. "Processing the Future." *Science,* 166 (5 December 1969), pp. 1257-258.

Taylor, Gordon Rattray. *The Biological Time Bomb.* New York: World, 1968.

Taylor, Joshua C. *Futurism.* Garden City: Doubleday, 1961.

Teich, Albert (ed.). *Technology and Man's Future.* New York: St. Martin's Press, 1972.

Theobald, Robert. *An Alternative Future for America.* Chicago: Swallow Press, 1968.

Theobald, Robert (ed.). *Futures Conditional.* Indianapolis: Bobbs-Merrill, 1972.

Theobald, Robert (ed.). *Social Policies for America in the Seventies.* Garden City: Doubleday, 1968.

Thomson, George. *The Foreseeable Future.* Cambridge: Cambridge University Press, 1955.

Toffler, Alvin. "The Future As a Way of Life." *Horizon,* 7 (Summer, 1965), pp. 108-15.

Toffler, Alvin. *Future Shock.* New York: Random House, 1970.

Toynbee, Arnold. *Surviving the Future.* New York: Oxford University Press, 1971.

Wallia, C. S. (ed.). *Toward Century 21: Technology, Society, and Human Values.* New York: Basic Books, 1970.

Wells, H. G. *The Future in America.* New York: Harper, 1906.

Welty, Gordon. "A Note on the Optimism of Futurologists." *International Social Science Journal, 22* (1970), pp. 502-4.

Winthrop, Henry. "The Sociologist and the Study of the Future." *American Sociologist,* 3 (May, 1968), pp. 136-45.

Wynn, Mark. "Who Are the Futurists?" *The Futurist,* 6 (April, 1972), pp. 73-77.

Young, Richard (ed.). *Yearbook of Science and the Future.* Chicago: Encyclopedia Brittanica, 1968.

322 / Bibliography

II. Political Futuristics

Akzin, Benjamin. "On Conjecture in Political Science." *Political Studies,* 14 (1966), pp. 1-14.
Banfield, Edward. *The Unheavenly City.* Boston: Little, Brown, 1970.
Basiuk, Victor. "Technology, Western Europe's Alternative Futures, and American Policy." *Orbis,* 15 (Summer, 1971), pp. 484-506.
Bell, Daniel (ed.). *Toward the Year 2000.* New York: Houghton Mifflin, 1968.
Benn, Anthony W. "Politics in a Technological Age." *New Scientist,* 38 (June 6, June 13), pp. 506, 572-73.
Bennis, Warren. "Future of the Social Sciences." *The Antioch Review,* 28 (Summer, 1968), pp. 227-55.
Bennis, Warren. "Post Bureaucratic Leadership." *Trans-Action,* 6 (July-August, 1969), pp. 44-52.
Black, Cyril, and Falk, Richard (eds.). *The Future of the International Legal Order.* Five volumes. Princeton: Princeton University Press.
Vol. 1. "Trends and Patterns." 1969.
Vol. 2. "Wealth and Resources," 1970.
Vol. 3. "Conflict Management," 1971.
Vol. 4. "Structure of the International Environment," 1972.
Vol. 5. "Toward an International Consensus," forthcoming.
Brown, Lester. *Seeds of Change: The Green Revolution and Development in the 1970's.* New York: Praeger, 1970.
Brzezinski, Zbigniew. "America in the Technetronic Age." *Encounter,* 30 (January, 1968), pp. 16-26.
Brzezinski, Zbigniew. *Between Two Ages: America's Role in the Technetronic Era.* New York: Viking Press, 1970.
Calder, Nigel. "Tomorrow's Politics, the Control and Use of Technology." *Nation,* 200 (January 4, 1965), pp. 3-5.
Charlesworth, James. *A Design for Political Science.* Philadelphia: American Academy of Political and Social Science, 1966.
Chevalier, Michel, and Choukron, Jean-Marc. "Urban Change and the Urban Future." *Canadian Public Administration,* 14 (Fall, 1971), pp. 426-51.
Deutsch, Karl. "The Future of World Politics." *Political Quarterly,* 37 (January, 1966), pp. 9-32.
Deutsch, Karl W. "Outer Space and International Politics: A Look to 1988." In Joseph Goldsen (ed.), *Outer Space in World Politics.* New York: Praeger, 1963.
Draper, Theodore. "World Politics: A New Era?" *Encounter,* 31 (August, 1968), pp. 3-16.
Dror, Yehezkel. *Futures in Government.* Santa Monica: Rand Corporation, 1968.
Dror, Yehezkel. "The Prediction of Political Feasiblity." *Futures,* 1 (June, 1969), pp. 282-88.
Dror, Yehezkel. *Public Policy Making Reexamined.* San Francisco: Chandler, 1968.
Dror, Yehezkel. "The Role of Futures in Government." *Futures,* 1 (September, 1968), pp. 40-46.
Eldredge, H. Wentworth. "Futurism in Planning for Developing Countries." *Journal of the American Institute of Planners,* 34 (November, 1968), pp. 382-84.
Galtung, Johan. "On the Future of the International System." *Journal of Peace Research,* 4 (1967), pp. 305-33.
Galtung, Johan. "Peace Research—Past Experiences and Future Perspectives." *International Problems,* 23 (1971), pp. 69-86.
Giglio, Ernest D., and Schrems, John J. (eds.). *Future Politics.* Berkeley: McCutchan, 1971.
Greenberg, Stuart. *Forecasting in International Relations.* Washington: George Washington, 1970.

Gregg, Robert W., and Kegley, Charles W. (eds.). *After Vietnam: The Future of American Foreign Policy*. Garden City: Doubleday, 1971.

Gross, Bertram (ed.). *A Great Society*. New York: Basic Books, 1968.

Gross, Bertram (ed.). "Social Goals and Indicators for American Society." *Annals of the American Academy of Political and Social Science*, 371, 373 (June, September, 1967), entire issue.

Gross, Bertram, and Neustadter, Bonnie (eds.). "The City of the Future." *American Behavioral Scientist*, 14 (July-August, 1971), entire issue.

Gross, Bertram, and Springer, Michael (ed.). *Social Intelligence for America's Future*. Boston: Allyn and Bacon, 1969.

Haas, Ernst. *Collective Security and the Future International System*. Denver: University of Denver Press, 1967.

Hancock, M. Donald, and Sjoberg, Gideon (eds.). *The Politics of Post Welfare Society*. New York: Columbia University Press, 1972.

Hellman, Donald *et al. Forecast for Japan: Security in the 1970's*. Princeton: Princeton University Press, 1972.

Hyneman, Charles. *The Study of Politics*. Urbana: University of Illinois Press, 1959.

Jenks, C. *Space Law*. New York: Praeger, 1965.

Jungk, Robert. "The Need for Social Invention." *Center Diary*, 18 (May-June, 1967), pp. 48-51.

Jungk, Robert, and Galtung, Johan (eds.). *Mankind 2000*. London: Allen and Unwin, 1969.

Kahn, Herman. *The Emerging Japanese Superstate*. Englewood Cliffs: Prentice-Hall, 1970.

Kahn, Herman. "On Alternative World Futures." In Morton Kaplan (ed.), *New Approaches to International Relations*. New York: St. Martin's Press, 1968.

Kahn, Herman, and Wiener, Anthony. "Technological Innovation and the Future of Strategic Warfare." *Astronautics and Aeronautics*, 5 (December, 1967), pp. 128-48.

Kahn, Herman, and Wiener, Anthony (eds.). *The Year 2000*. New York: Macmillan, 1967.

Kerimov, D. A. "Future Applicability of Cybernetics to Jurisprudence in the USSR." *M.U.L.L.*, 5 (December, 1963), pp. 153-61.

La Porte, Todd. "Politics and Inventing the Future." *Public Administration Review*, 27 (June, 1967), pp. 117-27.

Lane, Robert. "The Decline of Politics and Ideology in a Knowledgeable Society." *American Sociological Review*, 31 (October, 1966), pp. 649-62.

Lasswell, Harold. The Political Science of Science." *American Political Science Review*, 50 (December, 1956), pp. 961-79.

Lasswell, Harold. "The Changing Image of Human Nature, the Socio-Cultural Aspect (Future Oriented Man)." *American Journal of Psychoanalysis*, 26 (1966), pp. 157-66.

Lasswell, Harold. *The Future of Political Science*. New York: Atherton Press, 1963.

Lasswell, Harold. *A Pre-View of Policy Sciences*. New York: Elsevier, 1971.

Lichtheim, George. "Ideas of the Future." *Partisan Review*, 33 (Summer, 1966), pp. 396-410.

Lompe, Klaus. "Problems of Futures Research in the Social Sciences." *Futures*, 1 (1968), pp. 47-53.

McDougal, Myres; Lasswell, Harold; and Vlasic, Ivan. *Law and Public Order in Space*. New Haven: Yale University Press, 1963.

Mayo, Lewis, and Jones, Ernest. "Legal-Policy Decision Process: Alternative Thinking and the Prediction Functions." *George Washington Law Review*, 33 (October, 1964), pp. 318-456.

Meyer, Marshall. "Automation and Bureaucratic Structures." *American Journal of Sociology*, 74 (November, 1968), pp. 256-64.

Meynaud, Jean. "A propos des spéculations sur l'avenir." *Revue Française de Science Politique*, 13 (1963), pp. 666-68.

Michael, Donald. "Speculations on the Relation of the Computer to Individual Freedom and the Right to Privacy." *The George Washington Law Review*, 33 (October, 1964), 270-86.

Miller, S. M. "Goals for American Society." *World Future Society Bulletin*, 3 (August, 1970).

Mushkat, Marion. "From the Law of Nations through Peace Research and Planning to Futurology." *Co-Existence*, 8 (1971), pp. 1-13.

Perloff, Harvey S. (ed.) *The Future of the U.S. Government*. New York: George Braziller, 1971.

Petersen, John. "Municipal Bonds and Future Shock." *Governmental Finance*, 1 (February, 1972), pp. 26-28.

Pirages, Dennis (ed.). *Seeing Beyond: Personal, Social, and Political Alternatives*. Reading: Addison-Wesley, 1971.

Pool, Ithiel de Sola. "Social Trends." *Science and Technology*, 76 (April, 1968), pp. 87-101.

Ranney, Austin. *Political Science and Public Policy*. Chicago: Markham, 1968.

Rosecrance, Richard (ed.). *The Future of the International Strategic System*. San Francisco: Chandler, 1972.

Rotenstreich, N. "Technology and Politics." *International Philosophical Quarterly*, 7 (June, 1967), pp. 197-212.

Rothman, Stanley. "The Future of European Politics." Concluding chapter in *European Society and Politics*. Indianapolis: Bobbs-Merrill, 1970.

Rummel, Rudolph. "Forecasting International Relations." *Technological Forecasting*, 1 (1969), pp. 197-216.

Russett, Bruce. "The Ecology of Future International Politics." In James Rosenau (ed.), *International Politics and Foreign Policy*. New York: The Free Press, 1969.

Sills, David. "Some Futures for the Social Sciences." Lecture, Stanford University, May 23, 1968.

Smoker, Paul. "Anarchism, Peace and Control: Some Ideas for Future Experiment." *Peace Research Reviews*, 4 (February, 1972), pp. 52-69.

Stover, Carl. "Technology and Law—A Look Ahead." *M.U.L.L.*, 4 (March, 1963, pp. 1-8.

Sullivan, David S., and Sattler, Martin J. (eds.). *Change in the Future International System*. New York: Columbia University Press, 1972.

Szalai, Alexander. "The Future of International Organizations." *Social Science Information*, 10 (June, 1971), pp. 151-71.

Tanter, Raymond. *Explanation, Prediction and Forecasting in International Politics*. Ann Arbor: University of Michigan, 1969.

Taviss, Irene. *Technology and the Polity*. Cambridge: Harvard University Press, 1969.

Taylor, Jean G., and Navarro, Joseph. "Simulation of a Court System for the Processing of Criminal Cases." *Simulation*, 10 (May, 1968), pp. 235-40.

Wright, Quincy. *On Predicting International Relations: The Year 2000*. Denver: University of Denver, 1969.

Wright, Theodore P. "Trends in American Political Science in the 1970's." *Political Science Review*, 10 (1971), pp. 110-12.

Young, Oran R. *The World System: Present Characteristics and Future Prospects*. Hudson Institute (HI-277-D), 1963.

III. Public Policy and Future Studies

Amara, Roy C. "Toward a Framework for National Goals and Policy Research." *Policy Sciences* 3 (March, 1972), pp. 59-70.

Bauer, Raymond, and Gergen, Kenneth. *The Study of Policy Formation*. New York: The Free Press, 1968.

Benne, Kenneth (ed.). "The Social Responsibilities of the Social Scientist." *Journal of Social Issues*, 21 (April, 1965), entire issue.

Caldwell, Lynton. "Managing the Scientific Superculture: The Task of Educational Preparation." *Public Administration Review*, 27 (June, 1967), pp. 128-33.

Coates, Joseph. "The Future of Crime in the United States from Now to the Year 2000." *Policy Sciences*, 3 (March, 1972), pp. 27-46.

Dror, Yehezkel. *A Policy Science's View of Future Studies: Alternative Futures and Present Action*. Santa Monica: Rand Corporation.

Dror, Yehezkel. *Teaching of Policy Sciences: Design for a Post-Graduate University Program*. Santa Monica: Rand Corporation, 1969.

DuBos, René. *The Dreams of Reason*. New York: Columbia University Press, 1961.

Dupre, J. Stefan, and Lakoff, Sanford A. *Science and the Nation: Policy and Politics*. Englewood Cliffs: Prentice-Hall, 1962.

Enzer, Selwyn *et al. Futures Research as an Aid to Government Planning in Canada*. Middletown: Institute of the Future, 1971.

Ewald, William (ed.). *Environment and Policy: The Next 50 Years*. Bloomington: Indiana University Press, 1968.

Feinberg, Gerald. *The Prometheus Project: Mankind's Search for Long-Range Goals*. Garden City: Doubleday, 1969.

Ferry, Wilbur. "Must We Rewrite the Constitution to Control Technology?" *Saturday Review*, 51 (March 2, 1968), pp. 50-54.

Gilpin, Robert, and Wright, Christopher (eds.). *Science and National Policy-Making*. New York: Columbia University Press, 1964.

Green, Thomas (ed.). *Educational Planning in Perspective Forecasting and Policy-Making*. New York: I.P.C., 1971.

Gross, Bertram M. "Planning in an Era of Social Revolution." *Public Administration Review*, 31 (May-June, 1971), 259-96.

Gross, Bertram. *The State of the Nation: Social Systems Accounting*. London: Tavistock, 1966.

Haberer, Joseph. "Politics and the Community of Science." *American Behavioral Scientist*, 10 (May, 1967), pp. 10ff.

Hearle, Edward F. R. (ed.). "Computers and Public Administration." *Public Administration Review* 28 (November-December, 1968) entire issue.

Hogg, Quintin, and Crossman, Richard. "A Science-Based Government." *International Science and Technology*, 33 (September, 1964), pp. 33-40.

La Porte, Todd. "Diffusion and Discontinuity in Science, Technology, and Public Affairs." *American Behavioral Scientist*, 10 (May, 1967), pp. 23-29.

Lear, John (ed.). "Science, Technology, and the Law." *Saturday Review*, 51 (August 3, 1968), pp. 39-52.

Mertins, Herman. "National Transportation Planning: Dimensions and Challenges." *Public Administration Review*, 31 (May-June, 1971), pp. 352-63.

Mesthene, Emmanuel. "The Impact of Science on Public Policy." *Public Administration Review*, 27 (June, 1967), pp. 117-27.

Myrdal, Gunnar. "Too Late To Plan?" *Bulletin of the Atomic Scientists*, 24 (January, 1968), pp. 5-9.

Nelson, Richard *et al. Technology, Economic Growth, and Public Policy*. Washington: Brookings Institution, 1967.

Rescher, Nicholas. *Value Considerations in the Public Policy Issues of the Year 2000*. Santa Monica: Rand Corporation, 1967.

Shils, Edward. *Criteria for Scientific Development: Public Policy and National Goals*. Cambridge: M.I.T. Press, 1968.

Vickers, Geoffrey. *The Art of Judgment: A Study of Policy-Making*. New York: Basic Books, 1965.

Vickers, Geoffrey. "Planning and Policy-Making." *Political Quarterly*, 38 (July, 1967), pp. 253-65.

Wheeler, Harvey. "The Logic and Limits of Technology." *Nation*, 204 (January 2, 1967), pp. 9-16.

Wolfle, Dael. *Science and Public Policy*. Lincoln: University of Nebraska Press, 1959.

IV. Methods of Future Studies

——. *Approaches to Long Range Forecasting.* Washington: Government Printing Office, 1969.

Allen, D. H. "Credibility Forecasts and Their Application to the Economic Assessment of Novel Research and Development Prospects." *Operational Research Quarterly*, 19 (March, 1968), pp. 25-42.

Apter, Michael J. *The Computer Simulation of Behavior.* New York: Hillary, 1970.

Arnfield, R. V. (ed.). *Technological Forecasting.* Edinburgh: Edinburgh University Press, 1969.

Bauer, Raymond (ed.). "Forecasting the Future." *Science Journal*, 3 (October, 1967), entire issue.

Bauer, Raymond (ed.). *Social Indicators.* Cambridge: M.I.T. Press, 1966.

Bauer, Raymond; Rosenbloom, Richard; and Sharp, Laure. *Second Order Consequences.* Cambridge: M.I.T. Press, 1969.

Bell, Daniel. "The Idea of a Social Report." *Public Interest*, 15 (Spring, 1969), pp. 72-84.

Bennis, Warren (ed.). *The Planning of Change.* New York: Holt, Rinehart, and Winston, 1969.

Bright, James R. (ed.). *Technological Forecasting for Industry and Government.* Englewood Cliffs: Prentice-Hall, 1968.

Brown, Murray. *On the Theory and Measurement of Social Change.* New York: Cambridge University Press, 1966.

Cetron, Marvin J. *Technological Forecasting: A Practical Approach.* New York: Gordon and Breach, 1969.

Crane, Dwight, and Crotty, James. "A Two-Stage Forecasting Model: Exponential Smoothing and Multiple Regression." *Management Science*, 13-B (April, 1967), pp. 501-8.

Dalkey, N. C. *Experiments in Group Prediction.* Santa Monica: Rand Corporation, 1968.

Dalkey, N. C. *Predicting the Future.* Santa Monica: Rand Corporation, 1968.

Enzer, Selwyn. "Cross-Impact Techniques in Technology Assessment." *Futures*, 4 (March, 1972), pp. 30-51.

Enzer, Selwyn. "Delphi and Cross-Impact Techniques: An Effective Combination for Systematic Futures Analysis." *Futures*, 3 (March, 1971), pp. 48-61.

Fairweather, George. *Methods for Experimental Social Innovation.* New York: Wiley, 1967.

Good, I. J. *The Estimation of Probabilities.* Cambridge: M.I.T. Press, 1969.

Gordon, Theodore J. "Forecasters Turn to Delphi." *The Futurist*, 1 (February, 1967), p. 6.

Hart, Hornell. "Predicting Future Trends." In Allen Hart (ed.), *Technology and Social Change.* New York: Appleton-Century-Crofts, 1957.

Helmer, Olaf. *Analysis of the Future: The Delphi Method.* Santa Monica: Rand Corporation, 1967.

Helmer, Olaf. *Methodology of Society Studies.* Santa Monica: Rand Corporation, 1967.

Helmer, Olaf. *New Developments in the Early Forecasting of Public Problems.* Santa Monica: Rand Corporation, 1967.

Helmer, Olaf. *A Use of Simulation for the Study of Future Values.* Santa Monica: Rand Corporation, 1966.

Kirby, Robert. "A Comparison of Short and Medium Range Statistical Forecasting Methods." *Management Science*, 13-B (December, 1966), pp. 202-11.

Lanford, H. W. *Technological Forecasting Methodologies: A Synthesis.* New York: American Management Association, 1971.

Lewinsohn, Richard. *Science, Prophecy, and Prediction.* New York: Harper, 1961.

Lovewell, P. J., and Bruce, R. D. "How We Predict Technological Change." *New Scientist*, 13 (1962), pp. 370-74.

Martino, Joseph (ed.). *An Introduction to Technological Forecasting.* New York: Gordon and Breach, 1972.

Moreland, Frank L. "Dialectic Methods in Forecasting." *The Futurist*, 5 (August, 1971), pp. 169-71.

Olson, Mancur. "Economics, Sociology, and the Best of All Possible Worlds." *Public Interest*, 12 (Summer, 1962), pp. 96-118.

Sheldon, Eleanor, and Moore, Wilbert. *Indicators of Social Change*. New York: Russell Sage Foundation, 1968.

Shostak, A. B., and Pennington, A. S. "Methodology: Futurism Pro and Con." *Futures*, 3 (June, 1971), pp. 173-75.

Sulc, Oto. *Forecasting the Interactions Between Technical and Social Change*. Manchester: Manchester Business School, 1968.

Sulc, Oto. "A Methodological Approach to the Integration of Technological and Social Forecasts." *Technological Forecasting*, 1 (1969), pp. 105-8.

Theobald, R. "Alternative Methods of Predicting the Future." *The Futurist*, 3 (1969), pp. 43-45.

Toch, Hans. "The Perception of Future Events: Case Studies in Social Prediction." *Public Opinion Quarterly*, 22 (Spring, 1958). pp. 57-66.

U.S. Department of Health Education and Welfare. *Toward a Social Report*. Washington, D.C.: Government Printing Office, 1969.

Von Leeuwen, Arend T. *Prophecy in a Technocratic Era*. New York: Scribner's, 1968.

Young, Michael. *Forecasting and the Social Sciences*. London: Heineman, 1968.

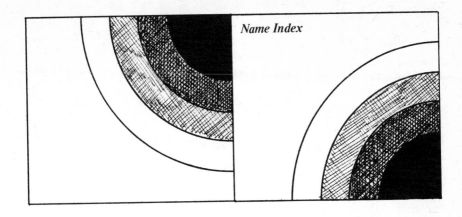

Name Index

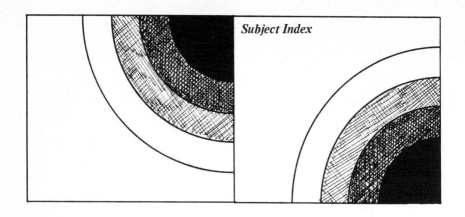